Clean C++20

Sustainable Software Development
Patterns and Best Practices

Second Edition

Stephan Roth

Apress®

Clean C++20: Sustainable Software Development Patterns and Best Practices

Stephan Roth
Bad Schwartau, Schleswig-Holstein, Germany

ISBN-13 (pbk): 978-1-4842-5948-1
https://doi.org/10.1007/978-1-4842-5949-8

ISBN-13 (electronic): 978-1-4842-5949-8

Managing Director, Apress Media LLC: Welmoed Spahr
Acquisitions Editor: Steve Anglin
Development Editor: Matthew Moodie
Coordinating Editor: Mark Powers

Cover designed by eStudioCalamar

Cover image by Jay Mantri on Unsplash (www.unsplash.com)

Distributed to the book trade worldwide by Apress Media, LLC, 1 New York Plaza, New York, NY 10004, U.S.A. Phone 1-800-SPRINGER, fax (201) 348-4505, e-mail orders-ny@springer-sbm.com, or visit www. springeronline.com. Apress Media, LLC is a California LLC and the sole member (owner) is Springer Science + Business Media Finance Inc (SSBM Finance Inc). SSBM Finance Inc is a **Delaware** corporation.

For information on translations, please e-mail booktranslations@springernature.com; for reprint, paperback, or audio rights, please e-mail bookpermissions@springernature.com.

Apress titles may be purchased in bulk for academic, corporate, or promotional use. eBook versions and licenses are also available for most titles. For more information, reference our Print and eBook Bulk Sales web page at http://www.apress.com/bulk-sales.

Any source code or other supplementary material referenced by the author in this book is available to readers on GitHub via the book's product page, located at www.apress.com/9781484259481. For more detailed information, please visit http://www.apress.com/source-code.

Printed on acid-free paper

To Caroline and Maximilian: my beloved and marvelous family.

Table of Contents

About the Author

Stephan Roth, born on May 15, 1968, is a passionate coach, consultant, and trainer for Systems and Software Engineering with the German consultancy company *oose Innovative Informatik eG,* located in Hamburg. Before he joined oose, Stephan worked for many years as a software developer, software architect, and systems engineer in the field of radio reconnaissance and communication intelligence systems. He has developed sophisticated applications, especially for distributed systems with ambitious performance requirements, and graphical user interfaces using C++ and other programming languages. Stephan is also a speaker at professional conferences and the author of several publications. As a member of the *Gesellschaft für Systems Engineering e.V.,* the German chapter of the international Systems Engineering organization INCOSE, he is also engaged in the Systems Engineering community. Furthermore, he is an active supporter of the Software Craftsmanship movement and concerned with principles and practices of Clean Code Development (CCD).

Stephan Roth lives with his wife Caroline and their son Maximilian in Bad Schwartau, a spa in the German federal state of Schleswig-Holstein near the Baltic Sea.

You can visit Stephan's website and blog about systems engineering, software engineering, and software craftsmanship via the URL roth-soft.de. Please note that the articles there are mainly written in German.

On top of that, you can contact him via email or follow him at the networks listed here.
Email: stephan@clean-cpp.com
Twitter: @_StephanRoth (https://twitter.com/_StephanRoth)
LinkedIn: www.linkedin.com/in/steproth

About the Technical Reviewer

Marc Gregoire is a software engineer from Belgium. He graduated from the University of Leuven, Belgium, with a degree in "Burgerlijk ingenieur in de computer wetenschappen" (equivalent to a master of science degree in computer engineering). The year after, he received the *cum laude* degree of master in artificial intelligence at the same university. After his studies, Marc started working for a software consultancy company called Ordina Belgium. As a consultant, he worked for Siemens and Nokia Siemens Networks on critical 2G and 3G software running on Solaris for telecom operators. This required working on international teams stretching from South America and the United States to Europe, the Middle East, and Asia. Currently, Marc works for Nikon Metrology on industrial 3D laser scanning software.

Acknowledgments

Writing a book like this one is never just the work of an individual person, the author. There are always numerous, fabulous people who contribute significantly to such a great project.

First, there was Steve Anglin of Apress. Steve contacted me in March 2016 for the first edition of *Clean C++*. He persuaded me to continue my book project with Apress Media LLC, which had been self-published at Leanpub. The self-publishing platform Leanpub served as a kind of "incubator" for a few years, but then I decided to finish and publish the book with Apress. Steve was also the one who contacted me in 2019 and asked me if I wanted to release a second edition that would take into account the emerging C++20 language standard. Well, he was obviously quite successful.

Next, I would like to thank Mark Powers, Editorial Operations Manager at Apress, for his great support during the writing of the manuscript for both editions. Mark was not only always available to answer questions, but his incessant follow-up on the progress of the manuscript was a positive incentive for me. I am very grateful to you, dear Mark.

In addition, many thanks also to Matthew Moodie, Lead Development Editor at Apress, who has provided proper help throughout the whole book development process.

A special thank you goes out to my technical reviewer Marc Gregoire. Marc critically examined every single chapter of both editions. He found many issues that I probably would have never found. He pushed me hard to improve several sections, and that was really valuable to me. Thank you!

Of course, I would also like to say a big thank you to the whole production team at Apress. They've done an excellent job regarding the finalization (copy editing, indexing, composition/layout, cover design, etc.) of the whole book up to the distribution of the final print (and eBook) files.

Last but not least, I would like to thank my beloved and unique family, especially for their understanding that a book project takes a great deal of time. Maximilian and Caroline, you're just wonderful.

CHAPTER 1

Introduction

"How it is done is as important as having it done."

—Eduardo Namur

Dear readers, I introduced the first edition of this book with the words: "It is still a sad reality that many software development projects are in bad condition, and some might even be in a serious crisis." That was a little over three years ago, and I am pretty sure that the general situation has not improved significantly since then.

The reasons that many software development projects are still having difficulties are manifold. There are a lot of risk factors that can cause software development projects to fail. Some projects, for example, are afflicted because of lousy project management. In other projects, the conditions and requirements constantly and rapidly change, but the development process does not support this high-dynamic environment. Furthermore, the all-important requirements elicitation and use case analysis is given little space in some projects. In particular, communication between external stakeholders, such as between domain experts and developers, can be difficult, leading to misunderstandings and the development of unnecessary features. And as if all this were not bad enough, quality assurance measures, such as testing, are given too little importance.

STAKEHOLDER

The term stakeholder in systems and software engineering is commonly used to refer to individuals or organizations that can potentially contribute requirements to a development project or that define important constraints for the project.

Usually, a distinction is made between external and internal stakeholders. Examples of *external stakeholders* are the customers, all users of the system, domain experts, system administrators, regulatory authorities, the legislators, etc. *Internal stakeholders* are those

© Stephan Roth 2021
S. Roth, *Clean C++20*, https://doi.org/10.1007/978-1-4842-5949-8_1

from within the development organization and can be the developers and software architects, business analysts, product management, requirements engineers, quality assurance, marketing personnel, etc.

The previously listed points are all typical and well-known problems in professional software development, but beyond that, another fact exists: **In some projects the code base is poor quality!**

That does not necessarily mean that the code is not working correctly. Its *external quality,* measured by the quality assurance (QA) department using integration or acceptance tests, can be pretty high. It can pass QA without complaints, and the test report might state that they found nothing wrong. The software users might also possibly be satisfied and happy, and the development may even have been completed on time and on budget (... which is rare, I know). Everything seems to be fine on first sight ... really, everything?!

Nevertheless, the *internal quality* of this code, which works correctly, can be very poor. Often the code is difficult to understand and horrible to maintain and extend. Countless software units, like classes or functions, are very large, some of them with thousands of lines of code, making their comprehensibility and adaptability a serious challenge. Too many dependencies between software units lead to unwanted side effects if something changes. The software has no perceivable architecture. Its structure seems to be randomly originated and some developers speak about "historically grown software" or "architecture by accident." Classes, functions, variables, and constants have bad and mysterious names, and the code is littered with lots of comments: some of them are outdated, just describe obvious things, or are plain wrong. Developers are afraid to change something or to extend the software because they know that it is rotten and fragile, and they know that unit test coverage is poor, if there are any unit tests at all. "Never touch a running system" is a statement that is frequently heard from people working within such kinds of projects. The implementation of a new feature doesn't just need a few hours or days until it is ready for deployment; it takes several weeks or even months.

This kind of bad software is often referred to as a *big ball of mud.* This term was first used in 1997 by Brian Foote and Joseph W. Yoder in a paper for the Fourth Conference on Patterns Languages of Programs (PLoP '97/EuroPLoP '97). Foote and Yoder describe the big ball of mud as "... a haphazardly structured, sprawling, sloppy, duct-tape-and-baling-wire, spaghetti-code jungle." Such software systems are costly and time-wasting maintenance nightmares, and they can bring a development organization to its knees!

The pathological phenomena just described can be found in software projects in all industrial sectors and domains. The programming language they use doesn't matter. You'll find big balls of mud written in Java, PHP, C, C#, C++, and other more or less popular languages. Why is that so?

Software Entropy

First of all, there is the natural law of entropy, or disorder. Just like any other closed and complex system, software tends to get messier over time. This phenomenon is called *software entropy*. The term is based on the second law of thermodynamics. It states that a closed system's disorder cannot be reduced; it can only remain unchanged or increase. Software seems to behave this way. Every time a new function is added or something is changed, the code gets a little bit more disordered. There are also numerous influencing factors that can contribute to software entropy:

- Unrealistic project schedules raise the pressure and abet developers to botch things and to do their work in a bad and unprofessional way.

- The immense complexity of today's software systems, both technically and in terms of the requirements to be satisfied.

- Developers with different skill levels and experience.

- Globally distributed, cross-cultural teams, enforcing communication problems.

- Development mainly pays attention to the functional aspects (functional requirements and the system's use cases) of the software, whereby the quality requirements (non-functional requirements), such as performance, efficiency, maintainability, availability, usability, portability, security, etc., are neglected or at worst are fully ignored.

- Inappropriate development environments and bad tools.

- Management is focused on earning money quickly and doesn't understand the value of sustainable software development.

- Quick and dirty hacks and non-design-conformable implementations (*broken windows*).

THE BROKEN WINDOW THEORY

The *Broken Window Theory* was developed in connection with American crime research. The theory states that a single destroyed window at an abandoned building can be the trigger for the dilapidation of an entire neighborhood. The broken window sends a fatal signal to the environment: "Look, nobody cares about this building!" This attracts further decay, vandalism, and other antisocial behavior. The Broken Window Theory has been used as the foundation for several reforms in criminal policy, especially for the development of zero-tolerance strategies.

In software development, this theory was taken up and applied to the quality of code. Hacks and bad implementations, which are not compliant with the software design, are called "broken windows." If these bad implementations are not repaired, more hacks to deal with them may appear in their neighborhood. And thus, code dilapidation is set into motion.

Don't tolerate "broken windows" in your code—*fix them!*

Why C++?

> *"C makes it easy to shoot yourself in the foot. C++ makes it harder, but when you do, you blow away your whole leg!"*
>
> —Bjarne Stroustrup, Bjarne Stroustrup's FAQ: Did you really say that?

First and foremost, phenomena like software entropy, code smells, anti-patterns, and other problems with the internal software quality, are basically independent of the programming language. However, it seems to be that C and C++ projects are especially prone to messiness and tend to slip into a bad state. Even the World Wide Web is full of bad, but apparently very fast and highly optimized, C++ code examples. They often have a cruel syntax that completely ignores elementary principles of good design and well-written code. Why is that?

One reason for this might be that C++ is a multi-paradigm programming language on an intermediate level; that is, it comprises both high-level and low-level language features. C++ is like a melting pot that blends many different ideas and concepts together. With this language, you can write procedural, functional, or object-oriented programs, or even a mixture of all three. In addition, C++ allows *template metaprogramming* (TMP), a technique in which so-called templates are used by a compiler to generate temporary source code that is merged with the rest of the source

4

code and then compiled. Ever since the release of ISO standard C++11 (ISO/IEC 14882:2011 [ISO11]) in September 2011, even more ways have been added; for example, functional programming with anonymous functions are now supported in a very elegant manner by lambda expressions. As a consequence of these diverse capabilities, C++ has a reputation for being very complex, complicated, and cumbersome. And with each standard after C++11 (C++14, C++17, and now C++20), a lot of new features were added, which have further increased the complexity of the language.

Another cause for bad software could be that many developers didn't have an IT background. Anyone can begin to develop software nowadays, no matter if they have a university degree or any other apprenticeship in computer science. A vast majority of C++ developers are (or were) non-experts. Especially in the technological domains automotive, railway transportation, aerospace, electrical/electronics, or mechanical engineering domains, many engineers slipped into programming during the last decades without having an education in computer science. As the complexity grew and technical systems contained more and more software, there was an urgent need for programmers. This demand was covered by the existing workforce. Electrical engineers, mathematicians, physicists, and lots of people from strictly nontechnical disciplines started to develop software. They learned to do it mainly by self-education and hands-on, by simply doing it. And they have done it to their best knowledge and belief.

Basically, there is absolutely nothing wrong with that. But sometimes just knowing the tools and the syntax of a programming language is not enough. Software development is not the same as programming. The world is full of software that was tinkered together by improperly trained software developers. There are many things on abstract levels a developer must consider to create a sustainable system, for example, architecture and design. How should a system be structured to achieve certain quality goals? What is this object-oriented thing good for and how do I use it efficiently? What are the advantages and drawbacks of a certain framework or library? What are the differences between various algorithms, and why doesn't one algorithm fit all similar problems? And what the heck is a deterministic finite automaton, and why does it help to cope with complexity?!

But there is no reason to lose heart! What really matters to a software program's ongoing health is that someone cares about it, and clean code is the key!

Clean Code

What, exactly, is meant by "clean code"?

A major misunderstanding is to confuse clean code with something that can be called "beautiful code." Clean code doesn't have necessarily to be beautiful (...whatever that means). Professional programmers are not paid to write beautiful or pretty code. They are hired by development companies as experts to create customer value.

Code is clean if it can be understood and maintained easily by any team member.

Clean code is the basis of fast code. If your code is clean and test coverage is high, it only takes a few hours or a couple of days to implement, test, and deploy a change or a new function—not weeks or months.

Clean code is the foundation for sustainable software; it keeps a software development project running over a long time without accumulating a large amount of technical debt. Developers must actively tend the software and ensure it stays in shape because the code is crucial for the survival of a software development organization.

Clean code is also the key to being a happier developer. It leads to a stress-free life. If your code is clean and you feel comfortable with it, you can keep calm in every situation, even when facing a tight project deadline.

All of the points mentioned here are true, but the key point is this: ***Clean code saves money!*** In essence, it's about economic efficiency. Each year, development organizations lose a lot of money because their code is in bad shape. Clean code ensures that the value added by the development organization remains high. Companies can earn money from its clean code for a long time.

C++11: The Beginning of a New Era

> *"Surprisingly, C++11 feels like a new language: The pieces just fit together better than they used to and I find a higher-level style of programming more natural than before and as efficient as ever."*
>
> —Bjarne Stroustrup, C++11 - the new ISO C++ standard [Stroustrup16]

After the release of the C++ language standard C++11 (ISO/IEC 14882:2011 [ISO11]) in September 2011, some people predicted that C++ would undergo a renaissance. Some even spoke of a revolution. They predicted that the idiomatic style of how development was done with this "modern C++" would be significantly different and not comparable to the "historical C++" of the early 1990s.

No doubt, C++11 has brought a bunch of great innovations and changed the way we think about developing software with this programming language. I can say with full confidence that C++11 has set such changes in motion. With C++11, we got move semantics, lambda expressions, automatic type deduction, deleted and defaulted functions, a lot of enhancements of the Standard Library, and many more useful things.

But this also meant that these new features came on top of the already existing features. It is not possible to remove a significant feature from C++ without breaking large amounts of existing code bases. This means that the complexity of the language increased, because C++11 is larger than its predecessor C++98, and thus it is harder to learn this language in its entirety.

Its successor, C++14, was an evolutionary development with some bug fixes and minor enhancements. If you plan to switch to modern C++, you should at least start with this standard and skip C++11.

Three years later, with C++17, numerous new features were added again, but this revision also removed a few. And in December 2020, the C++ standardization committee completed and published the new C++20 standard, which is called "the next big thing" by some people. This standard again adds lots of new features besides many extensions to the core language, the Standard Library, and other stuff, especially the so-called "big four": Concepts, Coroutines, Ranges Library, and Modules.

If we look at C++ development over the past 10 years, we can see that the complexity of the language has increased significantly. In the meantime, C++23 development has already begun. I question whether this is the right way to go about things in the long run. Perhaps it would be appropriate at some point not only to permanently add functionalities, but also to review the existing features, consolidate them, and simplify the language again.

Who This Book Is For

As a trainer and consultant, I have had the opportunity to look at many companies that are developing software. Furthermore, I observe very closely what is happening in the developer scene. And I've recognized a gap.

My impression is that C++ programmers have been ignored by those promoting software craftsmanship and clean code development. Many principles and practices, which are relatively well known in the Java environment and in the hip world of web or game development, seem to be largely unknown in the C++ world.

This book tries to close that gap a little, because even with C++, developers can write clean code! If you want to learn about writing clean C++, this book is for you. It is written for C++ developers of all skill levels and shows by example how to write understandable, flexible, maintainable, and efficient C++ code. Even if you are a seasoned C++ developer, there are interesting hints and tips in this book that you will find useful in your work.

This book is not a C++ primer! In order to use the knowledge in this book efficiently, you should already be familiar with the basic concepts of the language. If you just want to start with C++ development and still have no basic knowledge of the language, you should first learn the basic concepts, which can be done with other books or with a good C++ introduction training. This book also does not discuss every single new C++20 language feature, or the features of its predecessors, in detail. As I have already pointed out, the complexity of the language is now relatively high. There are other very good books that introduce the language from A to Z.

Furthermore, this book doesn't contain any esoteric hack or kludge. I know that a lot of nutty and mind-blowing things are possible with C++, but these are usually not in the spirit of clean code and should not be used to create a clean and modern C++ program. If you are really crazy about mysterious C++ pointer calisthenics, this book is not for you.

Apart from that, this book is written to help C++ developers of all skill levels. It shows by example how to write understandable, flexible, maintainable and efficient C++ code. The presented principles and practices can be applied to new software systems, sometimes called *greenfield projects*, as well as to legacy systems with a long history, which are often pejoratively called *brownfield projects*.

Note   Please consider that not every C++ compiler currently supports all of the new language features, especially not those from the latest C++20 standard, completely.

Conventions Used in This Book

The following typographical conventions are used in this book:

> *Italic font* is used to introduce new terms and names.

Bold font is used within paragraphs to emphasize terms or important statements.

`Monospaced font` is used within paragraphs to refer to program elements such as class, variable, or function names, statements, and C++ keywords. This font is also used to show command line inputs, an address of a website (URL), a keystroke sequence, or the output produced by a program.

Sidebars

Sometimes I pass on small bits of information that are tangentially related to the content around it, which can be considered separate from that content. Such sections are known as sidebars. Sometimes I use a sidebar to present an additional or contrasting discussion about the topic around it.

THIS HEADER CONTAINS THE TITLE OF A SIDEBAR

This is the text in a sidebar.

Notes, Tips, and Warnings

Another kind of sidebar for special purposes is used for notes, tips, and warnings. They are used to provide some special information, to provide a useful piece of advice, or to warn you about things that can be dangerous and should be avoided.

Note   This is the text of a note.

Code Samples

Code examples and code snippets appear separately from the text, syntax-highlighted (keywords of the C++ language are bold), and in a monospaced font. Longer code sections usually have numbered titles. To reference specific lines of the code example in the text, code samples sometimes include line numbers (see Listing 1-1).

Listing 1-1. A Line-Numbered Code Sample

```
01  class Clazz {
02  public:
03    Clazz();
04    virtual ~Clazz();
05    void doSomething();
06
07  private:
08    int _attribute;
09
10    void function();
11  };
```

To better focus on specific aspects of the code, irrelevant parts are sometimes obscured and represented by a comment with an ellipsis (…), like in this example:

```
void Clazz::function() {
  // ...
}
```

Coding Style

Just a few words about the coding style I use in this book.

You may get the impression that my programming style has a strong likeness to typical Java code, mixed with the Kernighan and Ritchie (K&R) style. I've spent nearly 20 years as a software developer, and even later in my career, I have learned other programming languages (for instance, ANSI-C, Java, Delphi, Scala, and several scripting languages). Hence, I've adopted my own programming style, which is a melting pot of these different influences.

Maybe you will not like my style, and you instead prefer Linus Torvald's Kernel style, the Allman style, or any other popular C++ coding standard. This is of course perfectly okay. I like my style, and you like yours.

C++ Core Guidelines

You may have heard of the *C++ Core Guidelines*, found at `https://isocpp.github.io/CppCoreGuidelines/CppCoreGuidelines.html` [Cppcore21]. This is a collection of guidelines, rules, and good practices for programming with modern C++. The project is hosted on GitHub and released under a MIT-style license. It was initiated by Bjarne Stroustrup, but has a lot more editors and contributors, e.g., Herb Sutter.

The number of rules and recommendations in the *C++ Core Guidelines* is pretty high. There are currently 30 rules on the subject of interfaces alone, about the same number on error handling, and no less than 55 rules on functions. And that is by no means the end of the story. Further guidelines exist on topics such as classes, resource management, performance, and templates.

I first had the idea of linking the topics in my book to the rules from the *C++ Core Guidelines*. But that would have led to countless references to the guidelines and might even have reduced the readability of the book. Therefore, I have largely refrained from doing so, but would like to explicitly recommend the *C++ Core Guidelines* at this point. They are a very good supplement to this book, even though I do not agree with every rule.

Companion Website and Source Code Repository

This book is accompanied by a companion website: `www.clean-cpp.com`.

The website includes:

- The discussion of additional topics not covered in this book.

- High-resolution versions of all the figures in this book.

Some of the source code examples in this book, and other useful additions, are available on GitHub at:

`https://github.com/Apress/clean-cpp20`

You can check out the code using Git with the following command:

`$> git clone https://github.com/clean-cpp/book-samples.git`

You can get a .ZIP archive of the code by going to `https://github.com/clean-cpp/book-samples` and clicking the Download ZIP button.

UML Diagrams

Some illustrations in this book are UML diagrams. The *Unified Modeling Language* (UML) is a standardized graphical language used to create models of software and other systems. In its current version, 2.5.1, UML offers 15 diagram types to describe a system entirely.

Don't worry if you are not familiar with all diagram types; I use only a few of them in this book. I present UML diagrams from time to time to provide a quick overview of certain issues that possibly cannot be understood quickly enough by just reading the code. Appendix A contains a brief overview of the used UML notations.

CHAPTER 2

Build a Safety Net

"Testing is a skill. While this may come as a surprise to some people, it is a simple fact.:

—Mark Fewster and Dorothy Graham,
Software Test Automation, 1999

That I start the main part of this book with a chapter about testing may be surprising to some readers, but this is for several good reasons. During the past few years, testing on certain levels has become an essential cornerstone of modern software development. The potential benefits of a good test strategy are enormous. All kinds of tests, if well engineered, can be helpful and useful. In this chapter, I describe why I think that unit tests, especially, are indispensable to ensure a fundamental level of high quality in software.

Note that this chapter is about what is sometimes called POUT ("plain old unit testing") and not the design-supporting tool test-driven development (TDD), which I cover in Chapter 8.

The Need for Testing

1962: NASA MARINER 1

The Mariner 1 spacecraft was launched on July 22, 1962, as a Venus flyby mission for planetary exploration. Due to a problem with its directional antenna, the Atlas-Agena B launching rocket worked unreliably and lost its control signal from ground control shortly after launch.

This exceptional case had been considered during design and construction of the rocket. The Atlas-Agena launching vehicle switched to automatic control by the on-board guidance computer. Unfortunately, an error in the software of that computer led to incorrect control commands that caused a critical course deviation and made steering impossible. The rocket was directed toward Earth and pointed to a critical area.

© Stephan Roth 2021
S. Roth, *Clean C++20*, https://doi.org/10.1007/978-1-4842-5949-8_2

At T+293 seconds, the Range Safety Officer sent the destruct command to blow the rocket. A NASA examination report[1] mentions a typo in the computer's source code, the lack of a hyphen (-), as the cause of the error. The total loss was $18.5 million, which was a huge amount of money in those days.

If software developers are asked why tests are good and essential, I suppose that the most common answer would be the reduction of bugs, errors, or flaws. No doubt this is basically correct: testing is an elementary part of quality assurance.

Software bugs are usually perceived as an unpleasant nuisance. Users are annoyed about the wrong behavior of the program, which produces invalid output, or they are seriously ticked off about regular crashes. Sometimes even odds and ends, such as a truncated text in a dialog box of a user interface, are enough to significantly bother software users in their daily work. The consequence may be an increasing dissatisfaction with the software, and at worst its replacement by another product. In addition to a financial loss, the image of the software manufacturer suffers from bugs. At worst, the company gets into serious trouble and many jobs are lost.

But the previously described scenario does not apply to every piece of software. The implications of bugs can be much more dramatic.

1986: THERAC-25 MEDICAL ACCELERATOR DISASTER

This case is probably the most consequential failure in the history of software development. The Therac-25 was a radiation therapy device. It was developed and produced from 1982 until 1985 by the state-owned enterprise Atomic Energy of Canada Limited (AECL). Eleven devices were produced and installed in clinics in the United States and Canada.

Due to bugs in the control software, an insufficient quality assurance process, and other deficiencies, three patients lost their lives caused due to radiation overdoses. Three other patients were irradiated and suffered permanent, heavy health problems.

An analysis of this case determined that, among other things, the software was written by only one person who was also responsible for the tests.

---

[1]NASA National Space Science Data Center (NSSDC): Mariner 1, `http://nssdc.gsfc.nasa.gov/nmc/spacecraftDisplay.do?id=MARIN1`, retrieved 2021-0305.

When people think of computers, they usually have a desktop PC, laptop, tablet, or smartphone in mind. And if they think about software, they usually think about web shops, office suites, or business IT systems.

But these kinds of software and computers make up only a very small percentage of all systems with which we have contact every day. Most software that surrounds us controls machines that physically interact with the world. Our whole life is managed by software. In a nutshell: **There is no life today without software!** Software is everywhere and an essential part of our infrastructure.

If we board an elevator, our lives are in the hands of software. Aircrafts are controlled by software, and the entire, worldwide air traffic control system depends on software. Our modern cars contain a significant amount of small computer systems with software that communicates over a network, responsible for many safety-critical functions of the vehicle. Air conditioning, automatic doors, medical devices, trains, automated production lines in factories ... no matter what we're doing nowadays, we permanently come in touch with software. And with the *digital revolution* and the *Internet of Things* (IoT), the relevance of software in our life will again increase significantly. This fact could not get more evident than with the autonomous (driverless) car.

It is unnecessary to emphasize that any bug in these software-intense systems could have catastrophic consequences. A fault or malfunction of an important system can be a threat to lives or physical condition. At worst, hundreds of people could lose their lives during a plane crash, possibly caused by a wrong `if` statement in a subroutine of the Fly-by-Wire subsystem. Quality is under no circumstances negotiable in these kinds of systems. **Never!**

But even in systems without functional safety requirements, bugs can have serious implications, especially if they are subtler in their destructiveness. It is easy to imagine that bugs in financial software could trigger a worldwide bank crisis. Imagine if the financial software of an arbitrary big bank completed every posting twice due to a bug, and this issue was not noticed for a few days.

1990: THE AT&T CRASH

On January 15th, 1990, the AT&T long distance telephone network crashed and 75 million phone calls failed for the following nine hours. The blackout was caused by a single line of code (a wrong `break` statement) in a software upgrade that AT&T deployed to all 114 of its computer-operated electronic switches (4ESS) in December 1989. The problem began the afternoon of January 15 when a malfunction in AT&T's Manhattan control center led to a chain reaction and disabled switches throughout half the network.

The estimated loss for AT&T was $60 million. There were also probably a huge amount of losses for businesses that relied on the telephone network.

Introduction to Testing

There are different levels of quality assurance measures in software development projects. These levels are often visualized in the form of a pyramid—the so-called *test pyramid*. The fundamental concept was developed by the American software developer Mike Cohn, one of the founders of the Scrum Alliance. He described the test automation pyramid in his book, *Succeeding with Agile* [Cohn09]. With the aid of the pyramid, Cohn describes the degree of automation required for efficient software testing. In the following years, the test pyramid has been further developed by different people. The one depicted in Figure 2-1 is my version.

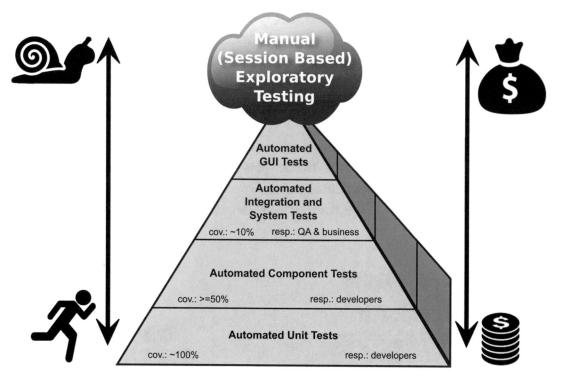

Figure 2-1. *The test pyramid*

The pyramid shape, of course, is no coincidence. The message behind it is that you should have many more low-level unit tests (approximately 100% code coverage) than any other kind of tests. But why is that?

Experience has shown that the total costs regarding implementation and maintenance of tests increase toward the top of the pyramid. Large system tests and manual user acceptance tests are usually complex, often require extensive organization, and cannot be automated easily. For instance, an automated UI test is hard to write, often fragile, and relatively slow. Therefore, these tests are often performed manually, which is suitable for customer approval (acceptance tests) and regular exploratory tests by QA, but far too time consuming and expensive for everyday use during development.

Furthermore, large system tests, or UI-driven tests, are totally improper to check all possible paths of execution through the whole system. There's lots of code in a software system that deals with alternative paths, exceptions and error-handling, cross-cutting concerns (security, transaction handling, logging …), and other auxiliary functions that are required, but often cannot be reached through the normal user interface.

Above all, if a test at the system level fails, the exact cause of the error can be difficult to locate. System tests typically are based on the system's use cases. During the execution of a use case, many components are involved. This means that many hundreds, or even thousands, of lines of code are executed. Which one of these lines was responsible for the failed test? This question often cannot be answered easily and requires a time-consuming and costly analysis.

Unfortunately, in several software development projects you'll find degenerated test pyramids, as shown in Figure 2-2. In such projects, enormous effort goes into the tests on the higher level, whereas the elementary unit tests are neglected (*ice cream cone anti-pattern*). In the extreme case, the unit tests are completely missing (*cupcake anti-pattern*).

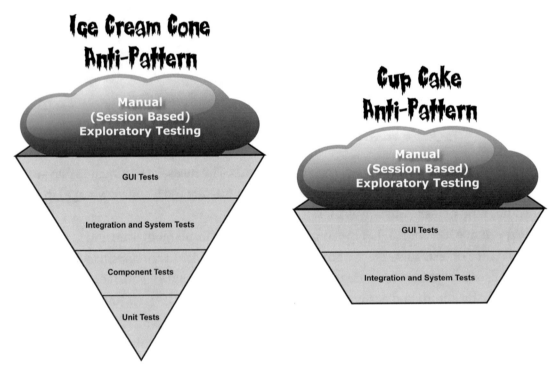

Figure 2-2. *Degenerated test pyramids (anti-patterns)*

Therefore, a broad base of inexpensive, well-crafted, very fast, regularly maintained, and fully automated unit tests, supported by a selection of useful component tests, can be a solid foundation to ensure a pretty high quality of a software system.

Unit Tests

"'Refactoring' without tests isn't refactoring, it is just moving shit around."

—Corey Haines (@coreyhaines), December 20, 2013, on Twitter

A unit test is a piece of code that executes a small part of your production code base in a particular context. The test will show you, in a split second, that your code works as you expect it to work. If unit test coverage is pretty high, and you can check in less than a minute that all parts of your system under development are working correctly, this will have numerous advantages:

- Numerous investigations and studies have proven that fixing bugs after software is shipped is much more expensive than having unit tests in place.

- Unit tests give you immediate feedback about your entire code base. Provided that test coverage is sufficiently high (approx. 100%), developers know in just a few seconds if the code works correctly.

- Unit tests give developers the confidence to refactor their code without fear of doing something wrong that breaks the code. In fact, a structural change in a code base without a safety net of unit tests is dangerous and should not be called refactoring.

- A high coverage with unit tests can prevent time-consuming and frustrating debugging sessions. The often hour-long searches for the causation of a bug using a debugger can be reduced dramatically. Of course, you will never be able to completely eliminate the use of a debugger. This tool can still be used to analyze subtle problems, or to find the cause of a failed unit test. But it will no longer be the pivotal developer tool to ensure the quality of your code.

- Unit tests are a kind of executable documentation because they show exactly how the code is designed to be used. They are, so to speak, something of a usage example.

- Unit tests can easily detect regressions; that is, they can immediately show things that used to work, but have unexpectedly stopped working after a change was made.

- Unit testing fosters the creation of clean and well-formed interfaces. It can help to avoid unwanted dependencies between units. A *design for testability* is also a good *design for usability*; that is, if a piece of code can easily be mounted against a test fixture, then it can usually also be integrated with less effort into the system's production code.

- Unit testing makes development go faster.

The last item in this list appears to be paradoxical and needs a little bit of explanation. Unit testing helps development go faster—how can that be? That doesn't seem logical.

No doubt about it: writing unit tests takes effort. First and foremost, managers just see that effort and do not understand why developers should invest time into these tests. Especially during the initial phase of a project, the positive effect of unit testing on development speed may not be visible. In these early stages, when the complexity of the system is relatively low and most everything works fine, writing unit tests seems at first just to take effort. But times are changing ...

When the system becomes bigger and bigger (+ 100,000 LOC) and the complexity increases, it becomes more difficult to understand and verify the system (remember software entropy described in Chapter 1). When many developers on different teams are working on a huge system, they are confronted with code written by other developers every day. Without unit tests in place, this can become a very frustrating job. I'm sure everyone knows those stupid, endless debugging sessions, walking through the code in single-step mode while analyzing the values of variables again and again and again. This is a huge waste of time and it will slow down development speed significantly.

Particularly in the mid-to-late stages of development, and in the maintenance phase after product delivery, good unit tests become very valuable. The greatest time savings from unit testing comes a few months or years after a test is written, when a unit or its API needs to be changed or extended.

If test coverage is high, it's nearly irrelevant whether a piece of code that is edited by a developer was written by himself or by another developer. Good unit tests help developers understand a piece of code written by another person quickly, even if it was written three years ago. If a test fails, it exactly shows where the behavior is broken. Developers can trust that everything still works correctly if all tests pass. Lengthy and annoying debugging sessions become a rarity, and the debugger serves mainly to find the cause of a failed test quickly if this cause is not obvious. And that's great because it's fun to work that way. It's motivating, and it leads to faster and better results. Developers will have greater confidence in the code base and will feel comfortable with it. Changing requirements or new feature requests? No problem, because they can ship the new product quick and often, and with excellent quality.

UNIT TEST FRAMEWORKS

There are several different unit test frameworks available for C++ development, for example, CppUnit, Boost.Test, CUTE, Google Test, Catch respectively Catch2, and a couple more.

In principle, all these frameworks follow the basic design of so-called *xUnit*, which is a collective name for several unit test frameworks that derive their structure and functionality from Smalltalk's *SUnit*. Apart from the fact that the content of this chapter is not fixated on a specific unit test framework, because its content is applicable to unit testing in general, a full and detailed comparison of all available frameworks is beyond the scope of this book. Furthermore, choosing a suitable framework is dependent on many factors. For instance, if it is very important to you to be able to add new tests with a minimal amount of work quickly, this might be knock-out criteria for certain frameworks.

What About QA?

A developer might have the following attitude: "Why should I test my software? We have testers and a QA department, it's their job."

The essential question is this: Is software quality a sole concern of the quality assurance department?

The simple and clear answer: **No!**

It would be extremely unprofessional to hand over a piece of software to QA knowing that it contains bugs. Professional developers never foist off the responsibility for a system's quality on other departments. On the contrary, professional software craftspeople build productive partnerships with the people from QA. They should work closely together and complement each other.

Of course, it is a very ambitious goal to deliver 100% defect-free software. From time to time, QA will find something wrong. And that's good. QA is our second safety net. They check whether the previous quality assurance measures were sufficient and effective.

We can learn from our mistakes and get better. Professional developers remedy those quality deficits immediately by fixing the bugs found by QA, and by writing automated unit tests to catch them in the future. Then they should carefully think about this: "How could it happen that we've overlooked this issue?" The result of this retrospective should serve as feedback to improve the development process.

Rules for Good Unit Tests

I've seen many unit tests that are pretty unhelpful. Unit tests should add value to your project. To achieve this goal, you need to follow some essential rules, which I describe in this section.

Test Code Quality

The same high-quality requirements for the production code have to be valid for the unit test code. I'll go even further. Ideally, there should be no distinction between production and test code—they are equal. If we say that there is production code on the one hand and test code on the other, we separate things that belong together. Don't do that! Thinking about production and test code in two categories lays the foundation to neglect tests later in the project.

Unit Test Naming

If a unit test fails, the developer wants to know immediately:

- What is the name of the unit; whose test failed?

- What was tested, and what was the environment of the test (the test scenario)?

- What was the expected test result, and what was the actual test result of the failed test?

Hence an expressive and descriptive naming standard for your unit tests is very important. My advice is to establish naming standards for all tests.

First of all, it's good practice to name the unit test module (depending on the unit test framework, they are called *test harnesses* or *test fixtures*) in such a way so that the tested unit can be easily derived from it. They should have a name like <Unit_under_Test>Test, whereby the placeholder `<Unit_under_Test>` is substituted with the name of the test subject. For instance, if your system under test (SUT) is the unit `Money`, the corresponding test fixture that attaches to that unit and contains all unit test cases should be named `MoneyTest` (see Figure 2-3).

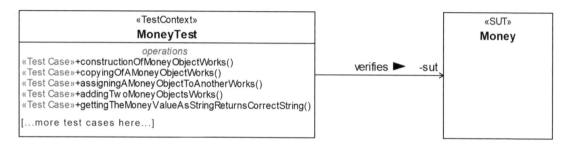

Figure 2-3. *The system under test, (SUT) Money and its test fixture, MoneyTest*

Beyond that, unit tests must have expressive and descriptive names. It is not helpful when unit tests have meaningless names like `testConstructor()`, `test4391()`, or `sumTest()`. Here are two suggestions for finding good names for them.

For general, multipurpose classes that can be used in different contexts, an expressive name could contain the following parts:

- The precondition of the test scenario, that is, the state of the SUT before the test was executed.

- The tested part of the unit under test, typically the name of the tested procedure, function, or method (API).

- The expected test result.

That leads to a name template for unit test procedures/methods like this one:

`<PreconditionAndStateOfUnitUnderTest>_<TestedPartOfAPI>_<ExpectedBehavior>`

Listing 2-1 shows a few examples.

Listing 2-1. Examples of Good and Expressive Unit Test Names

```
void CustomerCacheTest::cacheIsEmpty_addElement_sizeIsOne();
void CustomerCacheTest::cacheContainsOneElement_removeElement_sizeIsZero();
void ComplexNumberCalculatorTest::givenTwoComplexNumbers_add_Works();
```

```
void MoneyTest:: givenTwoMoneyObjectsWithDifferentBalance_Inequality
Comparison_Works();
void MoneyTest::createMoneyObjectWithParameter_getBalanceAsString_
returnsCorrectString();
void InvoiceTest::invoiceIsReadyForAccounting_getInvoiceDate_returnsToday();
```

Another possible approach to building expressive unit test names is to manifest a specific requirement in the name. These names typically reflect requirements of the application's domain. For instance, they could be derived from stakeholder requirements. See Listing 2-2.

Listing 2-2. More Examples of Unit Test Names that Verify Domain-Specific Requirements

```
void UserAccountTest::creatingNewAccountWithExisting
EmailAddressThrowsException();
void ChessEngineTest::aPawnCanNotMoveBackwards();
void ChessEngineTest::aCastlingIsNotAllowedIfInvolvedKingHasBeenMovedBefore();
void ChessEngineTest::aCastlingIsNotAllowedIfInvolvedRookHasBeenMovedBefore();
void HeaterControlTest::ifWaterTemperatureIsGreaterThan92DegTurnHeaterOff();
void BookInventoryTest::aBookThatIsInTheInventoryCanBeBorrowedByAuthorized
People();
void BookInventoryTest::aBookThatIsAlreadyBorrowedCanNotBeBorrowedTwice();
```

As you read these test method names, it should become clear that even if the implementation of the tests and the test methods are not shown here, a lot of useful information can be easily derived. This is also a great advantage if such a test fails. All known unit test frameworks either output the name of a failed test via stdout on the command-line interface or list it in a special output window of the IDE. Thus, error location is greatly facilitated.

Unit Test Independence

Each unit test must be independent of all the others. It would be fatal if tests had to be executed in a specific order because one test was based on the result of the previous one. Never write a unit test whose result is the prerequisite for a subsequent test. Never leave the unit under test in an altered state, which is a precondition for the following tests.

Major problems can be caused by global states, for example, the usage of Singletons or static members in your unit under test. Not only do Singletons increase the coupling between software units, they also often hold a global state that circumvents unit test independence. For instance, if a certain global state is the precondition for a successful test, but the previous test has mutated that global state, this can cause serious trouble.

Especially in legacy systems, which are often littered with Singletons, this begs the question: how can you get rid of all those nasty dependencies to those Singletons and make your code more easily testable? Well, that's an important question I discuss in the section entitled "Dependency Injection" in Chapter 6.

DEALING WITH LEGACY SYSTEMS

If you are confronted with so-called legacy systems and you are facing many difficulties while trying to add unit tests, I recommend the book *Working Effectively with Legacy Code* [Feathers07] by Michael C. Feathers. Feathers's book contains many strategies for working with large, untested legacy code bases. It also includes a catalogue of 24 dependency-breaking techniques. These strategies and techniques are beyond the scope of this book.

One Assertion per Test

My advice is to limit a unit test to one assertion only, as shown in Listing 2-3. I know that this is a controversial topic, but I will try to explain why I think this is important.

Listing 2-3. A Unit Test that Checks the not-equal-Operator of a Money Class

```
void MoneyTest::givenTwoMoneyObjectsWithDifferentBalance_
InequalityComparison_Works() {
  const Money m1(-4000.0);
  const Money m2(2000.0);
  ASSERT_TRUE(m1 != m2);
}
```

One could now argue that you could also check whether other comparison operators (e.g., Money::operator==()) are working correctly in this unit test. It would be easy to do that, by simply adding more assertions, as shown in Listing 2-4.

Listing 2-4. Question: Is It a Good Idea to Check All Comparison Operators in One Unit Test?

```
void MoneyTest::givenTwoMoneyObjectsWithDifferentBalance_
testAllComparisonOperators() {
  const Money m1(-4000.0);
  const Money m2(2000.0);
  ASSERT_TRUE(m1 != m2);
  ASSERT_FALSE(m1 == m2);
  ASSERT_TRUE(m1 < m2);
  ASSERT_FALSE(m1 > m2);
  // ...more assertions here...
}
```

I think the problems with this approach are obvious:

- If a test can fail for several reasons, it can be difficult for developers to find the cause of the error quickly. Above all, an early assertion that fails obscures additional errors, that is, it hides subsequent assertions, because the execution of the test is stopped.

- As explained in the section "Unit Test Naming," we should name a test in a precise and expressive way. With multiple assertions, a unit test tests many things (which is, by the way, a violation of the single responsibility principle; see Chapter 6), and it would be difficult to find a good name for it. The `...testAllComparisonOperators()` name is not precise enough.

Independent Initialization of Unit Test Environments

This rule is somewhat akin to unit test independence. When a cleanly implemented test completes, all states related to that test must disappear. In more specific terms, when running all unit tests, each test must be an isolated partial instantiation of an application. Each test has to set up and initialize its required environment completely on its own. The same applies to cleaning up after the execution of the test.

Exclude Getters and Setters

Don't write unit tests for usual getters and setters of a class, as shown in Listing 2-5.

Listing 2-5. A Simple Setter and Getter

```cpp
void Customer::setForename(const std::string& forename) {
  this->forename = forename;
}

const std::string& Customer::getForename() const {
  return forename;
}
```

Do you really expect that something could go wrong with such straightforward methods? These member functions are typically so simple that it would be foolish to write unit tests for them. Furthermore, usual getters and setters are implicitly tested by other and more important unit tests.

Attention, I just wrote that it is not necessary to test **usual and simple** getters and setters. Sometimes, getters and setters are not that simple. According to the information hiding principle (see the section about information hiding in Chapter 3) that we will discuss later, it should be hidden from the client if a getter is simple and stupid, or if it has to make complex things to determine its return value. Therefore, it can sometimes be useful to write an explicit test for a getter or setter.

Exclude Third-Party Code

Don't write tests for third-party code! We don't have to verify that libraries or frameworks do work as expected. For example, we can assume with a clear conscience that the used member function std::vector::push_back() from the C++ Standard Library works correctly. On the contrary, we can expect that third-party code comes with its own unit tests. It can be a wise architectural decision to not use libraries or frameworks in your project that don't have their own unit tests and whose quality is doubtful.

Exclude External Systems

The same is true for external systems. Don't write tests for external systems that are part of the context of your system to be developed, and thus are not in your responsibility. For instance, if your financial software uses an existing, external currency conversion system that is connected via the Internet, you should not test this. Besides the fact that such a system cannot provide a defined answer (the conversion factor between currencies varies minute by minute), and that such a system might be impossible to reach due to network issues, we are not responsible for the external system.

My advice is to mock (see the section "Test Doubles (Fake Objects)" later in this chapter) these things out and to test your code, not theirs.

What Do We Do with the Database?

Many IT systems contain (relational) databases nowadays. They are required to persist huge amounts of objects or data into longer-term storage, so that these objects or data can be queried in a comfortable way and survive a system shutdown.

An important question is this: what do you do with the database during unit testing?

> *"My first and overriding piece of advice on this subject is: When there is any way to test without a database, test without the database!"*
>
> —Gerard Meszaros, *xUnit Test Patterns*

Databases can cause diverse and sometimes subtle problems during unit testing. For instance, if many unit tests use the same database, the database tends to become a large central storage that those tests must share for different purposes. This sharing may adversely affect the independence of the unit tests I discussed earlier in this chapter. It could be difficult to guarantee the required precondition for each unit test. The execution of a single unit test can cause unwanted side effects for other tests via the commonly used database.

Another problem is that databases are basically slow. They are much slower than access to local computer memory. Unit tests that interact with the database tend to run magnitudes slower than tests that can run entirely in memory. Imagine you have a few hundred unit tests, and each test needs an extra time span of 500ms on average, caused by the database queries. In sum, all the tests take several minutes longer than without a database.

My advice is to mock out the database (see the section about test doubles/mock objects later in this chapter) and execute all the unit tests solely in memory. Don't worry: the database, if it exists, will be involved at the integration and system testing level.

Don't Mix Test Code with Production Code

Sometimes developers come up with the idea to equip their production code with test code. For example, a class might contain code to handle a dependency to a collaborating class during a test in the manner shown in Listing 2-6.

Listing 2-6. One Possible Solution to Deal with a Dependency During Testing

```cpp
#include <memory>
#include "DataAccessObject.h"
#include "CustomerDAO.h"
#include "FakeDAOForTest.h"

using DataAccessObjectPtr = std::unique_ptr<DataAccessObject>;

class Customer {
public:
  Customer() = default;
  explicit Customer(const bool testMode) : inTestMode(testMode) {}

  void save() {
    DataAccessObjectPtr dataAccessObject = getDataAccessObject();
    // ...use dataAccessObject to save this customer...
  }

  // ...

private:
  DataAccessObjectPtr getDataAccessObject() const {
    if (inTestMode) {
      return std::make_unique<FakeDAOForTest>();
    } else {
      return std::make_unique<CustomerDAO>();
    }
  }
  // ...more operations here...

  bool inTestMode{ false };
  // ...more attributes here...
};
```

DataAccessObject is the abstract base class of specific DAOs, in this case, CustomerDAO and FakeDAOForTest. The last one is a so-called fake object, which is simply a test double (see the section about test doubles later in this chapter). It is intended to replace the real DAO, since we do not want to test it, and we don't want to save the customer during the test (remember my advice about databases). The Boolean data member inTestMode determines which one of the DAOs is used.

Well, this code would work, but the solution has several disadvantages.

First of all, the production code is cluttered with test code. Although it does not appear dramatically at first sight, it can increase complexity and reduce readability. We need an additional member to distinguish between the test mode and production usage of our system. This Boolean member has nothing to do with a customer, not to mention with our system's domain. And it's easy to imagine that this kind of member is required in many classes in our system.

Moreover, the Customer class has dependencies to CustomerDAO and FakeDAOForTest. You can see it in the list of includes at the top of the source code. This means that the test dummy FakeDAOForTest is also part of the system in the production environment. It is to be hoped that the code of the test double is never called in production, but it is compiled, linked, and deployed.

Of course, there are more elegant ways to deal with these dependencies and to keep the production code free from test code. For instance, we can inject the specific DAO as a reference parameter in Customer::save(). See Listing 2-7.

Listing 2-7. Avoiding Dependencies to Test Code (1)

```
class DataAccessObject;

class Customer {
public:
  void save(DataAccessObject& dataAccessObject) {
    // ...use dataAccessObject to save this customer...
  }
  // ...
};
```

Alternatively, this can be done while constructing instances of type Customer. In this case, we must hold a reference to the DAO as an attribute of the class. Furthermore, we have to suppress the automatic generation of the default constructor through the compiler, because we don't want any user of Customer to be able to create an improperly initialized instance of it. See Listing 2-8.

Listing 2-8. Avoiding Dependencies to Test Code (2)

```
class DataAccessObject;

class Customer {
public:
  Customer() = delete;
  explicit Customer(DataAccessObject& dataAccessObject) :
  dataAccessObject_(dataAccessObject) {}
  void save() {
    // ...use member dataAccessObject to save this customer...
  }
  // ...
private:
  DataAccessObject& dataAccessObject_;
  // ...
};
```

DELETED FUNCTIONS

In C++, the compiler automatically generates the so-called *special member functions* (default constructor, copy constructor, copy-assignment operator, and destructor) for a type if it does not declare its own [C++11]. Since C++11, this list of special member functions is extended by the move constructor and move-assignment operator. C++11 (and higher) provides an easy and declarative way to suppress the automatic creation of any special member function, as well as normal member functions and non-member functions: you can delete them. For instance, you can prevent the creation of a default constructor this way:

```
class Clazz {
public:
  Clazz() = delete;
};
```

And another example: you can delete the new operator to prevent classes from being dynamically allocated on the heap:

```cpp
class Clazz {
public:
  void* operator new(std::size_t) = delete;
};
```

A third alternative could be that the specific DAO is created by a factory (see the section entitled "Factory" in Chapter 9 about design patterns) that the Customer knows. This factory can be configured from the outside to create the kind of DAO that is required if the system runs in a test environment. No matter which one of these possible solutions you choose, the Customer is free of test code. There are no dependencies to specific DAOs in Customer.

Tests Must Run Fast

In large projects, one day you will reach the point where you have thousands of unit tests. This is great in terms of software quality. But an awkward side effect might be that people will stop running these tests before they're doing a check-in into the source code repository, because they take too long.

It is easy to imagine that there is a strong correlation between the time it takes to run tests and a team's productivity. If running all unit tests takes 15 minutes, 1/2 hour, or more, developers are impeded in doing their work and waste their time waiting for the test results. Even if the execution of each unit test takes "only" half a second on average, it takes more than eight minutes to carry out 1,000 tests. That means that the execution of the whole test suite 10 times a day will result in almost 1.5 hours of waiting time. As a result, developers will run the tests less often.

My advice is: **Tests must run fast!** Unit tests should establish a rapid feedback loop for developers. The execution of all unit tests for a large project should not last longer than about three minutes, and rather less time than that. For a faster, local test execution (a few seconds) during development, the test framework should provide an easy way to temporarily turn off irrelevant groups of tests.

On the automated build system, all tests must be executed without exception continuously every time before the final product will be built. The development team should get an immediate notification if one or more tests fail on the build system. For instance, this can be done via email or with the help of an optical visualization (e.g., due to a flat screen on the wall, or a "traffic light" controlled by the build system) in a prominent place. If even just one test fails, under no circumstances should you release and ship the product!

How Do You Find a Test's Input Data?

A piece of software can react very differently depending on the data used as input. If unit tests should add value to your project, you may come quickly to the question: How do I find all test cases that are necessary to ensure good fault detection?

On the one hand, you want to have a very high, ideally complete test coverage. On the other hand, economic aspects such as project duration and budget must also be kept in mind. That means that it is often not possible to perform extensive testing for each set of test data, especially when there is a large set of input combinations and you will end up with an almost infinite number of test cases.

To find a sufficient number of test cases, there are two central and important concepts in the quality assurance of software: *equivalence partitioning,* sometimes also called equivalence class partitioning (ECP), and the *boundary value analysis.*

Equivalence Partitioning

An equivalence partition, sometimes also called equivalence class, is a set or portion of input data for which a piece of software, both in a test environment and in its operational environment, should exhibit similar behavior. In other words, the behavior of a system, component, class, or function/method is assumed to be the same, based on its specification.

The result of an equivalence partitioning can be used to derive test cases from these partitions of similar input data. In principle, the test cases are designed so that each partition is covered at least once.

As a specification-driven approach, the technique of equivalence partitioning is properly speaking a blackbox test design technique, i.e. the innards of the software to be tested are usually not known. However, it is also a very useful approach for whitebox testing techniques, i.e. unit testing and test-first approaches like TDD (see Chapter 8).

Let's look at an example. Suppose we have to test a C++ class that calculates the interest on a bank account. According to the requirements specification, the account should exhibit the following behavior:

- The bank charges 4 percent penalty interest on overdrafts.

- The bank offers 0.5 percent interest for the first 5,000 USD savings.

- The bank offers 1 percent interest for the next 5,000 USD savings.

- The bank offers 2 percent interest for the rest.

- Interest is calculated on a daily basis.

According to these specifications, the interest calculator's API therefore has two parameters: the amount of money and, as interest is calculated on a daily basis, the number of days for which this amount is valid. This means we have to build equivalence classes for two input parameters.

The equivalence partitioning for the amount of money is depicted in Figure 2-4.

Figure 2-4. The equivalence classes of the input parameter for the monetary amount

The equivalence classes for the validity period in days are a bit simpler and are depicted in Figure 2-5.

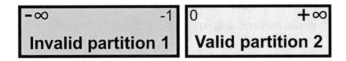

Figure 2-5. The equivalence classes of the input parameter for the number of days

What insights can we now derive from this for test case creation?

First of all, note that the input parameter for the monetary amount allows infinitely large positive or infinitely large negative values. In contrast, negative values for the number of days are not allowed.

This is the moment when it would be advisable to involve the business stakeholders and the domain experts.

First, it should be clarified whether the upper or lower limit for the amount of money is really infinite. The answer to this question not only affects the test cases, but also the data type to be used for this parameter. Furthermore, the specification does not clarify what should happen if a negative value is used for the number of days. A negative value would be invalid, yes, but what kind of reaction should the interest calculator show?

Another question that could be answered by such an analysis would be, for example, whether the interest rates are really as fixed (constants) as the specification requires. Perhaps the interest rates are variable, and possibly also the amounts of money associated with them.

However, test cases can now be systematically derived from this analysis. The idea behind equivalence partitioning is that it is enough to pick only one value from each partition for testing. The hypothesis behind this technique is that **if one condition/value in a partition passes a test, all others in the same partition will also pass**. Likewise, if one condition/value in a partition fails, all other conditions/values in that partition will also fail. If there is more than one parameter, as in our case, appropriate combinations should be formed.

Boundary Value Analysis

"Bugs lurk in corners and congregate at boundaries."

—Boris Beizer, Software Testing Techniques [Beizer90]

Many software bugs can be traced back to difficulties in the border areas of the equivalence classes, for example at the transition between two valid equivalence classes, between a valid and an invalid equivalence class, or due to an extreme value that was not taken into account. Therefore, building equivalence classes is complemented by boundary value analysis.

In the discipline of testing, boundary value analysis is a technique that finds the switch-over points between equivalence classes and deals with extreme values. The result of such an analysis is useful to select the input values of a numerical parameter for the tests:

- Exactly on its minimum.

- Just above the minimum.

- A nominal value taken somewhere from the middle of the equivalence partition.

- Just below the maximum.

- Exactly on its maximum.

These values can also be depicted on a number line, as shown in Figure 2-6.

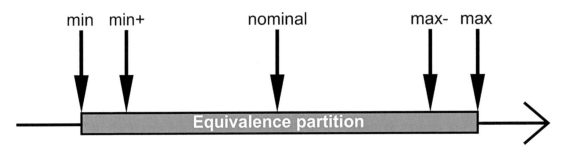

Figure 2-6. *The input parameters derived from a boundary value analysis*

If the boundary values are determined and tested for each equivalence partition, then very good test coverage can be achieved in practice with relatively little effort.

Test Doubles (Fake Objects)

Unit tests should only be called "unit tests" if the units to be tested are completely independent from collaborators during test execution, that is, the unit under test does not use other units or external systems. For instance, while the involvement of a database during an integration test is uncritical and required, because that's the purpose of an integration test, access (e.g., a query) to this database during a real unit test is proscribed (see the section "What Do We Do with the Database?" earlier in this chapter). Thus, dependencies of the unit to be tested with other modules or external systems should be replaced with so-called *test doubles*, also known as *fake objects*, or *mock-ups*.

In order to work in an elegant way with such test doubles, we should strive for loose coupling of the unit under test (see the section entitled "Loose Coupling" in Chapter 3). For instance, an abstraction (e.g., an interface in the form of a pure abstract class) can be introduced at the access point to an unwanted collaborator, as shown in Figure 2-7.

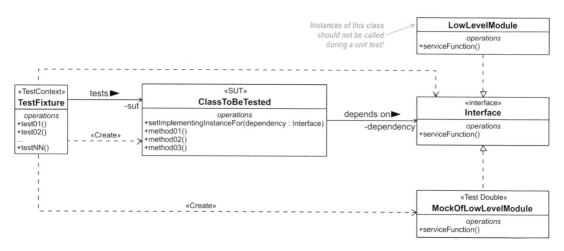

Figure 2-7. *An interface makes it easy to replace the LowLevelModule with a test double*

Let's assume that you want to develop an application that uses an external web service for real-time currency conversions. During a unit test you cannot use this external service naturally, because it delivers different conversion factors every minute. Furthermore, the service is queried via the Internet, which is basically slow and can fail. And it is impossible to simulate borderline cases. Hence, you have to replace the real currency conversion with a test double during the unit test.

First, we have to introduce a variation point in the code to be able to replace the module that communicates with the currency conversion service with a test double. This can be done with the help of an interface, which in C++ is an abstract class with solely pure virtual member functions. See Listing 2-9.

Listing 2-9. An Abstract Interface for Currency Converters

```cpp
class CurrencyConverter {
public:
  virtual ~CurrencyConverter() { }
  virtual long double getConversionFactor() const = 0;
};
```

The access to the currency conversion service via the Internet is encapsulated in a class that implements the CurrencyConverter interface. See Listing 2-10.

Listing 2-10. The Class that Accesses the Realtime Currency Conversion Service

```cpp
class RealtimeCurrencyConversionService : public CurrencyConverter {
public:
  virtual long double getConversionFactor() const override;
  // ...more members here that are required to access the service...
};
```

For testing purposes, a second implementation exists: The CurrencyConversionServiceMock test double. Objects of this class will return a defined and predictable conversion factor as it is required for unit testing. Furthermore, objects of this class provide the capability to set the conversion factor from the outside, for example, to simulate borderline cases. See Listing 2-11.

Listing 2-11. The Test Double

```cpp
class CurrencyConversionServiceMock : public CurrencyConverter {
public:
  virtual long double getConversionFactor() const override {
    return conversionFactor;
  }

  void setConversionFactor(const long double value) {
    conversionFactor = value;
  }
private:
  long double conversionFactor{0.5};
};
```

At the place in the production code where the currency converter is used, the interface is now used to access the service. Due to this abstraction, it is totally transparent to the client's code which kind of implementation is used during runtime— either the real currency converter or its test double. See Listings 2-12 and 2-13.

Listing 2-12. The Header of the Class that Uses the Service

```cpp
#include <memory>

class CurrencyConverter;
```

```
class UserOfConversionService {
public:
  UserOfConversionService() = delete;
  explicit UserOfConversionService(const std::shared_
  ptr<CurrencyConverter>& conversionService);
  void doSomething();
  // More of the public class interface follows here...

private:
  std::shared_ptr<CurrencyConverter> conversionService_;
  //...internal implementation...
};
```

Listing 2-13. An Excerpt from the Implementation File

```
UserOfConversionService::UserOfConversionService     (const std::shared_
ptr<CurrencyConverter>& conversionService) :
  conversionService_(conversionService) { }

void UserOfConversionService::doSomething() {
  long double conversionFactor = conversionService_->getConversionFactor();
  // ...
}
```

In a unit test for the UserOfConversionService class, the test case can now pass in the mock object through the initialization constructor. On the other hand, during normal operations, the real service can be passed through the constructor. This technique is a design pattern called *dependency injection,* which is discussed in detail in the eponymous section of Chapter 9. See Listing 2-14.

Listing 2-14. UserOfConversionService Gets its Required CurrencyConverter Object

```
auto serviceToUse =
  std::make_shared</* name of the desired class here */>();
UserOfConversionService user(serviceToUse);
// The instance of UserOfConversionService is ready for use...
user.doSomething();
```

CHAPTER 3

Be Principled

"I would advise students to pay more attention to the fundamental ideas rather than the latest technology. The technology will be out-of-date before they graduate. Fundamental ideas never get out of date."

—David L. Parnas

In this chapter, I introduce the most important and fundamental principles of well-designed and well-crafted software. What makes these principles special is the fact that they are not tied to certain programming paradigms or programming languages. Some of them are not even specific to software development. For instance, the discussed KISS principle, an acronym for "keep it simple, stupid," can be relevant to many areas of life. Generally speaking, it is not a bad idea to make everything as simple in life as possible—not only software development.

This means that you should not learn the following principles once and then forget them. I strongly recommend you internalize them. These principles are so important that they should ideally become second nature to every developer. Many of the more concrete principles I discuss later in this book have their roots in these basic principles.

What Is a Principle?

In this book you will find various principles for better C++ code and well-designed software. But what is a principle in general?

Many people have principles that guide them through their life. For example, if you're against eating meat for several reasons, that would be a principle. If you want to protect your child, you give him principles along the way, guiding him to make the right decisions on their own, for example "Be careful and don't talk to strangers!" With this principle in mind, the child can deduce the correct behavior in certain specific situations.

© Stephan Roth 2021
S. Roth, *Clean C++20*, https://doi.org/10.1007/978-1-4842-5949-8_3

A principle is a kind of rule, belief, or idea that guides you. Principles are often directly coupled to values or a value system. For instance, we don't need to be told that cannibalism is wrong because humans have an innate value regarding human life. And as a further example, the well-known "Manifesto for Agile Software Development" [Beck01] contains 12 principles that guide project teams in uncovering better ways to develop software.

Principles are not irrevocable laws. They are not carved in stone. Willful violations of principles are sometimes necessary in programming. If you have very good reasons to violate principles, do so, but do so very carefully! It should be an exception.

Some of the following basic principles are, at various points later in the book, revisited and deepened.

KISS

"Everything should be made as simple as possible, but not simpler."

—Albert Einstein, theoretical physicist, 1879 - 1955

KISS is an acronym for "keep it simple, stupid" or "keep it simple and stupid" (okay, I know, there are other meanings for this acronym, but these two are the most common ones). In eXtreme Programming (XP), this principle is represented by a practice called "do the simplest thing that could possibly work" (DTSTTCPW). The KISS principle states that simplicity should be a major goal in software development, and that unnecessary complexity should be avoided.

I think that KISS is one of those principles that developers often forget when they are developing software. Software developers tend to write code in some elaborate way and make things more complicated than they should be. I know we are all excellently skilled and highly motivated developers, and we know everything about design and architecture patterns, frameworks, technologies, tools, and other cool and fancy stuff. Crafting cool software is not just our 9-to-5 job—it is our mission and we achieve fulfillment through our work.

But we have to keep in mind that any software system has an intrinsic complexity that is already challenging in itself. No doubt, complex problems often require complex code. The intrinsic complexity cannot be reduced. This kind of complexity is just there, due to the requirements to be fulfilled by the system. But it would be fatal to add unnecessary, homemade complexity to this intrinsic complexity. Therefore, it is advisable not to use every fancy feature of your language or cool design patterns just because you can. On the other hand, do not overplay simplicity. If 10 decisions are necessary in a `switch-case` statement and there is no better, alternative solution, that's just how it is.

Keep your code as simple as you can! Of course, if there are high prioritized quality requirements about flexibility and extensibility, you have to add complexity to fulfill these requirements. For instance, you can use the well-known **strategy pattern** (see Chapter 9 about design patterns) to introduce a flexible variation point into your code when requirements demand it. But be careful and add only the amount of complexity that makes such things easier.

> *"Focusing on simplicity is probably one of the most difficult things for a programmer to do. And it is a life long learning experience."*
>
> —Adrian Bolboaca (@adibolb), April 3, 2014, on Twitter

YAGNI

> *"Always implement things when you actually need them, never when you just foresee that you need them."*
>
> —Ron Jeffries, *You're NOT gonna need it!* [Jeffries98]

This principle is tightly coupled to the previously discussed KISS principle. YAGNI is an acronym for "you aren't gonna need it!" or is sometimes translated to "you ain't gonna need it!". YAGNI is the declaration of war against speculative generalization and over-engineering. It states that you should not write code that is not necessary at the moment, but might be in the future.

Probably every developer knows these kinds of tempting impulses in their daily work: "Maybe we could use it later...", or "We're going to need..." **No, we aren't gonna need it!** We should under all circumstances avoid producing anything today for an uncertain and speculative future. In most cases, this code is simply not needed. But if we have implemented that unnecessary thing, we've wasted our precious time and the code gets more complicated than it should be! And of course, we also violate the previously discussed KISS principle. Even worse, these code pieces could be buggy and could cause serious problems!

My advice is this: Trust in the power of refactoring and build things only when you know that they are actually necessary, not before.

DRY

"Copy and paste is a design error."

—David L. Parnas

Although this principle is one of the most important, I'm quite sure that it is often violated, unintentionally or intentionally. DRY is an acronym for "don't repeat yourself!" and states that we should avoid duplication, because duplication is evil. Sometimes this principle is also referred to as "once and only once" (OAOO).

The reason that duplication is very dangerous is obvious: when one piece is changed, its copies must be changed accordingly. And don't have high hopes. It is a safe bet that change will occur. I think it's unnecessary to mention that any copied piece will be forgotten sooner or later and we can say hello to bugs.

Okay, that's it—nothing more to say? Wait, there is still something and we need to go deeper. In fact, I believe that the DRY principle is often misunderstood and also construed too pedantically by many developers! Thus, we should refresh our understanding of this principle.

It's About Knowledge!

"Don't Repeat Yourself (or DRY) is probably one of the most misunderstood parts of the book."

—Dave Thomas, Orthogonality and the DRY Principle, 2003

In their brilliant book, *The Pragmatic Programmer* [Hunt99], Dave Thomas and Andy Hunt state that applying the DRY principle means that we have to ensure that "every piece of knowledge must have a single, unambiguous, authoritative representation within a system." It is noticeable that Dave and Andy did not explicitly mention the code, but they talk about the knowledge.

First of all, a system's knowledge is far broader than just its code. For instance, the DRY principle is also valid for business processes, requirements, database schemes, documentation, project plans, test plans, or the system's configuration data. DRY affects everything! Perhaps you can imagine that strict compliance with this principle is not as easy as it might seem at first sight.

Building Abstractions Is Sometimes Hard

Moreover, an exaggerated application of the DRY principle at all costs in a code base can lead to some fiddly problems. The reason is that creating an adequate common abstraction from duplicated code pieces can quickly become a tricky task, sometimes deteriorating the readability and comprehensibility of the code.

The annoyance becomes really big if there are requirement changes or functional enhancements that affect only one locus of usage of a multiple used abstraction, as the following example demonstrates.

Let's look at the following two (simplified) classes (Listings 3-1 and 3-2) from software for an online mail order business.

Listing 3-1. The Class for the Shopping Cart

```cpp
#include "Product.h"
#include <algorithm>
#include <vector>

class ShoppingCart {
public:
  void addProduct(const Product& product) {
    goods.push_back(product);
  }

  void removeProduct(const Product& product) {
    std::erase(goods, product);
  }

private:
  std::vector<Product> goods;
};
```

Listing 3-2. The Class Used to Ship the Ordered Products

```
#include "Product.h"
#include <algorithm>
#include <vector>

class Shipment {
public:
  void addProduct(const Product& product) {
    goods.push_back(product);
  }

  void removeProduct(const Product& product) {
    std::erase(goods, product);
  }

private:
  std::vector<Product> goods;
};
```

I'm pretty sure you would agree that these two classes are duplicated code and that they therefore violate the DRY principle. The only difference is the class name; all other lines of code are identical.

THE ERASE-REMOVE IDIOM (UNTIL C++20)

Before C++20, if developers wanted to eliminate elements from a container, such as a std::vector, they often applied the so-called Erase-Remove idiom on that container.

In this idiom, two steps were successively applied to the container. First, the algorithm std::remove was used to move those elements that did **not** match the removal criteria, to the front of the container. The name of this function is misleading, as no elements are actually removed by std::remove, but are shifted to the front of the container.

After that, std::remove returns an iterator pointing to the first element of the tail elements in the container. This iterator, as well as the container's end iterator, have then been passed to the std::vector::erase member function of the container to physically remove the tail elements. Applied to an arbitrary vector named vec, it looked like this:

```
// Removing all elements that match 'value' from a vector before C++20:
vec.erase(std::remove(begin(vec), end(vec), value), end(vec));
```

Since C++20, the Remove-Erase idiom is no longer necessary for this purpose. Instead, the two template functions `std::erase` and `std::erase_if`, both defined in header `<vector>`, can do the job. These functions not only physically delete the elements that match the deletion criteria, but can also be used easier because it is not necessary anymore to pass two iterators. Instead, the entire container can be passed, like this:

```
// Removing all elements that match 'value' from a vector since C++20:
std::erase(vec, value);
```

A suitable solution to get rid of the duplicated code seems to be to refactor the code and create a common abstraction, for instance by using inheritance, as shown in Listing 3-3.

Listing 3-3. The Base Class ProductContainer, from which ShoppingCart and Shipment Is Derived

```
#include "Product.h"
#include <algorithm>
#include <vector>

class ProductContainer {
public:
  void addProduct(const Product& product) {
    products.push_back(product);
  }

  void removeProduct(const Product& product) {
    std::erase(goods, product);
  }

private:
  std::vector<Product> products;
};

class ShoppingCart : public ProductContainer { };
class Shipment : public ProductContainer { };
```

Alternative solutions would be to use C++ templates, or to use composition instead of inheritance, i.e., `ShoppingCart` and `Shipment` use `ProductContainer` for their implementation (see the section entitled "Favor Composition over Inheritance" in Chapter 6).

So, the code for the shopping cart and for the shipment of goods has been identical, and we have removed the duplication now ... but wait! Maybe we should stop and ask ourselves the question: **Why was the code identical?!**

From the perspective of the business stakeholders, there may be very good reasons for making a very clear distinction between the two domain-specific concepts of a shopping basket and the product shipment. It is therefore highly recommended to ask the business people what they think of our idea to map the shopping basket and product shipping to the same piece of code. They might say, " Well, yes, on first sight a nice idea, but remember that customers can order certain products by any number, but for safety reasons we have to make sure that we never ship more than a certain number of these products with the same delivery."

By sharing the same code for two (or more) different domain concepts, we have coupled them very closely together. Often there are additional requirements to fulfill, which only affect one of both usages. In such a case, exceptions and special case handlings must be implemented for the several uses of the `ProductContainer` class. This can become a very tedious task, the readability of the code can suffer, and the initial advantage of the shared abstraction is quickly lost.

The conclusion is this: Reusing code is not basically a bad thing. But overzealous de-duplication of code creates the risk that we reuse code that only "accidentally" or "superficially" behaves the same, but that in fact has different meanings in the different places it is used. Mapping different domain concepts to the same piece of code is dangerous, because there are different reasons that this code needs to be changed.

The DRY principle is only marginally about code. In fact, it's about knowledge.

Information Hiding

Information hiding is a long-known and fundamental principle in software development. It was first documented in the seminal paper "On the Criteria to Be Used in Decomposing Systems Into Modules," [Parnas72] written by David L. Parnas in 1972.

The principle states that one piece of code that calls another piece of code should not "know" the internals about that other piece of code. This makes it possible to change internal parts of the called piece of code without being forced to change the calling piece of code accordingly.

David L. Parnas describes information hiding as the basic principle for decomposing systems into modules. Parnas argued that system modularization should concern the hiding of difficult design decisions or design decisions that are likely to change. The fewer internals a software unit (e.g., a class or component) exposes to its environment, the lesser is the coupling between the implementation of the unit and its clients. As a result, changes in the internal implementation of a software unit will not be propagated to its environment.

There are numerous advantages of information hiding:

- Limitation of the consequences of changes in modules

- Minimal influence on other modules if a bug fix is necessary

- Significantly increasing the reusability of modules

- Better testability of modules

Information hiding is often confused with encapsulation, but it's not the same. I know that both terms have been used in many noted books synonymously, but I don't agree. Information hiding is a design principle for aiding developers in finding good modules. The principle works at multiple levels of abstraction and unfolds its positive effect, especially in large systems.

Encapsulation is often a programming-language dependent technique for restricting access to the innards of a module. For instance, in C++ you can precede a list of class members with the `private` keyword to ensure that they cannot be accessed from outside the class. But just because we use these guards for access control, we are still far away from getting information hiding automatically. Encapsulation facilitates, but does not guarantee, information hiding.

The code example in Listing 3-4 shows an encapsulated class with poor information hiding.

Listing 3-4. A Class for Automatic Door Steering (Excerpt)

```
class AutomaticDoor {
public:
  enum class State {
    closed = 1,
    opening,
    open,
    closing
  };

private:
  State state;
  // ...more attributes here...

public:
  State getState() const;
  // ...more member functions here...
};
```

This is not information hiding, because parts of the internal implementation of the class are exposed to the environment, even if the class looks well encapsulated. Note the type of the return value of getState. The enumeration class State is required by clients using this class, as Listing 3-5 demonstrates.

Listing 3-5. An Example of How AutomaticDoor Must Be Used to Query the Door's Current State

```
#include "AutomaticDoor.h"

int main() {
  AutomaticDoor automaticDoor;
  AutomaticDoor::State doorsState = automaticDoor.getState();
  if (doorsState == AutomaticDoor::State::closed) {
    // do something...
  }
  return 0;
}
```

ENUMERATION CLASS (STRUCT) [C++11]

With C++11 there has also been an innovation on enumerations types. For downward compatibility to earlier C++ standards, there is still the well-known enumeration with its keyword enum. Since C++11, there are also the enumeration classes.

One problem with those old C++ enumerations is that they export their enumeration literals to the surrounding namespace, causing name clashes, such as in the following example:

```
const std::string bear;
// ...and elsewhere in the same namespace...
enum Animal { dog, deer, cat, bird, bear }; // error: 'bear' redeclared as
                                            different kind of symbol
```

Furthermore, old C++ enums implicitly convert to int, causing subtle errors when such a conversion is not expected or wanted:

```
enum Animal { dog, deer, cat, bird, bear };
Animal animal = dog;
int aNumber = animal; // Implicit conversion: works
```

These problems no longer exist when using enumeration classes, also called "new enums" or "strong enums." Their enumeration literals are local to the enumeration, and their values do not implicitly convert to other types (like to another enumeration or an int).

```
const std::string bear;
// ...and elsewhere in the same namespace...
enum class Animal { dog, deer, cat, bird, bear }; // No conflict with the
                                                  string named 'bear'
Animal animal = Animal::dog;
int aNumber = animal; // Compiler error!
```

It is strongly recommended to use enumeration classes instead of plain old enums for a modern C++ program, because it makes the code safer. And because enumeration classes are also classes, they can be forward declared.

What will happen if the internal implementation of AutomaticDoor must be changed and the enumeration class State is removed from the class? It is easy to see that this will have a significant impact on the client's code. It will result in changes everywhere that member function AutomaticDoor::getState() is used.

Listings 3-6 and 3-7 show an encapsulated AutomaticDoor with good information hiding.

Listing 3-6. A Better Designed Class for Automatic Door Steering

```cpp
class AutomaticDoor {
public:
  bool isClosed() const;
  bool isOpening() const;
  bool isOpen() const;
  bool isClosing() const;
  // ...more operations here...

private:
  enum class State {
    closed = 1,
    opening,
    open,
    closing
  };

  State state;
  // ...more attributes here...
};
```

Listing 3-7. An Example of How Elegant Class AutomaticDoor Can Be Used After it Was Changed

```cpp
#include "AutomaticDoor.h"

int main() {
  AutomaticDoor automaticDoor;
  if (automaticDoor.isClosed()) {
    // do something...
  }
  return 0;
}
```

Now it's much easier to change the innards of `AutomaticDoor`. The client code does not depend on internal parts of the class anymore. You can remove the `State` enumeration and replace it with another kind of implementation without users of the class noticing this.

Strong Cohesion

A general piece of advice in software development is that any software entity (i.e., module, component, unit, class, function, etc.) should have a strong (or high) cohesion. In very general terms, cohesion is strong when the module does a well-defined job.

To dive deeper into this principle, let's look at two examples where cohesion is weak, starting with Figure 3-1.

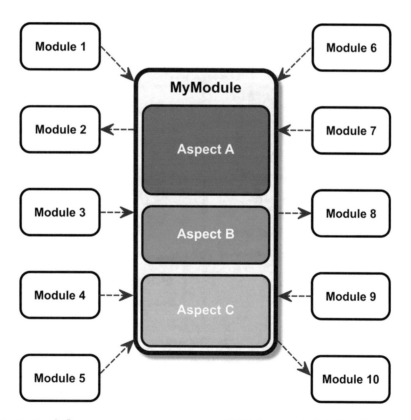

Figure 3-1. *`MyModule` has too many responsibilities, and this leads to many dependencies from and to other modules*

In this illustration of the modularization of an arbitrary system, three different aspects of the business domain are placed inside one single module. Aspects A, B, and C have nothing, or nearly nothing, in common, but all three are placed inside MyModule. Looking at the module's code could reveal that the functions of A, B, and C are operating on different, and completely independent, pieces of data.

Now look at all the dashed arrows in that picture. Each of them is a dependency. The element at the tail of such an arrow requires the element at the head of the arrow for its implementation. In this case, any other module of the system that wants to use services offered by A, or B, or C will make itself dependent from the whole module MyModule. The major drawback of such a design is obvious: it will result in too many dependencies and the maintainability goes down the drain.

To increase cohesion, the aspects of A, B, and C should be separated from each other and moved into their own modules (Figure 3-2).

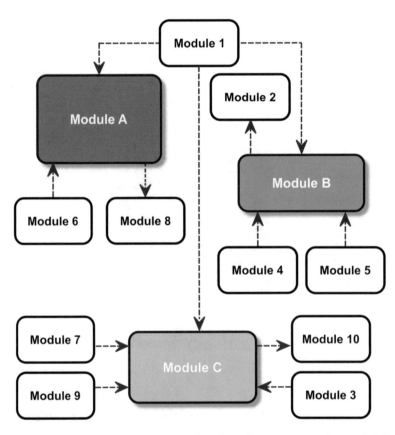

Figure 3-2. *High cohesion: The previously mixed aspects A, B, and C have been separated into discrete modules*

Now it is easy to see that each of these modules has far fewer dependencies than the old MyModule. It is clear that A, B, and C have nothing to do with each other directly. The only module that depends on all three modules A, B, and C is Module 1.

Another form of weak cohesion is called the *shot gun anti-pattern*. I think it is generally known that a shot gun is a firearm that shoots a huge amount of small spherical pellets. The weapon typically has a large scatter. In software development, this metaphor is used to express that a certain domain aspect, or single logical idea, is highly fragmented and distributed across many modules. Figure 3-3 depicts such a situation.

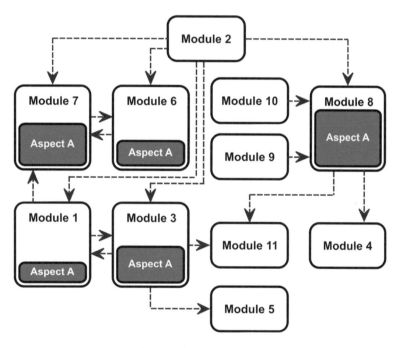

Figure 3-3. *Aspect A is scattered over five modules*

Even with this form of weak cohesion, many unfavorable dependencies arise. The distributed fragments of Aspect A must work closely together. That means that every module that implements a subset of Aspect A must interact at least with one other module containing another subset of Aspect A. This leads to a large number of dependencies crosswise through the design. At worst, it can lead to cyclic dependencies, like between Modules 1 and 3, or between Modules 6 and 7. This has, once again, a negative impact on the maintainability and extendibility. Furthermore, the testability is also very poor due to this design.

This kind of design will lead to something that is called *shotgun surgery*. A certain type of change regarding Aspect A leads to making lots of small changes to many modules. That's really bad and should be avoided. We have to fix this by pulling all the parts of the code that are fragments of the same logical aspect together into a single cohesive module.

There are certain other principles—for instance, the single responsibility principle (SRP) of object-oriented design (see Chapter 6)—that foster high cohesion. High cohesion often correlates with loose coupling and vice versa.

Loose Coupling

Consider the small example in Listing 3-8.

Listing 3-8. A Switch That Powers a Lamp On and Off

```cpp
class Lamp {
public:
  void on() {
    //...
  }

  void off() {
    //...
  }
};

class Switch {
private:
  Lamp& lamp;
  bool state {false};

public:
  Switch(Lamp& lamp) : lamp(lamp) { }

  void toggle() {
    if (state) {
      state = false;
      lamp.off();
```

```
    } else {
      state = true;
      lamp.on();
    }
  }
};
```

Basically, this piece of code will work. You can first create an instance of the Lamp class. Then this is passed by reference when instantiating the Switch class. Visualized with UML, this small example would look like Figure 3-4.

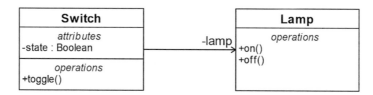

Figure 3-4. *A class diagram of Switch and Lamp*

What's the problem with this design?

The problem is that the Switch contains a direct reference to the concrete class Lamp. In other word, the switch knows that there is a lamp.

Maybe you would argue, "Well, but that's the purpose of the switch. It has to power on and off lamps." That's true if that is the one and only thing the switch should do. If that's the case, this design might be adequate. But go to a DIY store and look at the switches that you can buy there. Do they know that lamps exist?

And what do you think about the testability of this design? Can the switch be tested independently as it is required for unit testing? No, this is not possible. And what will we do when the switch has to power on not only a lamp, but also a fan or an electric roller blind?

In this example, the switch and the lamp are *tightly coupled*.

In software development, a loose coupling (also known as low or weak coupling) between modules is best. That means that you should build a system in which each of its modules has, or makes use of, little or no knowledge of the definitions of other separate modules.

The key to achieve loose coupling in object-oriented software designs is to use interfaces. An interface declares publicly accessible behavioral features of a class without committing to a particular implementation of that class. An interface is like a contract. Classes that implement an interface are committed to fulfill the contract, that is, these classes must provide implementations for the method signatures of the interface.

In C++, interfaces are implemented using abstract classes, as shown in Listing 3-9.

Listing 3-9. The Switchable Interface

```cpp
class Switchable {
public:
  virtual void on() = 0;
  virtual void off() = 0;
};
```

The Switch class doesn't contain a reference to the lamp any more. Instead, it holds a reference to our new interface class called Switchable, as shown in Listing 3-10.

Listing 3-10. The Modified Switch Class, Whereby Lamp Is Gone

```cpp
class Switch {
private:
  Switchable& switchable;
  bool state {false};

public:
  Switch(Switchable& switchable) : switchable(switchable) {}

  void toggle() {
    if (state) {
      state = false;
      switchable.off();
    } else {
      state = true;
      switchable.on();
    }
  }
};
```

The Lamp class implements our new interface, as shown in Listing 3-11.

Listing 3-11. The Lamp Class Implements the Switchable Interface

```cpp
class Lamp : public Switchable {
public:
  void on() override {
    // ...
  }

  void off() override {
    // ...
  }
};
```

Expressed in UML, the new design looks like Figure 3-5.

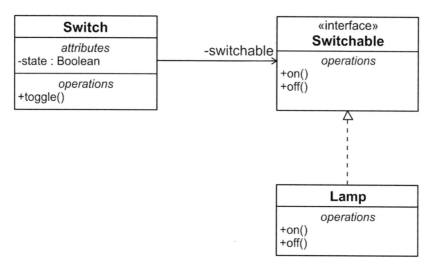

Figure 3-5. *Loosely coupled Switch and Lamp via an interface*

The advantages of such a design are obvious. Switch is completely independent from concrete classes that will be controlled by it. Furthermore, Switch can be tested independently by providing a test double implementing the Switchable interface. You want to control a fan instead of a lamp? No problem, as this design is open for extension. Just create a Fan class or other classes representing electrical devices that implement the Switchable interface, as depicted in Figure 3-6.

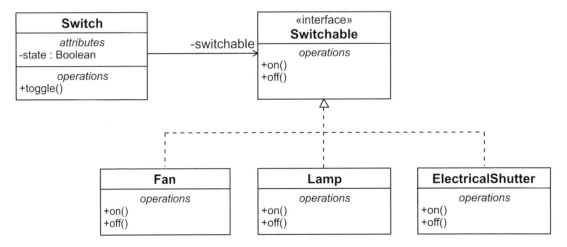

Figure 3-6. *Via an interface, a Switch can control different classes for electrical devices*

Attention to loose coupling can provide a high degree of autonomy for individual modules of a system. The principle can be effective at different levels: both at the smallest modules, as well as on the system's architecture level for large components. High cohesion fosters loose coupling, because a module with a clearly defined responsibility usually depends on fewer collaborators.

Be Careful with Optimizations

"Premature optimization is the root of all evil (or at least most of it) in programming."

—Donald E. Knuth, American computer scientist [Knuth74]

I've seen developers starting time-wasting optimizations just with vague ideas of overhead, but not really knowing where the performance is lost. They often fiddled with individual instructions or tried to optimize small, local loops, to squeeze out even the last drop of performance. Just as a footnote, one of these programmers I'm talking about was me.

The success of these activities is generally marginal. The expected performance advantages usually do not arise. In the end it's just a waste of precious time. On the contrary, often the understandability and maintainability of the allegedly optimized code suffers drastically. Particularly bad is that sometimes it even happens that bugs are subtly slipped into the code during such optimization measures. My advice is this: **As long as there are no explicit performance requirements to satisfy, keep your hands off optimizations.**

The comprehensibility and maintainability of our code should be our first goal. And as I explain in the section "But the Call Time Overhead!" in Chapter 4, compilers are nowadays very good at optimizing code. Whenever you feel a desire to optimize something, think about YAGNI.

You should spring into action only when explicit performance requirements (requested by a stakeholder) are not satisfied. First carefully analyze where the performance gets lost. Don't make any optimizations on the basis of a gut feeling. For instance, you can use a profiler to find out where the bottlenecks are. After using such a tool, developers are often surprised to find that the performance gets lost at a completely different location than where they assumed it to be.

Note   A *profiler* is a tool for dynamic program analysis. It measures, among other metrics, the frequency and duration of function calls. The gathered profiling information can be used to aid program optimization.

Principle of Least Astonishment (PLA)

The principle of least astonishment (POLA/PLA), also known as the principle of least surprise (POLS), is well known in user interface design and ergonomics. The principle states that the user should not be surprised by unexpected responses of the user interface. The user should not be puzzled by appearing or disappearing controls, confusing error messages, unusual reactions on established keystroke sequences or other unexpected behavior. For example, Ctrl+C is the de facto standard for the Copy command on Windows operating systems, and not to exit a program.

This principle can also be well transferred to API design in software development. Calling a function should not surprise the caller with unexpected behavior or mysterious side effects. A function should do exactly what its function name implies (see the section entitled "Function Naming" in Chapter 4). For instance, calling a getter on an instance of a class should not modify the internal state of that object.

The Boy Scout Rule

This principle is about you and your behavior. It reads as follows: **Always leave the campground cleaner than you found it.**

Boy scouts are very principled. One of their principles states that they should clean up a mess or pollution in the environment immediately, once they've found such issues. As responsible software craftspeople, we should apply this principle to our daily work. Whenever we find something in a piece of code that needs to be improved, or that's a bad code smell, we should do one of two things. We should fix it immediately if it is a simple change (e.g., renaming a bad named variable). Or we should create a ticket in the issue tracker if it would result in a major refactoring, for example, in the case of a design or architecture problem. It does not matter who the original author of this piece of code was.

The advantage of this behavior is that we continuously prevent code dilapidation. If we all behave this way, the code simply cannot rot. The tendency of growing software entropy has little chance to dominate our system. And the improvement doesn't have to be a big deal. It may be a very small cleanup, such as these:

- Renaming a poorly named class, variable, function, or method (see the sections "Good Names" and "Function Naming" in Chapter 4).

- Cutting the innards of a large function into smaller pieces (see the section entitled "Let Them Be Small" in Chapter 4).

- Deleting a comment by making the commented piece of code self-explanatory (see the section entitled "Avoid Comments" in Chapter 4).

- Cleaning up a complex and puzzling `if-else` compound.

- Removing a small bit of duplicated code (see the section about the DRY principle in this chapter).

Since most of these improvements are code refactorings, a solid safety net consisting of good unit tests, as described in Chapter 2, is essential. Without unit tests in place, you cannot be sure that you won't break something.

Besides good unit test coverage, we still need a special culture on our team: *collective code ownership.*

Collective Code Ownership

This principle was first formulated in the context of the eXtreme Programming (XP) movement and addresses the corporate culture as well as the team culture. Collective code ownership means that we should work as a community. Every team member, at any time, is allowed to make a change or extension to any piece of code. There should be no attitude like "this is Sheila's code, and that's Fred's module. I don't touch them!" It should be considered valueable that other people can easily take over the code we wrote. A set of well-crafted unit tests (see Chapter 2) supports this, as it allows safe refactorings and thus takes away the fear of change. Nobody on a real team should be afraid, or have to obtain permission, to clean up code or add new features to it. With a culture of collective code ownership, the Boy Scout rule explained in the previous section works fine.

CHAPTER 4

Basics of Clean C++

As I have explained in Chapter 1, lots of C++ code out there is not clean. In many projects, software entropy has gotten the upper hand. Even if you are dealing with an ongoing development project, for example, with a piece of software under maintenance, large parts of the code base are often very old. The code looks as if it were written in the last century. This is not surprising, since most of that code *was* literally written in the last century! There are many projects with a long lifecycle, and they have their roots in the 1990s or even the 1980s. Furthermore, many programmers copy code snippets out of legacy projects and modify them to get things done in their daily work.

Some programmers treat the language just like one of many tools. They see no reason to improve something, because what they cobble together works somehow. It should not be that way because this approach will quickly lead to increased software entropy, and the project will turn into a big mess quicker than you think.

In this chapter, I describe the general basics of clean C++. These are universal topics that are often programming language independent. For example, paying attention to good names for any kind of software unit is essential in all programming languages. Several other aspects, like const correctness, using smart pointers, or the great advantages of move semantics, are specific for C++.

But before I discuss specific topics, I want to point out a general piece of advice, which is to use the latest version of C++ if at all possible.

Tip   If you are not already doing so, start to develop your software using modern C++ now. Skip C++11 and start right away with C++14, C++17, or even better: C++20!

Why should you skip C++11? Well, C++11 was a big hit, no doubt, but it was also not perfect and in certain areas a bit flawed. For instance, C++11 lacked generic and variadic lambdas and didn't support full auto return type deduction. Thus, it is reasonable and

© Stephan Roth 2021
S. Roth, *Clean C++20*, https://doi.org/10.1007/978-1-4842-5949-8_4

advisable to start with C++14, which was essentially a bugfix release of C++11, or even start with a higher standard right away.

Now let's explore the key elements of clean and modern C++, step by step.

Good Names

"Programs must be written for people to read, and only incidentally for machines to execute."

—Hal Abelson and Gerald Jay Sussman, 1984

The following piece of source code is taken from *Apache OpenOffice* version 3.4.1, a well-known open source office software suite. Apache OpenOffice has a long history, which dates back to the year 1984. It descends from Oracle's OpenOffice.org (OOo), which was an open sourced version of the earlier *StarOffice*. In 2011, Oracle stopped the development of OpenOffice.org, fired all developers, and contributed the code and trademarks to the *Apache Software Foundation*. Therefore, be tolerant and keep in mind that the Apache Software Foundation has inherited a nearly 30-year-old ancient beast and vast technical debt.

Listing 4-1. An Excerpt from Apache's OpenOffice 3.4.1 Source Code

```cpp
// Building the info struct for single elements
SbxInfo* ProcessWrapper::GetInfo( short nIdx )
{
    Methods* p = &pMethods[ nIdx ];
    // Wenn mal eine Hilfedatei zur Verfuegung steht:
    // SbxInfo* pResultInfo = new SbxInfo( Hilfedateiname, p->nHelpId );
    SbxInfo* pResultInfo = new SbxInfo;
    short nPar = p->nArgs & _ARGSMASK;
    for( short i = 0; i < nPar; i++ )
    {
        p++;
        String aMethodName( p->pName, RTL_TEXTENCODING_ASCII_US );
        sal_uInt16 nInfoFlags = ( p->nArgs >> 8 ) & 0x03;
```

```
    if( p->nArgs & _OPT )
        nInfoFlags |= SBX_OPTIONAL;
    pResultInfo->AddParam( aMethodName, p->eType, nInfoFlags );
  }
  return pResultInfo;
}
```

I have a simple question for you: **What does this function do?**

It seems easy to give an answer at first sight, because the code snippet is small (less than 20 LOC) and the indentation is okay. But in fact, it is not possible to say at a glance what this function really does, and the reason for this is not only the domain of office software, which is possibly unknown to us.

This short code snippet has many bad smells (e.g., commented-out code, comments in German, magic literals like 0x03, etc.), but a major problem is the poor naming. The function's name GetInfo() is very abstract and gives us at most a vague idea of what this function actually does. Also the namespace name ProcessWrapper is not very helpful. Perhaps you can use this function to retrieve information about a running process? Well, wouldn't RetrieveProcessInformation() be a much better name for it? The comment on the first line ("Building the info struct...") indicates that something is created.

After an analysis of the function's implementation you will also notice that the name is misleading, because GetInfo() is not just a simple getter as you might suspect. There is also something created with the new operator. In other words, the call site will receive a resource that was allocated on the heap and the caller must take care of it. To emphasize this fact, wouldn't a name like CreateProcessInformation() or BuildProcessInfoFromIndex() be much better?

Next, take a look at the parameter and the return value of the function. What is SbxInfo? What is nIdx? Maybe the argument nIdx holds a value that is used to access an element in a data structure (that is, an index), but that would just be a guess. In fact, we don't know exactly.

Developers very often read source code, usually more often even than they write new code. Therefore, source code should be readable, and good names are a key factor of readability. If you are working on a project with multiple people, good naming is essential so that you and your teammates can understand the code quickly. If you have to edit or read a piece of code you wrote a few weeks or months later, good module, class, method, and variable names will help you recall what you meant.

Note   Any entity in a source code base, e.g., files, modules, namespaces, classes, templates, functions, arguments, variables, constants, type aliases, etc., should have meaningful and expressive names.

When I'm designing software or write code, I spend a lot of time thinking about names. I am convinced that it is well-invested time to think about good names, even if it's sometimes not easy and takes five minutes or longer. I seldom find the perfect name for a thing immediately. Therefore, I rename often, which is easy with a good editor or an Integrated Development Environment (IDE) with refactoring capabilities.

If finding a proper name for a variable, function, or class seems to be difficult or nearly impossible, that might indicate that something else is wrong. Perhaps a design issue exists and you should find and solve the root cause of your naming problem.

The next section includes a few bits of advice for finding good names.

Names Should Be Self-Explanatory

I've committed myself to the concept of self-explanatory code. Self-explanatory code is code when no comments are required to explain its purpose (see the following section on comments and how to avoid them). Self-explanatory code requires self-explanatory names for its namespaces, modules, classes, variables, constants, and functions. See Listing 4-2.

Tip   Use simple but descriptive and self-explaining names.

Listing 4-2. Some Examples of Bad Names

```cpp
unsigned int num;
bool flag;
std::vector<Customer> list;
Product data;
```

Variable naming conventions can often turn into a religious war, but I am very sure that there is broad agreement that num, flag, list, and data are really bad names. What is data? Everything is data. This name has absolutely no semantics. It's as if you boxed your goods into moving boxes and, instead of writing on them what they really contain, for example, "cookware," you wrote write the word "things" on every single carton. When the cartons arrive at the new house, this information is completely useless.

Listing 4-3 shows an example of how we could better name the four variables in the previous code example.

Listing 4-3. Some Examples of Good Names

```cpp
unsigned int numberOfArticles;
bool isChanged;
std::vector<Customer> customers;
Product orderedProduct;
```

One can now argue that names are better the longer they are. Consider the example in Listing 4-4.

Listing 4-4. A Very Exhaustive Variable Name

```cpp
unsigned int totalNumberOfCustomerEntriesWithIncompleteAddressInformation;
```

No doubt, this name is extremely expressive. Even without knowing where this code comes from, the reader knows quite well what this variable is used for. However, there are problems with names like this. For example, you cannot easily remember such long names. And they are difficult to type if you don't use an IDE that has auto completion. If such extremely verbose names are used in expressions, the readability of the code may even suffer, as shown in Listing 4-5.

Listing 4-5. Naming Chaos, Caused By Too Verbose Names

```cpp
totalNumberOfCustomerEntriesWithIncompleteAddressInformation =
  amountOfCustomerEntriesWithIncompleteOrMissingZipCode +
  amountOfCustomerEntriesWithoutCityInformation +
  amountOfCustomerEntriesWithoutStreetInformation;
```

Too long and verbose names are not appropriate or desirable when trying to make our code clean. If the context is clear in which a variable is used, shorter and less descriptive names are possible. If the variable is a member (attribute) of a class, for instance, the class's name usually provides sufficient context for the variable. See Listing 4-6.

Listing 4-6. The Class's Name Provides Enough Context Information for the Attribute

```cpp
class CustomerRepository {
private:
  unsigned int numberOfIncompleteEntries;
  // ...
};
```

> *"You're creating a vocabulary, not writing a program. Be a poet for a moment. The simple, the punchy, the easily remembered will be far more effective in the long run than some long name that says it all, but in such a way that no one wants to say it at all."*
>
> —Kent Beck, Smalltalk Best Practice Patterns, 1995

Use Names from the Domain

Maybe you have already heard of software design methodologies like *object-oriented analysis and design* (OOAD) or *domain-driven design* (DDD)? OOAD was first described by Peter Coad and Edward Yourdon in the early 1990s. It was one of the first software design methodologies in which the so-called domain of the system to be developed plays a central role. More than 10 years later, Eric Evans coined the term "domain-driven design" in his eponymous book from 2004 [Evans04]. Like OOAD, DDD is an approach in the complex object-oriented software development that primarily focuses on the core domain and domain logic.

WHAT IS A DOMAIN?

A *domain* in the realm of systems and software engineering commonly refers to the subject area—the sphere of knowledge, influence, or activity—in which a system of interest is intended to be used. Some examples of domains are Automotive, Medical, Healthcare, Agriculture, Space and Aviation, Online Shopping, Music Production, Railway-Transportation, Energy Economy, etc.

When a system of interest is operated just in a subarea of a domain, this is called a subdomain. For instance, subdomains of the Medical domain are Intensive Care Medicine, and imaging techniques like radiography or magnetic resonance imaging (MRI).

Simply put, both methodologies (OOAD and DDD) are about trying to make your software a model of a real-life system by mapping business domain things and concepts into the code. For instance, if the software to be developed will support the business processes in a car rental, then things and concepts of car rental (e.g., rented car, car pool, rentee, rental period, rental confirmation, car usage report, accounting, etc.) should be discoverable in the design of this software. If, on the other hand, the software is developed for a certain area in the aerospace industry, things and concepts from this domain should be reflected in it.

The advantages of such an approach are enormous: the use of terms from the domain facilitates, above all, the communication between the developers and other stakeholders. DDD helps the software development team create a common model between the business and IT stakeholders in the company that the team can use to communicate about the business requirements, data entities, and process models.

A detailed introduction to OOAD and DDD is far beyond the scope of this book. If you are interested, I recommend a good, practice-oriented training to learn these methodologies.

However, it is basically always a very good idea to name modules, classes, and functions in a way that elements and concepts from the application's domain can be rediscovered. This enables you to communicate software designs as naturally as possible. It will make code more understandable to anyone involved in solving a problem, for example, a tester or a business expert.

Take, for example, the aforementioned car rental. The class that is responsible for the use case of the reservation of a car for a certain customer could be as shown in Listing 4-7.

Listing 4-7. The Interface of a Use Case Controller Class to Reserve a Car

```cpp
class ReserveCarUseCaseController {
public:
  Customer identifyCustomer(const UniqueIdentifier& customerId);
  CarList getListOfAvailableCars(const Station& atStation,
    const RentalPeriod& desiredRentalPeriod) const;
  ConfirmationOfReservation reserveCar(const UniqueIdentifier& carId,
    const RentalPeriod& rentalPeriod) const;

private:
  Customer& inquiringCustomer;
};
```

Now take a look at all those names used for the class, the methods, the arguments, and return types. They represent things that are typical for the car rental domain. If you read the methods from top to bottom, these are the individual steps that are required to rent a car. This is C++ code, but there is a great chance that nontechnical stakeholders with domain knowledge can also understand it.

Note   Software developers should speak the language of their stakeholders and use domain-specific terms in their code whenever possible.

Choose Names at an Appropriate Level of Abstraction

To keep the complexity of today's software systems under control, these systems are usually hierarchically decomposed. Hierarchical decomposition of a software system means that the entire problem is broken down and partitioned into smaller parts as subtasks, until developers get the confidence that they can manage these smaller parts. I will deepen this topic again in Chapter 6, when covering modularization of a software system.

With such decomposition, software modules are created at different levels of abstraction: starting from large components or subsystems down to very small building blocks like classes. The task, which a building block at a higher abstraction level fulfills, should be fulfilled by an interaction of the building blocks on the next lower abstraction level.

The abstraction levels introduced by this approach also have an impact on naming. Every time we go one step deeper down the hierarchy, the names of the elements get more concrete.

Imagine a web shop. On the top level there might exist a large component whose single responsibility is to create invoices. This component could have a short and descriptive name like `Billing`. Usually, this component consists of further smaller components or classes. For instance, one of these smaller modules could be responsible for calculating a discount. Another module could be responsible for creating invoice line items. Thus, good names for these modules could be `DiscountCalculator` and `LineItemFactory`. If we now dive deeper into the decomposition hierarchy, the identifiers for components, classes, and functions or methods become more and more concrete, verbose, and thus also longer. For example, a small method in a class at the deepest level could have a very detailed and elongated name, like `calculateReducedValueAddedTax()`.

Note   Always choose names that reflect the level of abstraction of the module, class, or (member-) function you are working in. Look to it that all instructions within a function are on the same abstraction level.

Avoid Redundancy When Choosing a Name

It is redundant to pick up a class name or other names that provide a clear context and use them as a part to build the name of a member variable. Listing 4-8 shows an example of this.

Listing 4-8. Don't Repeat the Class's Name in its Attributes

```cpp
#include <string>

class Movie {
private:
  std::string movieTitle;
  // ...
};
```

Don't do that! It is an, albeit, only very tiny violation of the DRY principle we discussed in Chapter 3. Instead, just name it `title`. The member variable is in the namespace of class `Movie`, so it's clear without ambiguity whose title is meant: the movie's title!

Listing 4-9 shows another example of redundancy.

Listing 4-9. Don't Include the Attribute's Type in its Name

```cpp
#include <string>

class Movie {
  // ...
private:
  std::string stringTitle;
};
```

It is the title of a movie, so obviously it is a string and not an integer! Do not include the type of a variable or constant in its name. In a following section on Hungarian notation, I will take up this topic again.

Avoid Cryptic Abbreviations

When choosing a name for your variables or constants, use full words instead of cryptic abbreviations. There should only be rare exceptions to this rule and only in the case that an abbreviation is very well known in a certain domain, for example, IBAN (short for International Bank Account Number) in the financial world.

The reason is obvious: cryptic abbreviations reduce the readability of your code significantly. Furthermore, when developers talk about their code, variable names should be easy to pronounce.

Remember the variable named nPar on Line 8 from our OpenOffice code snippet? Neither is its meaning clear, nor can it be pronounced in a good manner.

Listing 4-10 shows a few more examples of Dos and Don'ts.

Listing 4-10. Some Examples of Good and Bad Names

```
std::size_t idx;           // Bad!
std::size_t index;         // Good; might be sufficient in some cases
std::size_t customerIndex; // To be preferred, especially in situations where
                           // several objects are indexed

Car rcar;         // Bad!
Car rentedCar;    // Good

Polygon ply1;            // Bad!
Polygon firstPolygon;    // Good

unsigned int nBottles;        // Bad!
unsigned int bottleAmount;    // Better
unsigned int bottlesPerHour;  // Ah, the variable holds a work value,
                              // and not an absolute number. Excellent!

const double GOE = 9.80665;              // Bad!
const double gravityOfEarth = 9.80665;  // More expressive, but misleading.
                                        //  The constant is
```

```
// not a gravitation, which would be a force in physics.
const double gravitationalAccelerationOnEarth = 9.80665; // Good.
constexpr Acceleration gravitationalAccelerationOnEarth = 9.80665_ms2;
// Wow!
```

Look at the last line, which I have commented with "Wow!" That looks pretty convenient, because it is a familiar notation for scientists. It looks almost like teaching physics at school. And yes, that's really possible in C++, as you will learn in one of the sections about type-rich programming in Chapter 5.

Avoid Hungarian Notation and Prefixes

Do you know Charles Simonyi? He is a Hungarian-American computer software expert who worked as a Chief Architect at Microsoft in the 1980s. Maybe you remember his name in a different context. Charles Simonyi is a space tourist and has made two trips to space, one of them to the International Space Station (ISS).

He also developed a notation convention for naming variables in computer software, named the *Hungarian notation,* which has been widely used inside Microsoft and later also by other software manufacturers.

When using Hungarian notation, the type, and sometimes also the scope, of a variable are used as a naming prefix for that variable. Listing 4-11 shows a few examples.

Listing 4-11. Some Examples of Hungarian Notation with Explanations

```
bool fEnabled;        // f = a boolean flag
int nCounter;         // n = number type (int, short, unsigned, ...)
char* pszName;        // psz = a pointer to a zero-terminated string
std::string strName;  // str = a C++ stdlib string
int m_nCounter;       // The prefix 'm_' marks that it is a member variable,
                      // i.e. it has class scope.
char* g_pszNotice;    // That's a global(!) variable. Believe me, I've seen
                      // such a thing.
int dRange;           // d = double-precision floating point. In this case
                         it's
                      // a stone-cold lie!
```

Note   Do not use Hungarian notation, or any other prefix-based notation, by encoding the type of a variable in its name!

Hungarian notation was potentially helpful in a weakly typed language like C. It may have been useful at a time when developers used simple editors for programming, and not IDEs that have a feature like "IntelliSense."

Modern and sophisticated development tools today support the developer very well and show the type and scope of a variable. There are no good reasons anymore to encode the type of a variable in its name. Far from it, such prefixes can impede the train of readability of the code.

At worst, it may even happen that during development the type of a variable is changed without adapting the prefix of its name. In other words, the prefixes tend to turn into lies, as you can see from the last variable in the previous example. That's really bad!

Another problem is that in object-oriented languages that support polymorphism, the prefix cannot be specified easily, or a prefix can even be puzzling. Which Hungarian prefix is suitable for a polymorphic variable that can be an integer or a double? idX? diX? How do we determine a suitable and unmistakable prefix for an instantiated C++ template?

By the way, meanwhile even Microsoft's so-called *general naming conventions* stress that one should not use Hungarian notation anymore.

If you want to mark the member variables of a class, I recommend you use an appended underscore instead of prefixes like the widely used m_..., as in this example:

```cpp
#include <string>

class Person {
  //...
private:
  std::string name_;
};
```

Avoid Using the Same Name for Different Purposes

Once you've introduced a meaningful and expressive name for any kind of software entity (e.g., a class or component), a function, or a variable, you should ensure that its name is never used for any other purpose.

I think it is pretty obvious that using the same name for different purposes can be puzzling and can mislead readers. Don't do that. That's all I have to say about that topic.

Comments

"If the code and the comments disagree, then both are probably wrong."

—Norm Schryer, Computer Scientist and Division
Manager at AT&T Labs Research

Do you remember your beginnings as a professional software developer? Do you still remember the coding standards of your company during those days? Maybe you're still young and not long in business, but the older ones will confirm that most of those standards contained a rule that professional code must always be properly commented. The absolutely comprehensible reasoning for this rule was so that any other developer, or a new team member, could easily understand the intent of the code.

On first sight, this rule seems like a good idea. In many companies, the code was therefore commented extensively. In some projects, the ratio between productive lines of code and comments was almost 50:50.

Unfortunately, it was not a good idea. On the contrary: **This rule was an absolutely bad idea!**

It is completely wrong in several respects, because comments are a code smell in most cases. Comments are necessary when there is need for explanation and clarification. And that often means that the developer was not able to write simple and self-explanatory code.

Do not misunderstand: there are some reasonable use cases for comments. In some situations, a comment might actually be helpful. I present a few of these rather rare cases at the end of this section. But for any other case, this rule should apply, and that's also the heading of the next section: "Let the Code Tell the Story".

Let the Code Tell the Story

Just imagine watching a movie that's only understandable when individual scenes are explained using a textual description below the picture. This film would certainly not be a success. On the contrary, the critics would pick it to pieces. No one would watch such a bad movie. Good films are therefore successful because they tell a gripping story only through the pictures and the dialogues of the actors.

Storytelling is basically a successful concept in many domains, not only in film production. When you think about building a great software product, you should think about it as telling the world a great and enthralling story. It's not surprising that Agile project management frameworks like Scrum use phrases called "user stories" as a way to capture requirements from the perspective of the user. And as I've explained in a section about preferring domain-specific names, you should talk to stakeholders in their own language.

Note Code should tell a story and be self-explanatory. Comments must be avoided whenever possible.

Comments are not subtitles. Whenever you feel the desire to write a comment in your code because you want to explain something, you should think about how you can write the code better so that it is self-explanatory and the comment is therefore superfluous. Modern programming languages like C++ have everything that's necessary to write clear and expressive code. Good programmers take advantage of that expressiveness to tell stories.

> *"Any fool can write code that a computer can understand. Good programmers write code that humans can understand."*
>
> —Martin Fowler, 1999

Do Not Comment Obvious Things

Once again, we take a look at a small and typical piece of source code that was commented extensively. See Listing 4-12.

Listing 4-12. Are These Comments Useful?

```
customerIndex++;                                    // Increment index
Customer* customer = getCustomerByIndex(customerIndex); // Retrieve the customer
                                                       at the given index
CustomerAccount* account = customer->getAccount();  // Retrieve the
                                                       customer's account
account->setLoyaltyDiscountInPercent(discount);     // Grant a 10% discount
```

Please don't insult the reader's intelligence! It is obvious that these comments are totally useless. The code itself is largely self-explanatory. They don't add new or relevant information. Much worse is that these useless comments are a kind of duplication of the code. They violate the DRY principle discussed in Chapter 3.

Maybe you've noticed another detail. Take a look at the last line. The comment speaks literally of a 10% discount, but in the code there is a variable or constant named `discount` that is passed into the function or method `setLoyaltyDiscountInPercent()`. What has happened here? Remember the quote by Norm Schryer from the beginning of this section? A reasonable suspicion is that this comment has turned into a lie because the code was changed, but the comment was not adapted. That's really bad and misleading.

Comments defy any quality assurance measure. You cannot write a unit test for a comment. Thus, they can become misleading and outright wrong very quickly without anyone noticing.

Don't Disable Code with Comments

Sometimes comments are used to disable a bunch of code that should not be translated by the compiler. A reason often mentioned by developers for this practice is that one could possibly use this piece of code again later. They think, "Maybe one day ... we'll need it again." What could happen then is that from time to time you'll find a stone-old piece of code from ancient times, commented out and forgotten for years, as shown in Listing 4-13.

Listing 4-13. An Example of Commented-Out Code

```
// This function is no longer used (John Doe, 2013-10-25):
/*
double calcDisplacement(double t) {
  const double goe = 9.81;              // gravity of earth
  double d = 0.5 * goe * pow(t, 2);   // calculation of distance
  return d;
}
*/
```

A major problem with commented-out code is that it adds confusion with no real benefit. Just imagine that the disabled function in the example in Listing 4-13 is not the only one, but one of many places where code has been commented out. The code will soon turn into a big mess and the commented-out code snippets will add a lot of noise that impedes readability. Furthermore, commented-out code snippets are not quality assured, that is, they are not translated by the compiler, not tested, and not maintained.

Note   Except for the purpose to try out something quickly, don't use comments to disable code. There is a version control system!

If code is no longer used, simply delete it. Let it go. You have a "time machine" to get it back, if necessary: your version control system. However, it often turns out that this case is very rare. Just take a look at the timestamp the developer added in the example in Listing 4-13. This piece of code is age old. What is the likelihood that it will ever be needed again?

To try out something quickly during development, such as when searching for the cause of a bug, it is of course helpful to comment out a code section temporarily. But it must be ensured that such modified code is not checked into the version control system and accidentally comes into production.

Don't Write Block Comments

Comments like the ones shown in Listing 4-14 are found in many projects.

Listing 4-14. An Example of Block Comments

```
#ifndef _STUFF_H_
#define _STUFF_H_

// -------------------------------------
// stuff.h: the interface of class Stuff
// John Doe, created: 2007-09-21
// -------------------------------------

class Stuff {
public:
  // ----------------
  // Public interface
  // ----------------
```

```
  // ...

protected:
  // -------------
  // Overrideables
  // -------------

  // ...

private:
  // -----------------------
  // Private member functions
  // -----------------------

  // ...

  // -----------------
  // Private attributes
  // -----------------

  // ...

};

#endif
```

These kinds of comments (and I do not mean the ones I used to obscure irrelevant parts) are called "block comments," or "banners." They are often used to add a summary about the content at the top of a source code file. Or they are used to mark a special position in the code. For instance, they introduce a code section where all private member functions of a class can be found.

These kinds of comments are mostly pure clutter and should be deleted immediately!

There are very few exceptions where such comments could have a benefit. In some rare cases, a bunch of functions of a special category can be gathered together underneath such a comment. But then you should not use noisy character trains consisting of hyphens (-), slashes (/), number signs (#), or asterisks (*) to envelop them. A comment like the one in Listing 4-15 is absolutely sufficient to introduce such a region.

Listing 4-15. Sometimes Useful: a Comment to Introduce a Category of Functions

```
private:
  // Event handlers:
  void onUndoButtonClick();
  void onRedoButtonClick();
  void onCopyButtonClick();
  // ...
```

#PRAGMA REGION/#PRAGMA ENDREGION

So-called #pragma directives provide a way to specify compiler-, machine-, and operating system-specific functionality while maintaining overall compatibility with the C++ language. For example, many C++ compilers support the #pragma once directive, which ensures that a (header) file is included only once and thus offers an alternative to macro-based include guards.

Using the #pragma region <name-of-region> directive and its corresponding #pragma endregion directive, developers can specify a block of code that can be expanded or collapsed when the IDE has a so-called folding editor that supports it. The code example from Listing 4-15 would then look like this:

```
#pragma region EventHandler
void onUndoButtonClick();
void onRedoButtonClick();
void onCopyButtonClick();
#pragma endregion
```

In some projects the coding standards say that big headers with copyright and license text at the top of any source code file are mandatory. They can look like Listing 4-16.

Listing 4-16. The License Header in Any Source Code File of Apache OpenOffice 3.4.1

```
/************************************************************
 *
 * Licensed to the Apache Software Foundation (ASF) under one
 * or more contributor license agreements.  See the NOTICE file
 * distributed with this work for additional information
 * regarding copyright ownership.  The ASF licenses this file
 * to you under the Apache License, Version 2.0 (the
 * "License"); you may not use this file except in compliance
 * with the License.  You may obtain a copy of the License at
 *
 *   http://www.apache.org/licenses/LICENSE-2.0
 *
 * Unless required by applicable law or agreed to in writing,
 * software distributed under the License is distributed on an
 * "AS IS" BASIS, WITHOUT WARRANTIES OR CONDITIONS OF ANY
 * KIND, either express or implied.  See the License for the
 * specific language governing permissions and limitations
 * under the License.
 *
 ************************************************************/
```

First, I want to say something fundamental about copyrights. You don't need to add comments about the copyright, or do anything else, to have copyright over your works. According to the *Berne Convention for the Protection of Literary and Artistic Works* [Wipo1886] (or *Berne Convention* in short), such comments have no legal meaning.

There were times where such comments were required. Before the United States had signed the Berne Convention in 1989, such copyright notices were mandatory if you wanted to enforce your copyright in the United States. But that is a thing of the past. Nowadays these comments are no longer needed.

My advice is to simply omit them. They are just cumbersome and useless baggage. However, if you want to, or even need to offer copyright and license information in your project, you better write them in separate files, like `license.txt` and `copyright.txt`. If a software license requires under all circumstances that license information has to be included in the head area of every source code file, you can hide these comments if your IDE has a so-called folding editor.

Don't Use Comments to Substitute Version Control

Sometimes—and this is extremely bad—banner comments are used for a change log, as shown in Listing 4-17.

Listing 4-17. Managing the Change History in the Source Code File

```
// ###############################################################################
// Change log:
// 2016-06-14 (John Smith) Change method rebuildProductList to fix bug #275
// 2015-11-07 (Bob Jones) Extracted four methods to new class ProductListSorter
// 2015-09-23 (Ninja Dev) Fixed the most stupid bug ever in a very smart way
// ###############################################################################
```

Don't do this! One of the main tasks of your version control system is tracking the change history of every file in your project. If you are using Git for example, you can use `git log -- [filename]` to get the history of file changes. The programmers who wrote the comments above are more than likely those who always leave the Check-In Comments box empty on their commits.

The Rare Cases Where Comments Are Useful

Of course, not all source code comments are basically useless, false, or bad. There are some cases where comments are important or even indispensable.

In a few very specific cases it may happen that, even if you used perfect names for all your variables and functions, some sections of your code need further explanation to support the reader. For example, a comment is justified if a section of the code has a high degree of inherent complexity and cannot be understood easily by anyone without deep expert knowledge. This can be the case, for example, when using a sophisticated mathematical algorithm or formula. Or the software system deals with an uncommon (business) domain, i.e., an area or field of application that is not easily comprehensible to everyone. This could include areas such as experimental physics, complex simulations of natural phenomena, or ambitious ciphering methods. In such cases, some well-written comments explaining things can be very valuable.

Another good reason to write a comment is when you're deliberately deviating from a good design principle. For example, the DRY principle (see Chapter 3) is, of course, valid in most circumstances. However, there may be some very rare cases in which you willfully duplicate a piece of code, such as to meet certain quality requirements. This justifies a comment explaining why you have violated the principle; otherwise, your teammates may not be able to comprehend your decision.

The challenge is this: Good and meaningful comments are hard to write. It can be more difficult than writing the code. Just as not every member of a development team is good at designing a user interface, not everyone is good at writing either. Technical writing is a skill for which usually there are specialists.

So, here are a few bits of advice for writing useful and necessary comments:

- **Make sure that your comments add value to the code.** Value in this context means that comments add important pieces of information for other human beings (usually other developers) that are not evident from the code itself.

- **Always explain the why, not the how.** How a piece of code works should be pretty clear from the code itself, and meaningful names for variables and functions are the keys to achieve this goal. Use comments solely to explain **why** a certain piece of code exists. For example, you can provide a rationale for why you chose a particular algorithm or method.

- **Try to be as short and expressive as possible.** Choose short and concise comments, ideally one-liners, and avoid long and garrulous texts. Always keep in mind that comments need to be maintained. It is actually much easier to keep short comments up to date than extensive and wordy explanations.

Tip   In integrated development environments (IDE) with syntax coloring, the text color for comments is usually preconfigured to something like light green or teal. You should change this color to loud red! A comment in the source code should be something special, and it should attract the attention of the developers.

Documentation Generation from Source Code

A special form of comments is an annotation that can be extracted by a documentation generator. An example of such a tool is Doxygen (`https://doxygen.org`). It's widespread in the C++ world and is published under a GNU General Public License (GPLv2). Such a tool parses the annotated C++ source code and can create documentation in the form of a readable and printable document (e.g., PDF), or a set of cross-referenced and navigable web documents (HTML) that can be viewed with a browser. In combination with a visualization tool, Doxygen can even generate class diagrams, include dependency graphs, and call graphs. Thus, Doxygen can also be used for static code analysis.

In order for such a tool to generate meaningful documentation, the source code must be annotated intensely with specific comments. Listing 4-18 shows a not-so-good example with annotations in Doxygen style.

Listing 4-18. A Class Annotated with Documentation Comments for Doxygen

```cpp
//! Objects of this class represent a customer account in our system.
class CustomerAccount {
  // ...

  //! Grant a loyalty discount.
  //! @param discount is the discount value in percent.
  void grantLoyaltyDiscount(unsigned short discount);

  // ...
};
```

What? Objects of class `CustomerAccount` represent customer accounts? Oh really?! And `grantLoyaltyDiscount` grants a loyalty discount? You don't say!

But seriously folks! For me, this form of documentation cuts both ways.

On the one hand, it may be very useful to annotate, especially the public interface (API) of a C++ module, a library or a framework with these comments and to generate documentation from them. Particularly if the clients of the software are unknown (the typical case with publically available libraries and frameworks), such documentation can be very helpful if they want to use the software in their projects.

On the other hand, such comments add a huge amount of noise to your code. The ratio of code to comment lines can quickly reach 50:50. As seen in Listing 4-18, such comments also tend to explain obvious things (remember the earlier section in this chapter, "Do Not Comment Obvious Things"). Finally, the best documentation ever—an "executable documentation"—is a set of well-crafted unit tests (see the section about unit tests in Chapter 2 and the section about test-driven development in Chapter 8) that exactly show how the module's or library's API has to be used.

Anyway, I have no final opinion about this topic. If you want to, or have to, annotate the public API of your software components with Doxygen-style comments at all costs, then, for God's sake, do it. If it is well done, and those comments are regularly maintained, it can be pretty helpful. I strongly advise you to pay sole attention to your public API headers! For all other parts of your software, for instance, internally used modules, or private functions, I recommend that you not equip them with Doxygen annotations.

The previous example can be significantly improved if terms and explanations from the application's domain are used, as shown in Listing 4-19.

Listing 4-19. A Class Annotated with Comments from a Business Perspective for Doxygen

```
//! Each customer must have an account, so bookings can be made. The account
//! is also necessary for the creation of monthly invoices.
//! @ingroup entities
//! @ingroup accounting
class CustomerAccount {
  // ...

  //! Regular customers can get a discount on their purchases.
  void grantDiscount(const PercentageValue& discount);

  // ...
};
```

Maybe you've noticed that I do not comment the method's parameter with Doxygen's @param tag anymore. Instead, I changed its type from a meaningless unsigned short to a const reference of a custom type named PercentageValue. Due to this, the parameter is now self-explanatory. Why this is a much better approach than any comment, you can read in a section about type-rich programming in Chapter 5.

Here are a few final tips for Doxygen-style annotations in source code:

- Don't use Doxygen's `@file` [`<name>`] tag to write the name of the file somewhere into the file itself. For one, this is useless, because Doxygen reads the name of the file automatically. In addition, it violates the DRY principle (see Chapter 3). It is redundant information, and if you have to rename the file, you must remember to rename the `@file` tag as well.

- Do not edit the `@version`, `@author`, and `@date` tags manually, because your version control system can manage and keep track of this information a lot better than any developer who would edit them manually. If such management information should appear in the source code file under all circumstances, these tags should be filled automatically by the version control system. In all other cases, I would do without them entirely.

- Do not use the `@bug` or `@todo` tags. Instead, either fix the bug immediately, or use an issue-tracking software to file bugs for later troubleshooting or to manage open points.

- It is strongly recommended to provide a descriptive project home page using the `@mainpage` tag (ideally in a separate header file just for this purpose), since such a home page serves as a getting started guide and orientation aid for new developers. Comprehensive concepts and high-level architecture decisions can also be documented here.

- The interface of a class or library consists not only of method signatures with their parameters and return values. There are more things that belong to an interface but may not be visible to its users: preconditions, postconditions, exceptions, and invariants. Especially if a library is delivered in binary format and users have only header files, such properties of an interface should be documented. For this purpose, Doxygen offers the following tags:

  - `@pre` for the preconditions of an entity.

  - `@invariant` for a description of the properties that remain stable throughout the lifetime of an entity.

- @post for the postconditions of an entity.

- @throws to document the exception object an entity can throw
  and the reasons for the exception.

- I would not use the @example tag to provide a comment block
  containing a source code example about how to use an API. As
  mentioned, such comments add a lot of noise to the code. Instead, I
  would offer a suite of well-crafted unit tests (see Chapter 2 about unit
  tests and Chapter 8 about test-driven development), as these are the
  best examples of use—executable examples! In addition, unit tests
  are always correct and up to date, as they must be adjusted when the
  API changes (otherwise the tests will fail). A comment with a usage
  example, on the other hand, can become wrong without anyone
  noticing it.

- Once a project has been grown to a particular size, it is advisable to
  pool certain categories of software units with the help of Doxygen's
  grouping mechanisms (Tags: @defgroup <name>, @addtogroup
  <name>, and @ingroup <name>). This is, for example, very useful when
  you want to express the fact that certain software units belong to a
  cohesive module on a higher level of abstraction (e.g., a component
  or subsystem). This mechanism also allows certain categories of
  classes to be grouped together, for example all entities, all adapters
  (see the section entitled "Adapter Pattern" in Chapter 9), or all object
  factories (see the section entitled "Factory Pattern" in Chapter 9).
  The CustomerAccount class from the previous code example is, for
  instance, in the group of entities (a group that contains all business
  objects), but it is also part of the accounting component.

Functions

Functions (methods, procedures, services, operations) are the heart of any software
system. They represent the first organizational unit above the lines of code. Well-written
functions foster the readability and maintainability of a program considerably. For this
reason, they should be well crafted in a careful manner. In this section, I give several
important clues for writing good functions.

However, before I explain the things that I consider to be important for well-crafted functions, let's examine a deterrent example again, taken from Apache's OpenOffice 3.4.1. See Listing 4-20.

Listing 4-20. Another Excerpt from Apache's OpenOffice 3.4.1 Source Code

```
1780  sal_Bool BasicFrame::QueryFileName(String& rName, FileType nFileType,
      sal_Bool bSave )
1781  {
1782      NewFileDialog aDlg( this, bSave ? WinBits( WB_SAVEAS ) :
1783                           WinBits( WB_OPEN ) );
1784      aDlg.SetText( String( SttResId( bSave ? IDS_SAVEDLG : IDS_LOADDLG
          ) ) );
1785
1786      if ( nFileType & FT_RESULT_FILE )
1787      {
1788        aDlg.SetDefaultExt( String( SttResId( IDS_RESFILE ) ) );
1789        aDlg.AddFilter( String( SttResId( IDS_RESFILTER ) ),
1790              String( SttResId( IDS_RESFILE ) ) );
1791         aDlg.AddFilter( String( SttResId( IDS_TXTFILTER ) ),
1792              String( SttResId( IDS_TXTFILE ) ) );
1793         aDlg.SetCurFilter( SttResId( IDS_RESFILTER ) );
1794      }
1795
1796      if ( nFileType & FT_BASIC_SOURCE )
1797      {
1798          aDlg.SetDefaultExt( String( SttResId( IDS_NONAMEFILE ) ) );
1799          aDlg.AddFilter( String( SttResId( IDS_BASFILTER ) ),
1800              String( SttResId( IDS_NONAMEFILE ) ) );
1801          aDlg.AddFilter( String( SttResId( IDS_INCFILTER ) ),
1802              String( SttResId( IDS_INCFILE ) ) );
1803          aDlg.SetCurFilter( SttResId( IDS_BASFILTER ) );
1804      }
1805
1806      if ( nFileType & FT_BASIC_LIBRARY )
1807      {
```

```
1808          aDlg.SetDefaultExt( String( SttResId( IDS_LIBFILE f) ) );
1809          aDlg.AddFilter( String( SttResId( IDS_LIBFILTER ) ),
1810              String( SttResId( IDS_LIBFILE ) ) );
1811          aDlg.SetCurFilter( SttResId( IDS_LIBFILTER ) );
1812      }
1813
1814      Config aConf(Config::GetConfigName( Config::GetDefDirectory(),
1815          CUniString("testtool") ));
1816      aConf.SetGroup( "Misc" );
1817      ByteString aCurrentProfile = aConf.ReadKey( "CurrentProfile",
          "Path" );
1818      aConf.SetGroup( aCurrentProfile );
1819      ByteString aFilter( aConf.ReadKey( "LastFilterName") );
1820      if ( aFilter.Len() )
1821          aDlg.SetCurFilter( String( aFilter, RTL_TEXTENCODING_UTF8 ) );
1822      else
1823          aDlg.SetCurFilter( String( SttResId( IDS_BASFILTER ) ) );
1824
1825      aDlg.FilterSelect(); // Selects the last used path
1826  //  if ( bSave )
1827      if ( rName.Len() > 0 )
1828          aDlg.SetPath( rName );
1829
1830      if( aDlg.Execute() )
1831      {
1832          rName = aDlg.GetPath();
1833  /*      rExtension = aDlg.GetCurrentFilter();
1834          var i:integer;
1835          for ( i = 0 ; i < aDlg.GetFilterCount() ; i++ )
1836              if ( rExtension == aDlg.GetFilterName( i ) )
1837                  rExtension = aDlg.GetFilterType( i );
1838  */
1839          return sal_True;
1840      } else return sal_False;
1841  }
```

Question: What did you expect when you saw the member function named
`QueryFileName()` the first time?

Would you expect that a file selection dialog box is opened (remember the principle
of least astonishment discussed in Chapter 3)? Probably not, but that is exactly what is
done here. The user is obviously asked to interact with the application, so a better name
for this member function would be `AskUserForFilename()`.

But that's not enough. If you look at the first lines in detail, you will see that there is a
Boolean parameter `bSave` used to distinguish between a file dialog box for opening, and
a file dialog box for saving files. Did you expect that? And how does the term `Queryf` in
the function name match that fact? So, a better name for this member function may be
`AskUserForFilenameToOpenOrSave()`. And while looking at this more expressive method
name, it should immediately strike you that this method does at least two things and
thus violates the single responsibility principle (discussed in detail in Chapter 6).

The following lines deal with the function's argument `nFileType`. Apparently,
three different file types are distinguished. The `nFileType` parameter is masked out
with something named `FT_RESULT_FILE`, `FT_BASIC_SOURCE`, and `FT_BASIC_LIBRARY`.
Depending on the result of this bitwise AND operation, the file dialog box is configured
differently, for example, filters are set. As the Boolean parameter `bSave` has done before,
the three `if` statements introduce alternative paths. That increases what is known as the
cyclomatic complexity of the function.

CYCLOMATIC COMPLEXITY

The quantitative software metric *cyclomatic complexity* was developed by Thomas J. McCabe,
a U.S. mathematician, in 1976.

The metric is a direct count of the number of linearly independent paths through a section of
source code, for example, a function. If a function contains no `if` or `switch` statement, and
no `for` or `while` loop, there is just one single path through the function and its cyclomatic
complexity is 1. If the function contains one `if` statement representing a single decision point,
there are two paths through the function and the cyclomatic complexity is 2.

If cyclomatic complexity is high, the affected piece of code is typically more difficult to
understand, test, and modify, and thus more prone to bugs.

The three `if` statements raise another question: Is this function the right place to do such configurations? Definitely not! This does not belong over here.

The following lines (starting from 1814) are taking access to additional configuration data. It cannot be determined exactly, but it looks as if the last used file filter (`LastFilterName`) is loaded from a source that contains configuration data, either a configuration file or the Windows registry. Especially confusing is that the already defined filter, which was set in the previous three `if` blocks (`aDlg.SetCurFilter(...)`), will **always** be overwritten at this place (see lines 1820-1823). So, what is the sense of setting this filter in the three `if` blocks before?

Shortly before the end, the reference parameter `rName` comes into play. Hold it ... name of what, please?! It is probably the filename, yes, but why is it not named `filename` to exclude all possibilities of doubt? And why is the filename not the return value of this function? (The reason you should avoid so-called output arguments is a topic that is discussed later in this chapter.)

As if this were not bad enough, the function also contains commented-out code.

This function consists of only about 50 lines, but it has many bad code smells. The function is too long, has a high cyclomatic complexity, mixes different concerns, has many arguments, and contains dead code. The function name `QueryFileName()` is unspecific and can be misleading. Who is queried? A database? `AskUserForFilename()` would be much better, because it emphasizes the interaction with the user. Most of the code is hard to read and difficult to understand. What does `nFileType & FT_BASIC_LIBRARY` mean?

But the essential point is that the task to be performed by this function (filename selection) justifies an own class, because the class `BasicFrame`, which is part of the application's UI, is definitely not responsible for such things.

Enough of that. Let's take a look at what has to be considered by a software crafter while designing good functions.

One Thing, No More!

A method or function should have a very precisely defined task represented by its significant name. In other words, a function or method should do exactly one logical thing.

You may ask now: But how do I know when a function does too many things? Here are some possible indications:

- The function is too long, that is, it contains too many lines of code (see the following section about small functions).

- You try to find a meaningful and expressive name for the function that exactly describes its purpose, but you cannot avoid using conjunctions, such as "and" or "or," to build the name. (See one of the following sections on names.)

- The code in the body of a method or function has been grouped by its developer using blank lines. These code groups represent the individual process steps that make up the method. Often these groups are also introduced with comments that are like headlines. In other words, the developer already thought that the method would consist of partial steps without introducing sub-methods for these steps.

- The cyclomatic complexity is high. That means it has deeply nested control structures. The function contains many `if`, `else`, or `switch-case` statements.

- The function has many arguments (see the section about arguments and return values later in this chapter), especially one or more flag arguments of type `bool`.

The indicator mentioned in the first bullet point, that the method or function contains too many lines of code, leads us directly to the topic in the following section.

Let Them Be Small

A central question regarding functions is this: What is the maximum length of a function? (When I talk about functions in the following section, I also mean methods.)

There are many rules of thumb and heuristics for the length of a function. For example, some say that a function should fit on the screen vertically. Okay, at first glance that seems to be a not-so-bad rule. If a function fits on the screen, there is no need for the developer to scroll. On the other hand, should the height of my screen really determine the maximum size of a function? Screen heights are not all the same. So, I personally don't think that it is a good rule.

Note   Functions or methods should be pretty small. Ideally 4–5 lines, maximum 12–15 lines, but not more.

Panic! I can already hear the outcry of many developers: "Lots of tiny functions? ARE YOU SERIOUS?!"

Yes, I am serious.

Large functions usually have a high complexity. Developers often cannot tell at a glance what such a function does. If a function is too large, it typically has too many responsibilities (see the previous section) and does not do only one thing. The larger a function is, the harder it is to understand and maintain. Such functions often contain many, mostly nested decisions (`if`, `else`, or `switch`) and loops. This is also known as high cyclomatic complexity.

Of course, as with any rule, there can be few justified exceptions. For instance, a function that contains a single large `switch` statement might be acceptable if it is extremely clean and straightforward to read. You can have a 400-line `switch` statement in a function (sometimes required to handle different kinds of incoming data in telecommunication systems), and it is perfectly okay.

"But the Call Time Overhead!"

People now might raise the objection that many small functions reduce the execution speed of a program. They might argue that any function call is costly.

Let me explain why I think that these fears are unfounded in most cases.

Yes, there were times when C++ compilers were not very good at optimizing, and CPUs were comparatively slow. It was at a time when the myth was spread that C++ is generally slower than C. Such myths were propagated by individuals who did not know the language very well. And the times have changed.

Nowadays, modern C++ compilers are very good at optimizing. For instance, they can perform manifold local and global speed-up optimizations. They can reduce many C++ constructs, like loops or conditional statements, to functionally similar sequences of very efficient machine code. And they are now smart enough to inline functions automatically, if those functions can be basically inlined (… of course, sometimes it is not possible to do that).

And even the Linker can perform optimizations. For example, many modern C++ compilers nowadays offer a feature such as *whole program optimization* (Microsoft

Visual-Studio Compiler/Linker) and *link-time optimization* (gcc or LLVM/Clang), which allows the compiler and linker to perform global optimizations with information on all modules in the program. And with another Visual-Studio feature called *profile-guided optimizations*, the compiler optimizes a program using gathered data from profiling test runs of the .EXE or .DLL file.

Even if we do not want to use the optimization options of the compiler, what are we talking about when we consider a function call?

An Intel Core i7 2600K CPU can perform 128,300 million instructions per second (MIPS) at a clock speed of 3.4GHz. Ladies and gentleman, when we are talking about function calls, we are talking about a few nanoseconds! Light travels approximately 30cm in one nanosecond (0.000000001 sec). Compared to other operations on a computer, like memory access outside of the cache, or hard disk access, a function call is magnitudes faster.

Developers should rather spend their precious time on real performance issues, which usually have their roots in bad architecture and design. Only under very special circumstances do you have to worry about function call overhead.

Function Naming

In general, it can be said that the same naming rules that apply to variables and constants are also applicable to functions and methods. Function names should be clear, expressive, and self-explanatory. You should not have to read the body of a function to know what it does. Because functions define the behavior of a program, they typically have a verb in their name. Some special kinds of functions are used to provide information about a state. Their names often start with "is ..." or "has...".

Tip   The name of a function should start with a verb. Predicates, that is, statements about an object that can be true or false, should start with "is" or "has."

Listing 4-21 shows some examples of expressive method names.

Listing 4-21. A Few Examples of Expressive and Self-Explanatory Names for Member Functions

```
void CustomerAccount::grantDiscount(DiscountValue discount);
void Subject::attachObserver(const Observer& observer);
void Subject::notifyAllObservers() const;
int Bottling::getTotalAmountOfFilledBottles() const;
bool AutomaticDoor::isOpen() const;
bool CardReader::isEnabled() const;
bool DoubleLinkedList::hasMoreElements() const;
```

Use Intention-Revealing Names

Take a look at the following line of code, which is, of course, just a small excerpt from a larger program:

```
std::string head = html.substr(startOfHeader, lengthOfHeader);
```

This line of code looks good in principle. There is a C++ string (header <string>) named html, containing a piece of HTML (Hypertext Mark-Up Language) obviously. When this line is executed, a copy of a substring of html is retrieved and assigned to a new string named head. The substring is defined by two parameters: one that sets the starting index of the substring and another that defines the number of characters to include in the substring.

Okay, I've just explained in detail **how** the header from a piece of HTML is extracted. Listing 4-22 shows another version of the same code.

Listing 4-22. After Introducing an Intention-Revealing Name the Code Is More Understandable

```
std::string ReportRenderer::extractHtmlHeader(const std::string& html) {
  return html.substr(startOfHeader, lengthOfHeader);
}

// ...

std::string head = extractHtmlHeader(html);
```

Can you see how much clarity a small change like this could bring to your code? We introduced a small member function that explains its intention by its semantic name. And at the place where the string operation originally could be found, we've replaced the direct invocation of `std::string::substr()` by a call of the new function.

Note   The name of a function should express its intention/purpose, and not explain how it works.

How the job is done—that's what you should learn from the code in the function's body. Don't explain the how in a function's name. Instead, express the purpose of the function from a business perspective.

In addition, we have another advantage. The partial functionality of how the header is extracted from the HTML page has been quasi-isolated and is now more easily replaceable without fumbling around at those places where the function is called.

Parameters and Return Values

After we discussed function names in detail, there is another aspect that is important for good and clean functions: the function's parameters and return values. These both also contribute significantly to the fact that a function or method can be well understood and is easily usable by clients.

Number of Parameters

How many parameters should a function or method have at most? Two? Three? Or just one?

Well, methods of a class often have no parameter at all. The explanation for this is that these always have an additional implicit "argument" available: `this`! The `this` pointer represents the context of execution. With the help of `this`, a member function can access the attributes of its class, read, or manipulate them. In other words, from the perspective of a member function, attributes of a class feel like global variables.

When we think of a function in the pure mathematical sense ($y = f(x)$), it always has at least one parameter (see Chapter 7 about functional programming).

But why are too many parameters bad?

First, every parameter in a function's parameter list can lead to a dependency, with the exception of parameters of standard built-in types like `int` or `double`. If you use a complex type (e.g., a class) in a function's parameter list, your code depends on that type. The header file containing the used type must be included.

Furthermore, every parameter must be processed somewhere inside of a function (if not, it is unnecessary and should be deleted immediately). Three parameters can lead to a relatively complex function, as we have seen by example of member function `BasicFrame::QueryFileName()` from Apache's OpenOffice.

In procedural programming it may sometimes be very difficult not to exceed three parameters. In C, for instance, you will often see functions with more parameters. A deterrent example is the hopelessly antiquated Windows Win32 API, as shown in Listing 4-23.

Listing 4-23. The Win32 CreateWindowEx Function to Create Windows

```
HWND CreateWindowEx
(
  DWORD dwExStyle,
  LPCTSTR lpClassName,
  LPCTSTR lpWindowName,
  DWORD dwStyle,
  int x,
  int y,
  int nWidth,
  int nHeight,
  HWND hWndParent,
  HMENU hMenu,
  HINSTANCE hInstance,
  LPVOID lpParam
);
```

Well, this ugly code comes from ancient times, obviously. I'm pretty sure that if it were designed nowadays, the Windows API would not look like that any more. Not without reason, there are numerous frameworks, such as *Microsoft Foundation Classes* (MFC), *Qt* (`https://www.qt.io`), and *wxWidgets* (`https://www.wxwidgets.org`), that wrap this creepy interface and offer simpler and more object-oriented ways to create a graphical user interface (UI).

And there are few possibilities to reduce the number of parameters. You could combine x, y, nWidth, and nHeight to a new structure named Rectangle, but then there are still nine parameters. An aggravating factor is that some of the parameters of this function are pointers to other complex structures, which for their part are composed of many attributes.

In good object-oriented designs, such long parameter lists are usually not required. But C++ is not a pure object-oriented language, such as Java or C#. In Java, everything must be embedded in a class, which sometimes leads to much boilerplate code. In C++ this is not required. You are allowed to implement free-standing functions in C++, that is, functions that are not members of a class. And that's quite okay.

Tip   Methods and functions should have as few parameters as possible. One parameter is the ideal number. Member functions (methods) of a class sometimes have no parameters at all. Usually those functions manipulate the internal state of the object, or they are used to query something from the object.

Avoid Flag Parameters

A flag parameter is a kind of parameter that tells a function to perform a different operation depending on its value. Flag parameters are mostly of type bool, and sometimes even an enumeration. See Listing 4-24.

Listing 4-24. A Flag Parameter to Control the Level of Detail on an Invoice

```cpp
Invoice Billing::createInvoice(const BookingItems& items, const bool
withDetails) {
  if (withDetails) {
    //...
  } else {
    //...
  }
}
```

The basic problem with flag parameters is that you introduce two (or sometimes even more) paths through your function and hence increase its cyclomatic complexity.

The value of such a parameter is typically evaluated somewhere inside the function in an if or switch/case statement. It is used to determine whether to take a certain action. It means that the function is not doing one thing exactly right, as it should be (see the section "One Thing, No More," earlier in this chapter). It's a case of weak cohesion (see Chapter 3) and violates the single responsibility principle (see Chapter 6 about object orientation).

And if you see the function call somewhere in the code, you do not know exactly what a true or false means without analyzing the Billing::createInvoice()function in detail. See Listing 4-25.

Listing 4-25. Baffling: What Does the True in the Argument List Mean?

```
Billing billing;
Invoice invoice = billing.createInvoice(bookingItems, true);
```

My advice is that you should simply avoid flag parameters. Such kinds of parameters are always necessary if the concern of performing an action is not separated from its configuration.

One solution could be to provide separate, well-named functions instead, as shown in Listing 4-26.

Listing 4-26. Easier to Comprehend: Two Member Functions with Intention-Revealing Names

```
Invoice Billing::createSimpleInvoice(const BookingItems& items) {
  //...
}

Invoice Billing::createInvoiceWithDetails(const BookingItems& items) {
  Invoice invoice = createSimpleInvoice(items);
  //...add details to the invoice...
}
```

Another solution is a specialization hierarchy of billings, as shown in Listing 4-27.

Listing 4-27. Different Levels of Details for Invoices, Realized the Object-Oriented Way

```cpp
class Billing {
public:
  virtual Invoice createInvoice(const BookingItems& items) = 0;
  // ...
};

class SimpleBilling : public Billing {
public:
  Invoice createInvoice(const BookingItems& items) override;
  // ...
};

class DetailedBilling : public Billing {
public:
  Invoice createInvoice(const BookingItems& items) override;
  // ...
private:
  SimpleBilling simpleBilling;
};
```

The private member variable of type SimpleBilling is required in the DetailedBilling class to be able to first perform a simple invoice creation without code duplication, and to add the details to the invoice afterward.

OVERRIDE SPECIFIER [C++11]

Since C++11, it can explicitly be specified that a virtual function should override a base class virtual function. For this purpose, the override identifier has been introduced.

If override appears immediately after the declaration of a member function, the compiler will check that the function is virtual and is overriding a virtual function from a base class. Thus, developers are protected from subtle errors that can arise when they merely think that they have overridden a virtual function, but in fact they have altered/added a new function, for example, due to a typo.

Avoid Output Parameters

An output parameter, sometimes also called a *result parameter*, is a function parameter that is used for the function's return value.

One of the frequently mentioned benefits of using output parameters is that functions that use them can pass back more than one value at a time. Here is a typical example:

```
bool ScriptInterpreter::executeCommand(const std::string& name,
                          const std::vector<std::string>& arguments,
                          Result& result);
```

This member function of the ScriptInterpreter class returns not only a bool. The third parameter is a non-const reference to an object of type Result, which represents the real result of the function. The Boolean return value determines whether the execution of the command was successful by the interpreter. A typical call of this member function might look like this:

```
ScriptInterpreter interpreter;
// Many other preparations...
Result result;

if (interpreter.executeCommand(commandName, argumentList, result)) {
  // Continue normally...
} else {
  // Handle failed execution of command...
}
```

Tip   Avoid output parameters at all costs.

Output parameters are unintuitive and can lead to confusion. The caller can sometimes not determine whether a passed object is treated as an output parameter and will possibly be mutated by the function.

Furthermore, output parameters complicate the easy composition of expressions. If functions have only one return value, they can be interconnected quite easily to chained function calls. In contrast, if functions have multiple output parameters, developers are forced to prepare and handle all the variables that will hold the resultant values. Therefore, the code that calls these functions can turn into a mess quickly.

Especially if immutability should be fostered and side effects must be reduced, output parameters are an absolutely terrible idea. Unsurprisingly, it is still impossible to pass an immutable object (see Chapter 9) as an output parameter.

If a method should return something to its callers, let the method return it as the method's return value. If the method must return multiple values, redesign it to return a single instance of an object that holds the values.

Alternatively, the class template `std::pair` can be used. The first member variable is assigned the Boolean value indicating success or fail, and the second member variable is assigned the real return value. However, both `std::pair` and its "big brother" `std::tuple` (available since C++11) are, from my point of view, always a design smell. A `std::pair<bool, Result>` is not really a speaking name. If you decide to use something like that, and I would not recommend it anyway, you should at least introduce a meaningful alias name with the help of the `using` declaration.

Another possibility is to use a `std::optional`, a class template that is defined in the `<optional>` header and available since C++17. As its name suggest, objects of this class template can manage an optional contained value, i.e., a value that may or may not be present.

In addition to the aforementioned solutions, there is one more. You can use the so-called *special case object pattern* to return an object representing an invalid result. Since this is a object-oriented design pattern, I introduce it in Chapter 9.

Here is my final advice about how to deal with return parameters: As mentioned, avoid output parameters. If you want to return multiple values from a function or method, introduce a small class with well-named member variables to bundle all the data that you want to return to the call site. You may find after a short while that this class should have existed anyway and you can put some logic in it.

Don't Pass or Return 0 (NULL, nullptr)

THE BILLION DOLLAR MISTAKE

Sir Charles Antony Richard Hoare, commonly known as Tony Hoare or C. A. R. Hoare, is a famous British computer scientist. He is primarily known for the Quick Sort algorithm. In 1965, Tony Hoare worked with the Swiss computer scientist Niklaus E. Wirth on the further development of the programming language ALGOL. He introduced null references in the programming language ALGOL W, which was the predecessor of PASCAL.

More than 40 years later, Tony Hoare regrets this decision. In a talk at the QCon 2009 Conference in London, he said that the introduction of null references had probably been a billion dollar mistake. He argued that null references have caused so many problems in the past decades that the cost could be approximated at $USD 1 billion.

In C++, pointers can point to NULL or 0. Concretely, this means that the pointer points to the memory address 0. NULL is just a macro definition:

```
#define NULL    0
```

Since C++11, the language provides the new keyword called nullptr, which is of type std::nullptr_t.

Sometimes I see functions like this one:

```
Customer* findCustomerByName(const std::string& name) const {
  // Code that searches the customer by name...
  // ...and if the customer could not be found:
  return nullptr; // ...or NULL;
}
```

Receiving NULL or nullptr as a return value from a function can be confusing. (Starting from here, I will only use nullptr in the following text, because the C-style macro NULL has no place in modern C++ anymore.) What should the caller do with it? What does it mean? In the previous example, it might be that a customer with the given name does not exist. But it can also mean that there has been a critical error. A nullptr can mean failure, can mean success, and can mean almost anything.

Note   If it is inevitable to return a regular pointer as the result from a function or method, do not return nullptr!

In other words, if you're forced to return a regular pointer as the result from a function (we will see later that there may be better alternatives), ensure that the pointer you're returning always points to a valid address. Here are my reasons why I think this is important.

The main rationale why you should not return nullptr from a function is that you shift the responsibility to decide what to do to your callers. They have to check it. They have to deal with it. If functions can potentially return `nullptr`, this leads to many null checks, like this:

```
Customer* customer = findCustomerByName("Stephan");

if (customer != nullptr) {
  OrderedProducts* orderedProducts = customer->getAllOrderedProducts();
  if (orderedProducts != nullptr) {
    // Do something with orderedProducts...
  } else {
    // And what should we do here?
  }
} else {
  // And what should we do here?
}
```

Many null checks reduce the readability of the code and increase its complexity. And there is another visible problem that leads us directly to the next point.

If a function can return a valid pointer or `nullptr`, it introduces an alternative flow path that needs to be continued by the caller. And it should lead to a reasonable and sensible reaction. This is sometimes quite problematic. What would be the correct, intuitive response in our program when our pointer to `Customer` is not pointing to a valid instance, but `nullptr`? Should the program abort the running operation with a message? Are there any requirements that a certain type of program continuation is mandatory in such cases? These questions sometimes cannot be answered well. Experience has shown that it is often relatively easy for stakeholders to describe all the so-called *happy day cases* of their software, which are the positive cases during normal operation. It is much more difficult to describe the desired behavior of the software during the exceptions, errors, and special cases.

The worst consequence may be this: If any null check is forgotten, this can lead to critical runtime errors. Dereferencing a null pointer will lead to a segmentation fault and your application will crash.

In C++ there is still another problem to consider: **object ownership**.

For the caller of the function, it is unclear what to do with the resource pointed to by the pointer after its usage. Who is its owner? Is it required to delete the object? If yes, how is the resource to be disposed? Must the object be deleted with `delete`, because it was allocated with the `new` operator somewhere inside the function? Or is the ownership of the resource object managed differently, so that a delete is forbidden and will result in undefined behavior (see the section "Don't Allow Undefined Behavior" in Chapter 5)? Is it perhaps even an operating system resource that has to be handled in a very special manner?

According to the *information hiding principle* (see Chapter 3), this should have no relevance for the callers, but in fact we've imposed the responsibility for the resource to them. And if the callers do not handle the pointer correctly, it can lead to serious bugs, for example, memory leaks, double deletion, undefined behavior, and sometimes security vulnerabilities.

Strategies for Avoiding Regular Pointers

Choose simple object construction on the stack instead of on the heap

The simplest way to create a new object is simply by creating it on the stack, like so:

```cpp
#include "Customer.h"
// ...
Customer customer;
```

In this example, an instance of the Customer class (defined in the Customer.h header) is created on the stack. The line of code that creates the instance can usually be found somewhere inside a function's or method's body. That means that the instance is destroyed automatically if the function or method runs out of scope, which happens when we return from the function or method.

So far, so good. But what shall we do if an object that was created in a function or method must be returned to the caller?

In old-style C++, this challenge was often coped with in such a way that the object was created on the heap (using the new operator) and then returned from the function as a pointer to this allocated resource.

```cpp
Customer* createDefaultCustomer() {
  Customer* customer = new Customer();
  // Do something more with customer, e.g. configuring it, and at the end...
  return customer;
}
```

The comprehensible reason for this approach is that, if we are dealing with a large object, an expensive copy construction can be avoided this way. But we have already discussed the drawbacks of this solution in the previous section. For instance, what will the caller do if the returned pointer is `nullptr`? Furthermore, the caller of the function is forced to be in charge of the resource management (e.g., deleting the returned pointer in the correct manner).

COPY ELISION

Almost all, especially commercial-grade C++ compilers today, support so-called *copy elision* techniques. These are optimizations to prevent extra copies of objects in certain situations (depending on optimization settings; as of C++17, copy elision is guaranteed when an object is returned directly).

On the one hand, this is great, because we can get more performant software with less to no effort this way. And it makes returning by value or passing by value large and costly objects, apart from some exceptions, much simpler in practice. These exceptions are limitations of copy elision where this optimization won't be able to kick in, such as having multiple exit points (`return` statements) in a function returning different named objects.

On the other hand, we have to keep in mind that copy elision—depending on the compiler and its settings—can influence the program's behavior. If the copying an object is optimized away, any copy constructor that may be present is also not executed. Furthermore, if fewer objects are created, you can't rely on a specific number of destructors being called. You shouldn't put critical code inside copy- or move-constructors or destructors, as you can't rely on them being called. (You will learn that you should avoid implementing these so-called special member functions by hand anyway, in Chapter 5, in the section "The Rule of Zero"!)

Common forms of copy elision are *return value optimization* (RVO) and *named return value optimization* (NRVO).

Named Return Value Optimization

NRVO eliminates the copy constructor and destructor of a named stack-based object that is returned. For instance, a function could return an instance of a class by value like in this simple example:

```
class SomeClass {
public:
  SomeClass();
  SomeClass(const SomeClass&);
  SomeClass(SomeClass&&);
  ~SomeClass();
};

SomeClass getInstanceOfSomeClass() {
  SomeClass object;
  return object;
}
```

RVO happens if a function returns a nameless temporary object, as with this modified form of the getInstanceOfSomeClass() function:

```
SomeClass getInstanceOfSomeClass() {
  return SomeClass ();
}
```

Important: Even when copy elision takes place and the call of a copy-/move-constructor is optimized away, they must be present and accessible, either hand-crafted or compiler-generated; otherwise, the program is considered ill-formed!

Good news: Since C++11, we can simply return large objects as values without being worried about a costly copy construction.

```
Customer createDefaultCustomer() {
  Customer customer;
  // Do something with customer, and at the end...
  return customer;
}
```

The reason that we no longer have to worry about resource management in this case are the so-called **move semantics**, which are supported since C++11. Simply speaking, the concept of move semantics allows resources to be "moved" from one object to another instead of copying them. The term "move" means, in this context, that the internal data of an object is removed from the old source object and placed into a new object. It is a transfer of ownership of the data from one object to another object, and this can be performed extremely fast. (C++11 move semantics are discussed in detail in Chapter 5.)

With C++11, all Standard Library container classes have been extended to support move semantics. This not only has made them very efficient, but also much easier to handle. For instance, you can return a large vector containing strings from a function in a very efficient manner, as shown in the example in Listing 4-28.

Listing 4-28. Since C++11, a Locally Instantiated and Large Object Can Be Easily Returned by Value

```
#include <vector>
#include <string>

using StringVector = std::vector<std::string>;
const StringVector::size_type AMOUNT_OF_STRINGS = 10'000;

StringVector createLargeVectorOfStrings() {
  StringVector theVector(AMOUNT_OF_STRINGS, "Test");
  return theVector; // Guaranteed no copy construction here!
}
```

The exploitation of move semantics is one very good way to get rid of lots of regular pointers. But we can do much more...

In a function's argument list, use (const) references instead of pointers

Instead of writing...

```
void function(Type* argument);
```

...you should use C++ references, like this:

```
void function(Type& argument);
```

The main advantage of using references instead of pointers for arguments is that there's no need to check that the reference is not a `nullptr`. The simple reason for this is that references are never `"NULL."` (Okay, I know that there are some subtle possibilities where you can still end up with a null reference, but these presuppose a very foolish or amateurish programming style.)

And another advantage is that you don't need to dereference anything inside the function with the help of the dereference operator (*). That will lead to cleaner code. The reference can be used inside the function as it has been created locally on the stack. Of course, if you don't want to have any side effects, you should make it a `const` reference (see the upcoming section about `const` correctness).

If it is inevitable to deal with a pointer to a resource, use a smart one

If you cannot avoid using a pointer because the resource must be created on the heap, you should wrap it immediately and take advantage of the so-called RAII idiom (resource acquisition is initialization).

```
Customer* customer1 = new Customer(); // Bad! Don't do that.
auto customer2 = std::make_unique<Customer>(); // Good: the heap-allocated
customer is owned by a smart pointer
```

That means that you should use a smart pointer for it. Since smart pointers and the RAII idiom play an important role in modern C++, there is a section dedicated to this topic in Chapter 5. Always follow rule R.3 from the *C++ Core Guidelines* [Cppcore21]: A raw pointer (a T*) is non-owning.

If an API returns a raw pointer...

..., well, then we have an "it-depends-problem."

Pointers are often returned from APIs that are more or less out of our hands. Typical examples are third-party libraries.

In the lucky case that we are confronted with a well-designed API that provides factory methods to create resources and provides methods to hand them back to the library for safe and proper disposal, we have won. In this case we can once again take advantage of the RAII idiom (resource acquisition is initialization; see Chapter 5). We can create a custom smart pointer to wrap the regular pointer, whose allocator and deallocator could handle the managed resource as expected by the third-party library.

The Power of const Correctness

const correctness is a powerful approach to better and safer code in C++. The use of const can save a lot of trouble and debugging time, because violations of const cause compile-time errors. And as a kind of side effect, the use of const can also support the compiler in applying some of its optimization algorithms. That means that the proper use of this qualifier is also an easy way to raise the execution performance of the program a little bit.

Unfortunately, many developers don't appreciate the benefits of an intense use of const.

Tip   Pay attention to const correctness. Use const as much as possible, and always choose a proper declaration of variables or objects as mutable or immutable.

In general, the const keyword in C++ prevents objects from being mutated by the program. But const can be used in different contexts. This keyword has many faces.

Its simplest use is to define a variable as a constant:

```
const long double PI = 3.141592653589794;
```

MATHEMATICAL CONSTANTS [C++20]

Since C++20, the C++ numerics library has been extended, among others by a number of mathematical constants, which are defined in the <numbers> header. Here is a small selection:

```
#include <numbers>

auto pi = std::numbers::pi;      // the Archimedes constant aka PI:
                                 //    3.141592653589794
auto e = std::numbers::e;        // Euler's number: 2.718281828459045
auto phi = std::numbers::phi;    // the golden ratio Φ constant:
                                 //    1.618033988749895
```

The C-style defined mathematical constants in the <cmath> header, which had to be made accessible by defining _USE_MATH_DEFINES before including the header, are thus obsolete.

Another use of const is to prevent parameters that are passed into a function from being mutated. Since there are several variations, it often leads to confusion. Here are some examples:

```
unsigned int determineWeightOfCar(Car const* car);          // 1
void lacquerCar(Car* const car);                            // 2
unsigned int determineWeightOfCar(Car const* const car);    // 3
void printMessage(const std::string& message);              // 4
void printMessage(std::string const& message);              // 5
```

- The pointer car points to a **constant object** of type Car, that is, the Car object (the "pointee") cannot be modified.

- The pointer car is a **constant pointer** of type Car, that is, you can modify the Car object, but you cannot modify the pointer (e.g., assign a new instance of Car to it).

- In this case, both the pointer and the pointee (the Car object) cannot be modified.

- The argument message is passed by reference-to-const to the function, that is, the string variable being referenced is not allowed to be changed inside the function.

- This is just an alternative notation for a const reference argument. It is functionally equivalent to line 4 (...which I prefer, by the way).

Tip   There is a simple rule of thumb to read const qualifiers in the right manner. If you read them from right to left, then any appearing const qualifier modifies the thing to the left of it. **Exception:** If there is nothing on the left, for example, at the beginning of a declaration, then const modifies the thing to its right.

Another use of the const keyword is to declare a (non-static) member-function of a class as const, like in this example on line 5:

```
01  #include <string>
02
03  class Car {
```

```
04  public:
05    const std::string& getRegistrationCode() const;
06    void setRegistrationCode(const std::string& registrationCode);
07    // ...
08
09  private:
10    std::string registrationCode_;
11    // ...
12  };
```

As opposed to the setter on line 6, the getRegistrationCode member function on line 5 cannot modify member variables of the Car class. The following implementation of getRegistrationCode will cause a compiler error, because the function tries to assign a new string to registrationCode_:

```
const std::string& Car::getRegistrationCode() {
  std::string toBeReturned = registrationCode_;
  registrationCode_ = "foo"; // Compile-time error!
  return toBeReturned;
}
```

About Old C-Style in C++ Projects

If you take a look at relatively new C++ programs (for example, on GitHub or SourceForge), you will be surprised at how many of these allegedly "new" programs still contain countless lines of old C code. Well, C is still a subset of the C++ language. This means that the language elements of C are still available. Unfortunately, many of these old C constructs have significant drawbacks when it comes to writing clean, safe, and modern code. And there are clearly better alternatives.

Therefore, a basic piece of advice is to quit using those old and error-prone C constructs wherever better C++ alternatives exist. And there are many of these possibilities. Nowadays you can nearly completely do without C programming in modern C++.

Choose C++ Strings and Streams over Old C-Style char*

A so-called C++ string is part of the C++ Standard Library and is of type std::string, std::wstring, std::u8string, std::u16string, or std::u32string (all defined in the <string> header). In fact, all are type aliases of the std::basic_string<T> class template and are (simplified) defined this way:

```
using string = basic_string<char>;
using wstring = basic_string<wchar_t>;
using u8string = basic_string<char8_t>;
using u16string = basic_string<char16_t>;
using u32string = basic_string<char32_t>;
```

Note   To simplify things, from now on I will only speak about C++ strings in general, by which I mean all the previously mentioned, different string types.

To create such a string, an object of one of these two templates must be instantiated, for example, with the initialization constructor:

```
std::string name("Stephan");
```

Compared to this, a so-called C-style string is simply an array of characters (type char or wchar_t) that ends with a so-called zero terminator (sometimes also called a null terminator). A zero terminator is a special character ('\0', ASCII code 0) used to indicate the end of the string. A C-style string can be defined this way:

```
char name[] = "Stephan";
```

In this case, the zero terminator is automatically added at the end of the string, that is, the length of the string is eight characters. An important point is that we have to keep in mind that we're still dealing with an array of characters. This means, for instance, that it has a fixed size. You can change the content of the array using the index operator, but no characters can be added to the end of the array. And if the zero terminator at the end is accidentally overwritten, this can cause various issues.

The character array is often used with the help of a pointer pointing to the first element, for example, when it is passed as a function argument:

```
char* pointerToName = name;

void function(char* pointerToCharacterArray) {
  //...
}
```

However, in many C++ programs as well as in textbooks, C strings are still frequently used. Are there any good reasons to use C-style strings in C++ nowadays?

Yes, there are some situations where you can still use C-style strings. I will present a few of these exceptions later. Apart from that, the vast majority of strings in a modern and clean C++ program should be implemented using C++ strings. Objects of type std::string, as well as all the other C++ string types, provide numerous advantages compared to old C-style strings:

- C++ string objects manage their memory by themselves, so you can copy, create, and destroy them easily. That means that they free you from managing the lifetime of the string's data, which can be a tricky and daunting task using C-style character arrays.

- They are mutable. The string can be manipulated easily in various ways: adding strings or single characters, concatenating strings, replacing parts of the string, etc.

- C++ strings provide a convenient iterator interface. As with all other Standard Library container types, std::string and std::wstring allow you to iterate over their elements (i.e., over their characters). This also means that all suitable algorithms that are defined in the <algorithm> header can be applied to the string.

- C++ strings work perfectly together with C++ I/O streams (e.g., ostream, stringstream, fstream, etc.) so you can take advantage of all those useful stream facilities easily.

- Since C++11, the Standard Library uses move semantics extensively. Many algorithms and containers are now move-optimized. This also applies to C++ strings. For example, an instance of a `std::string` can simply be returned as the return value of a function. The formerly still necessary approaches with pointers or references to efficiently return large string objects from a function—that is, without costly copying of the string's data—are no longer required.

Note   Apart from a few exceptions, strings in modern C++ programs should be represented by C++ strings taken from the Standard Library.

So, what are the few exceptions that justify the use of old C-style strings?

On the one hand, there are string constants, that is, immutable strings. If you just need a fixed array of fixed characters, then `std::string` provides little advantage. For instance, you can define such a string constant this way:

```
const char* const PUBLISHER = "Apress Media LLC";
```

In this case, neither the value being pointed to nor the pointer itself can be modified (see the section about `const` correctness).

Another reason to work with C strings is compatibility with C-style API's libraries. Many third-party libraries often have low-level interfaces to ensure backward compatibility and to keep their area of application as broad as possible. Strings are often expected as C-style strings by such an API. However, even in this case, the use of the C-style strings should be locally limited to the handling of this interface. Follow rule CPL.3 of the C++ *Core Guidelines* [Cppcore20]: If you must use C for interfaces, use C++ in the calling code using such interfaces.

Avoid Using printf( ), sprintf( ), gets( ), etc.

`printf()`, which is part of the C library to perform input/output operations (defined in the `<cstdio>` header), prints formatted data to standard output (stdout). Some developers still use a lot of `printf`s for tracing/logging purposes in their C++ code. They often argue that `printf` is ... no ... it must be much faster than C++ I/O streams, since the whole C++ overhead is missing.

First, I/O is a bottleneck anyway, no matter if you're using `printf()` or `std::cout`. To write anything on standard output is generally slow, with magnitudes slower than most of the other operations in a program. Under certain circumstances, `std::cout` can be slightly slower than `printf()`, but in relation to the general cost of an I/O operation, those few microseconds are usually negligible. At this point I would also like to remind everyone to be careful with (premature) optimizations (remember the section "Be Careful with Optimizations" in Chapter 3).

Second, `printf()` is fundamentally type-unsafe and thus prone to error. The function expects a sequence of non-typed arguments that are related to a C string filled with format specifiers, which is the first argument. Functions that cannot be used safely should never be used, because this can lead to subtle bugs, undefined behavior (see the section about undefined behavior in Chapter 5), and security vulnerabilities.

TEXT FORMATTING LIBRARY [C++20]

With the new standard C++20, a text formatting library is available that offers a safe, faster, and more extensible alternative to the outdated and potentially dangerous `printf` family of functions. The header file of this library is `<format>`. The style of formatting looks very similar to string formatting in the Python programming language.

Unfortunately, it is also one of the new libraries that's currently not supported by any C++ compiler while I'm writing this book. A temporary and good alternative, which was also the template for the new C++20 library, is the open source library called {fmt} (`https://github.com/fmtlib/fmt`), which provides, among other features, a C++20 compatible implementation of `std::format`.

Here are some usage examples:

```cpp
#include "fmt/format.h" // Can be replaced by <format> when available.
#include <numbers>
#include <iostream>

int main() {
  // Note: replace namespace fmt:: by std:: once the compiler supports <format>.
  const auto theAnswer = fmt::format("The answer is {}.", 42);  std::cout <<
  theAnswer << "\n";
```

```
// Many different format specifiers are possible.
const auto formattedNumbers =
  fmt::format("Decimal: {:f}, Scientific: {:e}, Hexadecimal: {:X}",
    3.1415, 0.123, 255);
std::cout << formattedNumbers << "\n";

// Arguments can be reordered in the created string by using an index {n:}:
const auto reorderedArguments =
  fmt::format("Decimal: {1:f}, Scientific: {2:e}, Hexadecimal: {0:X}",
    255, 3.1415, 0.123);
std::cout << reorderedArguments << "\n";

// The number of decimal places can be specified as follows:
const auto piWith22DecimalPlaces = fmt::format("PI = {:.22f}",
  std::numbers::pi);
std::cout << piWith22DecimalPlaces << "\n";

return 0;
}
```

The output of this small demo program is as follows:

```
The answer is 42.
Decimal: 3.141500, Scientific: 1.230000e-01, Hexadecimal: FF
Decimal: 3.141500, Scientific: 1.230000e-01, Hexadecimal: FF
PI = 3.1415926535897931159980
```

Third, unlike printf, C++ I/O streams allow complex objects to be easily streamed by providing a custom insertion operator (operator<<). Suppose we have a class called Invoice (defined in a header file named Invoice.h) that looks like Listing 4-29.

Listing 4-29. An Excerpt from the Invoice.h File with Line Numbers

```
01  #ifndef INVOICE_H_
02  #define INVOICE_H_
03
04  #include <chrono>
05  #include <memory>
06  #include <ostream>
07  #include <string>
08  #include <vector>
```

```
09
10  #include "Customer.h"
11  #include "InvoiceLineItem.h"
12  #include "Money.h"
13  #include "UniqueIdentifier.h"
14
15  using InvoiceLineItemPtr = std::shared_ptr<InvoiceLineItem>;
16  using InvoiceLineItems = std::vector<InvoiceLineItemPtr>;
17
18  using InvoiceRecipient = Customer;
19  using InvoiceRecipientPtr = std::shared_ptr<InvoiceRecipient>;
20
21  using DateTime = std::chrono::system_clock::time_point;
22
23  class Invoice {
24  public:
25    explicit Invoice(const UniqueIdentifier& invoiceNumber);
26    void setRecipient(const InvoiceRecipientPtr& recipient);
27    void setDateTimeOfInvoicing(const DateTime& dateTimeOfInvoicing);
28    Money getSum() const;
29    Money getSumWithoutTax() const;
30    void addLineItem(const InvoiceLineItemPtr& lineItem);
31    // ...possibly more member functions here...
32
33  private:
34    friend std::ostream& operator<<(std::ostream& outstream, const
        Invoice& invoice);
35    std::string getDateTimeOfInvoicingAsString() const;
36
37    UniqueIdentifier invoiceNumber;
38    DateTime dateTimeOfInvoicing;
39    InvoiceRecipientPtr recipient;
40    InvoiceLineItems invoiceLineItems;
41  };
42  // ...
```

The class has dependencies to an invoice recipient (which in this case is an alias for the Customer defined in the Customer.h header; see line 18), and it uses an identifier (type UniqueIdentifier) representing an invoice number that is guaranteed to be unique among all invoice numbers. Furthermore, the invoice uses a data type that can represent money amounts (see the section entitled "Money Class" in Chapter 9 about design patterns), as well as a dependency to another data type that represents a single invoice line item. The latter is used to manage a list of invoice items inside the invoice using a std::vector (see lines 16 and 41). To represent the time of invoicing, we use the data type time_point from the Chrono library (defined in the <chrono> header), which has been available since C++11.

Now let's imagine that we also want to stream the entire invoice with all its data to standard output. Wouldn't it be pretty simple and convenient if we could write something like this:

```
std::cout << instanceOfInvoice;
```

Well, that's possible with C++. The insertion operator (<<) for output streams can be overloaded for any class. We just have to add an operator<< function to our class declaration in the header. It is important to make this function a friend of the class in our case (see line 34) because it accesses private member variables directly. See Listing 4-30.

Listing 4-30. The Insertion Operator for the Invoice Class

```
43  // ...
44  std::ostream& operator<<(std::ostream& outstream, const Invoice& invoice) {
45      outstream << "Invoice No.: " << invoice.invoiceNumber << "\n";
46      outstream << "Recipient: " << *(invoice.recipient) << "\n";
47      outstream << "Date/time: " << invoice.getDateTimeOfInvoicingAsString()
            << "\n";
48      outstream << "Items:" << "\n";
49      for (const auto& item : invoice.invoiceLineItems) {
50          outstream << "    " << *item << "\n";
51      }
52      outstream << "Amount invoiced: " << invoice.getSum() << std::endl;
53      return outstream;
54  }
55  // ...
```

All structural components of the Invoice class are written into an output stream inside the function. This is possible, because the UniqueIdentifier, InvoiceRecipient, and InvoiceLineItem classes also have their own insertion operator functions (not shown here) for output streams. To print all line items in the vector, a C++11 range-based for loop is used. And to get a textual representation of the date of invoicing, we use an internal helper method named getDateTimeOfInvoicingAsString() that returns a well-formatted date/time string.

Tip   Avoid using printf() and other unsafe C functions, such as sprintf(), puts(), scanf(), sscanf(), etc.

Choose Standard Library Containers over Simple C-Style Arrays

Instead of using C-style arrays, you should use the std::array<TYPE, N> template has been available since C++11 (in the <array> header). Instances of std::array<TYPE, N> are fixed-size sequence containers and are as efficient as ordinary C-style arrays.

The problems with C-style arrays are more or less the same as with C-style strings (see the previous section). C arrays are bad because they are passed around as raw pointers to their first element. This could be potentially dangerous, because there are no bound checks that protect users of that array to access nonexistent elements. Arrays built with std::array are safer, because they don't decay to pointers (see the section entitled "Strategies to Avoid Regular Pointers," earlier in this chapter).

An advantage of using std::array is that it knows its size (number of elements). When working with arrays, the size of the array is important information that is often required. Ordinary C-style arrays don't know their own size. Thus, the size of the array must often be handled as an additional piece of information, for example, in an additional variable. For example, the size must be passed as an additional argument to function calls like in the following example.

```
const std::size_t arraySize = 10;
MyArrayType cStyleArray[arraySize];

void function(MyArrayType const* pArray, const std::size_t arraySize) {
  // ...
}
```

Strictly speaking, in this case the array and its size don't form a cohesive unit (see the section entitled "Strong Cohesion" in Chapter 3). Furthermore, we already know from a previous section about parameters and return values that the number of function arguments should be as small as possible.

In contrast, instances of `std::array` carry their size and any instance can be queried about it. Thus, the parameter lists of functions or methods don't require additional parameters about the array's size:

```
#include <array>

using MyTypeArray = std::array<MyArrayType, 10>;

void function(const MyTypeArray& array) {
  const std::size_t arraySize = array.size();
  //...
}
```

Another noteworthy advantage of `std::array` is that it has a Standard Library compatible interface. The class template provides public member functions so it looks like every other container in the Standard Library. For example, users of an array can get an iterator pointing to the beginning and the end of the sequence using `std::array::begin()` and `std::array::end()`, respectively. This also means that algorithms from the `<algorithm>` header can be applied to the array (see the section about algorithms in the following chapter).

```
#include <array>
#include <algorithm>

using MyTypeArray = std::array<MyArrayType, 10>;
MyTypeArray array;

void doSomethingWithEachElement(const MyArrayType& element) {
  // ...
}

std::for_each(std::cbegin(array), std::cend(array),
doSomethingWithEachElement);
```

NON-MEMBER STD::BEGIN() AND STD::END() [C++11/14]

Every C++ Standard Library container has a begin() and cbegin() and an end() and cend() member function to retrieve iterators and const-iterators for that container. Apart from some some exceptions, many containers also provide corresponding const and non-const reverse iterators (rbegin()/rend() and crbegin()/crend()).

C++11 has introduced free non-member functions for that purpose: std::begin(<container>) and std::end(<container>). With C++14, the still missing functions std::cbegin(<container>), std::cend(<container>), std::rbegin(<container>), std::rend(<container>), std::crbegin(<container>), and std::crend(<container>) have been added. Instead of using the member functions, it is now recommended to use these non-member functions (all defined in the <iterator> header) to get iterators and const-iterators for a container, like so:

```
#include <vector>

std::vector<AnyType> aVector;
auto iter = std::begin(aVector);  // ...instead of 'auto iter = aVector.
                                              begin();'
```

The reason is that those free functions allow a more flexible and generic programming style. For instance, many user-defined containers don't have a begin() and end() member function, which makes them impossible to use with the Standard Library algorithms (see the section about algorithms in Chapter 5) or any other user-defined template function that requires iterators. The non-member functions to retrieve iterators are extensible in the sense of that they can be overloaded for any type of sequence, including old C-style arrays. In other words, non-Standard-Library-compatible (custom) containers can be retrofitted with iterator capabilities.

For instance, assume that you have to deal with a C-style array of integers, like this one:

```
int fibonacci[] = { 1, 1, 2, 3, 5, 8, 13, 21, 34, 55, 89, 144 };
```

This type of array can now be retrofitted with a Standard Library-compliant iterator interface. For C-style arrays, such functions are already provided in the Standard Library, so you do not have to program them yourself. They look more or less like this:

```
template <typename Type, std::size_t size>
constexpr Type* begin(Type (&cArray)[size]) noexcept {
  return cArray;
}

template <typename Type, std::size_t size>
constexpr Type* end(Type (&cArray)[size]) noexcept {
  return cArray + size;
}
```

To insert all elements of the array into an output stream, for example, to print them on standard output, we can now write:

```
using namespace std;

int main() {
  for (auto it = begin(fibonacci); it != end(fibonacci); ++it) {
    std::cout << *it << ", ";
  }
  std::cout << std::endl;
  return 0;
}
```

Providing overloaded begin() and end() functions for custom container types, or old C-style arrays, enables the application of all Standard Library algorithms to these types.

Furthermore, std::array can access elements including bound checks with the help of the std::array::at(size_type n) member function. If the given index is out of bounds, an exception of type std::out_of_bounds is thrown.

Use C++ Casts Instead of Old C-Style Casts

Before a false impression emerges, I would first like to state an important warning.

Warning   Type casts are basically bad and should be avoided whenever possible! They are a trustworthy indication that there must be, albeit a relatively tiny, design problem.

However, if a type cast cannot be avoided in a certain situation, then under no circumstances should you use a C-style cast:

```
double d { 3.1415 };
int i = (int)d;
```

In this case, the double is demoted to an integer. This explicit conversion is accompanied with a loss of precision since the decimal places of the floating-point number are thrown away. The explicit conversion with the C-style cast says something like this: "The programmer who wrote this line of code was aware about the consequences."

Well, this is certainly better than an implicit type conversion. Nevertheless, instead using old C-style casts, you should use C++ casts for explicit type conversions, like this:

```
int i = static_cast<int>(d);
```

The simple explanation for this advice is, with the exception of the dynamic_cast<T>, the compiler checks C++ style casts during compile time! C-style casts are not checked this way and thus they can fail at runtime, which may cause ugly bugs or application crashes. For instance, an improvident used C-style cast can cause a corrupted stack, like in the following case.

```
int32_t i { 200 };                  // Reserves and uses 4 byte memory
int64_t* pointerToI = (int64_t*)&i; // Pointer points to 8 byte

*pointerToI = 9223372036854775807;  // Can cause run-time error through
                                    //             stack corruption
```

Obviously, in this case it is possible to write a 64-bit value into a memory area that is only 32 bits in size. The problem is that the compiler cannot draw our attention to this potentially dangerous piece of code. The compiler translates this code, even with very conservative settings (g++ -std=c++17 -pedantic -pedantic-errors -Wall -Wextra -Werror -Wconversion), without complaints. This can lead to very insidious errors during program execution.

Now let's see what will happen if we use a C++ static_cast on the second line instead of the old and bad C-style cast:

```
int64_t* pointerToI = static_cast<int64_t*>(&i); // Pointer points to 8 byte
```

The compiler can now spot the problematic conversion and report a corresponding error message:

```
error: invalid static_cast from type 'int32_t* {aka int*}' to type
'int64_t* {aka long int*}'
```

Another reason that you should use C++ casts instead of old C-style casts is that C-style casts are very hard to spot in a program. In addition, developers cannot easily discover them, nor can they search them conveniently using an ordinary editor or word processor. In contrast, it is very easy to search for terms such as static_cast<>, const_cast<>, or dynamic_cast<>.

At a glance, here is the advice regarding type conversions for a modern and well-designed C++ program:

- **Try to avoid type conversions (casts) under all circumstances.** Instead, try to eliminate the underlying design error that forces you to use the conversion.

- If an explicitly type conversion cannot be avoided, **use C++ style casts** (static_cast<> or const_cast<>) **only**, because the compiler checks these casts. **Never use old and bad C-style casts.**

- **Notice that dynamic_cast<> should also never be used because it is considered bad design**. The need of a dynamic_cast<> is a reliable indication that something is wrong within a specialization hierarchy. (This topic will be deepened in Chapter 6 about object orientation.)

- Do not use reinterpret_cast<> **under any circumstances.** This kind of type conversion marks an unsafe, non-portable, and implementation-dependent cast. Its long and inconvenient name is a broad hint to make you think about what you're currently doing. If you have to interpret an object bit by bit as another object, use std::bit_cast<> (new since C++20) instead of reinterpret_cast<> or std::memcpy(). std::bit_cast<> (defined in the <bit> header) can be evaluated at compile-time (constexpr) and requires that the objects involved be trivially copied and be the same size.

Avoid Macros

Maybe one of the severest legacies of the C language is macros. A macro is a code fragment that can be identified by a name. If the so-called preprocessor finds the name of a macro in the program's source code while compiling, the name is replaced by its related code fragment.

One kind of macro is the object-like macro often used to give symbolic names to numeric constants, as shown in Listing 4-31.

Listing 4-31. Two Examples of Object-Like Macros

```
#define BUFFER_SIZE 1024
#define PI 3.14159265358979
```

Other typical examples of macros are shown in Listing 4-32.

Listing 4-32. Two Examples of Function-Like Macros

```
#define MIN(a,b) (((a)<(b))?(a): (b))
#define MAX(a,b) (((a)>(b))?(a): (b))
```

MIN and MAX compare two values and returns the smaller and larger one, respectively. Such macros are called function-like macros. Although these macros look almost like functions, they are not. The C preprocessor merely substitutes the name with the related code fragment (in fact, it is a textual find-and-replace operation).

Macros are potentially dangerous. They often do not behave as expected and can have unwanted side effects. For instance, let's assume that you defined a macro like this one:

```
#define DANGEROUS 1024+1024
```

And somewhere in your code you write this:

```
int value = DANGEROUS * 2;
```

Probably someone expects that the variable value contains 4096, but actually it would be 3072. Remember the order of mathematical operations, which tells us that division and multiplication, from left to right, should happen first.

Another example of unexpected side effects due to using a macro is using MAX in the following way:

```
int maximum = MAX(12, value++);
```

The preprocessor will generate the following:

```
int maximum = (((12)>(value++))?(12):(value++));
```

As can easily be seen now, the post-increment operation on value will be performed twice. This was certainly not the intention of the developer who wrote the piece of code.

Don't use macros anymore! At least since C++11, they are almost obsolete. With some very rare exceptions, macros are simply no longer necessary and should no longer be used in a modern C++ program. Maybe the introduction of so-called *reflection* (i.e., the ability of a program to examine, introspect, and modify its own structure and behavior at runtime) as a possible part of a future C++ standard can help to get rid of macros entirely. But until the time comes, macros are still currently needed for some special purposes, for example, when using a unit test or logging framework.

STD::SOURCE_LOCATION [C++20]

Since C++20, it is also possible to do without the probably well-known C macros __FILE__ and __LINE__. As a reminder: The preprocessor expands the macro __FILE__ to the filename of the source code file and the macro __LINE__ to the current line number. Both macros were typically used when log statements and error messages intended for programmers were generated.

With C++20 we now get a modern replacement in the form of a class: std::source_location (defined in the <source_location> header). The class has a static factory method called std::source_location::current(), which is designed as a so-called immediate function (consteval). It can be used to create a new std::source_location object at compile-time that contains information corresponding to the location of the call site:

```
#include <source_location>;
// ...and somewhere in the code:
const auto& location = std::source_location::current();
```

The class provides four public member functions (file_name(), function_name(), column(), and line()), which can then be used to retrieve the information for output or logging purposes.

```
std::cout << "Filename: " << location.file_name()
   << ", Function: " << location.function_name()
   << ", Line/Column: (" << location.line() << "," << location.column() << ")\n";
```

Instead of object-like macros, use constant expressions to define constants:

```
constexpr int HARMLESS = 1024 + 1024;
```

And instead of function-like macros, simply use true functions, for example, the function templates std::min or std::max, which are defined in the <algorithm> header (see the section about the <algorithm> header in Chapter 5):

```
#include <algorithm>
// ...
int maximum = std::max(12, value++);
```

CHAPTER 5

Advanced Concepts of Modern C++

In Chapters 3 and 4, we discussed the basic principles and practices that build a solid foundation for clean and modern C++ code. With these principles and rules in mind, a developer can raise the internal C++ code quality of a software project and, thus often its external quality, significantly. The code becomes more understandable, more maintainable, more easily extensible, and less susceptible to bugs. This leads to a better life for any software crafter, because it is more fun to work with a sound code base. In Chapter 2, we learned that, above all, a well-maintained suite of well-crafted unit tests can further improve the quality of the software as well as the development efficiency.

But can we do better? Of course we can.

As I explained in this book's introduction, the good old dinosaur C++ has experienced some considerable improvements during the last decade. The C++11 language standard (short for ISO/IEC 14882:2011) has fundamentally revolutionized the way developers think about C++ programming. After the rather evolutionary developments C++14 and C++17, and now with C++20, the standard contains many innovations and changes.

I have used a few of the C++ standards and features in the previous chapters and explained them in sidebars. Now it is time to dive deeper into some of them and explore how they can help you write exceptionally sound and modern C++ code. Of course, it is not possible to discuss all the language features of the newer C++ standards completely. That would go far beyond the scope of this book, leaving aside the fact that this is covered by numerous other books. Furthermore, it should not be the goal to use every fancy feature of the new C++ standards in every program. Always think about the KISS principle described in Chapter 3. Therefore, I have selected a few topics that I believe support the goal of writing clean C++ code very well.

© Stephan Roth 2021
S. Roth, *Clean C++20*, https://doi.org/10.1007/978-1-4842-5949-8_5

Managing Resources

Managing resources is the bread-and-butter business of software developers. A multitude of miscellaneous resources must be regularly allocated, used, and returned after use. These include the following:

- Memory (either on the stack or on the heap)

- File handles that are required to access files (read/write) on hard disk or other media

- Network connections (e.g., to a server, a database, etc.)

- Threads, locks, timers, and transactions

- Other operational system resources, like GDI handles on Windows operating systems[1]

The proper handling of resources can be a tricky task. Consider the example in Listing 5-1.

Listing 5-1. Dealing with a Resource That Was Allocated on the Heap

```
void doSomething() {
  ResourceType* resource = new ResourceType();
  try {
    // ...do something with resource...
    resource->foo();
  } catch (...) {
    delete resource;
    throw;
  }
  delete resource;
}
```

What's the problem here? Perhaps you've noticed the two identical delete statements. The catch-all exception handling mechanism introduces at least two possible paths in our program. This also means that we have to ensure that the resource

---

[1]GDI stands for Graphics Device Interface. GDI is a core operating system component of Microsoft Windows and is responsible for representing graphical objects.

is freed in two places. Under normal circumstances such catch-all exception handlers are frowned upon. But in this case, we have no other chance than to catch all possible occurring exceptions here, because we must free the resource first, before we throw the exception object further to treat it elsewhere (e.g., at the call site of the function).

I this simplified example, we have only two paths. In real programs, significantly more execution paths can exist. The probability that one delete is forgotten is much higher. Any forgotten delete will result in a dangerous resource leakage.

Warning   Do not underestimate resource leaks! Resource leaks are a **serious problem**, particularly for long-lived processes, and for processes that rapidly allocate many resources without deallocating them after usage. If an operating system has a lack of resources, this can lead to critical system states. Furthermore, resource leaks can be a security issue, because they can be exploited by assaulters during denial-of-service attacks.

The simplest solution for our small example could be that we allocate the resource on the stack, instead of allocating it on the heap, as shown in Listing 5-2.

Listing 5-2. Much Easier: Dealing with a Resource on the Stack

```
void doSomething() {
  ResourceType resource;

  // ...do something with resource...
  resource.foo();
}
```

With this change the resource is safely removed in any case. But sometimes it is not possible to allocate everything on the stack, as we've discussed in the section "Don't Pass or Return 0 (nullptr)" in Chapter 4. What about file handles, OS resources, etc.?

The central question is this: **How can we guarantee that allocated resources are always freed?**

Resource Acquisition Is Initialization (RAII)

Resource acquisition is initialization (RAII) is an idiom (see Chapter 9 about idioms) that can help cope with resources in a safe way. The idiom is also known as *constructor acquires, destructor releases* (CADRe) and *scope-based resource management* (SBRM).

RAII takes advantage of the symmetry of a class between its constructor and its corresponding destructor. We can allocate a resource in the constructor of a class, and we can deallocate it in the destructor. If we create such a class as a template, it can be used for different types of resources. See Listing 5-3.

Listing 5-3. A Very Simple Class Template That Can Manage Several Types of Resources

```cpp
template <typename RESTYPE>
class ScopedResource final {
public:
  ScopedResource() { managedResource = new RESTYPE(); }
  ~ScopedResource() { delete managedResource; }

  RESTYPE* operator->() const { return managedResource; }
  RESTYPE& operator*() const { return *managedResource; }

private:
  RESTYPE* managedResource;
};
```

Now we can use the class template called ScopedResource, as shown in Listing 5-4.

Listing 5-4. Using ScopedResource to Manage an Instance of ResourceType

```cpp
#include "ScopedResource.h"
#include "ResourceType.h"

void doSomething() {

  ScopedResource<ResourceType> resource;

  try {
    // ...do something with resource...
    resource->foo();
```

```
  } catch (...) {
    // Perform error handling here...
  }
}
```

As it can be easily seen, no new or delete is required. If resource runs out of scope, which can happen at various points in this method, the wrapped instance of type ResourceType is deleted automatically through the destructor of ScopedResource.

But there is usually no need to reinvent the wheel and to implement such a wrapper, which is also called a smart pointer.

Smart Pointers

Since C++11, the Standard Library offers different, efficient smart-pointer-implementations for easy use. These pointers have been developed over a long period within the well-known Boost library project before they were introduced into the C++ standard, and can be regarded as foolproof as possible. Smart pointers reduce the likelihood of memory leaks. Furthermore, their reference counter mechanism is designed to be thread-safe.

This section provides a brief overview.

Unique Ownership with std::unique_ptr<T>

The class template std::unique_ptr<T> (defined in the <memory> header) manages a pointer to an object of type T. As the name suggests, this smart pointer provides unique ownership, that is, an object can be owned by only one instance of std::unique_ptr<T> at a time, which is the main difference of the std::shared_ptr<T>, which is explained next. This also means that copy construction and copy assignment are not allowed.

Its use is pretty simple:

```
#include <memory>

class ResourceType {
  //...
};

//...
std::unique_ptr<ResourceType> resource1 { std::make_unique<ResourceType>() };
```

```
// ... or shorter with type deduction ...
auto resource2 { std::make_unique<ResourceType>() };
```

After this construction, resource can be used very much like a regular pointer to an instance of ResourceType. (std::make_unique<T> is explained in the section entitled "Avoid new and delete"). For example, you can use the * and -> operators for dereferencing:

```
resource->foo();
```

Of course, if resource runs out of scope, the contained instance of type ResourceType is freed safely. But the best part is that resource can be easily put into containers, for example, in a std::vector:

```
#include "ResourceType.h"
#include <memory>
#include <vector>

using ResourceTypePtr = std::unique_ptr<ResourceType>;
using ResourceVector = std::vector<ResourceTypePtr>;

//...

ResourceTypePtr resource { std::make_unique<ResourceType>() };
ResourceVector aCollectionOfResources;
aCollectionOfResources.push_back(std::move(resource));
// IMPORTANT: At this point, the instance of 'resource' is empty!
```

Note that we ensure that std::vector::push_back() calls the move constructor and the move assignment operator of std::unique_ptr<T> (see the section about move semantics in the next chapter). As a consequence, resource does not manage an object anymore and is denoted as empty.

As mentioned, copy construction of std::unique_ptr<T> is not allowed. However, the exclusive ownership of the managed resource can be transferred to another instance of std::unique_ptr<T>, using move semantics (we will discuss move semantics in detail in a later section) in the following way:

```
std::unique_ptr<ResourceType> pointer1 { std::make_unique<ResourceType>() };
std::unique_ptr<ResourceType> pointer2; // pointer2 owns nothing yet

pointer2 = std::move(pointer1);          // Now pointer1 is empty, pointer2
                                         // is the new owner
```

Shared Ownership with std::shared_ptr<T>

Instances of class template `std::shared_ptr<T>` (defined in the `<memory>` header) can take ownership of a resource of type T and can share this ownership with other instances of `std::shared_ptr<T>`. In other words, the ownership for a **single** instance of type T, and thus the responsibility for its deletion, can be taken over by **many** shared owners.

`std::shared_ptr<T>` provides something like simple limited garbage collector functionality. The smart pointer's implementation has a reference counter that monitors how many pointer instances owning the shared object still exist. It releases the managed resource if the last instance of the pointer is destroyed.

Figure 5-1 depicts a class diagram, as well as an object diagram. The lower area of the figure, where the object diagram can be seen, depicts a situation (snapshot) in a running system where three anonymous instances of the class `Client` share the same resource (:Resource) using three `std::shared_ptr` instances. The `_M_use_count` attribute represents the reference counter of `std::shared_ptr`.

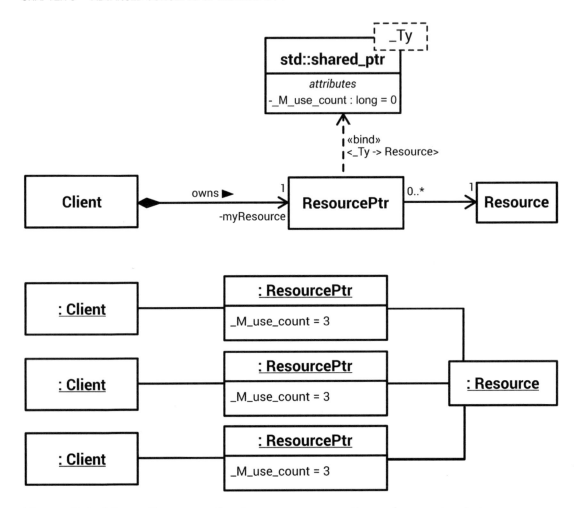

Figure 5-1. *Three clients are sharing one resource through smart pointers*

In contrast to the previously discussed std::unique_ptr<T>, std::shared_ptr<T> is of course copy-constructible as expected. But you can ensure that the managed resource is moved by using std::move<T>:

```
std::shared_ptr<ResourceType> pointer1 { std::make_shared<ResourceType>() };
std::shared_ptr<ResourceType> pointer2;

pointer2 = std::move(pointer1); // The reference count does not get
modified, pointer1 is empty
```

In this case, the reference counter is not modified, but you must be careful when using the variable pointer1 after the move, because it is empty, that is, it holds a nullptr. Move semantics and the utility function std::move<T> are discussed in a later section.

No Ownership, but Secure Access with std::weak_ptr<T>

Sometimes it is necessary to have a non-owning pointer to a resource that is owned by one or more shared pointers. At first you might say, okay, but what's the problem? I simply can obtain the raw pointer from an instance of std::shared_ptr<T> at any time by calling its get() member function. See Listing 5-5.

Listing 5-5. Retrieving the Regular Pointer from an Instance of std::shared_ptr<T>

```
std::shared_ptr<ResourceType> resource {
std::make_shared<ResourceType>() };
// ...
ResourceType* rawPointerToResource { resource.get() };
```

Watch your step! This could be dangerous. What will happen if the last instance of std::shared_ptr<ResourceType> gets destroyed somewhere in your program and this raw pointer is still in usage somewhere? The raw pointer will point to No-Man's-Land and using it can cause serious problems (remember my warning about undefined behavior in the previous chapter). You have absolutely no chance to determine that the raw pointer points to a valid address of a resource, or to an arbitrary location in memory.

If you need a pointer to the resource without having ownership, you should use std::weak_ptr<T> (defined in the <memory> header), which has no influence on the resource's lifetime. std::weak_ptr<T> merely "observes" the managed resource and can be interrogated that it is valid. See Listing 5-6.

Listing 5-6. Using std::weak_ptr<T> to Deal with Resources That Are Not Owned

```
01  #include <memory>
02
03  void doSomething(const std::weak_ptr<ResourceType>& weakResource) {
04    if (! weakResource.expired()) {
05      // Now we know that weakResource contains a pointer to a valid object
06      std::shared_ptr<ResourceType> sharedResource = weakResource.lock();
07      // Use sharedResource...
08    }
09  }
10
```

```
11  int main() {
12    auto sharedResource{ std::make_shared<ResourceType>() };
13    std::weak_ptr<ResourceType> weakResource{ sharedResource };
14
15    doSomething(weakResource);
16    sharedResource.reset(); // Deletes the managed instance of ResourceType
17    doSomething(weakResource);
18
19    return 0;
20  }
```

As you can see on Line 4 in Listing 5-6, we can interrogate the weak pointer object if it manages a valid resource. This is done by calling its expired() member function. std::weak_ptr<T> does not provide dereference operators, like *, or ->. If we want to use the resource, we first must call the lock() function (see line 6) to obtain a shared pointer object from it.

You might be asking yourself now what the use cases of this smart pointer type are. Why is it necessary, because you could readily also take a std::shared_ptr<T> everywhere a resource is needed?

First of all, with std::shared_ptr<T> and std::weak_ptr<T>, you are able to distinguish between owners of a resource and users of a resource in a software design. Not every software unit that requires a resource just for a certain and time-limited task wants to become its owner. As we can see in the function doSomething() in the previous example, sometimes it is sufficient just to "promote" a weak pointer to a strong pointer for a limited amount of time.

A good example would be an object cache that for the purpose of performance efficiency keeps recently accessed objects in memory for a certain amount of time. The objects in the cache are held with std::shared_ptr<T> instances, together with a last-used timestamp. Periodically, a kind of garbage collector process is running that scans the cache and decides to destroy those objects that have not been used for a defined time span.

At those places where the cached objects are used, instances of std::weak_ptr<T> are used to hold non-owning pointers to these objects. If the expired() member function of those std::weak_ptr<T> instances returns true, the garbage collector process has cleared the objects from the cache. In the other case, the std::weak_ptr<T>::lock() function can be used to retrieve a std::shared_ptr<T> from it. Now the object can be safely used, even if the garbage collector process gets active. The process could evaluate the usage counter of the `std::shared_ptr<T>` and ascertain that the object has currently at least one user outside the cache. As a consequence, the object's lifetime would be extended. Or the process could delete the object from the cache, which does not interfere with its users.

Another example is to deal with circular dependencies. For instance, if you have a class A that needs a pointer to another class B and vice versa, you will end up with a circular dependency. If you use `std::shared_ptr<T>` to point to the respective class, as shown in Listing 5-7, you can end up with a memory leak. The reason for this is that the usage counter in the respective shared pointer instance will never count down to 0. Thus, the objects will never be deleted.

Listing 5-7. The Problem with Circular Dependencies Caused Through Careless Use of std::shared_ptr<T>

```
#include <memory>

class B; // Forward declaration

class A {
public:
  void setB(std::shared_ptr<B>& pointerToB) {
    myPointerToB = pointerToB;
  }

private:
  std::shared_ptr<B> myPointerToB;
};

class B {
public:
  void setA(std::shared_ptr<A>& pointerToA) {
    myPointerToA = pointerToA;
  }

private:
  std::shared_ptr<A> myPointerToA;
};
```

```
int main() {
  { // Curly braces build a scope
    auto pointerToA = std::make_shared<A>();
    auto pointerToB = std::make_shared<B>();
    pointerToA->setB(pointerToB);
    pointerToB->setA(pointerToA);
  }
  // At this point, one instance each of A and B is "lost in space"
    (memory leak!)

  return 0;
}
```

If the std::shared_ptr<T> member variables in the classes are replaced with non-owning weak pointers (std::weak_ptr<T>) to the respective other class, the issue with the memory leak is solved. See Listing 5-8.

Listing 5-8. Circular Dependencies Implemented the Right Way with std::weak_ptr<T>

```
class B; // Forward declaration

class A {
public:
  void setB(std::shared_ptr<B>& pointerToB) {
    myPointerToB = pointerToB;
  }

private:
  std::weak_ptr<B> myPointerToB;
};

class B {
public:
  void setA(std::shared_ptr<A>& pointerToA) {
    myPointerToA = pointerToA;
  }
```

```
private:
  std::weak_ptr<A> myPointerToA;
};
// ...
```

Basically, circular dependencies are bad design in application code and should be avoided whenever possible. There might be a few exceptions in low-level libraries where circular dependencies cause no serious issues. But apart from that, you should follow the *acyclic dependency principle,* which is discussed in a dedicated section in Chapter 6.

Atomic Smart Pointers

As I mentioned briefly, the implementations of std::shared_ptr<T> and std::weak_ptr<T> are thread-safe by design. But this only applies to the reference count block of the pointers, not to the resource that is managed and shared by them! std::shared_ptr<T> guarantees that counting up and down the reference counter, as well as deleting the managed resource if necessary, are atomic operations.

ATOMIC OPERATION

In computer science and software development, an *atomic operation* is a compound of single operations that can be seen as one undividable logical unit. This means that they can only be successful or fail as a whole. Atomic operations play an important role in database changes (so-called transaction safety), as well as in the implementation of locking mechanisms to avoid data races in parallel programming.

In contrast, these pointers cannot guarantee that the uses of the resources they manage are atomic, nor that non-const method calls (e.g., assigning a new resource) invoked on them are atomic (and thus thread-safe). The second problem is now solved by the two new partial specializations of std::atomic<T> introduced with C++20: std::atomic<std::shared_ptr<T>> and std::atomic<std::weak_ptr<U>> (both defined in the <memory> header). To prevent data races and undefined behavior in a concurrent environment with the standard smart pointers, atomic, smart pointer types should be used instead. **However, be careful:** You should always keep in mind that the managed resource is still not protected from data races even with these atomic pointers!

Avoid Explicit New and Delete

In a modern C++ program, when writing application code you should avoid calling new and delete explicitly. Why? Well, the simple and short explanation is this: new and delete increase complexity.

The more detailed answer is this: every time when it is inevitable to call new and delete, one has to deal with an exceptional, non-default situation, a situation that requires special treatment. To understand these exceptional cases, let's take a look on the default cases—the situations any C++ developer should strive for.

Explicit calls of new and/or delete can be avoided using the following measures:

- **Use allocations on the stack wherever possible.** Allocations on the stack are simple (remember the KISS principle discussed in Chapter 3) and safe. It's impossible to leak any of that memory that was allocated on the stack. The resource will be destroyed once it goes out of scope. You can even return the object from a function by value, thus transferring its contents to the calling function.

- **To allocate a resource on the heap, use "make functions."** Use std::make_unique<T> or std::make_shared<T> to instantiate the resource and wrap it immediately into a manager object that takes care of the resource, a smart pointer.

- **Use containers (Standard Library, Boost, or others) wherever appropriate.** These well-designed containers are bullet-proof and manage the storage space for their elements in the correct manner. Instead, in the case of self-developed data structures and sequences, you are forced to implement the entire storage management on your own, which can be a complex and error-prone task.

- **Provide wrappers for resources from proprietary third-party libraries** that require a specific memory management (see the next section).

Managing Proprietary Resources

As mentioned in the introduction to this section about resource management, sometimes other resources need to be managed that are not allocated or deallocated on the heap using the default new or delete operator. Examples of such kinds of resources are opened files from a file system, database connections, a dynamically loaded module (e.g., a Dynamic Link Library [DLL] on Windows operating systems), or platform-specific objects of a graphical user interface (e.g., Windows, Buttons, Text input fields, etc.).

Often these kinds of resources are managed through something that is called a *handle*. A handle is an abstract and unique reference to an operational system resource. On Windows, the data type HANDLE is used to define such handles. In fact, this data type is defined as follows in the WinNT.h header, a C-style header file that defines various Win32 API macros and types:

```cpp
typedef void *HANDLE;
```

For instance, if you want to access a running Windows process with a certain process ID, you can retrieve a handle to this process using the Win32 API function called OpenProcess().

```cpp
#include <windows.h>
// ...
const DWORD processId = 4711;
HANDLE processHandle = OpenProcess(PROCESS_ALL_ACCESS, FALSE, processId);
```

After you are finished with the handle, you have to close it by using the CloseHandle() function:

```cpp
BOOL success = CloseHandle(processHandle);
```

Hence, we have symmetry similar to the new operator and its corresponding delete operator. It should therefore also be possible to take advantage of the RAII idiom and use smart pointers for such resources. First, we just have to exchange the default deleter (which calls delete) by a custom deleter that calls CloseHandle():

```cpp
#include <windows.h> // Windows API declarations

class Win32HandleCloser {
public:
  void operator()(HANDLE handle) const {
    if (handle != INVALID_HANDLE_VALUE) {
      CloseHandle(handle);
    }
  }
};
```

145

Be careful! If you define a type alias by writing something like the following, the std::shared_ptr<T> will manage something that is of type void**, because HANDLE is defined as a void-pointer:

```
using Win32SharedHandle = std::shared_ptr<HANDLE>; // Caution!
```

Therefore, smart pointers for the Win32 HANDLE must be defined as follows:

```
using Win32SharedHandle = std::shared_ptr<void>;
using Win32WeakHandle = std::weak_ptr<void>;
```

Note   You cannot define a std::unique_ptr<void> in C++! This is because std::shared_ptr<T> implements type-erasure, while std::unique_ptr<T> does not. If a class supports type-erasure, it means that it can store objects of an arbitrary type and destruct them correctly.

If you want to use the shared handle, you have to pay attention that you pass an instance of the custom deleter Win32HandleCloser as a parameter during construction:

```
const DWORD processId = 4711;
Win32SharedHandle processHandle { OpenProcess(PROCESS_ALL_ACCESS, FALSE,
processId),
  Win32HandleCloser() };
```

We Like to Move It

If someone asked me which C++11 feature has the most profound impact on how modern C++ programs are written now and in the future, I would clearly nominate *move semantics*. I discussed C++ move semantics briefly in Chapter 4, in the section about strategies to avoid regular pointers. But I think that they are so important that I want to deepen this language feature here.

What Are Move Semantics?

In many cases where the old C++ language forced us to use a copy constructor, we actually did not really want to create a deep copy of an object. Instead, we simply wanted to "move the object's payload." An object's payload is nothing else than the embedded data that the object carries around with it, so nothing else than other objects or member variables of primitive types like int.

These cases where we had to copy an object instead of moving it were, for example, the following:

- Returning a local object instance as a return value from a function or method. To prevent the copy construction in these cases prior C++11, pointers were frequently used.

- Inserting an object into a std::vector or other containers.

- The implementation of the std::swap<T> template function.

In many of the before-mentioned situations, it is unnecessary to keep the source object intact, that is, to create a deep, and in terms of runtime efficiency often costly, copy so that the source objects remains usable.

C++11 introduced a language feature that makes moving an object's embedded data a first-class operation. In addition to the copy constructor and copy assignment operator, the class's developer can now implement *move constructors* and *move assignment operators* (we will see later why we actually should **not** do that!). The move operations are usually very efficient. In contrast to a real copy operation, the source object's data is just handed over to the target object, and the argument (the source object) of the operation is put into a kind of "empty" or initial state.

The example in Listing 5-9 shows an arbitrary class that explicitly implements both types of semantics: copy constructor (line 6) and assignment operator (line 8), as well as move constructor (line 7) and assignment operator (line 9).

Listing 5-9. An Example Class That Explicitly Declares Special Member Functions for Copy and Move

```
01  #include <string>
02
03  class Clazz {
04  public:
05    Clazz() noexcept;                    // Default constructor
06    Clazz(const Clazz& other);           // Copy constructor
07    Clazz(Clazz&& other) noexcept;       // Move constructor
08    Clazz& operator=(const Clazz& other); // Copy assignment operator
```

```
09    Clazz& operator=(Clazz&& other) noexcept; // Move assignment operator
10    virtual ~Clazz() noexcept;                 // Destructor
11
12  private:
13    // ...
14  };
```

Note   The **noexcept** specifier specifies whether a function can throw exceptions or not and is explained in more detail in the section entitled "The No-Throw Guarantee" later in this chapter.

As you will see later in the section "The Rule of Zero," it should be a major goal of any C++ developer to **not** declare and define such constructors and assignment operators explicitly.

The move semantics are closely related to something that is called *rvalue references* (see the next section). The constructor or assignment operator of a class is called a "move constructor" or a "move assignment operator," respectively, when it takes an *rvalue reference* as a parameter. An rvalue reference is marked through the double ampersand operator (&&). For better distinction, the ordinary reference with its single ampersand (&) is now also called an *lvalue reference*.

The Matter with Those lvalues and rvalues

The *lvalues* and *rvalues* are historical terms (inherited from language C), because lvalues could usually appear on the left side of an assignment expression, whereas rvalues could usually appear on the right side of an assignment expression. In my opinion, a much better explanation for lvalue is that it is a **locator value**. This makes it clear that an lvalue represents an object that occupies a location in memory (i.e., it has an accessible and identifiable memory address).

In contrast, rvalues are all those objects in an expression that are not lvalues. They are temporary objects, or subobjects thereof. Hence, it is not possible to assign anything to an rvalue.

Although these definitions come from the old C world, and C++11 still has introduced more categories (*xvalue*, *glvalue*, and *prvalue*) to enable move semantics, they are pretty good for everyday use.

The simplest form of an lvalue expression is a variable declaration:

```
Type var1;
```

The expression `var1` is an lvalue of type `Type`. The following declarations represent lvalues too:

```
Type* pointer;
Type& reference;
Type& function();
```

An lvalue can be the left operand of an assignment operation, like the integer-variable `theAnswerToAllQuestions` in this example:

```
int theAnswerToAllQuestions = 42;
```

The assignment of a memory address to a pointer also makes clear that the pointer is an lvalue:

```
Type* pointerToVar1 = &var1;
```

The literal "42" instead is an rvalue. It doesn't represent an identifiable location in memory, so it is not possible to assign anything to it (of course, rvalues also occupy memory in the data section on the stack, but this memory is allocated temporarily and released immediately after completion of the assignment operation):

```
int number = 23; // Works, because 'number' is an lvalue
42 = number; // Compiler error: lvalue required as left operand of
                assignment
```

You don't believe that `function()` on the third line from the above generic examples is an lvalue? It is! You can write the following (without doubt, some kind of weird) piece of code and the compiler will compile it without complaints:

```
int theAnswerToAllQuestions = 42;

int& function() {
  return theAnswerToAllQuestions;
}
```

```
int main() {
  function() = 23; // Works!
  return 0;
}
```

rvalue References

As mentioned, C++11 move semantics are closely related to something that is called
rvalue references. These rvalue references make it possible to address the memory
location of rvalues. In the following example, temporary memory is assigned to an rvalue
reference and thus makes it "permanent." You can even retrieve a pointer pointing to
this location and manipulate the memory referenced by the rvalue reference using this
pointer.

```
int&& rvalueReference = 25 + 17;
int* pointerToRvalueReference = &rvalueReference;
*pointerToRvalueReference = 23;
```

By introducing rvalue references, these can of course also appear as parameters in
functions or methods. Table 5-1 shows the possibilities.

Table 5-1. *Different Function and Method Signatures and Their Allowed
Parameter Types*

Function/Method Signature	Allowed Parameter Types
void function(Type param) **void** X::method(Type param)	Both **lvalues and rvalues** can be passed as parameters.
void function(Type& param) **void** X::method(Type& param)	Only **lvalues** can be passed as parameters.
void function(**const** Type& param) **void** X::method(**const** Type& param)	Both **lvalues and rvalues** can be passed as parameters.
void function(Type&& param) **void** X::method(Type&& param)	Only **rvalues** can be passed as parameters.

Table 5-2 shows the situation for return types of a function or method and what is permitted for the function's/method's return statement.

Table 5-2. *Possible Return Types of Functions and Methods*

Function/Method Signature	Possible Data Types Returned by the return Statement
Type function() Type X::method()	[const] int, [const] int&, or [const] int&&.
Type& function() Type& X::method()	Non-const int or int&.
Type&& function() Type&& X::method()	Literals (e.g., return 42), or a rvalue reference (obtained with std::move()) to an object with a lifetime longer than the function's or method's scope.

Although, of course, rvalue references are allowed to be used for parameters in any function or method, their predestined field of application is in move constructors and move assignment operators. See Listing 5-10.

Listing 5-10. A Class That Explicitly Defines Both Copy and Move Semantics

```
#include <utility> // std::move<T>

class Clazz {
public:
  Clazz() noexcept = default;
  Clazz(const Clazz& other) {
    // Classical copy construction for lvalues
  }

  Clazz(Clazz&& other) noexcept {
    // Move constructor for rvalues: moves content from 'other' to this
  }

  Clazz& operator=(const Clazz& other) {
    // Classical copy assignment for lvalues
    return *this;
  }
```

```cpp
  Clazz& operator=(Clazz&& other) noexcept {
    // Move assignment for rvalues: moves content from 'other' to this
    return *this;
  }
  // ...
};

int main() {
  Clazz anObject;
  Clazz anotherObject1(anObject);            // Calls copy constructor
  Clazz anotherObject2(std::move(anObject)); // Calls move constructor
  anObject = anotherObject1;                 // Calls copy assignment
                                             //   operator

  anotherObject2 = std::move(anObject);      // Calls move assignment
                                             //   operator

  return 0;
}
```

Don't Enforce Move Everywhere

Maybe you've noticed the use of the helper function std::move<T>() (defined in the <utility> header) in the code example to force the compiler to use move semantics.

First of all, the name of this small helper function is misleading. std::move<T>() doesn't move anything. It is more or less a cast that produces an rvalue reference to an object of type T.

In most cases, it is not necessary to do that. Under normal circumstances, the selection between the copy and the move versions of constructors or assignment operators is done automatically at compile time through overload resolution. The compiler ascertains whether it is confronted with an lvalue or an rvalue, and then selects the best fitting constructor or assignment operator accordingly. The container classes of the C++ Standard Library also take into account the level of exception safety that is guaranteed by the move operations (we will discuss this topic in more detail later in the section entitled "Prevention Is Better Than Aftercare").

Note this especially—don't write code like the example in Listing 5-11.

Listing 5-11. Improper Use of std::move()

```cpp
#include <string>
#include <utility>
#include <vector>

using StringVector = std::vector<std::string>;

StringVector createVectorOfStrings() {
  StringVector result;
  // ...do something that the vector is filled with many strings...
  return std::move(result); // Bad and unnecessary, just write "return
  result;"!
}
```

Using `std::move<T>()` with the `return` statement is completely unnecessary, because the compiler knows that the variable is a candidate to be moved out of the function (since C++11, move semantics is supported by all Standard Library containers as well as by many other classes of the Standard Library, like `std::string`). A possibly even worse impact could be that it can interfere with the RVO (*return value optimization*), a special form of *copy elision* performed by nearly all compilers nowadays. RVO allows compilers to optimize a costly copy construction when returning values from a function or method (remember the sidebar about copy elision in Chapter 4).

Think always about the important principle from Chapter 3: **Be careful with optimizations!** Don't mess up your code with `std::move<T>()` statements everywhere, just because you think that you can be smarter than your compiler with the optimization of your code. You are not! The readability of your code will suffer with all those `std::move<T>()` everywhere, and your compiler might not be able to perform its optimization strategies properly.

The Rule of Zero

As an experienced C++ developer, you may know the *Rule of Three* and the *Rule of Five*. The Rule of Three [Koenig01], originally coined by Marshall Cline in 1991, states that if a class defines a destructor explicitly, it should almost always define a copy constructor and a copy assignment operator. With the advent of C++11 this rule was extended and became the Rule of Five, because the move constructor and the move assignment operator were added to the language, and these two special member functions must be defined as well if a class defines a destructor.

The reason that the Rule of Three and the Rule of Five were good pieces of advice for a long time in C++ class design is that subtle errors can occur when developers are not considering them, as demonstrated in the intentionally bad code example in Listing 5-12.

Listing 5-12. An Improper Implementation of a String Class

```cpp
#include <cstring>

class MyString {
public:
  explicit MyString(const std::size_t sizeOfString) : data { new
  char[sizeOfString] } { }
  MyString(const char* const charArray ) {
    data = new char[strlen(sizeOfArray) + 1];
    strcpy(data, charArray);
  }
  virtual ~MyString() { delete[] data; };

  char& operator[](const std::size_t index) {
    return data[index];
  }
  const char& operator[](const std::size_t index) const {
    return data[index];
  }
  // ...

private:
  char* data;
};
```

This is indeed a very amateurish implemented string class with some flaws, for example, a missing check that not a nullptr is passed into the initialization constructor, and totally ignoring the fact that strings can grow and shrink. Of course, no one has to implement a string class nowadays, and thus reinvent the wheel. With std::string, a bullet-proofed string class is available in the C++ Standard Library. On the basis of this example, however, it is very easy to demonstrate why adhering to the Rule of Five is important.

In order that the memory allocated by the initialization constructors for the internal string representation is freed safely, an explicit destructor must be defined and has to be implemented to do this. In the previous class, however, the Rule of Five is violated and the explicit copy/move constructors, as well as the copy/move assignment operators, are missing.

Now, let's assume that we're using the MyString class in the following way:

```
int main() {
  MyString aString("Test", 4);
  MyString anotherString { aString }; // Uh oh! :-(
  return 0;
}
```

Due to the fact that the MyString class does not explicitly define a copy or move constructor, the compiler will synthesize these special member functions; that is, the compiler will generate a default copy constructor and a default move constructor. These default implementations only create a shallow copy of the member variables of the source object. In our case, the address value stored in the character pointer data is copied, but not the area in memory where this pointer points.

That means the following: after the automatically generated default copy constructor has been called to create anotherString, both instances of MyString share the same data, as it can easily be seen in a debugger's variables view shown in Figure 5-2.

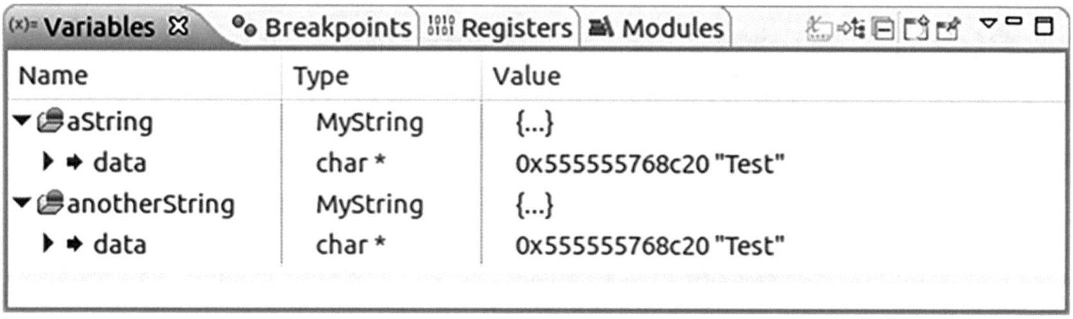

Figure 5-2. Both character pointers are pointing to the same memory address

This will result in double deletion of the internal data if the string objects are destroyed, which can cause critical issues, like segmentation faults or undefined behavior.

Under normal circumstances, there is no reason to define an explicit destructor for a class. Every time you are compelled to define a destructor, this is a noticeable exception, because it indicates that you need to do something special with resources at the end of the lifetime of an object that requires considerable effort. A non-trivial destructor is usually required to deallocate resources, for example, memory on the heap. As a consequence, you also need to define explicit copy/move constructors and copy/move assignment operators in order to handle these resources correctly while copying or moving. That's what the Rule of Five implies.

There are different approaches to dealing with this problem. For instance, we can provide explicit copy/move constructors and copy/move assignment operators to handle the allocated memory correctly, for example, by creating a deep copy of the memory area the pointer is pointing to, or by moving the ownership of the memory from the source object to the target object.

Another approach would be to prohibit copying and moving, and prevent the compiler from generating default versions of these functions. This can be done since C++11 by deleting these special member functions so that any use of a deleted function is ill formed, that is, the program will not compile. See Listing 5-13.

Listing 5-13. A Modified MyString Class That Explicitly Deletes the Copy Constructor and Copy Assignment Operators

```cpp
class MyString {
public:
  explicit MyString(const std::size_t sizeOfString) : data { new
  char[sizeOfString] } { }
  MyString(const char* const charArray ) {
    data = new char[strlen(sizeOfArray) + 1];
    strcpy(data, charArray);
  }
  virtual ~MyString() { delete[] data; };
  MyString(const MyString&) = delete;
  MyString(MyString&&) = delete;
  MyString& operator=(const MyString&) = delete;
```

```
MyString& operator=(MyString&&) = delete;

// ...
};
```

The problem is that by deleting the special member functions, the class now has a very limited area of use. For instance, MyString cannot be used in a std::vector now, because std::vector requires that its element type T implements move semantics and some operations of a vector also require that it is copy-assignable and copy-constructible.

Okay, it's time now to choose a different approach and to think differently. What we have to do is get rid of the destructor that frees the allocated resource. If this succeeds, it is also not necessary, according to the Rule of Five, to provide the other special member functions explicitly. See Listing 5-14.

Listing 5-14. Replacing the char Pointer with a Vector of Char Makes an Explicit Destructor Superfluous

```
#include <vector>

class MyString {
public:
  explicit MyString(const std::size_t sizeOfString) {
    data.resize(sizeOfString, ' ');
  }

  MyString(const char* const charArray, const size_t sizeOfArray) :
  MyString(sizeOfArray) {
    if (charArray != nullptr) {
      for (size_t index = 0; index < sizeOfArray; index++) {
        data[index] = charArray[index];
      }
    }
  }

  char& operator[](const std::size_t index) {
    return data[index];
  }
```

```
  const char& operator[](const std::size_t index) const {
    return data[index];
  }
  // ...

private:
  std::vector<char> data;
};
```

Once again: I know that this is an impractical and amateurish implementation of a self-made string, but it is for demonstration purposes only.

What has changed now? Well, we've replaced the private member of type char* with a std::vector of element type char. Thus, we do not need an explicit destructor anymore, because we have nothing to do if an object of our type MyString is destroyed. There is no need to deallocate any resource. As a result, the compiler-generated special member functions, like the copy/move constructor or the copy/move assignment operator, do the right things automatically if they are used, and we do not have to define them explicitly. And that's good news, because we've followed the KISS principle (see Chapter 3).

That leads us to the Rule of Zero! The Rule of Zero was coined by R. Martinho Fernandes in a blog post in 2012 [Fernandes12]. The rule was also promoted by ISO standard committee member Prof. Peter Sommerlad in a conference talk on *Meeting C++ 2013* [Sommerlad13].

Note   The Rule of Zero states: Write your classes in a way that you do not need to declare/define neither a non-virtual destructor (Exception: Base classes of an inheritance hierarchy should define a public virtual destructor or a protected non-virtual destructor; see rule C.35 of the *C++ Core Guidelines* [Cppcore21]!), not a copy/move constructor or copy/move assignment operator. Use C++ smart pointers and Standard Library classes and containers for managing resources.

In other words, the Rule of Zero states that your classes should be designed in a way that the compiler-generated member functions for copying, moving, and destruction automatically do the right things. This makes your classes easier to understand (think always of the KISS principle from Chapter 3), less error prone, and easier to maintain. The principle behind it is doing more by writing less code.

The Compiler Is Your Colleague

As I have written elsewhere, the advent of the C++11 language standard fundamentally changed the way that modern and clean C++ programs are designed. Styles, patterns, and idioms that programmers are using while writing modern C++ code are totally different than before. Besides the fact that the newer C++ standards offer many useful new features to write C++ code that is well maintainable, understandable, efficient, and testable, something else has still changed: **the role of the compiler!**

In former times, the compiler was just a tool to translate the source code into executable machine instructions (object code) for a computer; but now it is increasingly becoming a tool to support the developer on different levels. The three guiding principles for working with a C++ compiler are the following:

- Everything that can be done at compile time should be done at compile time.

- Everything that can be checked at compile time should be checked at compile time.

- Everything the compiler can know about a program should be determined by the compiler.

In former chapters and sections, you've experienced in some spots how the compiler can support you. For instance, in the section about move semantics, we've seen that modern C++ compilers are able to perform manifold sophisticated optimizations (e.g., copy elision) that we don't have to care about anymore. In the following sections, I show you how the compiler can support developers and make many things much easier.

Automatic Type Deduction

Do you remember the meaning of the C++ keyword auto before C++11? I'm pretty sure that it was probably the least-known and used keyword in the language. Maybe you remember that auto in C++98 or C++03 was a so-called storage class specifier and has been used to define that a local variable has "automatic duration," that is, the variable is created at the point of definition and destroyed when the block it was part of is exited. Since C++11, all variables have automatic duration per default unless otherwise specified. Thus, the previous semantics of auto were becoming useless, and the keyword got a completely new meaning.

Nowadays, auto is used for *automatic type deduction*, sometimes also called *type inference*. If it is used as a type specifier for a variable, it specifies that the type of the variable that is being declared will be automatically deduced (or inferred) from its initializer, like in the following examples:

```
auto theAnswerToAllQuestions = 42;
auto iter = begin(myMap);
const auto gravitationalAccelerationOnEarth = 9.80665;
constexpr auto sum = 10 + 20 + 12;
auto strings = { "The", "big", "brown", "fox", "jumps", "over", "the",
"lazy", "dog" };
auto numberOfStrings = strings.size();
```

ARGUMENT DEPENDENT NAME LOOKUP (ADL)

Argument Dependent (Name) Lookup (ADL), also known as *Koenig Lookup* (named after the American computer scientist Andrew Koenig), is a compiler technique to look up an unqualified function name (that is, a function name without a prefixed namespace qualifier) depending on the types of the arguments passed to the function at its call site.

Suppose you have a std::map<K, T> (defined in the <map> header) like the following one:

```
#include <map>
#include <string>
std::map<unsigned int, std::string> words;
```

Due to ADL, it is not necessary to specify the namespace std if you use the begin() or end() function to retrieve an iterator from the container. You can simply write:

```
auto wordIterator = begin(words);
```

The compiler does not just look at the local scope, but also the namespaces that contain the argument's type (in this case, the namespace of map<K, T>, which is std). Thus, in the previous example, the compiler finds a fitting begin() function for maps in the std-namespace.

In some cases, you need to explicitly define the namespace, for example, if you want to use std::begin() and std::end() with a simple C-style array.

On first sight, using auto instead of a concrete type seems to be a convenience feature. Developers are no longer forced to remember a type's name. They simply write auto, const auto, auto& (for references), or const auto& (for const references), and the compiler does the rest, because it knows the type of the assigned value. Automatic type deduction can of course also be used in conjunction with constexpr (see the section about computations at compile time).

Do not be afraid to use auto (or auto& and const auto&) as much as possible. The code is still statically typed, and the types of the variables are clearly defined. For instance, the type of the variable strings from the previous example is std::initializer_list<const char*>, the type of numberOfStrings is std::initializer_list<const char*>::size_type.

The only thing that developers should be aware of is that auto will strip const and reference qualifiers, and hence a careless use of it can result in unwanted copies being made. Especially in range-based for loops, this can easily be overlooked:

```cpp
#include <string>
#include <vector>

// And somewhere in the code...
std::vector<std::string> aLotOfStrings { .......... };

for (auto str : aLotOfStrings) {
  // Attention: A copy of each string will be made!
}
for (const auto& str : aLotOfStrings) {
  // Copies are avoided.
}
```

STD::INITIALIZER_LIST<T> [C++11]

In former days (prior C++11), if we wanted to initialize a Standard Library container using literals, we had to do the following:

```cpp
std::vector<int> integerSequence;
integerSequence.push_back(14);
integerSequence.push_back(33);
integerSequence.push_back(69);
// ...and so on...
```

Since C++11, we can simply do it this way:

```
std::vector<int> integerSequence { 14, 33, 69, 104, 222, 534 };
```

The reason for this is that `std::vector<T>` has an overloaded constructor that accepts a so-called initializer list as a parameter. An initializer list is an object of type `std::initializer_list<T>` (defined in the `<initializer_list>` header).

An instance of type `std::initializer_list<T>` is automatically constructed when you use a list of comma-separated literals that are surrounded with a pair of curly braces, a so-called *braced-init-list*. You can equip your own classes with constructors that can accept initializer lists, as shown in this example:

```cpp
#include <string>
#include <vector>

using WordList = std::vector<std::string>;

class LexicalRepository {
public:
  explicit LexicalRepository(const std::initializer_list<const char*>& words) {
    wordList.insert(begin(wordList), begin(words), end(words));
  }
  // ...

private:
  WordList wordList;
};

int main() {

LexicalRepository repo { "The", "big", "brown", "fox", "jumps", "over",
"the", "lazy", "dog" };
  // ...
  return 0;
}
```

Note   This initializer list should not be confused with a class of its constructor member initializer list!

Since C++14, the automatic return type deduction for functions is also supported. This is especially helpful when a return type has a difficult-to-remember or unutterable name, which is often the case when dealing with complex non-standard data types as return types.

```cpp
auto function() {
  std::vector<std::map<std::pair<int, double>, int>> returnValue;
  // ...fill 'returnValue' with data...
  return returnValue;
}
```

We haven't discussed lambda expressions until now (they will be discussed in detail in Chapter 7), but C++11 and higher lets you store lambda expressions in named variables:

```cpp
auto square = [](const int x) { return x * x; };
```

Maybe you're wondering why, in Chapter 4, I told you that an expressive and good name is important for the readability of the code and should be a major goal for every professional programmer. Now I promote the use of the keyword auto, which makes it more difficult to recognize the type of a variable quickly just by reading the code. Isn't that a contradiction?

My clear answer is this: no, quite the contrary! Apart from a few exceptions, auto can raise the readability of the code. Look at the two alternatives of a variable assignment in Listing 5-15.

Listing 5-15. Which One of the Following Two Versions Would You Prefer?

```cpp
// 1st version: without auto
std::shared_ptr<controller::CreateMonthlyInvoicesController>
createMonthlyInvoicesController =
  std::make_shared<controller::CreateMonthlyInvoicesController>();

// 2nd version: with auto:
auto createMonthlyInvoicesController =
  std::make_shared<controller::CreateMonthlyInvoicesController>();
```

From my point of view, the version using auto is easier to read. There is no need to repeat the type explicitly, because it is pretty clear from its initializer what type createMonthlyInvoicesController will be. By the way, repeating the explicit type would also be a kind of violation of the DRY principle (see Chapter 3). And if you think of the lambda expression named square, whose type is a unique, unnamed non-union class type, how can such a type be explicitly defined?

Tip   If it doesn't obscure the intent of your code, use auto wherever possible!

Computations During Compile Time

Fans of high-performance computing (HPC)—as well as developers of embedded software and programmers who prefer to use static, constant tables to separate data and code—want to compute as much as possible at compile time. The reasons for this are very easy to comprehend: everything that can be computed or evaluated at compile time does not have to be computed or evaluated at runtime. In other words, the computation of as much as possible at compile time is low-hanging fruit to raise the runtime efficiency of your program. This advantage is sometimes accompanied by a drawback, which is the more or less increasing time that it takes to compile the code.

Since C++11, the constexpr (constant expression) specifier makes it possible to evaluate the value of a function or a variable at compile time. With the subsequent standard C++14, some of the stringent restrictions for constexpr were lifted. For instance, a constexpr-specified function was allowed to have exactly one return statement only. This restriction has been abolished since C++14.

One of the simplest examples is that a variable's value is calculated from literals by arithmetic operations at compile time, like this:

```cpp
constexpr int theAnswerToAllQuestions = 10 + 20 + 12;
```

The theAnswerToAllQuestions variable is also a constant if it was declared with const; thus, you cannot manipulate it during runtime:

```cpp
int main() {
  // ...
  theAnswerToAllQuestions = 23;   // Compiler error: assignment of read-only
                                  //                 variable!

  return 0;
}
```

There are also `constexpr` functions:

```cpp
constexpr int multiply(const int multiplier, const int multiplicand) {
  return multiplier * multiplicand;
}
```

Such functions can be called at compile time, but they can also be used like ordinary functions with non-`const` arguments at runtime. This is necessary to test those functions with the help of unit tests (see Chapter 2).

```cpp
constexpr int theAnswerToAllQuestions = multiply(7, 6);
```

Unsurprisingly, `constexpr` specified functions can also be called recursively, as shown in the example in Listing 5-16, which shows a function that calculates factorials.

Listing 5-16. Calculating the Factorial of a Non-Negative Integer 'n' at Compile Time

```cpp
01  #include <iostream>
02
03  constexpr unsigned long long factorial(const unsigned short n) {
04    return n > 1 ? n * factorial(n - 1) : 1;
05  }
06
07  int main() {
08    unsigned short number = 6;
09    auto result1 = factorial(number);
10    constexpr auto result2 = factorial(10);
11
12    std::cout << "result1: " << result1 << ", result2: " << result2 <<
      std::endl;
13    return 0;
14  }
```

The previous example works under C++11. The `factorial()` function consists of only one statement, and recursion was allowed from the beginning in `constexpr` functions. The `main()` function contains two calls of the `factorial()` function. It is worth it to take a closer look at these two function calls.

The first call on line 9 uses the variable number as the argument for the function's parameter n, and its result is assigned to a non-const variable result1. The second function call on line 10 uses a number literal as the argument, and its result is assigned to a variable with a constexpr specifier. The difference between these two function calls at runtime can best be seen in the disassembled object code. Figure 5-3 shows the object code at the key spot in the Disassembly window of Eclipse CDT.

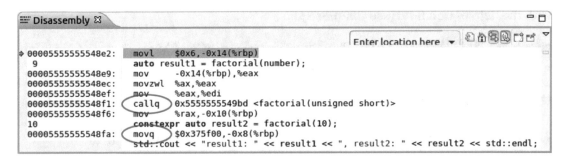

Figure 5-3. *The disassembled object code*

The first function call on line 9 results in five machine instructions. The fourth of these instructions (callq) is the jump to the function factorial() at memory address 0x5555555549bd. In other words, it is obvious that the function is called at runtime. In contrast, we see that the second call of factorial() at line 10 results in just one simple machine instruction. The movq instruction copies a quadword from the source operand to the destination operand. There is no costly function call at runtime. The result of factorial(10), which is 0x375f00 in hexadecimal and 3,628,800 in decimal, has been calculated at compile time and is available like a constant in the object code.

As I mentioned earlier, some restrictions for contexpr specified functions in C++11 have been repealed since C++14. For instance, a constexpr specified function can now have more than one return statement; it can have conditionals like if-else-branches, local variables of "literal" type, or loops. Basically, almost all C++ statements are allowed if they do not presuppose or require something that is only available in the context of a runtime environment, for example, allocating memory on the heap, or throwing exceptions.

Variable Templates

I think it is less surprising that constexpr can also be used in templates, as shown in the example in Listing 5-17.

Listing 5-17. A Variable Template for the Mathematical Constant pi

```
#include <concepts>

template<typename T>
concept FloatingPoint = std::floating_point<T>;

template <typename T> requires FloatingPoint<T>
constexpr T pi = T(3.141592653589793238462643L);
```

For the moment, we ignore the first lines of code in Listing 5-17 and focus on the last two lines only. What we can see there is known as a *variable template*. It is a good and flexible alternative to the archaic style of constant definitions using #define macros (see the section entitled "Avoid Macros" in Chapter 4). Depending on its usage context during template instantiation, the mathematical constant pi is typed as float, double, or long double. See Listing 5-18.

Listing 5-18. Calculating a Circle's Circumference at Compile Time Using the Variable Template pi

```
template <typename T>
constexpr T computeCircumference(const T radius) requires FloatingPoint<T>
{
  return 2 * radius * pi<T>;
}

int main() {
  constexpr long double radius { 10.0L };
  constexpr long double circumference = computeCircumference(radius);
  std::cout << circumference << std::endl;
  return 0;
}
```

Okay, but what do the other lines of code before the variable template pi in Listing 5-17 mean? Well, I've used a new and long-awaited feature of the C++20 language standard called *concepts*. Concepts are an extension to the C++ template mechanism that define requirements or constraints for template parameters. In this case I've defined a concept to enforce users of the variable template pi as well as the function template computeCircumference to instantiate both with a floating-point data type, otherwise the compiler will report an error. I will give a bit more detailed insight into C++20 concepts later in this chapter.

Last but not least, it is noteworthy that you can also use classes in computations at compile time. You can define constexpr constructors and member functions for classes. See Listing 5-19.

Listing 5-19. Rectangle Is a constexpr Class

```cpp
#include <cmath>
#include <iostream>

class Rectangle {
public:
  constexpr Rectangle() = delete;
  constexpr Rectangle(const double width, const double height) :
    width { width }, height { height } { }
  constexpr double getWidth() const { return width; }
  constexpr double getHeight() const { return height; }
  constexpr double getArea() const { return width * height; }
  constexpr double getLengthOfDiagonal() const {
    return std::sqrt(std::pow(width, 2.0) + std::pow(height, 2.0));
  }

private:
  double width;
  double height;
};

int main() {
  constexpr Rectangle americanFootballPlayingField { 48.76, 110.0 };
  constexpr double area = americanFootballPlayingField.getArea();
  constexpr double diagonal = americanFootballPlayingField.getLengthOfDiagonal();
```

```
std::cout << "The area of an American Football playing field is " <<
    area << "m^2 and the length of its diagonal is " << diagonal <<
    "m." << std::endl;
  return 0;
}
```

constexpr classes can be used at compile time and at runtime. In contrast to ordinary classes, however, you cannot define virtual member functions (there is no polymorphism at compile time), and a constexpr class must not have an explicitly defined destructor.

Note   The code example in Listing 5-19 could fail to compile on some C++ compilers. By today's standards, the C++ standard does not specify common mathematical functions from the numerics library (the <cmath> header) as constexpr, like std::sqrt() and std::pow(). Compiler implementations are free to do it anyway, but it's not required.

However, how should these computations at compile time have been judged from a clean code perspective? Is it basically a good idea to add constexpr to anything that can possibly have it?

Well, my opinion is that constexpr does not reduce the readability of the code. The specifier is always in front of variables and constants definitions or in front of function or method declarations. Hence, it does not disturb so much. On the other hand, if I definitely know that something will never be evaluated at compile time, I should also renounce the specifier.

Don't Allow Undefined Behavior

In C++ (and in some other programming languages too), the language specification does not define the behavior in any possible situation. In some places the specification says that the behavior of a certain operation is undefined under certain circumstances. In such a situation, you cannot predict what will happen, because the behavior of the program depends on compiler implementation, the underlying operating system, or special optimization switches. That's really bad! The program could either crash or silently generate incorrect results.

Here is an example of undefined behavior, an incorrect use of a smart pointer:

```
const std::size_t NUMBER_OF_STRINGS { 100 };
std::shared_ptr<std::string> arrayOfStrings(new std::string[NUMBER_OF_
STRINGS]);
```

Let's assume that this std::shared_ptr<T> object is the last one pointing to the string array resource and it runs out of scope somewhere. What will happen?

The destructor of std::shared_ptr<T> decrements the number of shared owners and the counter reaches 0. As a consequence, the resource managed by the smart pointer (the array of std::string) is destroyed by calling its destructor. But it will do it wrong, because when you allocate the managed resource using new[], you need to call the array form delete[], and not delete, to free the resource, and the default deleter of std::shared_ptr<T> uses delete.

Deleting an array with delete instead of delete[] results in undefined behavior. It is not specified what happens. Maybe it results in a memory leak, but that's just a guess.

Caution   Avoid undefined behavior! It is a bad mistake and ends up with programs that silently misbehave.

There are several solutions to let the smart pointer delete the string array correctly. For example, you can provide a custom deleter as a function-like object (also known as a functor; see Chapter 7):

```
template <typename T>
struct CustomArrayDeleter {
  void operator() (T const* pointer) {
    delete [] pointer;
  }
};
```

Now you can use your own deleter as follows:

```
const std::size_t NUMBER_OF_STRINGS { 100 };
std::shared_ptr<std::string> arrayOfStrings(new std::string[NUMBER_OF_
STRINGS], CustomArrayDeleter<std::string>());
```

In C++11, there is a default deleter for array types defined in the <memory> header:

```
const std::size_t NUMBER_OF_STRINGS { 100 };
std::shared_ptr<std::string> arrayOfStrings(new std::string[NUMBER_OF_
STRINGS], std::default_delete<std::string[]>());
```

Depending on the requirements to satisfy, you should consider whether using a std::vector or std::array is not the best solution to implement an "array of things." And since C++20, you can avoid the explicit new for heap allocation and do it clean and simple like this:

```
auto arrayOfStrings{ std::make_shared<std::string[]>(NUMBER_OF_STRINGS) };
```

Type-Rich Programming

"Don't trust names.

Trust types.

Types don't lie.

Types are your friends!"

—Mario Fusco (@mariofusco), April 13, 2016, on Twitter

On September 23, 1999, NASA lost its *Mars Climate Orbiter I*, a robotic space probe, after a 10-month journey to the fourth planet of our solar system (Figure 5-4). As the spacecraft went into orbital insertion, the transfer of important data failed between the propulsion team at Lockheed Martin Astronautics in Colorado and the NASA mission navigation team in Pasadena (California). This error pushed the spacecraft too close to the atmosphere of Mars, where it burned immediately.

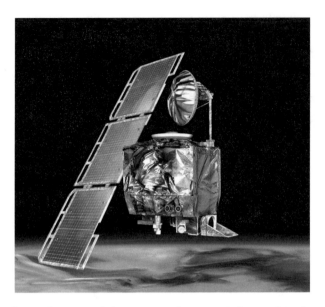

Figure 5-4. *Artist's rendering of the Mars Climate Orbiter (Author: NASA/JPL/ Corby Waste[2])*

The cause for the failed data transfer was that the NASA mission navigation team used the International System of Units (SI), while Lockheed Martin's navigation software used English units (the Imperial Measurement System). The software used by the mission navigation team sent values in pound-force-seconds (lbf·s), but the Orbiter's navigation software expected values in newton-seconds (N·s). NASA's total financial loss was 328 million in U.S. dollars. The lifetime work of around 200 good spacecraft engineers was destroyed in a few seconds.

This failure is not a typical example of a simple software bug. Both systems by themselves may have worked correctly. But it reveals an interesting aspect in software development. It seems that communication and coordination problems between the engineering teams to be the elementary reason for this failure. It is obvious: there were no joint system tests with both subsystems, and the interfaces between both subsystems had not been properly designed.

---

[2]https://solarsystem.nasa.gov/resources/2246/mars-climate-orbiter-artists-concept/; https://www.nasa.gov/multimedia/guidelines/index.html

"People sometimes make errors. The problem here was not the error, it was the failure of NASA's systems engineering, and the checks and balances in our processes to detect the error. That's why we lost the spacecraft."

—Dr. Edward Weiler, NASA Associate Administrator for
Space Science [JPL99]

In fact, I don't know anything about Mars Climate Orbiter's system software. But according to the examination report of the failure, I've understood that one piece of software produced results in an "English system" unit, while the other piece of software that used those results expected them to be in metric units.

I think everybody knows C++ member function declarations that look like the one in the following class:

```
class SpacecraftTrajectoryControl {
public:
  void applyMomentumToSpacecraftBody(const double impulseValue);
};
```

What does the double stand for? Of what unit is the value that is expected by the member function named applyMomentumToSpacecraftBody? Is it a value measured in Newtons (N), newton-seconds (N·s), pound-force-seconds (lbf·s), or any other unit? In fact, we don't know. The double can be anything. It is, of course, a type, but it is not a semantic type. Maybe it has been documented somewhere, or we could give the parameter a more meaningful and verbose name like impulseValueInNewtonSeconds, which would be better than nothing. But even the best documentation or parameter name cannot guarantee that a client of this class passes a value of an incorrect unit to this member function.

Can we do it better? Of course we can.

What we really want to have to define an interface properly, with rich semantics, is something like this:

```
class SpacecraftTrajectoryControl {
public:
  void applyMomentumToSpacecraftBody(const Momentum& impulseValue);
};
```

In mechanics, momentum is measured in newton-seconds (Ns). One newton-second (1 Ns) is the force of one Newton (which is 1 kg m/s² in SI base units) acting on a body (a physical object) for one second.

173

To use a type like Momentum instead of the unspecific floating-point type double, we have to introduce that type first. In the first step we define a template that can be used to represent physical quantities on the base of the MKS system of units. The abbreviation MKS stands for meter (length), kilogram (mass), and seconds (time). These three fundamental units can be used to express many physical measurements. See Listing 5-20.

Listing 5-20. A Class Template to Represent MKS Units

```
#include <type_traits>

template <int M, int K, int S>
struct MksUnit {
  enum { metre = M, kilogram = K, second = S};
};
```

You might wonder about why the Type Traits library (the <type_traits> header) is included on the first line? Well, type traits can be used to inspect the properties of types.

TYPE TRAITS [C++11]

Type traits can be regarded as one of the pillars of C++ template metaprogramming. When developers define a C++ template, the concrete types used to instantiate this template can theoretically be almost anything. For instance, when they define a class template like this:

```
template <typename T>
class MyClassTemplate {
  // ...
};
```

the template argument T can be substituted during instantiation with an int, a double, a std::string, or any other arbitrary data type that is defined by itself.

Using type traits, developers can let the compiler inspect which concrete data type is intended for the generic T during instantiation and can use the result of this check for conditional compiling. From a technical point of view, a type trait is a simple template struct, like this one:

```
template <typename T>
struct is_integral : bool_constant<> {
  // ...
};
```

This type trait checks whether T is an integral type (bool, char, int, unsigned int, ...). After its instantiation with a concrete data type for the template parameter T, the type trait holds a Boolean member constant, usually named value, containing the result of the check. This value can then be directly accessed (std::is_integral<T> ::value), but the more compact variant std::is_integral_v<T> is more common:

```cpp
#include <type_traits>

template <typename T>
class MyClassTemplate {
  static_assert(std::is_integral_v<T> , "T must be an integral type!");
};

int main() {
  MyClassTemplate<char8_t> foo; // OK!
  MyClassTemplate<float> bar;   // error: static assertion failed: T must be
                                //        an integral type!

  return 0;
}
```

Another category of type traits are those that alter the passed concrete type for template parameter T. For instance, the type trait std::remove_reference<T> transforms a reference type T& into T. The result of this transformation can be accessed through a member type alias usually named type.

In our case we need the Type Traits library to define a constraint with the help of C++ concepts. See Listing 5-21.

Listing 5-21. A C++ Concept to Check Whether a Type Is an Instantiation of the MksUnit Template

```cpp
template <typename T>
struct IsMksUnitType : std::false_type { };

template <int M, int K, int S>
struct IsMksUnitType<MksUnit<M, K, S>> : std::true_type { };

template <typename T>
concept MksUnitType = IsMksUnitType<T>::value;
```

STD::TRUE_TYPE AND STD::FALSE_TYPE (SINCE C++11)

Since C++11, there is a class template std::integral_constant (defined in the
<type_traits> header) available that takes an integral type and an integral value as
template parameters. Two type aliases, std::true_type and std::false_type, are also
defined in the <type_traits> header for the common case where the template parameter T
of std::integral_constant is of type bool. In simplified terms, they are defined like this:

```
using true_type  = integral_constant<bool, true>;
using false_type = integral_constant <bool, false>;
```

These two aliases are used to represent the Boolean values true and false as types and
serve as the base classes for many type traits. They can be used for so-called *tag dispatching*,
which is a technique to select an implementation of a function from a set of overloaded
functions that suits a given type. Here is a small example:

```
#include <type_traits>

template <typename T>
auto calculateImpl(T value, std::true_type) {
  // Implementation for arithmetic value types
}

template <typename T>
auto calculateImpl(T value, std::false_type) {
  // Implementation for non-arithmetic value types
}

template <typename T>
auto calculate(T value) {
  return calculateImpl(value, std::is_arithmetic<T>{});
}
```

Depending on whether the data type used to call the calculate() function is an
arithmetic type (that is, an integral type or a floating-point type) or not, the appropriate
calculateImpl() function template is selected at compile time.

With this concept (I discuss C++20 concepts in more detail later), we want to ensure under all circumstances that the template class Value presented in Listing 5-22 is always instantiated with a proper instantiated template class, MksUnit.

Listing 5-22. A Class Template to Represent Values of MKS Units

```
template <typename T> requires MksUnitType<T>
class Value {
public:
  explicit Value(const long double magnitude) noexcept :
  magnitude(magnitude) {}
  long double getMagnitude() const noexcept {
    return magnitude;
  }

private:
  long double magnitude{ 0.0 };
};
```

Next, we can use both class templates to define type aliases for concrete physical quantities. Here are some examples:

```
using DimensionlessQuantity = Value<MksUnit<0, 0, 0>>;
using Length = Value<MksUnit<1, 0, 0>>;
using Area = Value<MksUnit<2, 0, 0>>;
using Volume = Value<MksUnit<3, 0, 0>>;
using Mass = Value<MksUnit<0, 1, 0>>;
using Time = Value<MksUnit<0, 0, 1>>;
using Speed = Value<MksUnit<1, 0, -1>>;
using Acceleration = Value<MksUnit<1, 0, -2>>;
using Frequency = Value<MksUnit<0, 0, -1>>;
using Force = Value<MksUnit<1, 1, -2>>;
using Pressure = Value<MksUnit<-1, 1, -2>>;
// ... etc. ...
```

It is also possible to define the Momentum, which is required as the parameter type for our applyMomentumToSpacecraftBody member function:

```
using Momentum = Value<MksUnit<1, 1, -1>>;
```

After we've introduced the type alias Momentum, the following code will not compile, because there is no suitable constructor to convert from double to Value<MksUnit<1,1,-1>>:

```
SpacecraftTrajectoryControl control;
const double someValue = 13.75;
control.applyMomentumToSpacecraftBody(someValue); // Compile-time error!
```

The next example will also lead to compile-time errors, because a variable of type Force must not be used like a Momentum, and an implicit conversion between these different dimensions must be prevented:

```
SpacecraftTrajectoryControl control;
Force force { 13.75 };
control.applyMomentumToSpacecraftBody(force); // Compile-time error!
```

But this will work fine:

```
SpacecraftTrajectoryControl control;
Momentum momentum { 13.75 };
control.applyMomentumToSpacecraftBody(momentum);
```

The units can also be used to define constants. For this purpose, we need to slightly modify the class template Value. We add the keyword constexpr (see the section entitled "Computations During Compile Time" earlier in this chapter) to the initialization constructor and the getMagnitude() member function. This allows us to create compile-time constants of Value that don't have to be initialized during runtime. As you will see later, we can also perform computations with our physical values during compile time now.

```
template <typename T> requires MksUnitType<T>
class Value {
public:
  constexpr explicit Value(const long double magnitude) noexcept :
  magnitude { magnitude } {}
```

```
constexpr long double getMagnitude() const noexcept {
  return magnitude;
}

private:
  long double magnitude { 0.0 };
};
```

Thereafter, constants of different physical units can be defined, as in the following example:

```
constexpr Acceleration gravitationalAccelerationOnEarth { 9.80665 };
constexpr Pressure standardPressureOnSeaLevel { 1013.25 };
constexpr Speed speedOfLight { 299792458.0 };
constexpr Frequency concertPitchA { 440.0 };
constexpr Mass neutronMass { 1.6749286e-27 };
```

Furthermore, computations between units are possible if the necessary operators are implemented. For instance, these are the addition, subtraction, multiplication, and division operator templates that perform different calculations with two values of different MKS units:

```
template <int M, int K, int S>
constexpr Value<MksUnit<M, K, S>> operator+
  (const Value<MksUnit<M, K, S>>& lhs, const Value<MksUnit<M, K, S>>& rhs)
  noexcept {
  return Value<MksUnit<M, K, S>>(lhs.getMagnitude() + rhs.getMagnitude());
}

template <int M, int K, int S>
constexpr Value<MksUnit<M, K, S>> operator-
  (const Value<MksUnit<M, K, S>>& lhs, const Value<MksUnit<M, K, S>>& rhs)
  noexcept {
  return Value<MksUnit<M, K, S>>(lhs.getMagnitude() - rhs.getMagnitude());
}

template <int M1, int K1, int S1, int M2, int K2, int S2>
constexpr Value<MksUnit<M1 + M2, K1 + K2, S1 + S2>> operator*
```

```
(const Value<MksUnit<M1, K1, S1>>& lhs, const Value<MksUnit<M2, K2, S2>>&
rhs) noexcept {
return Value<MksUnit<M1 + M2, K1 + K2, S1 + S2>>(lhs.getMagnitude() *
rhs.getMagnitude());
}

template <int M1, int K1, int S1, int M2, int K2, int S2>
constexpr Value<MksUnit<M1 - M2, K1 - K2, S1 - S2>> operator/
(const Value<MksUnit<M1, K1, S1>>& lhs, const Value<MksUnit<M2, K2, S2>>&
rhs) noexcept {
return Value<MksUnit<M1 - M2, K1 - K2, S1 - S2>>(lhs.getMagnitude() /
rhs.getMagnitude());
}
```

Now you could write something like this:

```
constexpr Momentum impulseValueForCourseCorrection = Force { 30.0 } * Time
{ 3.0 };
SpacecraftTrajectoryControl control;
control.applyMomentumToSpacecraftBody(impulseValueForCourseCorrection);
```

That's obviously a significant improvement over a multiplication of two meaningless doubles and assigning the result to another meaningless double. It's pretty expressive. And it's safer, because you cannot assign the result of the multiplication to something different than a variable of type Momentum.

And the best part is this: **the type safety is ensured during compile time!** There is no overhead during runtime, because a C++11 (and higher)-compliant compiler can perform all the necessary type compatibility checks.

Let's go one step further. Would it not be very convenient and intuitive if we could write something like the following?

```
constexpr Acceleration gravitationalAccelerationOnEarth { 9.80665_ms2 };
```

Even that is possible with modern C++. Since C++11, we can provide custom suffixes for literals by defining special functions—so-called *literal operators*—for them:

```
constexpr Force operator"" _N(long double magnitude) {
  return Force(magnitude);
}
```

```cpp
constexpr Acceleration operator"" _ms2(long double magnitude) {
  return Acceleration(magnitude);
}

constexpr Time operator"" _s(long double magnitude) {
  return Time(magnitude);
}

constexpr Momentum operator"" _Ns(long double magnitude) {
  return Momentum(magnitude);
}

// ...more literal operators here...
```

USER-DEFINED LITERALS [C++11]

Basically, a literal is a compile-time constant whose value is specified in the source file. Since C++11, developers can produce objects of user-defined types by defining user-defined suffixes for literals. For instance, if a constant should be initialized with a literal of U.S. $145.67, this can be done by writing the following expression:

```cpp
constexpr Money amount = 145.67_USD;
```

In this case, _USD is the user-defined suffix (**Important:** They must always begin with an underscore!) for floating-point literals that represent money amounts. So that a user-defined literal can be used, a function that is known as a *literal operator* must be defined:

```cpp
constexpr Money operator"" _USD (const long double amount) {
  return Money(amount);
}
```

Once we've defined user-defined literals for our physical units, we can work with them in the following manner:

```cpp
Force force = 30.0_N;
Time time = 3.0_s;
Momentum momentum = force * time;
```

This notation is familiar to physicists and other scientists and it's even safer. With type-rich programming and user-defined literals, you are protected against assigning a literal expressing a value of seconds to a variable of type Force.

```
Force force1 = 3.0;      // Compile-time error!
Force force2 = 3.0_s;    // Compile-time error!
Force force3 = 3.0_N;    // Works!
```

It is, of course, also possible to use user-defined literals together with automatic type deduction and/or constant expressions:

```
auto force = 3.0_N;
constexpr auto acceleration = 100.0_ms2;
```

That's pretty convenient and quite elegant, isn't it? So, what follows is my advice for public interface design.

Tip   Create interfaces (APIs) that are strongly typed.

With other words, you should largely avoid general, low-level built-in types, like int, double, or—at worst—void*, in public interfaces and APIs. Such non-semantic types are dangerous under certain circumstances, because they can represent just about anything.

Tip   There are some template-based libraries available that provide types for physical quantities, including all SI units. A well-known example is Boost.Units (part of Boost since version 1.36.0; see http://www.boost.org). And with the UNITS project, a header-only library developed by Nic Holthaus is available on GitHub (https://github.com/nholthaus/units) that provides a set of data types, containers, and traits for physical quantities.

Know Your Libraries

Have you ever heard of the "Not invented here" (NIH) syndrome? It is an organizational anti-pattern. The NIH syndrome is a derogatory term for a stance in many development organizations that describes the ignoring of existing knowledge or tried-and-tested solutions based on their place of origin. It is a form of "reinventing the wheel," that is, reimplementing something (a library or a framework) that is available somewhere else. The reasoning behind this attitude is often the belief that in-house developments must be better in several respects. They are often mistakenly regarded as cheaper, more secure, more flexible, and more controllable than existing and well-established solutions.

In fact, only a few companies succeed in developing a truly equivalent, or even better alternative, to a solution that exists on the market. Often, the enormous effort of such developments does not justify the low benefit. And not infrequently is the self-developed library or framework clearly worse in quality compared to existing and mature solutions that have existed for years.

Over the past decades, many excellent libraries and frameworks have emerged in the C++ environment. These solutions had the chance to mature over a long time, and have been used successfully in tens of thousands of projects. There is no need to reinvent the wheel. Good software craftspeople should know about these libraries. It is not required to know every tiny detail about these libraries and their APIs. It is just good to know, however, that there are tried-and-tested solutions for certain fields of application, which are worth looking at to take into a narrower selection for your software development project.

Take Advantage of <algorithm>

"If you want to improve the code quality in your organization, replace all your coding guidelines with one goal: No raw loops!"

—Sean Parent, principal software architect with Adobe, at CppCon 2013

Fiddling with collections of elements is everyday business in programming. Regardless of whether we are dealing with collections of measurement data, with emails, strings, records from a database, or other elements, software must filter them, sort them, delete them, manipulate them, and more.

In many programs, we can find "raw loops" (e.g., hand-crafted for loops or while loops) for visiting some or all elements in a container, or sequence, in order to do something with them. A simple example is to reverse an order of integers stored in a std::vector this way:

```
#include <vector>

std::vector<int> integers { 2, 5, 8, 22, 45, 67, 99 };
```

```
// ...somewhere in the program:
std::size_t leftIndex = 0;
std::size_t rightIndex = integers.size() - 1;

while (leftIndex < rightIndex) {
  int buffer = integers[rightIndex];
  integers[rightIndex] = integers[leftIndex];
  integers[leftIndex] = buffer;
  ++leftIndex;
  --rightIndex;
}
```

Basically this code will work. But it has several disadvantages. It is difficult to see immediately what this piece of code is doing (in fact, the first three lines inside the while loop could be substituted with std::swap from the <utility> header). Furthermore, writing code this way is very tedious and error prone. Just imagine that, for any reason, we violate the boundaries of the vector and try to access an element at a position out of range. Unlike member function std::vector::at(), std::vector::operator[] does not raise a std::out_of_range exception then. It will lead to undefined behavior.

The C++ Standard Library provides more than 100 useful algorithms that can be applied to containers or sequences for searching, counting, and manipulating elements. They are collected in the <algorithm> header.

For example, to reverse the order of elements in any kind of Standard Library container, for example, in a std::vector, we can simply use std::reverse:

```
#include <algorithm>
#include <vector>

std::vector<int> integers = { 2, 5, 8, 22, 45, 67, 99 };
// ...somewhere in the program:
std::reverse(begin(integers), end(integers));
// The content of 'integers' is now: 99, 67, 45, 22, 8, 5, 2
```

Unlike our self-written solution before, this code is much more compact, less error prone, and easier to read. Since std::reverse is a function template (like all other algorithms too), it is universally applicable to all Standard Library sequence containers, associative containers, unordered associative containers, `std::string`, and primitive arrays (which, by the way, should not be used anymore in a modern C++ program; see the section "Prefer Standard Library Containers over Simple C-Style Arrays" in Chapter 4). See Listing 5-23.

Listing 5-23. Applying std::reverse to a C-Style Array and a String

```
#include <algorithm>
#include <string>

// Works, but primitive arrays should not be used in a modern C++ program
int integers[] = { 2, 5, 8, 22, 45, 67, 99 };
std::reverse(begin(integers), end(integers));

std::string text { "The big brown fox jumps over the lazy dog!" };
std::reverse(begin(text), end(text));
// Content of 'text' is now: "!god yzal eht revo spmuj xof nworb gib ehT"
```

The reverse algorithm can be applied, of course, also to sub-ranges of a container or sequence, as shown in Listing 5-24.

Listing 5-24. Only a Sub-Area of the String Is Reversed

```
std::string text { "The big brown fox jumps over the lazy dog!" };
std::reverse(begin(text) + 13, end(text) - 9);
// Content of 'text' is now: "The big brown eht revo spmuj xof lazy dog!"
```

Easier Parallelization of Algorithms Since C++17

> *"Your free lunch will soon be over."*
>
> —Herb Sutter [Sutter04]

The previous quote, which was addressed to software developers all over the world, is taken from an article published by Herb Sutter, member of the ISO C++ standardization committee, in 2004. It was at a time when the clock rates of processors stopped increasing from year to year. In other words, serial-processing speed has reached a physical limit. Instead, processors were increasingly equipped with more cores. This development in processor architectures leads to a heavy consequence: developers can no longer take advantage of ever-increasing processor performance by clock rates—the "free lunch" that Herb was talking about—but they will be forced to develop massively multithreaded programs as a way to better utilize modern multi-core processors. As a result, developers and software architects now need to consider parallelization in their software architecture and design.

Before the advent of C++11, the C++ standard supported only single-threaded programming, and you have to use third-party libraries (e.g., Boost.Thread) or compiler extensions (e.g., Open Multi-Processing—OpenMP) to parallelize your programs. Since C++11, the *Thread Support Library* is available to support multithreaded and parallel programming. This extension of the Standard Library has introduced threads, mutual exclusions, condition variables, and futures.

Parallelizing a section of code requires good problem knowledge and must be considered in the software design accordingly. Otherwise, subtle errors caused by race conditions can occur that could be very difficult to debug. Especially for the algorithms of the Standard Library, which often have to operate on containers that are filled with a huge number of objects, the parallelization should be simplified for developers in order to exploit today's modern multi-core processors.

Starting with C++17, parts of the Standard Library have been redesigned according to the *Technical Specification for C++ Extensions for Parallelism* (ISO/IEC TS 19570:2015), also known as the *Parallelism TS* (TS stands for technical specification). In other words, with C++17 these extensions became part of the mainline ISO C++ standard. Their main goal is to relieve developers a bit from the complex task of fiddling around with those low-level language features from the Thread Support Library, such as `std::thread`, `std::mutex`, etc.

In fact that means that about 70 well-known algorithms were overloaded and are now also available in one or more versions accepting an extra template parameter for parallelization called `ExecutionPolicy`. Some of these algorithms are, for instance, `std::for_each`, `std::transform`, `std::copy_if`, or `std::sort`. Furthermore, seven new algorithms have been added that can also be parallelized, like `std::reduce`, `std::exclusive_scan`, or `std::transform_reduce`. These new algorithms are particularly useful in functional programming, which is why I discuss them in Chapter 7.

EXECUTION POLICIES [C++17/C++20]

With the appearance of the standard C++17, a majority of algorithm templates from the
<algorithm> header have been overloaded and are also available in a parallelizable version.
For example, in addition to the existing template for the std::find function, another version
has been defined that takes an additional template parameter to specify the execution policy:

```
// Standard (single-threaded) version:
template< class InputIt, class T >
constexpr InputIt find( InputIt first, InputIt last, const T& value );
// Additional version with user-definable execution policy (since C++17):
template< class ExecutionPolicy, class ForwardIt, class T >
ForwardIt find(ExecutionPolicy&& policy, ForwardIt first, ForwardIt last,
const T& value);
```

The four standard policy tags that are available in C++20 for the template parameter
ExecutionPolicy are:

- std::execution::seq (since C++17). An execution policy type that defines
  that a parallel algorithm's execution may be sequentially. Hence, it is more or
  less the same as you would use the single-threaded standard version of the
  algorithm template function without an execution policy.

- std::execution::par (since C++17.) An execution policy type that
  defines that a parallel algorithm's execution may be parallelized. It permits the
  implementation to execute the algorithm on multiple threads. **Important:** The
  parallel algorithms do not automatically protect against critical data races or
  deadlocks! You are responsible for ensuring that no data race conditions can
  occur while executing the function.

- std::execution::par_unseq (since C++17). An execution policy type that
  defines that a parallel algorithm's execution may be vectorized, parallelized,
  or migrated across threads. Vectorization takes advantage of the SIMD (*Single
  Instruction, Multiple Data*) command set of modern CPUs. SIMD means
  that a processor can perform the same operation on multiple data points
  simultaneously.

- `std::execution::unseq` (since C++20). An execution policy type that defines that a parallel algorithm's execution may be vectorized, i.e., the algorithm takes advantage of SIMD and can perform the same operation on multiple data elements simultaneously.

Of course, it makes absolutely no sense to sort a small vector with a few elements in parallel. The overhead for thread management would be much higher than the gain on performance. Thus, an execution policy should also be selectable dynamically during runtime, for example, by taking the size of the vector into consideration. Unfortunately, as it was the case when the C++17 Standard was adopted, so-called *dynamic execution policies* are also not included in C++20.

A full discussion of all available algorithms is way beyond the scope of this book. But after this short introduction to the `<algorithm>` header and the advanced possibilities of parallelization with C++20, let's look at a few examples of what can be done with algorithms.

Sorting and Output of a Container

The following example uses two templates from the `<algorithm>` header: `std::sort` and `std::for_each`. Internally, `std::sort` is using the quicksort algorithm. By default, the comparisons inside `std::sort` are performed with the `operator<` function of the elements. This means that if you want to sort a sequence of instances of one of your own classes, you have to ensure that `operator<` is properly implemented on that type. See Listing 5-25.

Listing 5-25. Sorting a Vector of Strings and Printing Them on stdout

```cpp
#include <algorithm>
#include <iostream>
#include <string>
#include <string_view>
#include <vector>

void printCommaSeparated(std::string_view text) {
  std::cout << text << ", ";
}
```

```
int main() {
  std::vector<std::string> names = { "Peter", "Harry", "Julia", "Marc",
  "Antonio", "Glenn" };
  std::sort(begin(names), end(names));
  std::for_each(begin(names), end(names), printCommaSeparated);
  return 0;
}
```

But couldn't this be even easier? Yes it could!

More Convenience with Ranges

Maybe you have sometimes also asked yourself why there is no more comfortable API for the algorithms than always calling them with two iterators of a container, usually the start and the end iterator. After all, applying an algorithm to all elements in a container or sequence is probably the most common use case.

Maybe you've heard about the so-called *Range Library for C++14/17/20,* written by Eric Niebler, a member of the ISO C++ Standardization Committee. Eric's library code became the basis of a formal proposal to add range support to the C++ Standard Library. It was merged into the C++20 working drafts in November 2018 and finally became part of the C++20 standard.

C++20 Ranges is a header-only library that simplifies the dealing with containers of the C++ Standard Library or containers from other libraries (e.g., Boost). With the help of this library, you can get rid of the sometimes tricky juggling with iterators in various situations. For instance, instead of writing:

```
std::sort(std::begin(container), std::end(container));
```

you can simply write:

```
std::ranges::sort(container);
```

With the help of ranges, the example in Listing 5-25 can be implemented more simply and becomes much more readable, as shown in Listing 5-26.

Listing 5-26. Sorting and Printing a Vector of Strings with the Help of Ranges

```cpp
#include <algorithm>
#include <iostream>
#include <ranges>
#include <string>
#include <string_view>
#include <vector>

void printCommaSeparated(std::string_view text) {
  std::cout << text << ", ";
}

int main() {
  std::vector<std::string> names = { "Peter", "Harry", "Julia", "Marc",
  "Antonio", "Glenn" };
  std::ranges::sort(names);
  std::ranges::for_each(names, printCommaSeparated);
  return 0;
}
```

For many algorithms from the `<algorithm>` header that require iterators as parameters, there is a corresponding alternative with this simplified interface in the `std::ranges` namespace. But C++20 Ranges offers even more: Views!

Non-Owning Ranges with Views

Containers from the C++ Standard Library are owners of their elements. For instance, if you delete a `std::vector`, all the elements stored in it are also deleted.

In contrast, views are a category of ranges that do not own any element. Views can be applied to other ranges, or to subareas of these ranges, and provide a kind of "transformed view" onto the elements in the underlying range. These "transformed views" are generated by algorithms or operations.

It is important to know that views are lazy-evaluated, i.e. whatever transformation they apply to the underlying range, they do so at the moment users request an element, *not* when the view is created! In other words, applying the `std::reverse` algorithm on a container manipulates the ordering of its elements immediately, whereas applying `std::views::reverse` on the same container doesn't change it in this moment:

```
#include <iostream>
#include <ranges>
#include <vector>

std::vector<int> integers = { 2, 5, 8, 22, 45, 67, 99 };
auto view = std::views::reverse(integers); // does not change 'integers'
```

The proof that the view does not manipulate the underlying range can be provided by outputting the first element of the view and vector to stdout:

```
std::cout << *view.begin() << ", " << *integers.begin() << '\n';
```

The output is as follows:

```
99, 2
```

It must be emphasized again that the computation that the first element of the view view corresponds to the last element of the vector named integers is done on demand. This also reveals something that needs to be considered when using views: if the same element is requested again, the same transformation has to be performed again! This can lead to performance losses, especially with complex transformations.

That's all for now; you will learn about a few more features of ranges in Chapter 7 on functional programming.

Comparing Two Sequences

The example in Listing 5-27 compares two sequences of strings using std::equal.

Listing 5-27. Comparing Two Sequences of Strings

```
#include <algorithm>
#include <iostream>
#include <string>
#include <vector>

int main() {
  const std::vector<std::string> names1 { "Peter", "Harry", "Julia",
  "Marc", "Antonio", "Glenn" };
```

```cpp
  const std::vector<std::string> names2 { "Peter", "Harry", "Julia",
  "John", "Antonio", "Glenn" };

const bool isEqual = std::equal(begin(names1), end(names1), begin(names2),
end(names2));

  if (isEqual) {
    std::cout << "The contents of both sequences are equal.\n";
  } else {
    std::cout << "The contents of both sequences differ.\n";
  }
  return 0;
}
```

By default, std::equal compares elements using operator==. But you can define
"equalness" as you want. The standard comparison can be replaced with a custom
comparison operation, as shown in Listing 5-28.

Listing 5-28. Comparing Two Sequences of Strings Using a Custom Predicate
Function

```cpp
#include <algorithm>
#include <iostream>
#include <string>
#include <vector>

bool compareFirstThreeCharactersOnly(const std::string& string1,
                                     const std::string& string2) {
  return (string1.compare(0, 3, string2, 0, 3) == 0);
}

int main() {
  const std::vector<std::string> names1 { "Peter", "Harry", "Julia",
  "Marc", "Antonio", "Glenn" };
  const std::vector<std::string> names2 { "Peter", "Harold", "Julia",
  "Maria", "Antonio","Glenn" };
```

```
const bool isEqual = std::equal(begin(names1), end(names1),
begin(names2),
  end(names2), compareFirstThreeCharactersOnly);

if (isEqual) {
  std::cout << "The first three characters of all strings in both
  sequences are equal.\n";
} else {
  std::cout << "The first three characters of all strings in both
  sequences differ.\n";
}
  return 0;
}
```

If no reusability is required for the comparison function
compareFirstThreeCharactersOnly(), the line where the comparison takes place can
also be implemented using a lambda expression, like this:

```
// Compare just the first three characters of every string to ascertain
equalness:
const bool isEqual =
  std::equal(begin(names1), end(names1), begin(names2), end(names2),
  [](const auto& string1, const auto& string2) {
    return (string1.compare(0, 3, string2, 0, 3) == 0);
  });
```

We discuss lambda expressions in more detail in Chapter 7. This alternative may
appear more compact, but it does not necessarily contribute to the readability of the
code. The explicit function compareFirstThreeCharactersOnly() has a semantic
name that expresses very clearly what is compared (not the *how*; see the section "Use
Intention-Revealing Names" in Chapter 4). What exactly is compared cannot necessarily
be seen at first sight from the version with the lambda expression. Always keep in mind
that the readability of our code should be one of our first goals. Also keep in mind that
source code comments are basically a code smell and not suitable to explain hard-to-
read code (remember the section about comments in Chapter 4).

Take Advantage of Boost

I can't give a broad introduction into the famous Boost library (`www.boost.org`, distributed under the *Boost Software License*, Version 1.0) here. The library (in fact, it is a library of libraries) is too big and too powerful, and discussing it in detail is beyond the scope of this book. Furthermore, there are numerous good books and tutorials about Boost.

But I think that it is very important to know about this library and its content. Many problems and challenges that C++ developers face in their daily work can be pretty well solved with libraries from Boost.

Beyond that, Boost is a kind of "incubator" for several libraries that are sometimes accepted to become part of the C++ language standard, if they have a certain level of maturity. Be careful, that does not necessarily mean that they are fully compatible! For instance, `std::thread` (part of the standard since C++11) is partially equal to Boost. Thread, but there are some differences. For example, the Boost implementation supports thread cancellation, something that is available in the Standard Library only since C++20 (`std::jthread`). On the other hand, C++11 supports `std::async`, but Boost does not.

From my perspective, it is worth it to know the libraries from Boost, and to remember when you have a suitable problem that can be properly solved by them.

More Libraries That You Should Know About

Apart from Standard Library containers, `<algorithm>`, Ranges, and Boost, there are some more libraries out there that you might take into consideration when writing your code. Here is an incomplete list of libraries that are worth looking at when you are confronted with a certain suitable problem:

- **Atomic types** (`<atomic>`): A collection of templates and types available since C++11 that different threads can simultaneously operate on without raising undefined behavior (data races; see the sidebar about "Atomic Operations" in the section about smart pointers). The central element is the class template **std::atomic<T>**, which can be used to define atomic types. For all integral data types, corresponding aliases are predefined, for example **atomic_int32_t** for **std::atomic<int32_t>**.

- **Date and time utilities** (`<chrono>`): Since C++11, the language provides a collection of types to represent clocks, time points, and durations. And with the latest standard C++20, dates and time zones have also been added. For instance, you can represent time intervals with the help of `std::chrono::duration`. And with `std::chrono::system_clock`, a system-wide real-time clock is available. You can use the library since C++11 by just including the `<chrono>` header.

- **Pseudo-random number generator library** (`<random>`): A library available since C++11 that provides classes for generating random and pseudo-random numbers. This library is a much better, more modern, and more powerful alternative to the old C library function combination `srand()` with `rand()`. With the `<random>` header, developers get a selection of Random Number Generators (RNG) with different engines (Minimum standard, 32-bit and 64-bit Mersenne Twister, etc.) and distributions (Normal, Uniform, Bernoulli, etc.) at hand.

- **Regular expressions library** (`<regex>`): Since C++11, a regular expressions library is available that can be used to perform pattern matching within strings. Also the replacement of text within a string based on regular expressions is supported. You can use the library since C++11 by just including the `<regex>` header.

- **Filesystem library** (`<filesystem>`): Since C++17, the Filesystem library has become part of the standard. Before it became part of the mainline C++ standard, it was a technical specification (ISO/IEC TS 18822:2015). The operational system independent library provides various facilities for performing operations on file systems and their components. With the help of `<filesystem>` you can create directories, copy files, iterate over directory entries, retrieve the size of a file, etc. You can use the library since C++17 by just including the `<filesystem>` header.

Tip   If you are currently not working according to the C++17 standard or higher, *Boost.Filesystem* could be an alternative.

- **Concurrent data structures** (libcds): A mostly header-only C++ template library written by Max Khizhinsky, this provides lock-free algorithms and concurrent data structure implementations for parallel high-performance computing. The library is written using modern C++ (C++11 and higher) and published under a BSD license. libcds and its documentation can be found on SourceForge at http://libcds.sourceforge.net.

Proper Exception and Error Handling

Maybe you have heard the term *cross-cutting concerns*? This expression includes all those things that are difficult to address through a modularization concept and therefore require special treatment by software architecture and design. One of these typical cross-cutting concerns is *security*. If you have to take care of data security and access restrictions in your software system, because it is demanded by certain quality requirements, it is a sensitive topic that pervades the whole system. You have to deal with it nearly everywhere, in virtually every component.

Another cross-cutting concern is *transaction handling*. Especially in software applications that use databases, you have to ensure that a so-called *transaction*, which is a coherent series of single operations, must succeed or fail as a complete logical unit; it can never be only partially complete.

And as another example, *logging* is also a cross-cutting concern. Logging is typically needed everywhere in a software system. Sometimes the domain-specific and productive code is littered with log statements, which is detrimental to the readability and understandability of the code.

If the software architecture does not take care of these cross-cutting concerns, this could lead to inconsistent solutions. For instance, two different logging frameworks could be used in the same project, because two development teams working on the same system decided to choose different frameworks.

The exception and error handling is another cross-cutting concern. Dealing with errors and unpredictable exceptions that require special responses and treatments is mandatory in every software system. And, of course, the system-wide error-handling strategies should be uniform and consistent. Hence, it is very important that the people responsible for the software's architecture have to design and develop an error-handling strategy quite early in the project.

Well, but what are the principles that guide us in developing a good error-handling strategy? When is it justified to throw an exception? How do I deal with thrown exceptions? And for what purposes should exceptions never be used? What are the alternatives?

The following sections present some rules, guidelines, and principles that help C++ programmers design and implement a good error-handling strategy.

Prevention Is Better Than Aftercare

A fundamentally good basic strategy for dealing with errors and exceptions is to generally avoid them. The reason for this is obvious: everything that cannot happen does not have to be treated.

Maybe you will say now, well, this is a truism. Of course it is much better to avoid errors or exceptions, but sometimes it is not possible to prevent them. You're right, it sounds banal at first glance. And yes, especially when using third-party libraries, accessing databases, or accessing an external system, unforeseeable things can happen. But for your own code, meaning the parts of the system that you can design as you want, you can take appropriate measures to avoid exceptions as far as possible.

David Abrahams, an American programmer, former ISO C++ standardization committee member, and a founding member of Boost C++ Libraries, created an understanding of what is called *exception safety* and presented it in a paper [Abrahams98] in 1998. The set of contractual guidelines formulated in this paper, which are also known as the "Abrahams Guarantees," had a significant influence on the design of the C++ Standard Library and how this library deals with exceptions. But these guidelines are not only relevant to low-level library implementers. They can also be considered by software developers who are writing the application code on higher abstraction levels.

Exception safety is part of the interface design. An interface (API) does not only consist of function signatures, that is, a function's parameters and return types. The exceptions that might be thrown if a function is invoked are also part of its interface. Furthermore, there are three more aspects that must be considered:

- **Precondition:** A condition that must always be true before a function or a class's method is invoked. If a precondition is violated, no guarantee can be given that the function call leads to the expected result. The function call may succeed, may fail, can cause unwanted side effects, or show undefined behavior.

- **Invariant:** A condition that must always be true during the execution of a function or method. In other words, it is a condition that is true at the beginning and at the end of a function's execution. A special form of an invariant in object-orientation is a *class invariant*. If such an invariant is violated, the object (instance) of the class is left behind in an incorrect and inconsistent state after a method call.

- **Postcondition:** A condition that must always be true immediately after the execution of a function or method. If a postcondition is violated, an error must have occurred during execution of the function or method.

The idea behind exception safety is that functions, or a class and its methods, give their clients a kind of promise, or a guarantee, about invariants, postconditions, and about exceptions that might be thrown or not thrown. There are four levels of exception safety. In the following subsections, I discuss them shortly in increasing order of safety.

No Exception Safety

With this lowest level of exception safety—literally, no exception safety—absolutely nothing is guaranteed. Any occurring exception can have disastrous consequences. For instance, invariants and postconditions of the called function or method are violated, and a portion of your code, for example, an object, is possibly left behind in a corrupted state.

I think that there is no doubt that the code written by you should **never ever offer this inadequate level of exception safety!** Just pretend that there is no such thing as "no exception safety." That's all; there's nothing more to say about that.

Basic Exception Safety

The *basic exception safety* guarantee is the guarantee that any piece of code should offer at least. It is also the exception safety level that can be achieved with relatively little implementation effort. This level guarantees the following:

- If an exception is thrown during a function or method call, it is ensured that no resources are leaked! This guarantee includes memory resources as well as other resources. This can be achieved by applying RAII pattern (see the section about RAII and smart pointers).

- If an exception is thrown during a function or method call, all invariants are preserved.

- If an exception is thrown during a function or method call, there will be no corruption of data or memory afterward, and all objects are in a healthy and consistent state. However, it is **not** guaranteed that the data content is the same as before the function or method has been called.

Tip   The strict rule is this: Design your code, especially your classes, such that they guarantee at least the basic exception safety. This should always be the default exception-safety level!

It is important to know that the C++ Standard Library expects all user types to give at least the basic exception guarantee.

Strong Exception Safety

The *strong exception safety* guarantees everything that is also guaranteed by the basic exception safety level, but also ensures that in case of an exception, the data is recovered exactly as before the function or method was called. In other words, with this exception-safety level, we get commit or rollback semantics like in transaction handling on databases.

It is easy to comprehend that this exception-safety level leads to a higher implementation effort and can be costly at runtime. An example of this additional effort is the so-called *copy-and-swap* idiom that must be used to ensure strong exception safety for copy assignment.

Equipping your whole code with strong exception safety without any good reasons would violate the KISS and YAGNI principles (see Chapter 3). Hence, the guideline regarding this is in the following tip.

Tip   Issue the strong exception safety guarantee for your code only if it is absolutely required or if the implementation efforts are small compared to the benefits you get (see the Copy-and-Swap idiom discussed in Chapter 9).

Of course, if there are certain quality requirements regarding data integrity and data correctness that have to be satisfied, you have to provide the rollback mechanism that is guaranteed through strong exception safety.

The No-Throw Guarantee

This is the highest exception-safety level, also known as *failure transparency*. Simply speaking, this level means that as a caller of a function or method, you don't have to worry about exceptions. The function or method call will succeed. **Always!** It will never throw an exception, because everything is properly handled internally. There will never be violated invariants and postconditions.

This is the all-round carefree package of exception safety, but it is sometimes very difficult or even impossible to achieve, especially in C++. For instance, if you use any kind of dynamic memory allocation inside a function, like operator new, either directly or indirectly (e.g., via std::make_shared<T>), you have absolutely no chance to end up with a successfully processed function after an exception was encountered.

Here are the cases where the no-throw guarantee is either absolutely mandatory or at least explicitly advised:

- **Destructors of classes must guarantee to be no-throw under all circumstances!** The reason is that, among other situations, destructors are also called while stack unwinding after an exception has been encountered. It would be fatal if another exception would occur during stack unwinding, because the program would terminate immediately.

  As a consequence, any operation inside a destructor that deals with allocated resources and tries to close them, like opened files or allocated memory on the heap, must not throw.

- **Move operations** (move constructors and move assignment operators; see the earlier section about move semantics) **should guarantee to be no-throw.** If a move operation throws an exception, the probability is enormously high that the move has not taken place. Hence, it should be avoided at all costs that implementations of move operations allocate resources via resource allocation techniques that can throw exceptions. Furthermore, it is important to give the no-throw guarantee for types that are intended to be used with the C++ Standard Library containers. If the move constructor for an element type in a container doesn't give a no-throw guarantee (i.e., the move constructor is not declared with the noexcept specifier), then the container will prefer using the copy operations rather than the move operations.

- **Default constructors should be preferably no-throw.** Basically, throwing an exception in a constructor is not desirable, but it is the best way to deal with constructor failures. A "half-constructed object" does highly likely violate invariants. And an object in a corrupt state that violates its class invariants is useless and dangerous. Therefore, there is nothing speaking against throwing an exception in a default constructor when it is unavoidable. However, it is a good design strategy to largely avoid it. Default constructors should be simple. If a default constructor can throw, it is probably doing too many complex things. Hence, when designing a class, you should try to avoid exceptions in the default constructor.

- **A swap function must guarantee to be no-throw under all circumstances!** An expertly implemented swap() function should not allocate any resources (e.g., memory) using memory allocation techniques that potentially can throw exceptions. It would be fatal if swap() can throw, because it can end up with an inconsistent state. The best way to write an exception-safe operator=() is using a non-throwing swap() function for its implementation (see the Copy-and-Swap idiom in Chapter 9).

NOEXCEPT SPECIFIER AND OPERATOR [C++11]

Prior to C++11, the throw keyword could be in a function's declaration. It was used to list all exception types in a comma-separated list that a function might directly or indirectly throw, known as the *dynamic exception specification*. **The usage of** throw(exceptionType, exceptionType, ...) **is deprecated since C++11 and has been finally removed from the standard in C++17!** What was still available, but also marked as deprecated since C++11, was the throw() specifier without an exception type list. **This has now also been removed from the standard with C++20.** Its semantics are now the same as the noexcept(true) specifier.

The noexcept specifier in a function's signature declares that the function may not throw any exceptions. The same is valid for noexcept(true), which is just a synonym for noexcept. Instead, a function that is declared with noexcept(false) is potentially throwing, that is, it may throw exceptions. Here are some examples:

```
void nonThrowingFunction() noexcept;
void anotherNonThrowingFunction() noexcept(true);
void aPotentiallyThrowingFunction() noexcept(false); // The default if nothing
                                                     has been specified.
```

There are two good reasons for using noexcept: First, exceptions that a function or method could throw (or not) are parts of the function's interface. It is about semantics, and helps a developer who's reading the code to know what might happen and what not might happen. noexcept tells developers that they can safely use this function in their own non-throwing functions. Hence, the presence of noexcept is somewhat akin to const.

Second, it can be used by the compiler for optimizations. noexcept potentially allows a compiler to compile the function without adding the runtime overhead that was formerly required by the removed throw(...); that is, the object code that was necessary to call std::unexpected() when an exception that was not listed was thrown.

For template implementers, there is also a noexcept operator, which performs a compile-time check that returns true if the expression is declared to not throw any exceptions:

```
constexpr auto isNotThrowing = noexcept(nonThrowingFunction());
```

Note   constexpr functions (see the section entitled "Computations During Compile Time") can also throw when evaluated at runtime, so you may also need noexcept for some of those.

An Exception Is an Exception, Literally!

In Chapter 4, we discussed in the section "Do Not Pass or Return 0 (NULL, nullptr)," that you should not return nullptr as a return value from a function. As a code example, we had a small function that should perform a lookup for a customer by name, which of course leads to no result if this customer cannot be found. Someone could now come up with the idea that we could throw an exception for a non-found customer, as shown in the following code example.

```cpp
#include "Customer.h"
#include <string>
#include <exception>

class CustomerNotFoundException : public std::exception {
private:
  const char* what() const noexcept override {
    return "Customer not found!";
  }
};

// ...

Customer CustomerService::findCustomerByName(const std::string& name) const {
  // Code that searches the customer by name...
  // ...and if the customer could not be found:
  throw CustomerNotFoundException();
}
```

Now let's take a look at the invocation site of this function:

```cpp
Customer customer;
try {
  customer = findCustomerByName("Non-existing name");
} catch (const CustomerNotFoundException& ex) {
  // ...
}
  // ...
```

At first sight, this seems to look like a feasible solution. If we have to avoid returning `nullptr` from the function, we can throw a `CustomerNotFoundException` instead. At the invocation site, we are now able to distinguish between the happy case and the bad case with the help of a `try-catch` construct.

In fact, it is a really bad solution! Not finding a customer just because its name does not exist is definitely no exceptional case. These are things that will happen normally.

Just think about a search function for users of a software application that deals with customers and allows a free text search.

What has been done in the previous example is an abuse of exceptions. Exceptions are not there to control the normal program flow. **Exceptions should be reserved for what's truly exceptional!**

What does "truly exceptional" mean? Well, it means that there is nothing you can do about it, and you cannot really handle that exception. For instance, let's assume that you are confronted with a `std::bad_alloc` exception, which means that there was a failure to allocate memory. How should the program continue now? What was the root cause for this problem? Does the underlying hardware system have a lack of memory? Well, then we have a really serious problem! Is there any meaningful way to recover from this serious exception and resume the program's execution? Can we still take responsibility if the program simply continues running as if nothing happened?

These questions cannot be answered easily. Perhaps the real trigger for this problem was a dangling pointer, which has been used inexpertly millions of instructions before we've encountered the `std::bad_alloc` exception. All of this can seldom be reproduced at the time of the exception.

Tip   Throw exceptions only in very exceptional cases. Do not misuse exceptions to control the normal program flow.

You might wonder now, it is bad to use `nullptr` and `NULL` as a return value, and exceptions are also undesired, then what should I do instead? In the section entitled "Special Case Object (Null Object)" in Chapter 9 about design patterns, I present a feasible solution to handle these cases in a proper way.

If You Can't Recover, Get Out Quickly

If you are confronted with an exception from which you cannot recover, it is often the best approach to log the exception (if possible), or to generate a crash dump file for later analyzing purposes, and to terminate the program immediately. A good example where a quick termination can be the best reaction is a failed memory allocation. If a system lacks memory, well, what should you do in the context of your program?

The principle behind this strict handling strategy for some critical exceptions and errors is called "Dead Programs Tell No Lies" and is described in the book *Pragmatic Programmer* [Hunt99].

Nothing is worse than continuing after a serious error as if nothing had happened, and to produce, for example, tens of thousands of erroneous bookings, or to send the lift for the hundredth time from the cellar to the top floor and back. Instead, get out before too much consequential damage occurs.

Define User-Specific Exception Types

Although you can throw whatever you want in C++, like an `int` or a `const char*`, I would not recommend it. Exceptions are caught by types; hence it is a very good idea to create your custom exception classes for certain, mostly domain-specific, exceptions. As I explained in Chapter 4, good naming is crucial for the readability and the maintainability of the code, and exception types should have good names. Further principles, which are valid for designing the "normal" program code, are of course also valid for exception types (we discuss these principles in detail in the Chapter 6 about object orientation).

To provide your own exception type, you can simply create your own class and derive them from `std::exception` (defined in the `<stdexcept>` header):

```cpp
#include <stdexcept>

class MyCustomException : public std::exception {
public:
  const char* what() const noexcept override {
    return "Provide some details about what was going wrong here!";
  }
};
```

By overriding the virtual `what()` member function inherited from `std::exception`, we can provide some information to the caller about what went wrong. Furthermore, deriving our own exception class from `std::exception` will make it catchable by a generic `catch` clause (which, by the way, should only be regarded as the very last possibility to catch an exception), like this one:

```cpp
#include <iostream>

// ...
try {
  doSomethingThatThrows();
```

```
} catch (const std::exception& ex) {
  std::cerr << ex.what() << std::endl;
}
```

Basically, exception classes should have a simple design, but if you want to provide more details about the cause of the exception, you can also write more sophisticated classes, like the one in Listing 5-29.

Listing 5-29. A Custom Exception Class for Divisions by Zero

```cpp
class DivisionByZeroException : public std::exception {
public:
  DivisionByZeroException() = delete;
  explicit DivisionByZeroException(const int dividend) {
    buildErrorMessage(dividend);
  }

  const char* what() const noexcept override {
    return errorMessage.c_str();
  }

private:
  void buildErrorMessage(const int dividend) {
    errorMessage = "A division with dividend = ";
    errorMessage += std::to_string(dividend);
    errorMessage += ", and divisor = 0, is not allowed (Division by Zero)!";
  }

  std::string errorMessage;
};
```

Note that due to its implementation, the private member function buildErrorMessage() can only guarantee strong exception safety, that is, it may throw due to the use of std::string::operator+=()! Hence, the initialization constructor cannot give the no-throw guarantee. That's why exception classes generally should have a pretty simple design.

Here is a small example of the DivisionByZeroException class:

```
int divide(const int dividend, const int divisor) {
  if (divisor == 0) {
    throw DivisionByZeroException(dividend);
  }
  return dividend / divisor;
}

int main() {
  try {
    divide(10, 0);
  } catch (const DivisionByZeroException& ex) {
    std::cerr << ex.what() << std::endl;
    return 1;
  }
  return 0;
}
```

Throw by Value, Catch by const Reference

Sometimes I've seen exception objects allocated on the heap with the help of new and thrown as a pointer, like in this example:

```
try
{
  CFile f(_T("M_Cause_File.dat"), CFile::modeWrite);
  // If "M_Cause_File.dat" does not exist, the constructor of CFile throws
     an exception
  // this way: throw new CFileException()
}
catch(CFileException* e)
{
  if( e->m_cause == CFileException::fileNotFound)
    TRACE(_T("ERROR: File not found\n"));
  e->Delete();
}
```

Perhaps you have recognized this C++ coding style: throwing and catching exceptions in this manner can be found in the good old MFC (Microsoft Foundation Classes) library galore. And it is important that you don't forget to call the `Delete()` member function at the end of the `catch` clause; otherwise you can say "Hello!" to memory leaks.

Well, throwing exceptions with `new` and catching them as a pointer is possible in C++, but it is bad design. **Don't do it!** If you forget to delete the exception object, it will result in a memory leak. Throw the exception object by value, and catch them by const reference, as can be seen in all the previous examples.

Pay Attention to the Correct Order of Catch Clauses

If you provide more than one `catch` clause after a `try` block, for example to distinguish between different types of exceptions, it is important that you do so in the correct order. Catch clauses are evaluated in the order they appear. This means that the `catch` clauses for the more specific exception types must come first. In the example in Listing 5-30, exception classes `DivisionByZeroException` and `CommunicationInterruptedException` are both derived from `std::exception`.

Listing 5-30. The More Specific Exceptions Must Be Handled First

```
try {
  doSomethingThatCanThrowSeveralExceptions();
} catch (const DivisionByZeroException& ex) {
  // ...
} catch (const CommunicationInterruptedException& ex) {
  // ...
} catch (const std::exception& ex) {
  // Handle all other exceptions here that are derived from std::exception
} catch (...) {
  // The rest...
}
```

The reason is obvious, I think: let's assume that the `catch` clause for the general `std::exception` would be the first one, what would happen? The more specific ones below would never get a chance because they are "hidden" by the more general one. Therefore, developers must be sure to put them in the correct order.

Interface Design

"Since changing interfaces breaks clients, you should consider them as immutable once you've published them."

—Erich Gamma, Design Principles from Design Patterns, 2005

In our daily work as software craftspeople, we are constantly confronted with interfaces, either because we have to use them (e.g., from a library), or because we have to design them (e.g., when creating a class or a module). Probably one of the most demanding tasks in software design is to design *good* interfaces and APIs. But what makes a "good interface"?

Well, in previous chapters, you learned some principles and practices that can help you create well-designed interfaces:

- **Easy to use, even without documentation.** Think about the KISS principle from Chapter 3. An interface should not be too complicated. Furthermore, a good and expressive naming is important; if an interface is hard to name, that's generally a bad sign. Good names also make it easier to learn an interface. The API can quickly be memorized by developers who work with it constantly.

- **Users of an interface/API should not be surprised by unexpected behavior.** Avoid unexpected side effects! Think about the principle of least astonishment, discussed in Chapter 3.

- **An interface should be as small as possible.** Do not offer more services than necessary. You won't be able to please everyone anyway. You can always add something, but you can never remove it! If something has to be added, it should be done in a way that existing parts of the interface are not changed.

- **A well-designed interface/API hides the implementation.** Changes in the implementation of a software module should not be propagated outside via its interface. Think about the information hiding principle from Chapter 3. Make classes and their members as private as possible, because it fosters loose coupling.

- **Hard to misuse.** Use appropriate parameter and return types and avoid long parameter lists (see the section entitled "Arguments and Return Values" in Chapter 4). If values have semantics, strongly typed parameters instead of primitive data types (int, double, ...) should be used for them, as described in the section "Type-Rich Programming" in this chapter. Don't use a string if a better type exists.

- **Don't forget that exceptions are also part of an interface.** Throw exceptions only to indicate true exceptional conditions, i.e. don't force users of your interface to use exceptions for normal control flow. This aspect has been discussed in detail in the previous section entitled "Proper Exception and Error Handling."

- **Provide a suite of well-crafted unit tests for your API.** As discussed in Chapter 2, a suite of good tests is not only a sign of the quality awareness of the developers, but they are also good examples for users that can show how to use the API.

In addition to these general good practices for interface design, modern C++ offers further possibilities to specify interfaces, which I briefly discuss in the following and last sections of this chapter:

- Attributes (since C++11)

- Concepts (new since C++20)

Attributes

C++ Attributes were introduced with C++11 and regularly extended with the following language standards. Maybe you know a very similar concept in programming language Java, which is called *annotations*. Some attributes are part of the C++ language standard, others are compiler-specific.

In simple terms, an attribute is an expression surrounded with double square brackets to give instructions to the compiler, like this:

```
[[attr]]
```

Multiple attributes can be specified as a comma-separated list:

```
[[attr1, attr2, attr3]]
```

Specific kinds of attributes can also have an argument:

```
[[attr(argument)]]
```

With attributes, software developers can specify additional information or instructions for the compiler, e.g., to enforce constraints (conditions), optimize certain sections of code, or do some specific code generations. Basically, attributes can be applied to almost every C++ programming language construct, e.g., types, variables, functions/methods, names, code blocks, and so on. However, certain attributes only make sense for very specific parts of the code. And they can also be very useful to design interfaces.

In the following sections, I introduce some of the attributes that are defined in the C++ standard and that can be used in interface design.

noreturn (since C++11)

The attribute [[noreturn]] can be used to mark a function from which the program flow does not return.

```
[[noreturn]] void function() {
  while (true) {
    // ... do something ...
  }
}
```

Perhaps you might wonder what this is good for? Well, if you implement a function that should intentionally not return (e.g., an endless loop to process events), but does so anyway due to a programming error, you'll get a compiler warning:

```
warning: 'noreturn' function does return
```

deprecated (since C++14)

Sometimes it is necessary to take back parts of an already published interface. As mentioned, ideally this should not happen, because users of an interface have made themselves dependent on it. At the same time, it is sometimes unavoidable in reality.

A good idea is not to remove the published part of the interface immediately, but to prepare the users that this could happen in the future. In other words, it is advisable to give your API users a grace period. Therefore, you can mark such entities as deprecated, meaning their use is allowed, but discouraged for some reason.

```cpp
class SomeType {
public:
  [[deprecated]] void doSomething() {
    // ...
  }
};
```

It is also possible to specify a rationale as a string-literal to explain why the use is discouraged:

```cpp
class SomeType {
public:
  [[deprecated("This function will be removed in future versions, "
  "use SomeType::doSomethingNew() instead!")]]
  void doSomething() {
    // ...
  }

  void doSomethingNew() {
    // ...
  }
};
```

nodiscard (since C++17)

With the help of the [[nodiscard]] attribute interface, designers can indicate that a return value of a function shouldn't be ignored. If the return value is ignored at the call site, the compiler generates a warning. Since C++20, you can also specify a rationale as a string-literal to explain to users why ignoring the return value is discouraged. See Listing 5-31.

Listing 5-31. The [[nodiscard]] Attribute Reminds Users to Accept the Return Value

```cpp
#include <memory>

class SomeType { };

using SomeTypePtr = std::shared_ptr<SomeType>;

class ObjectFactory {
public:
  [[nodiscard]] SomeTypePtr createInstance() const {
    return std::make_shared<SomeType>();
  }
};

int main() {
  ObjectFactory factory;
  auto instance = factory.createInstance(); // OK!
  factory.createInstance(); // Compiler warning!
  return 0;
}
```

maybe_unused (since C++17)

This attribute can be used to mark entities that might not be used. Thus, a compiler warning can be suppressed, which is generated when variables, parameters of functions or methods, data types, and other entities are declared, but not used.

For instance, depending on the configured warning level of your compiler, the following piece of code will produce a warning like "'param2': unreferenced formal parameter":

```cpp
int function(const int param1, const int param2) {
  return param1 + param1;
}

int main() {
  function(10, 20);
  return 0;
}
```

With the attribute [[maybe_unused]], this parameter can be marked so that the compiler warning is suppressed.

```
int function(const int param1, [[maybe_unused]] const int param2) {
  return param1 + param1;
}
```

You might be wondering how you'd use this attribute. You might ask yourself, who intentionally introduces a function parameter that is not used inside the function?

Think about conditional compiling with C++ templates. Listing 5-32 shows a simple example.

Listing 5-32. If Only Param1 Is Needed, You'll Get No Warning

```
#include <type_traits>

template<typename T, typename U>
void function(T param1, [[maybe_unused]] U param2) {
  if constexpr (std::is_floating_point<U>::value) {
    // ...code that uses 'param1' and 'param2'...
  } else {
    // ...code that uses 'param1' only...
  }
}

int main() {
  function(10, 20.0);
  function(10, 20);
  return 0;
}
```

In the main() function, we see two instantiations of the template function(): the first with one int and one double, and the second one with two ints. In the implementation of function(), we can see a constexpr if, or in other words, a compile-time-if, a new language feature that was introduced with C++17. This feature allows template designers to discard branches of an if statement at compile-time based on a constant expression condition. In our case, it is a type trait (defined in the <type_traits> header) that inspects the type U of param2 and returns true if it is a floating-point type. So, instantiating the template with two ints would result in an unused param2.

Concepts: Requirements for Template Arguments

The C++ template mechanism is a Turing Complete metalanguage for generic programming, which calculates types and values at compile time. There is nothing comparable in other programming languages, which only come close to the power of C++ templates.

On the downside, data type independent (generic) programming with templates is inherently complex and demanding. Just take a look at an outstanding example, the template code of the C++ Standard Library, and you know what I mean. You will be confronted with code that in many ways does not conform to the clean code guidelines I've presented in this book. On the contrary, it looks complex and cumbersome.

Many developers who write domain-specific application code are often very intensive users of template libraries, but they rarely come into a situation to write a template class or template function. But even as a user of templates, you often get into a situation where you have instantiated a template with one or more concrete data types for its template arguments, and were confronted with a very long and verbose list of cryptic error messages.

Just an example: earlier in this chapter, in the section about the `<algorithm>` header, I presented a small code example (see Listing 5-25) where a `std::vector<T>` filled with strings was sorted and then printed on `stdout`. In Listing 5-33, I modify this example a little bit by using a `std::list<T>` instead of a `std::vector<T>`.

Listing 5-33. Using a std::list Instead of a std::vector for names

```cpp
#include <algorithm>
#include <iostream>
#include <string>
#include <string_view>
#include <list> // formerly: <vector>

void printCommaSeparated(std::string_view text) {
  std::cout << text << ", ";
}

int main() {
  std::list<std::string> names = { "Peter", "Harry", "Julia", "Marc",
  "Antonio", "Glenn" };
```

```
std::sort(begin(names), end(names));
std::for_each(begin(names), end(names), printCommaSeparated);
return 0;
}
```

If you now compile this example, the compiler confronts you with a long list of sometimes hard-to-understand error messages. Then you are faced with the question: What the heck went wrong? I only exchanged the container type; can't a std::list<T> be sorted?

The reason for that bunch of errors is that a std::list<T> only offers a bidirectional iterator; that is, an iterator that can be used to access the sequence of elements in both directions. However, the algorithm std::sort requires a random access iterator, i.e. an iterator that can be used to access elements at an arbitrary offset position relative to the element it points to.

The basic problem is that a template instantiation is first of all only an obtuse, textual replacement of the template arguments by concrete types. The compiler can only determine whether the template is at all suitable to work correctly with this type when it compiles the instantiated template. In addition, it is almost impossible to implement a function or class template in such a way that it fits every conceivable concrete data type.

With the new C++20 standard, template designers get a long-awaited feature: Concepts! *Concepts* are named sets of semantic requirements or constraints that can be applied on template parameters and are evaluated at compile-time. Thus, they become part of the template's interface. We also get improved error messages, because the compiler can check if the requirements specified in a concept are satisfied by the concrete template arguments.

A C++ concept can be specified completely by yourself (I've done this in some code examples in this chapter before), but there is also a collection of predefined core concepts in the <concepts> header. These can be combined to build higher-level concepts. Furthermore, several concepts are also defined in other headers of the Standard Library, such as in <iterator> and <ranges>.

Specifying a Concept

Let's assume that we want to develop a function template named `function()` whose one and only template parameter must be copyable. The corresponding C++ concept looks like this:

```cpp
#include <concepts>

template<typename T>
concept Copyable =
  std::copy_constructible<T> &&
  std::movable <T> &&
  std::assignable_from<T&, const T&> && &&
  std::assignable_from<T&, const T&> &&
  std::assignable_from<T&, const T>;
```

Note   The previous code snippet is for demonstration purposes only. It is not necessary to define a concept like `Copyable` by yourself, because it is included in the `<concept>`: `std::copyable<T>` header.

The specified requirement that a template parameter T should be copyable corresponds to a logical AND of five core concepts from the `<concepts>` header. Our new concept also got a good, semantic name: `Copyable`.

Another way to specify a concept is using the `requires` expression:

```cpp
template<typename T>
concept Addable = requires (T x) { x + x; };
```

In this case, we have specified that a concrete type for template argument T can be added.

Applying a Concept

Now we apply the concept `Copyable<T>` by specifying the requirements for the template parameter T of a function, as shown in Listing 5-34.

Listing 5-34. Using a C++20 Concept to Specify Requirements That T Must Satisfy

```
class CopyableType { };

class NonCopyableType {
public:
  NonCopyableType() = default;
  NonCopyableType(const NonCopyableType&) = delete;
  NonCopyableType& operator=(const NonCopyableType&) = delete;
};

template<typename T>
void function(T& t) requires Copyable<T> {
  // ...
};
int main() {
  CopyableType a;
  function(a); // OK!
  NonCopyableType b;
  function(b); // Compiler error!
  return 0;
}
```

Because I deleted the copy constructor and copy assignment operator of the NonCopyableType class, we get the following expressive error message (excerpt; compiler: Clang 13.0.0):

```
prog.cc:28:3: error: no matching function for call to 'function'
  function(b); // Compiler error!
  ^~~~~~~~
prog.cc:20:6: note: candidate template ignored: constraints not satisfied
[with T = NonCopyableType]
void function(T& t) requires Copyable<T> {
     ^
prog.cc:20:30: note: because 'NonCopyableType' does not satisfy 'Copyable'
void function(T& t) requires Copyable<T> {
                             ^
[...]
```

I highlighted the relevant line with bold font: The data type NonCopyableType does not satisfy the requirements of our concept named Copyable<T>. In the following lines of this error output (intentionally omitted here and replaced by an ellipsis: [...]), the compiler tells us which partial requirement of the concept was not satisfied. This is a significant improvement compared to those cryptic error messages from former times.

By the way, the function from Listing 5-34 can be written much more compact and elegant without the requires clause:

```
template<Copyable T>
void function(T& t) {
  // ...
};
```

Or even better, using the C++20 abbreviated function template syntax:

```
void function(Copyable auto& t) {
  // ...
};
```

Templates, concepts, and metaprogramming during compile time are extremely powerful features of modern C++ whose primary target group is clearly library developers. They justify a much more detailed introduction. Unfortunately, a deep dive into these language constructs is far beyond the scope of this book.

CHAPTER 6

Modularization

"I have absolutely no idea about space exploration. I'm a software guy. But because I'm a non-expert, I've been able to bring the software concept of modularity into the space sector, which was never done before."

—Naveen Jain, software engineer, entrepreneur and founder,
May 12, 2015

This quote is from a blog article [Jain15] by Naveen Jain, one of the three founders of the Florida-based private company *Moon Express Inc.*, which was founded in 2010. The business objective of Moon Express (MoonEx) is to mine natural resources of economic value, such as ore, on the moon. For this purpose, MoonEx engineers designed a family of flexible and scalable robotic explorers based on modular spacecraft architecture. The foundation for their modular architecture is NASA's *Modular Common Spacecraft Bus* (MCSB), which is a general-purpose spacecraft platform that can be configured as landers or orbiters. The MCSB not only reduces costs; NASA states that an uncrewed space mission that is built on the MCSB platform is roughly one-tenth the price of a conventional mission. Furthermore, by using a modular platform, NASA will no longer "reinvent the wheel," by being able to reuse many components.

Since the early days of software development, developers strove for well-modularized software. The reason for this is obvious: Once a piece of software has reached a certain size, it gets more and more difficult for humans to grasp it in its entirety. We do not modularize for the computer. A computer doesn't need a modularized version of the code to run it. It's our own cognitive limitations that force us to break down a software system in smaller pieces.

In addition, people expect further positive effects from well modularized software: reusable modules, better maintainability, and easier extensibility. Creating a scalable, configurable, and flexible product family like MoonEx did with its robotic space probes is the goal. Furthermore, modules with minimal interdependencies and well-designed interfaces are easier to test.

© Stephan Roth 2021
S. Roth, *Clean C++20*, https://doi.org/10.1007/978-1-4842-5949-8_6

This chapter covers the fundamentals and some good approaches to finding a suitable modularization for a software system. Furthermore, it also deals with the topic of object-orientation and covers a promising packaging mechanism called *modules*, introduced with C++20.

The Basics of Modularization

In general, modularization is an approach to divide a software system into multiple discrete and, ideally, independent building blocks (modules). Each module is expected to carry out a specific task of the software independently.

So far, so good, but of course this definition raises many more questions. Which properties must a module have to be considered a well-defined one? Is a module the same as a component, another term often used in software development? And what about classes, aren't they the same as modules? What criteria do we use to break down an entire software system into these modules? And if these modules should ideally be independent of each other, how can we then put them back together to build a running system?

Criteria for Finding Modules

Identifying or finding modules is usually part of the software design and architecture processes, and we know some important guiding principles for modularization from Chapter 3:

- Information hiding
- Strong cohesion
- Loose coupling

Perhaps these three fundamental principles are good, but not sufficient to achieve an appropriate modularization for a complex software system. The question is, which further criteria should be used?

Focus on the Domain of Your Software

In some of the projects that I looked at, the development team focused far too early on technical issues, such as the look of the UI, the database and its schemata, frameworks, libraries, network protocols, and other IT-specific topics. The consequence was that the modularization reflected this. The modules that were identified by the development team were mainly of a technical nature: central control unit, database interface, Internet communication module, logging, and similar stuff.

The problem with this is that virtually every software system in the world has something that could be called a "central control unit" in the broadest sense. It is a very unspecific term. What is a central control unit? What exactly is its responsibility? How does the central control unit of System A differ from the central control unit of System B?

On the other hand, how do you talk to external stakeholders about all this technical stuff? Normally, they are not IT experts. How can communication with these people work if the development team uses technical jargon? How can requirements be elicited, discussed, and clarified with these people if they have no clue about this weird thing called the "central control unit"? Have you ever heard financial experts, salespersons, farmers, or doctors talk about "central control units" when they discuss software that they use in their daily work?

A much better approach to a well-formed modularization is **a domain-centered or domain-driven approach**. You may remember that in Chapter 4, I recommended you name components, classes, and functions in a way that reflects the elements and concepts from the application's domain. I also mentioned two well-known software design methodologies there, OOAD and DDD, which focus on the domain of the system being developed.

One of the great benefits of domain-driven approaches is that they lead very clearly and directly to a meaningful modularization. In the *domain model*, that usually is one of the key results of these approaches, everything is considered as an object, and will, therefore, be quite modular and encapsulated. This means that a modular software design can be derived from it very easily, even though it must be enriched by further technical and architecture-motivated objects in order to build an executable software system.

Furthermore, with an early focus on the system's domain, teams will often find communication throughout the entire development process, especially the important communication with non-technical stakeholders and domain experts, to be much easier. Using terms from the system's domain reduces technical and IT-specific jargon when discussing requirements and other aspects of the system of interest. This enables developers to talk to the domain experts at eye level.

Abstraction

While performing an analysis of the domain, as recommended in the previous section, we should of course be careful not to model a reproduction of the entire real world. We should confine ourselves only to those things that must be represented in our software system to satisfy stakeholder needs and requirements. We only need an excerpt from the real world, reduced to the details that are relevant to realize the system's use cases. **This reduction to those details that are necessary to satisfy requirements is called** *abstraction.*

For instance, if we want to represent a customer in a bookstore system, it is of no interest which blood type this customer has. On the other hand, for a software system from the medical domain, for example a patient management system, blood type can be a very important detail.

Choose a Hierarchical Decomposition

Let's consider a well-known physical system from the automotive domain: a car. A car is a composition of several parts, for example, the body, engine, gears, wheels, seats, etc. Each of these parts consists of smaller parts. Take for instance the car's engine (let's assume that it is a combustion engine, and not an electric motor). The engine consists of the cylinder block, the gasoline ignition pump, the driving shaft, the camshaft, pistons, an engine control unit (ECU), a coolant subsystem, etc. The coolant subsystem again consists of a heat exchanger, coolant pump, coolant reservoir, fan, thermostat, and the heater core. The decomposition of the car can theoretically be continued to the smallest screw. And every identified subsystem or part has a well-defined responsibility. Only when you have all parts together, assembled in the right way, do you have a car that provides the services that drivers expect.

Complex software systems can be considered in the same way. They can be decomposed hierarchically into coarse-to-fine-grained modules. That helps developers cope with the system's complexity, provides more flexibility, and fosters reusability, maintainability, and testability. A generalized decomposition of such a software system is depicted in Figure 6-1.

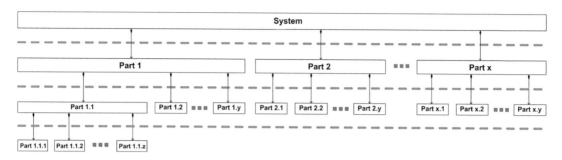

Figure 6-1. *The basic scheme of a hierarchically broken down system*

You may also have noticed the areas separated by horizontal, dashed grey lines in Figure 6-1. These are the **levels of abstraction**. The whole software system is on the highest abstraction level. This system is formed by interconnecting and orchestrating modules of the next lower level of abstraction, in this example designated as "Part 1," "Part 2," etc. These parts are again assembled from smaller modules of the next level of abstraction, just as it happened with our car example.

If one applies this hierarchical breaking down over different levels of abstraction to a software system, it is noticeable that the elements on the higher levels represent concepts of the domain, e.g. pure business logic, whereas it becomes more and more technical on the lower levels.

At this point, it's time to introduce two further principles important to finding a reasonable modularization for a software system: the **Single Responsibility Principle (SRP)** and the **Single Level of Abstraction (SLA).**

Single Responsibility Principle (SRP)

The *Single Responsibility Principle* (SRP) states that each software unit—and these include, among others, modules, classes, and functions—should have only one single, well-defined responsibility.

SRP is based on the general principle of cohesion discussed in Chapter 3. If a software module has a well-defined responsibility, also its cohesion is typically strong.

But what exactly is a responsibility? In literature we can often find the explanation that there must only be one reason to change a software unit. And a frequently mentioned example is that this rule is violated when the unit needs to be changed due to new or changed requirements of different aspects of the system.

These aspects can be, for example, device driver and UI. If the same software unit must be changed, either because the interface of a device driver has changed, or a new requirement regarding the graphical user interface has to be implemented, then this class has obviously too many responsibilities.

Another type of aspect relates to the system's domain. If the same software unit must be changed, either because there are new requirements regarding the customer management, or there are new requirements regarding the invoicing, this software unit has too many responsibilities.

If we look again at the general hierarchical decomposition of a system as depicted in Figure 6-1, we can see that on every hierarchy level, every depicted part and software unit should have one well-defined and clear responsibility.

Single Level of Abstraction (SLA)

The principle of *Single Level of Abstraction* (SLA) states that each software unit—and this includes all units mentioned in the section on the SRP—should be composed of parts that are all at the next lower level of abstraction.

Software units usually have different levels of abstraction. For example, take a method of a class. The instructions within this method should all be at the same level of abstraction. Assigning a value to one of the class's attribute is on a lower level of abstraction than calling another method from within that method. The reason for this is that a method call can conceal the execution of a significant amount of complex logic.

If you take a look at the literature, the SLA is always only explained on the basis of the lines of code within a function or method. However, the principle should also be applied to the software units above the functions and methods, e.g., to larger software components. The building blocks that make up the software component, maybe a bunch of collaborating classes, should all be at the same next lower level of abstraction.

Why is this principle important?

First of all, the *single level of abstraction* fosters the readability of the code significantly. Mixing levels of abstraction can be very challenging for readers of the code, because our brain must permanently handle a mental shift between thinking about higher-level concepts and low-level implementation details.

Another great advantage is that SLA harmonizes extremely well with the aforementioned principles SRP, the practice of hierarchical decomposition, and especially with the domain-centric approach.

The Whole Enchilada

Now that we have worked through all the principles helping developers find a good modularization for a software system, we lump them all together to see how they overlap, support each other, or interact with each other. Let's recap once again.

The *single responsibility principle* (SRP) is an amplification of the general principle of cohesion, which we know from Chapter 3. It states that each module we create should have a clearly defined responsibility and perform only one task. To discover these responsibilities, it is strongly recommended to use a domain-centered method and perform domain analysis to approach the problem from a stakeholder's perspective and to make the modules and their interactions a model of an excerpt of the real world. While doing this, we will discover modules that are on different levels of abstraction: Large components that are responsible for an entire sub-area, down to small modules that solve minor subtasks. This will lead us to a model as it is generally depicted in Figure 6-1; we get a hierarchical decomposition of our software system. Modules on the same hierarchy level should also have the same level of abstraction; remember the SLA principle.

After this general introduction to the topic of modularization, let's now look at a programming paradigm that has been included in C++ from the very beginning and that supports the formation of modules: object-orientation.

Object-Orientation

The historical roots of object-orientation (OO) can be found in the late 1950s. The Norwegian computer scientists Kristen Nygaard and Ole-Johan Dahl carried out simulation calculations for the development and construction of Norway's first nuclear reactor at the military research institute *Norwegian Defense Research Establishment* (NDRE). While developing the simulation programs, the two scientists noted that the procedural programming languages used for that task were not well suited for the complexity of the problems to be addressed. Dahl and Nygaard felt the need for suitable possibilities in those languages to abstract and reproduce the structures, concepts, and processes of the real world.

In 1960, Nygaard moved to the *Norwegian Computing Center* (NCC) that had been established in Oslo two years before. Three years later, Ole-Johan Dahl also joined the NCC. At this private, independent, and nonprofit research foundation, the two scientists developed first ideas and concepts for an—from today's point of view—object-oriented programming language. Nygaard and Dahl were looking for a language that was suitable for all domains and less specialized for certain fields of application, such as *Fortran* for numeric computations and linear algebra or *COBOL,* which is designed especially for business use.

The result of their research activities was the programming language *Simula-67,* an extension of the procedural programming language *ALGOL 60.* The new language introduced classes, subclassing, objects, instance variables, virtual methods, and even a garbage collector. Simula-67 is considered the first object-oriented programming language and has influenced many other programming languages, for example, the full object-oriented programming language Smalltalk, which was designed by Alan Kay and his team in the early 1970s.

While the Danish computer scientist Bjarne Stroustrup worked on his PhD thesis *Communication and Control in Distributed Computer Systems* at University of Cambridge in late 1970, he used Simula-67 and found it pretty useful, but far too slow for practical use. So, he began to search for possibilities to combine the object-oriented concepts of data abstraction from Simula-67 with the high efficiency of low-level programming languages. The most efficient programming language at that time was C, which had been developed by the American computer scientist Dennis Ritchie at *Bell Telephone Laboratories* in the early 1970s. Stroustrup, who joined the *Computer Science Research Center* of the *Bell Telephone Laboratories* in 1979, began to add object-oriented features, like classes, inheritance, strong type checking, and many other things to the C language and named it "C with Classes." In 1983, the name of the language was changed to C++, a word creation by Stroustrup's associate Rick Mascitti, whereby the ++ was inspired by the post-increment operator of the language.

In the following decades, object-orientation became the dominant programming paradigm.

Object-Oriented Thinking

There is a very important point that we need to bear in mind. Just because there are several programming languages available on the market supporting object-oriented concepts, there is absolutely no guarantee that developers using these languages will produce an object-oriented software design automatically. Especially developers who have worked with procedural languages for a long time often have difficulties with the transition to that programming paradigm. Object-orientation is not a simple concept to grasp. It requires that developers view the world in a new way.

Dr. Alan Curtis Kay, who developed object-oriented programming language Smalltalk with some colleagues at *Xerox PARC* in the early 1970s, is well known as one of the fathers of the term "object-orientation." In a documented discussion via email with the German university lecturer Dipl.-Ing. Stefan Ram from *Freie Universität Berlin* from the year 2003, Kay explained what makes object-orientation for him:

> *"I thought of objects being like biological cells and/or individual computers on a network, only able to communicate with messages (so messaging came at the very beginning – it took a while to see how to do messaging in a programming language efficiently enough to be useful). (...) OOP to me means only messaging, local retention and protection and hiding of state-process, and extreme late-binding of all things."*

—Dr. Alan Curtis Kay, American computer scientist,
July 23, 2003 [Ram03]

Biological cells are the smallest structural and functional units of all organisms. They are often called the "building blocks of life." Alan Kay considered software in the same way a biologist sees complex, living organisms. This perspective of Alan Kay should not be surprising, because he has a bachelor's degree in mathematics and molecular biology.

Alan Kay's cells are what we call objects in OO. An object can be considered a "thing" that has structure and behavior. A biological cell has a membrane that surrounds and encapsulates it. This can also be applied to objects in object-orientation. An object should be well encapsulated and offers its services solely through well-defined interfaces.

In addition, Alan Kay emphasized that "messaging" plays a central role for him in object-orientation. However, he does not define exactly what he means by that. Is calling a method named foo() on an object the same as sending a message named "foo" to that object? Or had Alan Kay a message passing infrastructure in mind, such as *CORBA* (Common Object Request Broker Architecture) and similar technologies? Dr. Kay is also a mathematician, so he could also mean a prominent mathematical model of message passing named *Actor model*, which is very popular in concurrent computation.

In any case and whatever Alan Kay had in mind when he talked about messaging, I consider this view interesting and, by and large, applicable to explain the typical structure of an object-oriented program on an abstract level. But Mr. Kay's elucidations are definitely not sufficient enough to answer the following important questions:

- How do I find and form the "cells" (objects)?

- How do I design the publically available interface of those cells?

- How do I govern who can communicate with whom (dependencies)?

Object-orientation (OO) is primarily a mindset, and less a matter of the language used. And it can also be abused and misapplied.

I've seen many programs written in C++, or in a pure OO-language like Java, where classes are used, but these classes only constitute large namespaces wrapping a procedural program. Or slightly sarcastically expressed: Fortran-like programs can be written in nearly any programming language, obviously. On the other hand, every developer who has internalized object-oriented thinking will be able to develop software with an object-oriented design even in languages like ANSI-C, Assembler, or using shell scripts.

Principles for Good Class Design

The widespread and well-known mechanism for the formation of the previously described modules in object-oriented languages is the concept of a class. *Classes* are considered encapsulated software modules that combine structural features (attributes, data members, fields) and behavioral features (member functions, methods, operations) together into one cohesive unit.

In programming languages with object-oriented facilities like C++, classes are the next higher structuring concept above functions. They are often described as the blueprints of the objects (instances). That's reason enough to investigate the concept of classes further. In this section, I give several important clues for designing and writing good classes in C++.

Keep Classes Small

In my career as a software developer, I have seen many classes that were very large. Many thousands of lines of code were no rarity. On closer inspection, I've noticed that these large classes often were only used as namespaces for a more or less procedural program, whose developers commonly did not understand object-orientation.

I think that the problems with such large classes are obvious. If classes contain several thousand lines of code, they are difficult to understand, and their maintainability and testability is usually bad, not to mention reusability. And according to several studies, large classes generally contain a higher number of defects. And, of course, they usually always violate the SRP.

THE GOD CLASS ANTI-PATTERN

In many systems, there are exceptionally large classes with many attributes and several hundred operations. The names of these classes often end with "…Controller," "…Manager," or "…Helpers." Developers often argue that somewhere in the system must be one central instance that pulls the strings and coordinates everything. The results of this way of thinking are such giant classes with very poor cohesion (see the section about strong cohesion in Chapter 3). They are like a convenience store that offers a colorful palette of goods.

Such classes are called *God Classes*, *God Objects*, or sometimes also *The Blob* (*The Blob* is a 1958 American horror/science-fiction film about an alien amoeba that eats the citizens of a village.) This is a so-called *anti-pattern*, a synonym for what is perceived as bad design. A God Class is an untamable beast, horrible to maintain, difficult to understand, not testable, error prone, and has also a huge amount of dependencies to other classes. During the lifecycle of the system, such classes get bigger and bigger. This makes the problems worse.

What has been proven as a good rule for a function's size (see the section entitled "Let Them be Small" in Chapter 4), seems to be also good advice for the size of classes: **Classes should be small!**

If small size is an objective in class design, then the immediate next question is this: How small?

For functions, I've given a number of lines of code in Chapter 4. Wouldn't it be even possible to define a number of lines for classes that would be perceived as good or proper?

In *The ThoughtWorks Anthology* [Thought08], Jeff Bay contributed an essay entitled "Object Calisthenics: 9 Steps to Better Software Design Today" that advises no more than 50 lines of code for a single class.

An upper limit of about 50 lines seems to be out of the question for many developers. It appears that they feel a kind of unexplainable resistance against creating classes. They often argue as follows: "Not more than 50 lines? But that will result in a huge amount of tiny little classes, with just a few members and functions." And then they will surely conjure up an example that is irreducible to classes of such a small size.

I'm convinced that those developers are totally wrong. I'm pretty sure that every software system can be decomposed into such small elementary building blocks.

Yes, if classes are to be small, you will have more of them. But that's OO! In object-oriented software development, a class is an equally natural language element such as a function or a variable. In other words, do not be afraid to create small classes. Small classes are much easier to use, to understand, and to test.

Nonetheless, that leads to a fundamental question: Is the definition of an upper limit for lines of code basically the right way? I think that the metric of lines of code (LOC) can be a helpful indicator. Too many LOCs are a smell. You can take a careful look at classes with more than 50 lines. But it is not necessarily the case that many lines of code are always a problem. A much better criterion is the amount of responsibilities of a class. Classes that follow the SRP are usually small and have few dependencies. They are clear, easy to understand, and can be tested easily.

Responsibility is a much better criterion than the amount of lines of code of a class. There can be classes with 100, 200, or even 500 lines, and it can be perfectly okay if those classes do not violate the single responsibility principle. Nonetheless, a high LOC count can be an indicator. It is a clue that says: "You should take a look at these classes! Maybe everything is fine, but maybe they are so big because they have too many responsibilities."

Open-Closed Principle (OCP)

> *"All systems change during their lifecycles. This must be borne in mind when developing systems expected to last longer than the first version."*
>
> —Ivar Jacobson, Swedish computer scientist, 1992

Another important guideline for any kind of software unit, but especially for class design, is the *open-closed principle* (OCP). It states that software entities (modules, classes, functions, etc.) should be open for extension, but closed for modification.

It is a simple fact that software systems evolve over time. New requirements must constantly be satisfied, and existing requirements must be changed according to customer needs or technology progress. These extensions should be made not only in an elegant manner and with as little effort as possible. They should be especially made in such a way that existing code does not need to be changed. It would be fatal if any new requirement led to a cascade of changes and adjustments in existing and well-tested parts of the software.

One way to support this principle in object-orientation is the concept of *inheritance* (we will discuss another way in the following section). With inheritance it is possible to add new functionality to a class without modifying that class. Furthermore, there are many object-oriented design patterns that foster OCP, such as strategy or decorator (see Chapter 9 about design patterns).

In the section about loose coupling in Chapter 3, we discussed a design that supports OCP very well (see Figure 3-6). There we decoupled a switch and a lamp through an interface. Through this step, the design is closed against modification but pleasantly open for extensions. We can add more switchable devices easily, and we don't need to touch the `Switch` and `Lamp` classes or the `Switchable` interface. And as you can easily imagine, another advantage of such a design is that it is very easy to provide a test double (e.g., a mock object) for testing purposes (see the section about test doubles in Chapter 2).

But is an interface, which in C++ is nothing but an abstract class as a base type of a type hierarchy, the only way to support the OCP?

A Short Comparison of Type Erasure Techniques

"Inheritance is the base class of evil."

—Sean Parent, GoingNative 2013

In January 2020, I was at the conference OOP in Munich, one of the most famous software developer conferences in German-speaking countries and beyond. One evening I had dinner at the hotel with Peter Sommerlad, member of the ISO C++ standardization committee and co-author of the seminal work *Pattern-Oriented Software Architecture*. When we came to talk about the first edition of Clean C++, he gave me an interesting feedback: "Too much virtual."

So, I think it is time to talk about inheritance and dynamic polymorphism—their advantages, disadvantages, and alternatives.

When developers are asked about the central core concept and killer feature of OO, they often mention dynamic polymorphism. Polymorphism, a compound word of the Greek prefix "poly-" for many, and the suffix "-morph" for the form or shape, means the provision of a single interface to entities of different types. In fact, dynamic polymorphism is just a special form of a more general concept in C++ called **type erasure**.

TYPE ERASURE

C++ *type erasure* is a set of techniques that provide a generic interface to various underlying types, while hiding the underlying type information from the client code. In other words, the client code does not know the concrete types; it only knows and uses some kind of abstract interface. Thus, it is also an application of the information hiding principle from Chapter 3 and also makes the code more open-closed.

Note that type erasure in C++ is different than what is known by the same term in Java.

In other words, introducing an OO-style type hierarchy with an abstract base class as the single interface to all derived classes is only one way to realize type erasure. It is certainly not always the best solution under all circumstances, because it has, for instance, a few disadvantageous, although mostly only with small effects on performance. The quality requirements that the software have to satisfy, as well as the constraints of the execution environment, play a very important role here. In a demanding environment with very ambitious performance requirements or limited memory, as is sometimes the case in embedded software development, an OO-based approach can quickly become problematic. Another disadvantage is that we are somehow forced to use them predominantly via pointers or references, and we have to take care about the resource management (memory allocation and deallocation).

This is what Peter Sommerlad meant with his above quoted point of criticism, "too much virtual." But what other forms of type erasure are there in C++?

C had a primitive form of type erasure, namely using a void pointer (void*). An example is the C Standard Library function qsort that uses the well-known QuickSort algorithm to sort a given array (although the C standard does not require it to implement as a QuickSort):

```
void qsort(void* base, size_t nitems, size_t size,
  int(*comparator)(const void*, const void*));
```

The last parameter of qsort() is the function that compares two elements. The idea is to provide a high degree of flexibility so that qsort() can be used for any given type and with user-defined sorting criteria. As you can see, these two elements are represented by two unsafe void pointers.

Even if this is another form of type erasure, functions of the C Standard Library should of course no longer be used in a modern C++ program; remember the section entitled "About Old C-style in C++ Projects" in Chapter 4.

A much safer way to implement type erasure is using C++ templates.

- The `std::function` class template (since C++11; header `<functional>`) is a general-purpose polymorphic function wrapper, i.e., it provides a uniform interface to a function, a function-like object, or a lambda expression with a specified call signature. We discuss this template in more detail in Chapter 7 on functional programming.

- The `std::variant` class template (since C++17; header `<variant>`) represents something like a type-safe union. An instance of a `std::variant` can hold a value typed by one of the types specified as its template arguments. For example, a `std::variant<int, double>` can hold either an integral value or a double precision floating-point value (and in some rare cases when something goes wrong, it can also hold nothing).

- The Algorithm Library (the `<algorithm>` header) defines numerous flexible function templates for a variety of purposes (see the section entitled "Take Advantage of `<algorithm>`" in Chapter 5). For example, there is also a type-safe replacement for the legacy C function `qsort()` discussed previously: `std::sort()`. This function template works for all data types and for different data containers, e.g., old C-style arrays. Furthermore, it is faster than C's `qsort()`, because C++ compilers can optimize templated code.

In addition to these possibilities provided by the C++ Standard Library, developers can of course implement type erasure with templates. Let's consider the example in Listings 6-1 and 6-2 with dynamic polymorphism in OO.

Listing 6-1. A Simple Class Hierarchy

```cpp
#include <string>
#include <memory>
```

```
class Fruit {
public:
  virtual ~Fruit() = default;
  virtual std::string getTypeOfInstanceAsString() const = 0;
};

class Apple final : public Fruit {
   std::string getTypeOfInstanceAsString() const override {
    return "class Apple";
  }
};

class Peach final : public Fruit {
  std::string getTypeOfInstanceAsString() const override {
    return "class Peach";
  }
};

using FruitPointer = std::shared_ptr<Fruit>;
```

Listing 6-2. Concrete Instances Used via Their Abstract Base Classes

```
#include "Fruits.h"
#include <iostream>
#include <vector>

using Fruits = std::vector<FruitPointer>;

int main() {
  FruitPointer fruit1 = std::make_shared<Apple>();
  FruitPointer fruit2 = std::make_shared<Peach>();
  Fruits fruits{ fruit1, fruit2 };

  for (const auto& fruit : fruits) {
    std::cout << fruit->getTypeOfInstanceAsString() << ", ";
  }
  std::cout << std::endl;

  return 0;
}
```

This object-oriented variant of type erasure is type-safe, simple, and straightforward, but has the known small disadvantage of dynamic polymorphism: each lookup in the virtual function table costs a tiny little bit of runtime performance. I think in most applications, this drawback is irrelevant (remember "Be Careful with Optimizations" in Chapter 3), but maybe in some time-critical environments it might be an issue. Furthermore, inheritance is one of the strongest forms of tight coupling; it is white-box-reuse because the derived classes know their base class and its implementation.

Let's now discuss an alternative implementation using C++ templates: The **erasure idiom,** also known as "duck-typing".

DUCK-TYPING

The U.S. writer and poet James Whitcomb Riley (1849 – 1916) was supposed to have coined the phrase: "When I see a bird that walks like a duck and swims like a duck and quacks like a duck, I call that bird a duck."

The so-called "duck test" is a form of abductive reasoning. The test says that people can identify an unknown subject by just studying that subject's behavior or its habitual characteristics. In object-oriented programming, this principle is used to specify the type of a thing or object by its behavioral characteristics, i.e., the functionality that the object has.

Let's first look at the two simple classes Apple and Peach, which now no longer have a common base class. See Listing 6-3.

Listing 6-3. The Apple and Peach Classes Without a Common Base Class Such as Fruit

```
#include <string>

class Apple {
public:
  std::string getTypeOfInstanceAsString() const {
    return "class Apple";
  }
};
```

```cpp
class Peach {
public:
  std::string getTypeOfInstanceAsString() const {
    return "class Peach";
  }
};
```

To enable clients to call the getTypeOfInstanceAsString() method without having to know whether it is an instance of an Apple or a Peach, we need the class template in Listing 6-4.

Listing 6-4. The PolymorphicObjectWrapper Class for Realizing Type Erasure

```cpp
#include <concepts>
#include <memory>
#include <string>

template<typename Class>
concept ClassWithConstCallableMethod = requires (const Class& c) {
  { c.getTypeOfInstanceAsString() } -> std::same_as<std::string>;
};

class PolymorphicObjectWrapper {
public:
  template<ClassWithConstCallableMethod T>
  PolymorphicObjectWrapper(const T& obj) :
    wrappedObject_(std::make_shared<ObjectModel<T>>(obj)) {}

  std::string getTypeOfInstanceAsString() const {
    return wrappedObject_->getTypeOfInstanceAsString();
  }

private:
  struct ObjectConcept {
    virtual ~ObjectConcept() = default;
    virtual std::string getTypeOfInstanceAsString() const = 0;
  };
```

```
  template< ClassWithConstCallableMethod T>
  struct ObjectModel final : ObjectConcept {
    ObjectModel(const T& obj) : object_(obj) {}
    std::string getTypeOfInstanceAsString() const override {
      return object_.getTypeOfInstanceAsString();
    }
  private:
    T object_;
  };

  std::shared_ptr<ObjectConcept> wrappedObject_;
};
```

The PolymorphicObjectWrapper class has a smart pointer named wrappedObject_ that is typed by the inner interface or abstract class ObjectConcept. The inner class template ObjectModel<T> implements this interface. Concrete implementations of ObjectModel<T> (such as ObjectModel<Apple> or ObjectModel<Peach>) are accessed via the abstract class ObjectConcept. The PolymorphicObjectWrapper class forwards calls of the getTypeOfInstanceAsString() method to its ObjectConcept interface, which is overridden by a concrete ObjectModel<T> subclass. That subclass ultimately calls getTypeOfInstanceAsString() on the underlying type. For this to work, all concrete types used for the template parameter T must fulfill an interface contract, i.e., they must have public methods that fit to those that are declared by the inner interface ObjectConcept. We ensure that this requirement is satisfied by defining a C++ concept named ClassWithConstCallableMethod (see the section about concepts in Chapter 5). See Listing 6-5.

Listing 6-5. An Exemplary Use of PolymorphicObjectWrapper

```
#include "Fruits.h"
#include "PolymorphicObjectWrapper.h"
#include <iostream>
#include <vector>

using Fruits = std::vector<PolymorphicObjectWrapper>;

int main() {
  Fruits fruits{ Apple(), Peach() };
```

```
for (const auto& fruit : fruits) {
  std::cout << fruit.getTypeOfInstanceAsString() << ", ";
}
std::cout << std::endl;
return 0;
}
```

The output of stdout, both the object-oriented variant in Listing 6-2 and the implementation with the type erasure idiom in Listing 6-5, are identical:

```
class Apple, class Peach,
```

The advantage of the template-based solution is that the types do not need a common base class and it is still type safe. The template works with all data types that have a public interface expected by them. The downside is that the type erasure idiom has a significant higher degree of complexity compared to the much simpler implementation using dynamic polymorphism. Another drawback is that it has a performance issue during object construction, since the created objects have to be copied into the ObjectModel, resulting in additional copy-constructor calls.

Liskov Substitution Principle (LSP)

> *"Basically, the Liskov Substitution Principle states that you cannot create an octopus by extending a dog with four additional fake legs."*
>
> —Mario Fusco (@mariofusco), September 15, 2013, on Twitter

The object-oriented key concepts of inheritance and polymorphism seem relatively simple at first glance. Inheritance is a taxonomical concept that should be used to build a specialization hierarchy of types, that is, subtypes are derived from a more general type. Polymorphism means in general, that one single interface is provided as an access possibility to objects of different types, as discussed in the former section about type erasure.

So far, so good. But sometimes you get into situations where a subtype does not want to fit into a type hierarchy. Let's discuss a very popular example that is often used to illustrate the problem.

The Square-Rectangle Dilemma

Suppose that we are developing a class library with primitive types of shapes for drawing on a canvas, for example, a `Circle`, a `Rectangle`, a `Triangle`, and a `TextLabel`. Visualized as an UML class diagram, this library might look like Figure 6-2.

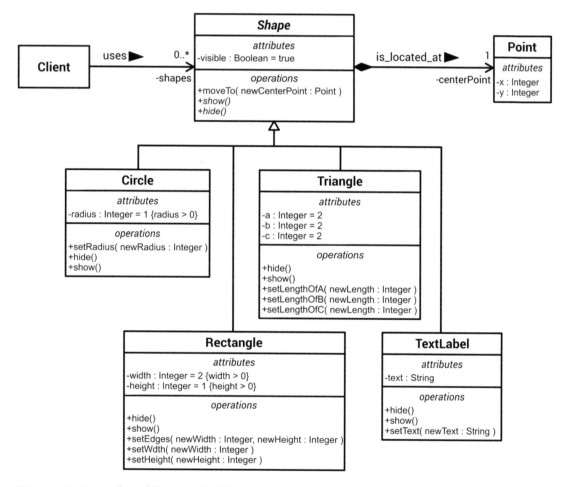

Figure 6-2. *A class library of different shapes*

The abstract base class Shape has attributes and operations that are the same for all specific shapes. For example, it is the same for all shapes how they can be moved from one position to another position on the canvas. However, the Shape cannot know how specific shapes can be shown (drawn) or hidden (erased). Therefore, these operations are abstract, that is, they cannot be (fully) implemented in Shape.

In C++, an implementation of the abstract class Shape (and the class Point that is required by Shape) might look like Listing 6-6.

Listing 6-6. The Point and Shape Classes

```cpp
class Point final {
public:
  Point() = default;
  Point(const unsigned int initialX, const unsigned int initialY) :
    x { initialX }, y { initialY } { }
  void setCoordinates(const unsigned int newX, const unsigned int newY) {
    x = newX;
    y = newY;
  }
  // ...more member functions here...

private:
  unsigned int x { 0 };
  unsigned int y { 0 };
};

class Shape {
public:
  Shape() = default;
  virtual ~Shape() = default;
  void moveTo(const Point& newCenterPoint) {
    hide();
    centerPoint = newCenterPoint;
    show();
  }
  virtual void show() = 0;
  virtual void hide() = 0;
  // ...

private:
  Point centerPoint;
  bool isVisible{ true };
};
```

```
void Shape::show() {
  isVisible = true;
}

void Shape::hide() {
  isVisible = false;
}
```

FINAL SPECIFIER [C++11]

The final specifier, available since C++11, can be used in two ways.

On the one hand, you can use this specifier to avoid individual virtual member functions from being overridden in derived classes, like in this example:

```
class AbstractBaseClass {
public:
  virtual void doSomething() = 0;
};

class Derived1 : public AbstractBaseClass {
public:
  void doSomething() override final {
    //...
  }
};

class Derived2 : public Derived1 {
public:
  void doSomething() override { // Causes a compiler error!
    //...
  }
};
```

In addition, you can also mark a complete class as final, like the class Point in our Shape library. This ensures that a developer cannot use such a class as a base class for inheritance.

```
class NotDerivable final {
  // ...
};
```

Of all concrete classes in the Shapes library, we take an exemplary look at one, the Rectangle. See Listing 6-7.

Listing 6-7. The Important Parts of the Rectangle Class

```cpp
class Rectangle : public Shape {
public:
  Rectangle() = default;
  Rectangle(const unsigned int initialWidth, const unsigned int
  initialHeight) :
    width { initialWidth }, height { initialHeight } { }

  void show() override {
    Shape::show();
    // ...code to show a rectangle here...
  }

  void hide() override {
    Shape::hide();
    // ...code to hide a rectangle here...
  }

  void setWidth(const unsigned int newWidth) {
    width = newWidth;
  }
  void setHeight(const unsigned int newHeight) {
    height = newHeight;
  }

  void setEdges(const unsigned int newWidth, const unsigned int newHeight) {
    width = newWidth;
    height = newHeight;
  }
  // ...

private:
  unsigned int width{ 2 };
  unsigned int height{ 1 };
};
```

The client code wants to use all shapes in a similar fashion, no matter which particular instance (Rectangle, Circle, etc.) it is confronted with. For instance, all shapes should be shown on a canvas at one blow, which can be achieved using the following code:

```
#include "Shapes.h" // Circle, Rectangle, etc.
#include <memory>
#include <vector>

using ShapePtr = std::shared_ptr<Shape>;
using ShapeCollection = std::vector<ShapePtr>;

void showAllShapes(const ShapeCollection& shapes) {
  for (auto& shape : shapes) {
    shape->show();
  }
}

int main() {

  ShapeCollection shapes;
  shapes.push_back(std::make_shared<Circle>());
  shapes.push_back(std::make_shared<Rectangle>());
  shapes.push_back(std::make_shared<TextLabel>());
  // ...etc...

  showAllShapes(shapes);
  return 0;
}
```

Now let's assume that users formulate a new requirement for our library: **they want to have a square!**

Probably everyone is immediately reminded of geometry lessons in school. At that time your teacher may have said that a square is a special kind of rectangle that has four sides of equal length. Thus, a first obvious solution seems to be that we derive a new class called Square from Rectangle, as depicted in Figure 6-3.

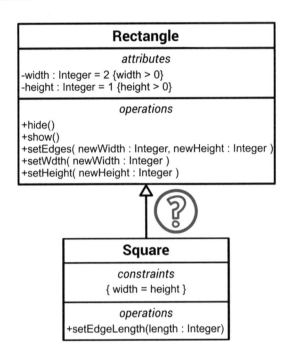

Figure 6-3. *Is deriving a square from the rectangle class a good idea?*

At first glance, this seems to be a feasible solution. The Square inherits the interface and the implementation of Rectangle. This is good to avoid code duplication (see the DRY principle discussed in Chapter 3), because the Square can easily reuse the behavior implemented in Rectangle.

A square just has to fulfill one additional and simple requirement that is shown in the UML diagram as a constraint in class Square: {width = height}. This constraint means that an instance of type Square ensures in all circumstances that its edges are always the same length.

So we first implement our Square by deriving it from our Rectangle:

```
class Square : public Rectangle {
public:
  //...
};
```

But in fact, this is not a good solution!

Note that the Square inherits all operations of the Rectangle. That means that we can do the following with an instance of Square:

```
Square square;
square.setHeight(10);      // Err...changing only the height of a square?!
square.setEdges(10, 20);   // Uh oh!
```

First of all, it would be very puzzling for users of Square to see that it provides a setter with two parameters (remember the principle of least astonishment in Chapter 3). They think: Why are there two parameters? Which parameter is used to set the length of all edges? Must I put both parameters to the same value? What happens if I don't?

The situation is even more dramatic when we do the following:

```
std::unique_ptr<Rectangle> rectangle = std::make_unique<Square>();
// ...and somewhere else in the code...
rectangle->setEdges(10, 20);
```

In this case, the client code uses a setter that makes sense. Both edges of a rectangle can be manipulated independently. That's not a surprise; it's exactly the expectation. However, the result may be weird. The instance of type Square would de facto not be a square after such a call anymore, because it has two different edge lengths. So we have once again committed a violation of the principle of least astonishment, and much worse: we violated the Square's class invariant.

However, one could now argue that we can declare setEdges(), setWidth(), and setHeight() as virtual in the Rectangle class and override these member functions in the Square class with an alternative implementation, which throws an exception in case of unsolicited use. Furthermore, we provide a new member function called setEdge() in the Square class instead, as shown in Listing 6-8.

Listing 6-8. A Bad Implementation of Square That Tries to "Erase" Unwanted Inherited Features

```
#include <stdexcept>
// ...

class IllegalOperationCall : public std::logic_error {
public:
```

```cpp
  explicit IllegalOperationCall(std::string_view message) :
  logic_error(message) { }
};

class Square : public Rectangle {
public:
  Square() : Rectangle { 2, 2 } { }
  explicit Square(const unsigned int edgeLength) :
    Rectangle { edgeLength, edgeLength } { }

  void setEdges([[maybe_unused]] const unsigned int newWidth,
    [[maybe_unused]] const unsigned int newHeight) override {
    throw IllegalOperationCall { ILLEGAL_OPERATION_MSG };
  }

  virtual void setWidth([[maybe_unused]] const unsigned int newWidth) override {
    throw IllegalOperationCall { ILLEGAL_OPERATION_MSG };
  }

  virtual void setHeight([[maybe_unused]] const unsigned int newHeight)
  override {
    throw IllegalOperationCall { ILLEGAL_OPERATION_MSG };
  }

  void setEdgeLength(const unsigned int length) {
    Rectangle::setEdges(length, length);
  }

private:
  static constexpr char* const ILLEGAL_OPERATION_MSG {
    "Unsolicited call of a prohibited   operation on an instance of class
    Square!" };
};
```

Well, I think it's obvious that that would be a terribly bad design. It violates a fundamental principle of object-orientation, that a derived class must not delete inherited properties of their base class. It is definitely not a solution to our problem. First, the new setter setEdge() would not be visible if we want to use an instance of Square as a Rectangle. Furthermore, all the other setters throw an exception if they are used. This is really abysmal! It ruined object-orientation.

So, what's the fundamental problem here? Why does the obviously sensible derivation of a Square class from a Rectangle cause so many difficulties?

The explanation is this: Deriving Square from Rectangle violates an important principle in object-oriented software design—the **Liskov Substitution Principle** (LSP)!

Barbara Liskov, an American computer scientist who is an institute professor at the *Massachusetts Institute of Technology* (MIT), and Jeannette Wing, who was the President's Professor of Computer Science at *Carnegie Mellon University* until 2013, formulated the principle in a 1994 paper as follows:

> *"Let q(x) be a property provable about objects x of type T. Then q(y) should be provable for objects y of type S, where S is a subtype of T."*
>
> —Barbara Liskov, Jeanette Wing [Liskov94]

Well, that's not necessarily a definition for everyday use. A definition suitable for everyday use is that derived classes must fully satisfy the contract of their base class, so that clients using a pointer or reference typed with this base class can use instances of the derived classes without knowing them.

In fact, that means the following: Derived types must be completely substitutable for their base types. In our example this is not possible. An instance of the Square type cannot substitute a Rectangle. The reason for that lies in the constraint {width = height} (a so-called class invariant) that would be enforced by the Square, but the Rectangle cannot fulfill that constraint.

The Liskov Substitution Principle stipulates the following rules for type and class hierarchies:

- The preconditions (see the section entitled "Prevention Is Better Than Aftercare" in Chapter 5 about preconditions) of a base class cannot be strengthened in a derived subclass.

- Postconditions (see the section entitled "Prevention Is Better Than Aftercare" in Chapter 5) of a base class cannot be weakened in a derived subclass.

- All invariants of a base class must not be changed or violated through a derived subclass.

- The history constraint (also known as the "history rule"): The internal state of an instance of a class should only be changed through its public interface, i.e., through public method calls (encapsulation). Of course, a newly derived class from this class is basically allowed to introduce new public methods. However, the history constraint states that these newly introduced methods in the derived class are not allowed to modify the state of its instances in a manner prohibited according to the base class. In other words, a derived class should never ignore the constraints imposed by its base class, because that would break any client code that relies on these constraints. For instance, if the base class is designed to be the blueprint for an immutable object (see Chapter 9 about immutable classes), the derived class should not invalidate this property of immutability with the help of newly introduced member functions. That's, by the way, the reason that immutable classes should be declared as `final`!

The interpretation of the generalization relationship (the arrow between Square and Rectangle) in the class diagram in Figure 6-2 is often translated with "...IS A...": Square IS A Rectangle. But that could be misleading. In mathematics it may be possible to say that a square is a special kind of rectangle, but in programming it is not!

To deal with this problem, the clients have to know with which specific type they are working. Some developers might now say, "No problem, this can be done by using *Run-Time Type Information* (RTTI)." See Listing 6-9.

RUN-TIME TYPE INFORMATION (RTTI)

The term *run-time type information* (sometimes also *run-time type identification*) denotes a C++ mechanism to access information about an object's data type at runtime. The general concept behind RTTI is called *type introspection* and is available also in other programming languages, like Java.

In C++, the `typeid` operator (defined in the `<typeinfo>` header) and `dynamic_cast<T>` (see the section about C++ casts in Chapter 4) belong to RTTI. For instance, to determine the class of an object at runtime, you can write:

```
const std::type_info& typeInformationAboutObject = typeid(instance);
```

The `const` reference of type `std::type_info` (also defined in the `<typeinfo>` header) now holds information about the object's class, for example, the class's name. Since C++11, a hash code is also available (`std::type_info::hash_code()`), which is identical to the `std::type_info` objects referring to the same type.

It is important to know that RTTI is available only to classes that are polymorphic, that is, for classes that have at least one virtual function, either directly or through inheritance. In addition, RTTI can be turned on or off on some compilers. For example, when using the gcc (GNU Compiler Collection), RTTI can be disabled by using the `-fno-rtti` option.

Listing 6-9. Another "Hack": Using RTTI to Distinguish Between Different Types of Shapes During Runtime

```
using ShapePtr = std::shared_ptr<Shape>;
using ShapeCollection = std::vector<ShapePtr>;
//...

void resizeAllShapes(const ShapeCollection& shapes) {
  try {
    for (const auto& shape : shapes) {
      const auto rawPointerToShape = shape.get();
      if (typeid(*rawPointerToShape) == typeid(Rectangle)) {
        Rectangle* rectangle = dynamic_cast<Rectangle*>(rawPointerToShape);
        rectangle->setEdges(10, 20);
        // Do more Rectangle-specific things here...
      } else if (typeid(*rawPointerToShape) == typeid(Square)) {
        Square* square = dynamic_cast<Square*>(rawPointerToShape);
        square->setEdge(10);
      } else {
        // ...
      }
    }
  } catch (const std::bad_typeid& ex) {
    // Attempted a typeid of NULL pointer!
  }
}
```

Don't do this! This cannot, and it should not, be the appropriate solution, especially not in a clean and modern C++ program. Many of the benefits of object-orientation, such as dynamic polymorphism, are counteracted.

Caution   Whenever you are compelled to use RTTI in your program to distinguish between different types, it is a distinct "design smell," that is, an obvious indicator of bad object-oriented software design!

In addition, our code will be heavily polluted with lousy if-else constructs and the readability will go down the drain. And as if this wasn't enough, the try-catch construct also makes it clear that something could go wrong.

But what can we do?

First of all, we should take another careful look at what a square really is.

From a pure mathematical point of view, a square can be regarded as a rectangle with equal edge lengths. So far, so good. But this definition cannot be directly transferred into an object-oriented type hierarchy. **A square is not a subtype of a rectangle!**

Instead, having a square shape is merely a special state of a rectangle. If a rectangle has identical edge lengths, which is solely a state of the rectangle, we usually give such particular rectangle a special name in our natural language: we then speak about a square!

That means that we just need to add an inspector method to our Rectangle class to query its state, allowing us to waive an explicit class Square. According to the KISS principle (see Chapter 3), this solution might be completely sufficient to satisfy the new requirement. Furthermore, we can provide a convenient setter method to clients to set both edge lengths equally. See Listing 6-10.

Listing 6-10. A Simple Solution Without an Explicit Class Called Square

```cpp
class Rectangle : public Shape {
public:
  // ...
  void setEdgesToEqualLength(const unsigned int newLength) {
    setEdges(newLength, newLength);
  }
```

```
  bool isSquare() const {
    return width == height;
  }
  //...
};
```

Favor Composition over Inheritance

But what can we do if an explicit class Square is uncompromisingly required, for example, because someone demands it? Well, if that is the case, we should never ever inherit from Rectangle, but from the Shape class, as depicted in Figure 6-4. In order not to violate the DRY principle, we use an instance of the Rectangle class for the Square's internal implementation.

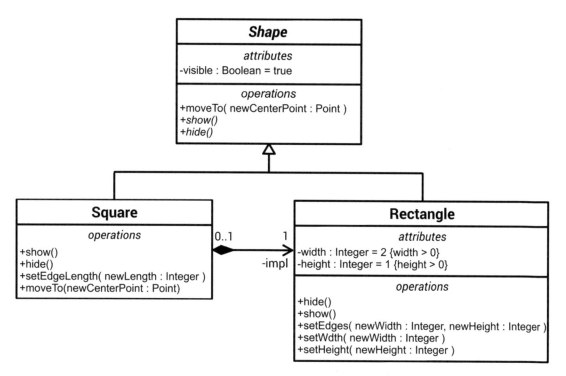

Figure 6-4. *The Square uses and delegates to an embedded instance of Rectangle*

Expressed in source code, the implementation of this Square class would look like Listing 6-11.

Listing 6-11. The Square Delegates All Method Calls to an Embedded Instance of Rectangle

```cpp
class Square : public Shape {
public:
  Square() {
    impl.setEdges(2, 2);
  }

  explicit Square(const unsigned int edgeLength) {
    impl.setEdges(edgeLength, edgeLength);
  }

  void setEdgeLength(const unsigned int length) {
    impl.setEdges(length, length);
  }

  virtual void moveTo(const Point& newCenterPoint) override {
    impl.moveTo(newCenterPoint);
  }

  virtual void show() override {
    impl.show();
  }

  virtual void hide() override {
    impl.hide();
  }

private:
  Rectangle impl;
};
```

Perhaps you've noticed that the moveTo() method was also overwritten. To this end, the moveTo() method must also be made virtual in the Shape class. We must override it, because the moveTo() inherited from Shape operates on the centerPoint of the base class Shape, and not on the embedded instance of the Rectangle used. This is one small drawback of this solution: some parts inherited from the base class Shape are idle.

Obviously, with this solution we will lose the possibility that an instance of Square can be assigned to a Rectangle:

```
std::unique_ptr<Rectangle> rectangle = std::make_unique<Square>();
// Compiler error!
```

The principle behind this solution to cope with inheritance problems in OO is called "favor composition over inheritance" (FCoI), sometimes also named "favor delegation over inheritance." For the reuse of functionality, object-oriented programming basically has two options: inheritance ("white box reuse") and composition or delegation ("black box reuse"). It is sometimes better to treat another type in a way as it would be a black box, that is, to use it only through its well-defined public interface, instead of deriving a subtype from this type. Reuse by composition/delegation fosters looser coupling between classes than reuse by inheritance.

Interface Segregation Principle (ISP)

We know interfaces as a way to foster loose coupling between classes. In a previous section about the open-closed principle, you learned that interfaces are a way to have an extension and variation point in the code. An interface is like a contract: classes may request services through this contract, which may be offered by other classes that fulfill the contract.

But what problems can arise when these contracts become too extensive, that is, if an interface becomes too broad or "fat"? The consequences can best be demonstrated with an example. Check out the interface in Listing 6-12.

Listing 6-12. An Interface for Birds

```
class Bird {
public:
  virtual ~Bird() = default;

  virtual void fly() = 0;
  virtual void eat() = 0;
  virtual void run() = 0;
  virtual void tweet() = 0;
};
```

This interface is implemented by several concrete birds, for example, by a `Sparrow`. See Listing 6-13.

Listing 6-13. The Sparrow Class Overrides and Implements All Pure Virtual Member Functions of Bird

```cpp
class Sparrow : public Bird {
public:
  void fly() override {
    //...
  }
  void eat() override {
    //...
  }
  void run() override {
    //...
  }
  void tweet() override {
    //...
  }
};
```

So far, so good. And now assume that we have another concrete `Bird`: a `Penguin`. See Listing 6-14.

Listing 6-14. The Penguin Class

```cpp
class Penguin : public Bird {
public:
  void fly() override {
    // ???
  }
    //...
};
```

Although a penguin is undoubtedly a bird, they cannot fly. Although our interface is relatively small, because it declares only four simple member functions, these declared services cannot, obviously, be offered by each bird species.

The *interface segregation principle* (ISP) states that an interface should not be bloated with member functions that are not required by implementing classes, or that these classes cannot implement in a meaningful way. In our example, the Penguin class cannot provide a meaningful implementation for Bird::fly(), but Penguin is enforced to overwrite that member function.

The interface segregation principle says that we should segregate a "fat interface" into smaller and highly cohesive interfaces. The resulting small interfaces are also referred to as *role interfaces*. See Listing 6-15.

Listing 6-15. The Three Role Interfaces as a Better Alternative to the Broad Bird Interface

```cpp
class Lifeform {
public:
  virtual ~Lifeform() = default;
  virtual void eat() = 0;
  virtual void move() = 0;
};

class Flyable {
public:
  virtual ~Flyable() = default;
  virtual void fly() = 0;
};

class Audible {
public:
  virtual ~Audible() = default;
  virtual void makeSound() = 0;
};
```

These small role interfaces can now be combined very flexibly. This means that the implementing classes only need to provide a meaningful functionality for those declared member functions, which they can implement in a sensible manner. See Listing 6-16.

Listing 6-16. The Sparrow and Penguin Classes Implement the Relevant Interfaces

```cpp
class Sparrow : public Lifeform, public Flyable, public Audible {
  //...
};

class Penguin : public Lifeform, public Audible {
  //...
};
```

Acyclic Dependency Principle

Sometimes there is the need for two classes to "know" each other. For example, let's assume that we're developing a web shop. So that certain use cases can be implemented, the class representing a customer in this web shop must know its related account. For other use cases, it is necessary that the account can access its owner, which is a customer.

In UML, this mutual relationship looks like Figure 6-5.

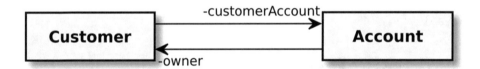

Figure 6-5. *The association relationships between the Customer and Account classes*

This is known as a *circular dependency*. Both classes, either directly or indirectly, depend on each other. In this case, there are only two classes. Circular dependencies can also occur with several software units involved.

Let's look at how that circular dependency shown in Figure 6-4 can be implemented in C++.

What definitely would not work in C++ is Listings 6-17 and 6-18.

Listing 6-17. The Contents of the Customer.h File

```
#pragma once

#include "Account.h"

class Customer {
// ...
private:
  Account account_;
};
```

Listing 6-18. The Contents of the Account.h File

```
#pragma once

#include "Customer.h"

class Account {
private:
  Customer owner_;
};
```

I think that the problem is obvious here. As soon as someone used the Account or Customer classes, they would trigger a chain reaction while compiling. For example, the Account owns an instance of Customer who owns an instance of Account who owns an instance of Customer, and so on, and so on... Due to the strict processing order of C++ compilers, this implementation will result in compiler errors.

These compiler errors can be avoided, for example, by using references or pointers in combination with forward declarations. A *forward declaration* is the declaration of an identifier (e.g., of a type, like a class) without defining the full structure of that identifier. Therefore, such types are sometimes also called *incomplete types*. Hence, they can only be used for pointers or references, but not for an instance member variable, because the compiler knows nothing about its size. See Listings 6-19 and 6-20.

Listing 6-19. The Modified Customer with a Forward-Declared Account

```
#pragma once

class Account;

class Customer {
public:
  // ...
  void setAccount(Account* account) {
    account_ = account;
  }
  // ...
private:
  Account* account_;
};
```

Listing 6-20. The Modified Account with a Forward-Declared Customer

```
#pragma once

class Customer;

class Account {
public:
  //...
  void setOwner(Customer* customer) {
    owner_ = customer;
  }
  //...
private:
  Customer* owner_;
};
```

Hand on heart: do you feel a little bit unwell with this solution? If yes, it's for good reasons! The compiler errors are gone, but this "fix" produces a bad gut feeling. Listing 6-21 shows how both classes are used.

Listing 6-21. Creating the Instances of Customer and Account and Wiring Them Circularly Together

```
#include "Account.h"
#include "Customer.h"
// ...
  Account* account = new Account { };
  Customer* customer = new Customer { };
  account->setOwner(customer);
  customer->setAccount(account);
// ...
```

I'm sure that a serious problem is obvious: what happens if, for example, the instance of Account will be deleted, but the instance of Customer still exists? Well, the instance of Customer will contain a dangling pointer then, that is, a pointer to No-Man's Land! Using or dereferencing such a pointer can cause serious issues, like undefined behavior and application crashes. Don't have high hopes: using std::shared_ptr<T> instead of regular pointers is not a solution either. On the contrary, that will result in memory leaks.

Forward declarations are pretty useful for certain things, but using them to deal with circular dependencies is a really bad practice. It is a creepy workaround that is supposed to conceal a fundamental design problem.

The problem is the circular dependency itself. This is bad design. The Customer and Account classes cannot be separated. Thus, they cannot be used independently of one another, nor are they testable independently of one another. This makes unit testing considerably more difficult.

The problem gets even worse if we have the situation depicted in Figure 6-6.

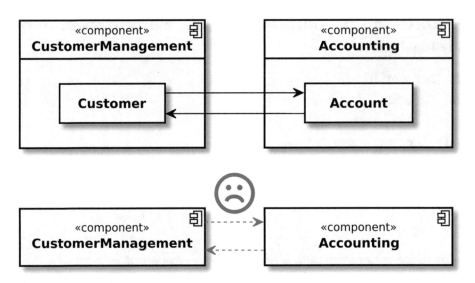

Figure 6-6. *The impact of circular dependencies between classes in different components*

The Customer and Account classes are each located in different components. Perhaps there are many more classes in each of these components, but these two classes have a circular dependency. The consequence is that this circular dependency has a impact on the architectural level. The circular dependency at the class level leads to a circular dependency at the component level. CustomerManagement and Accounting are tightly coupled (remember the section about loose coupling in Chapter 3) and cannot be reused independently. And of course, also, an independent component test is not possible anymore. The modularization on architecture level has been practically reduced to absurdity.

The *acyclic dependency principle* states that the dependency graph of components or classes should have no cycles. Circular dependencies are a bad form of tight coupling and should be avoided at all costs.

Don't sweat it! It is **always** possible to break a circular dependency, and the following section will show you how to avoid or break them.

Dependency Inversion Principle (DIP)

In the previous section, we experienced that circular dependencies are bad and should be avoided under all circumstances. As with many other problems related to unwanted dependencies, the concept of the interface (in C++, interfaces are simulated using abstract classes) is our friend when dealing with such troubles.

The goal should therefore be to break the circular dependency without losing the necessary possibility that the Customer class can access the Account class and vice versa.

The first step is that we no longer allow one of the two classes to have direct access to the other class. Instead we allow access only via an interface. Basically, it does not matter from which one of classes (Customer or Account) the interface is extracted. I've decided to extract an interface named Owner from Customer. Exemplary, the Owner interface declares just one pure virtual member function, which must be overridden by classes that implement this interface. See Listings 6-22 and 6-23.

Listing 6-22. An Exemplary Implementation of the New interface Owner (Owner.h)

```
#pragma once

#include <memory>
#include <string>

class Owner {
public:
  virtual ~Owner() = default;
  virtual std::string getName() const = 0;
};

using OwnerPtr = std::shared_ptr<Owner>;
```

Listing 6-23. The Customer Class Implements the Owner Interface (Customer.h)

```
#pragma once

#include "Owner.h"
#include "Account.h"

class Customer : public Owner {
public:
  void setAccount(AccountPtr account) {
    account_ = account;
  }
```

```cpp
  std::string getName() const override {
    // return the Customer's name here...
  }
  // ...

private:
  AccountPtr account_;
  // ...
};

using CustomerPtr = std::shared_ptr<Customer>;
```

As can easily be seen, the `Customer` class still knows its `Account`. But when we take a look at the changed implementation of the `Account` class, there is no dependency to `Customer` anymore. See Listing 6-24.

Listing 6-24. The Changed Implementation of the Account Class (Account.h)

```cpp
#pragma once

#include "Owner.h"

class Account {
public:
  void setOwner(OwnerPtr owner) {
    owner_ = owner;
  }
  //...

private:
  OwnerPtr owner_;
};

using AccountPtr = std::shared_ptr<Account>;
```

Depicted as an UML class diagram, the changed design at class level is shown in Figure 6-7.

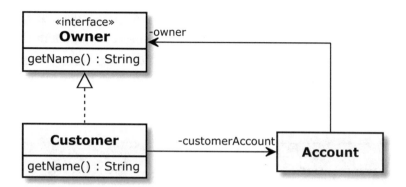

Figure 6-7. *Adding the interface has eliminated the circular dependency on class level*

Excellent! With this first step in the redesign, there are no more circular dependencies at the class level. The Account class knows absolutely nothing about the Customer class. But how does the situation look from the component level, as depicted in Figure 6-8?

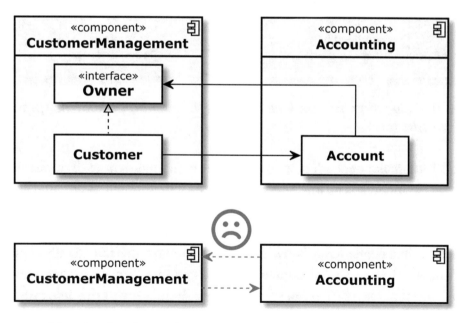

Figure 6-8. *The circular dependency between the components is still there*

Unfortunately, the circular dependency between the components has not been broken. The two association relationships still go from one element in the one component to one element in the other component. However, the step to achieve this goal is blindingly easy: we need to relocate the Owner interface to the other component, as depicted in Figure 6-9.

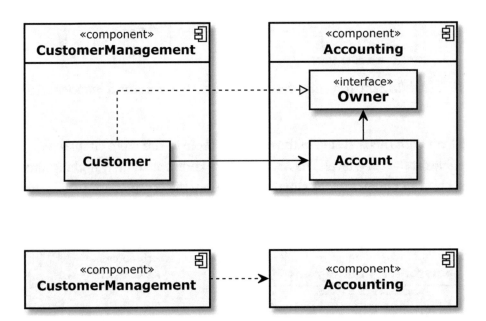

Figure 6-9. *Relocating the interface also fixes the circular dependency problem at the architecture level*

Great! The circular dependencies between the components have disappeared. The Accounting component is no longer dependent on CustomerManagement, and as a result, the quality of the modularization has been significantly improved. Furthermore, the Accounting component can now be tested independently.

In fact, the bad dependency between both components was not literally eliminated. On the contrary, through the introduction of the Owner interface, we have one additional dependency at the class level. **What we really have done is invert the dependency.**

The *dependency inversion principle* (DIP) is an object-oriented design principle that decouples software modules. The principle states that the basis of an object-oriented design is not the special properties of concrete software modules. Instead, their common features should be consolidated in a shared used abstraction (e.g., an interface). Robert C. Martin a.k.a. "Uncle Bob," formulated the principle as follows:

> *"A. High-level modules should not depend on low-level modules. Both should depend on abstractions.*
>
> *B. Abstractions should not depend on details. Details should depend on abstractions."*

—Robert C. Martin [Martin03]

Note   The terms "high-level modules" and "low-level modules" in this quote can be misleading. They refer not necessarily to their conceptual position within a layered architecture. A high-level module in this particular case is a software module that requires external services from another module, the so-called low-level module. High-level modules are those where an action is invoked; low-level modules are the ones where the action is performed. In some cases, these two categories may also be located on different levels of a software architecture (e.g., layers), or as in our example in different components.

The principle of dependency inversion is fundamental for what is perceived as a good object-oriented design. It fosters the development of reusable software modules by defining the provided and required external services solely through abstractions (e.g., interfaces). Consistently applied to our discussed case, we would also have to redesign the direct dependency between the Customer and the Account accordingly, as depicted in Figure 6-10.

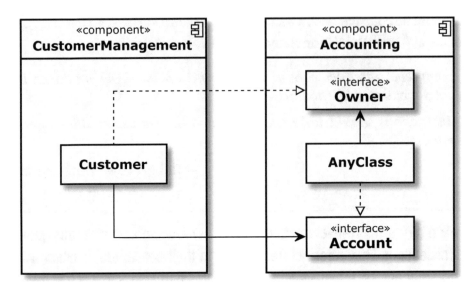

Figure 6-10. *Dependency inversion principle applied*

The classes in both components are solely dependent on abstractions. Therefore, it is no longer important to the client of the Accounting component which class requires the Owner interface or provides the Account interface (remember the section about information hiding in Chapter 3). I have insinuated this circumstance by introducing a class that is named AnyClass, which implements Account and uses Owner.

For instance, if we have to change or replace the Customer class now, for example, because we want to mount the Accounting against a test fixture for component testing, then nothing has to be changed in the AnyClass class to achieve it. This also applies to the reverse case.

The dependency inversion principle allows software developers to design dependencies between modules purposefully, that is, to define in which direction dependencies are pointing. You want to inverse the dependency between the components, that is, Accounting should be dependent on CustomerManagement? No problem: simply relocate both interfaces from Accounting to the CustomerManagement and the dependency turns around. Bad dependencies, which reduce the maintainability and the testability of the code, can be elegantly redesigned and reduced.

Don't Talk to Strangers (The Law of Demeter)

Do you remember the car I talked about earlier in this chapter? I described this car as a composition of several parts, for example, body, engine, gears, and so on. And I explained that these parts can consist of parts, which for themselves can also consist of several parts, etc. This leads to a hierarchical top-down decomposition of a car. Of course, a car can have a driver who wants to drive it.

Visualized as an UML class diagram, an excerpt from the car's decomposition can look like Figure 6-11.

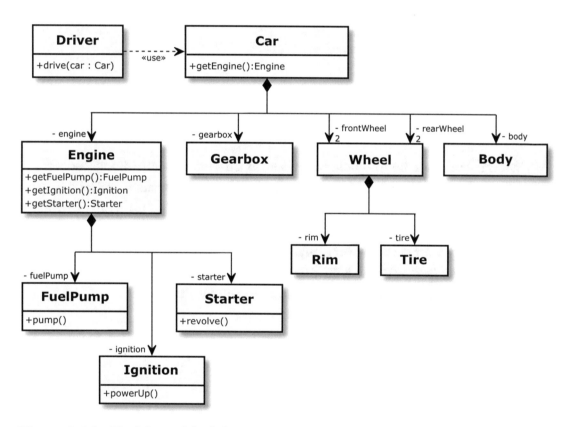

Figure 6-11. *The hierarchical decomposition of a simple car*

According to the single responsibility principle discussed in Chapter 5, everything is fine, because every class has a well-defined responsibility.

Now let's assume that the driver wants to drive the car. This could be implemented in the Driver class, as shown in Listing 6-25.

Listing 6-25. An Excerpt from the Implementation of the Driver Class

```
class Driver {
public:
// ...
  void drive(Car& car) const {
    Engine& engine = car.getEngine();
    FuelPump& fuelPump = engine.getFuelPump();
    fuelPump.pump();
    Ignition& ignition = engine.getIgnition();
    ignition.powerUp();
    Starter& starter = engine.getStarter();
    starter.revolve();
  }
// ...
};
```

What is the problem here? Would you expect as a driver of a car to directly access your car's engine, to turn on the fuel pump, turn on the ignition system, and let the starter revolve? I go even further: are you even interested in the fact that your car consists of these parts if you just want to drive it?!

I'm pretty sure your clear answer would be no!

Now let's take a look at Figure 6-12, depicting the relevant part from the UML class diagram to see what impact this implementation has on the design.

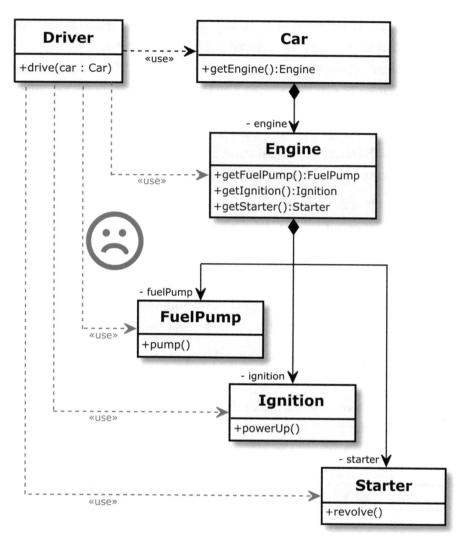

Figure 6-12. *The bad dependencies of the Driver class*

As can easily be seen in Figure 6-12, the Driver class has many awkward dependencies. The Driver is not only dependent from Engine. The class has also several dependency relationships to parts of the Engine. It is easy to imagine that this has some disadvantageous consequences.

What would happen, for example, if the combustion engine was replaced by an electric power train? An electric drive doesn't have a fuel pump, an ignition system, and a starter. Thus, the consequences would be that the implementation of the class driver would have to be adapted. This violates the open-closed principle (see the earlier section). Furthermore, all public getters that expose the innards of the Car and the Engine to their environment are violating the information hiding principle (see Chapter 3).

Essentially, the previous software design violates the *Law of Demeter* (LoD), also known as the *Principle of Least Knowledge*. The Law of Demeter can be regarded as a principle that says something like "don't talk to strangers", or "only talk to your immediate neighbors." This principle states that you should do shy programming, and the goal is to govern the communication structure within an object-oriented design.

The Law of Demeter postulates the following rules:

- A member function is allowed to call other member functions in its own class scope directly.

- A member function is allowed to call member functions on member variables that are in its class scope directly.

- If a member function has parameters, the member function is allowed to call the member functions of these parameters directly.

- If a member function creates local objects, the member function is allowed to call member functions on those local objects.

If one of these four aforementioned kinds of member function calls returns an object that is structurally farther than the immediate neighbors of the class, **it is forbidden to call a member function on that object.**

WHY THIS RULE IS NAMED LAW OF DEMETER

The name of this principle goes back to the *Demeter Project* about aspect-oriented software development, where these rules were formulated and strictly applied. The Demeter Project was a research project in the late 1980s with a main focus on making software easier to maintain and expand through adaptive programming. The Law of Demeter was discovered and proposed by Ian M. Holland and Karl Lieberherr who worked in that project. In Greek mythology, Demeter is the sister of Zeus and the goddess of agriculture.

So, what is now the solution in our example to get rid of the bad dependencies? Quite simply, we should ask ourselves what does a driver really want to do? The answer is easy: he wants to start the car! See Listing 6-26.

Listing 6-26. The Only Thing the Refactored Class Driver Has To Do Is Start the Car

```
class Driver {
public:
// ...
  void drive(Car& car) const {
    car.start();
  }
// ...
};
```

And what does the car do with this start command? Also, quite simple: it delegates this method call to its engine. See Listing 6-27.

Listing 6-27. The Car Delegates the Start Command to its Engine

```
class Car {
public:
// ...
  void start() {
    engine.start();
  }
// ...
private:
  Engine engine;
};
```

Last but not least, the engine knows how it can execute the start process by calling the appropriate member functions in the correct order on its parts, which are its immediate neighbors in the software design. See Listing 6-28.

Listing 6-28. The Engine Internally Causes Everything to Be Fired Up

```
class Engine {
public:
// ...
  void start() {
    fuelPump.pump();
    ignition.powerUp();
```

```
    starter.revolve();
  }
// ...
private:
  FuelPump fuelPump;
  Ignition ignition;
  Starter starter;
};
```

The positive effect of these changes on the object-oriented design can be very clearly seen in the class diagram depicted in Figure 6-13.

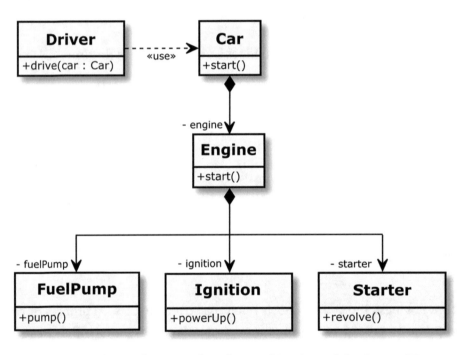

Figure 6-13. *Fewer dependencies after the application of the Law of Demeter*

The annoying dependencies of the driver to the car's parts are gone. Instead, the driver can start the car, regardless of the internal structure of the car. The Driver class doesn't know that there is an Engine, a FuelPump, etc. All those bad public getter functions, which revealed the innards of the car or the engine to all other classes, are gone. This also means that changes to the Engine and its parts have very local impacts and will not result in cascading changes straight through the whole design.

Following the Law of Demeter when designing software can reduce the number of dependencies significantly. This leads to loose coupling and fosters both the information hiding principle and the open-closed principle. As with many other principles and rules, too, there may be some justified exceptions, where a developer must vary from this principle for very good reasons.

Avoid Anemic Classes

In several projects, I've seen classes that looked like the one in Listing 6-29.

Listing 6-29. A Class Without Functionality that Serves Only as a Bucket for a Bunch of Data

```
class Customer {
public:
  void setId(const unsigned int id);
  unsigned int getId() const;
  void setForename(std::string_view forename);
  std::string getForename() const;
  void setSurname(std::string_view surname);
  std::string getSurname() const;
  //...more setters/getters here...

private:
  unsigned int id;
  std::string forename;
  std::string surname;
  // ...more attributes here...
};
```

This domain class, representing a customer in an arbitrary software system, does not contain any logic. The logic is in a different place, even that logic which represents exclusive functionality for the Customer, that is, operating only on attributes of the Customer.

Programmers who did this are using objects as bags for a bunch of data. This is just procedural programming with data structures, and it has nothing to do with object-orientation. Also all those setters/getters are totally foolish and violate the information hiding principle severely—actually we could use a simple C-structure (struct) here.

Such classes are called *anemic classes* and should be avoided at all costs. They can often be found in a software design that is an anti-pattern that has been called the *Anemic Domain Model* by Martin Fowler [Fowler03]. It is the exact opposite of the basic idea of object-oriented design, which is to combine data and the functionality that works with the data together into cohesive units.

As long as you do not violate the Law of Demeter, you should insert logic into (domain) classes, if this logic is operating on attributes of that class or collaborates only with the immediate neighbors of the class.

Tell, Don't Ask!

The principle *Tell, Don't Ask* has some similarities with the previously discussed Law of Demeter. This principle is the "declaration of war" to all those public get methods, which reveals something about the internal state of an object. Tell Don't Ask also fosters encapsulation and strengthens information hiding (see Chapter 3). But first and foremost, this principle is about strong cohesion.

Let's examine a small example. Let's assume that the member function Engine::start() from the Car example from the section about the Law Of Demeter is implemented as shown in Listing 6-30.

Listing 6-30. A Possible, But Not Recommendable, Implementation of the Engine::start() Member Function

```
class Engine {
public:
// ...
  void start() {
    if (! fuelPump.isRunning()) {
      fuelPump.powerUp();
      if (fuelPump.getFuelPressure() < NORMAL_FUEL_PRESSURE) {
        fuelPump.setFuelPressure(NORMAL_FUEL_PRESSURE);
      }
    }
    if (! ignition.isPoweredUp()) {
      ignition.powerUp();
    }
    if (! starter.isRotating()) {
```

```
      starter.revolve();
    }
    if (engine.hasStarted()) {
      starter.openClutchToEngine();
      starter.stop();
    }
  }
}
// ...
private:
  FuelPump fuelPump;
  Ignition ignition;
  Starter starter;
  static const unsigned int NORMAL_FUEL_PRESSURE { 120 };
};
```

As it is easy to see, the start() method of the Engine class queries many states from its parts and responds accordingly. Furthermore, the Engine checks the fuel pressure of the fuel pump and adjusts it if it is too low. This also means that the Engine must know the value for the normal fuel pressure. Due to the numerous if branches, the cyclomatic complexity (see Chapter 4) is high.

The Tell Don't Ask principle reminds us that we should not ask an object to expose information about its internal state and decide outside of this object what to do, if this object could decide it on its own. Basically, this principle reminds us that in object-orientation, data, and the operations operating on these data, are to be combined to cohesive units.

If we apply this principle to the example, the Engine::start() method would only tell its parts what they should do, as shown in Listing 6-31.

Listing 6-31. Delegating Stages of the Starting Procedure to the Responsible Parts of the Engine

```
class Engine {
public:
// ...
  void start() {
    fuelPump.pump();
    ignition.powerUp();
```

```
      starter.revolve();
  }
// ...
private:
  FuelPump fuelPump;
  Ignition ignition;
  Starter starter;
};
```

The parts can decide for themselves how they want to execute this command, because they have the knowledge about it. For example, the FuelPump can do all the things what it has to do to build up fuel pressure, as shown in Listing 6-32.

Listing 6-32. An Excerpt from the FuelPump Class

```
class FuelPump {
public:
// ...
  void pump() {
    if (! isRunning) {
      powerUp();
      setNormalFuelPressure();
    }
  }
// ...

private:
  void powerUp() {
    //...
  }

  void setNormalFuelPressure() {
    if (pressure != NORMAL_FUEL_PRESSURE) {
      pressure = NORMAL_FUEL_PRESSURE;
    }
  }
```

```
  bool isRunning;
  unsigned int pressure;
  static const unsigned int NORMAL_FUEL_PRESSURE { 120 };
};
```

Of course, not all getters are inherently bad. Sometimes it is necessary to retrieve information from an object, for example, if this information should be displayed on a graphical user interface.

Avoid Static Class Members

I can well imagine that many readers are wondering now: what is wrong with static member variables and static member functions?

Well, perhaps you still remember the God Class anti-pattern described in the earlier section on small classes. There I've described that utility classes typically tend to become such huge "God Classes." In addition, these utility classes usually also consist of many static member functions, often even without exception. The quiet comprehensible justification for this is: why should I force users of the utility class to create an instance of it? Because such classes offer a colorful assortment of different functions for different purposes, which is a sign of weak cohesion by the way, I have created a special pattern name for these cluttered things: the **Junk Shop anti-pattern**. According to the online encyclopedia *Wikipedia*, a junk shop is a retail outlet similar to a thrift store that offers a broad assortment of mostly used goods at cheap prices. See Listings 6-33 and 6-34.

Listing 6-33. Excerpt from Some Utility Class

```
class JunkShop {
public:
  // ...many public utility functions...
  static int oneOfManyUtilityFunctions(int param);
  // ...more public utility functions...
};
```

Listing 6-34. Another Class That Uses the Utility Class

```
#include "JunkShop.h"

class Client {
  // ...
  void doSomething() {
    // ...
    y = JunkShop::oneOfManyUtilityFunctions(x);
    // ...
  }
};
```

The first problem is that your code becomes hard-wired with all those static helper functions in these "junk shops." As it can easily be seen from the previous example, such static functions from utility classes are used somewhere in the implementation of another software module. Hence, there is no easy way to replace this function call with something else. But in unit testing (see Chapter 2), this is exactly what you want to do.

Furthermore, static member functions foster a procedural programming style. Using them in conjunction with static variables reduces object-orientation to absurdity. Sharing the same state across all instances of a class with the help of a static member variable is intrinsically not OOP because it breaks encapsulation, because an object is no longer in complete control of its state.

Of course, C++ is not a pure object-oriented programming language like Java or C#, and it is basically not forbidden to write procedural code in C++. But when you want to do that, you should be honest with yourself and consequently use simple free-standing procedures, functions, global variables, and namespaces.

My advice is to largely avoid static member variables and member functions.

One exception to this rule are private constants of a class, because they are read-only and do not represent an object's state. Another exception are factory methods, that is, static member functions that create instances of an object, usually instances of the class type that serve as the namespace of the static member function.

Modules

The programming language C++, which was first released in 1985, is now about 35 years old. The foundation of C++ is still the procedural language C, which was released in 1972. To this day, C++ is backward compatible with C. This also means that C++ dragged along the legacy of C until today. Especially with the latest developments in the direction of modern C++—i.e. the standards C++11, C++14, C++17 and now C++20—the legacy of C appears more and more anachronistic and fits less and less with a modern programming style. Nowadays, the old-fashioned and weak #include system for implementing the modularity system in C++ is simply no longer appropriate.

Newer programming languages, like D or Rust, often have a built-in module system. Java was retrofitted with the module system *Jigsaw* with the release of version 9 in 2017. So, it was high time that C++ also got a module system: modules.

The Drawbacks of #include

What are the disadvantages of the old #include system with header files? Well, these are relatively easy to understand when we think about what an #include really is. Every #include results in a simple text replacement by the preprocessor of the compiler, i.e. an #include directive leads to a simple copy-and-paste-operation of the contents of the included file, as depicted in Figure 6-14.

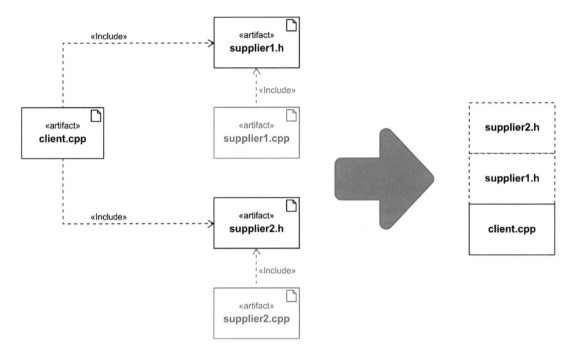

Figure 6-14. *#include causes the file contents to be included in the including file*

First of all, a major drawback to this approach is that the compilation time, especially in large projects, suffers greatly. If a header file is included in many translation units, the compiler must perform these copy-and-paste operations again and again. And the time-consuming part is not the text substitution alone, but mainly the subsequent generation of the so-called *Abstract Syntax Tree* (AST) by the compiler. Then it turns out that hundreds or even thousands of lines of code that have been included can be optimized away because they are not needed.

Furthermore, there are always two physical files, header and source file, to maintain the interface and the implementation of the same module. This basically results into consistency issues and many violations of the DRY principle.

But really unpleasant issues can be caused by multiple definitions of identical symbols and types in different header files, also known as ODR violations, and accidental code changes, e.g., redefinitions of symbols through macros. Imagine that two different header files, both defining a constant named PI in the global namespace, are included in the same translation unit. This requires that multiple inclusions of the same header file in the same translation unit be prevented through certain measures, e.g., with the help of an idiom called the *include guard macro;* otherwise, conflicts with multiple-defined symbols and types will occur.

ODR VIOLATION

ODR is the abbreviation for an important rule in C++ development: The *One Definition Rule*. The ODR is defined in the current ISO C++ Standard in Section 6.3. It states that no translation unit should contain more than one definition of any variable, function, class type, enumeration type, template, default argument for a parameter (for a function in a given scope), or default template argument.

A simple example of an ODR violation: A translation unit (`.cpp` file) includes two headers, both defining a class with an identical name. The compiler would terminate with an error message (e.g. "class type redefinition") then.

Some violations of the ODR must be diagnosed by the compiler. For other violations of this rule, the compiler may remain silent. These possibly undetected ODR violations can lead to very subtle side effects and errors in the running program.

Modules to the Rescue

With modules, which is one of the major new features of the C++20 standard, the separation of header files and implementation files, and thus many of the aforementioned problems, as well as C-style macros and the C preprocessor, should be a thing of the past. Ultimately, the aim of modules is to significantly speed up the compilation of the software and to make it easier for the software designer to build distributable components.

A NOTE ABOUT FILE EXTENSIONS

In the following sections I will use `*.mpp` as the file extension for module files, and `*.bmi` as extension for so-called Built Module Interface (BMI) files. In fact, these file extensions are not standardized and may vary between compilers. For example, if you're using the Microsoft Visual Studio C++ compiler, the module interface files end with `*.ixx`, and the BMI files generated by the compiler have the extension `*.ifc`. For Clang/LLVM compilers, the file extension for the module file is `*.cppm` and the BMI file ends with `*pcm`.

With modules, the situation presented in Figure 6-14 would change as depicted in Figure 6-15.

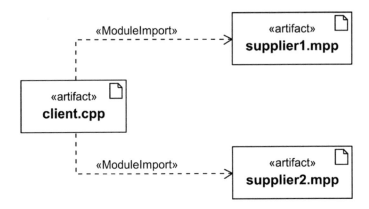

Figure 6-15. *Module import*

So, the solution is to do without the header files. Instead, one translation unit directly accesses the other translation units that it wants to use. Of course, this is not just easily done by throwing away the header file and instead using the implementation file directly as it is. You may have noticed while looking at Figure 6-15 that the file extension of the two artifacts to be imported in the `client.cpp` file has changed from `*.cpp` to `*.mpp`. Migration to modules is not for free, there are a lot of things that must be changed and taken into consideration. And sometimes you might not be able to do it for various reasons, e.g., if you are confronted with a third-party library that you cannot change.

Under the Hood

Before we go a bit more in detail, let's look at what happens "under the hood" when a C++ module is imported and what the basic difference to header file inclusion is.

As depicted in Figure 6-16, a module import is of course no copy&paste operation as with the content of header files. If the compiler encounters a module file—in this case the file named `mathLibrary.mpp`—imported by a translation unit (`main.cpp`), the module file is first translated into a *Built Module Interface* (BMI) file and an object file.

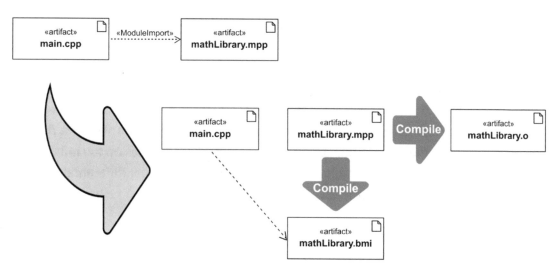

Figure 6-16. *A module file is first translated to a Binary Module Interface (BMI) file and an object file*

The BMI is a file on the filesystem that contains the metadata for the module and describes the exported interface of mathLibrary.mpp. The compiler also produces an object file (mathLibrary.o), which is required by the Linker to link the module to produce an executable.

So basically, when using modules, there is an additional processing step that is required to generate the intermediate artifacts BMI file and object file. This is also an essential difference compared to using header files: When using header file inclusions, we do not have any additional time-consuming generation step. The big advantage, however, is that this step only has to be performed once, no matter how many translation units are importing the module. For example, using "import <iostream>" instead of "#include <iostream>" everywhere in your program avoids compiling the thousands of lines of code from the <iostream> header over and over again.

But this also means that we have a strict chronological order. Importing a module creates a succession, i.e. the compiler has to process the module first to obtain the BMI file, before compiling the translation units that imports the module.

One of the most important aspects of increasing build performance, especially when building large projects, is parallelization. Especially in a CI/CD[1] environment where a continuous build chain is used to build the project very, very frequently, a single build has to run very fast. The development team needs fast feedback on whether the build

---

[1]Continuous Integration/Continuous Deployment

was successful and all automated tests ran without errors. Hence parallelization is the be-all and end-all here.

The fact that there are strict sequential processing steps when using C++ modules makes parallelization more difficult. Especially with more complex import graphs with a high DAG[2]-depth, i.e. with a long chain of modules that import each other, the potential to speed up compilation through parallelization can decrease significantly. Rene Rivera, who contributed to the famous Boost libraries, has carried out studies on the influence of the use of modules on the compiler performance, especially under different degrees of parallelization. He comes to the following conclusion:

> *"With the limitations of the capabilities of current compilers one can only conclude that modular builds are very advantageous at lower parallelism levels environments. But that it's unclear if they are an advantage in highly parallel build environments. In other words, that modules currently do not scale in the same ways as traditional compilation."*
>
> —Rene Rivera, "Are Modules Fast?" [Rivera19]

Three Options for Using Modules

Migration to C++ modules should also be easily possible in ongoing projects. It would be a big hurdle if there were no transition stages between the old concept of including header files on the one hand and importing modules on the other. For this reason, the new C++20 language standard provides three importing options, which I introduce briefly now.

Include Translation

The easiest step toward C++ modules in ongoing projects is to use the (header) include translation. Basically, *include translation* means treat the header includes like module imports. If certain constraints are fulfilled, especially that the header is importable, nothing in the code has to be adapted or changed, neither on the client's side nor on the supplier's side. However, it is important to point out that include translation is a compiler-dependent feature.

---

[2]Directed Acyclic Graph; a finite directed graph with no cycles

---

WHEN IS A HEADER FILE IMPORTABLE?

A header file that is suitable for both include translation and header importation must be sufficiently self-contained, i.e. it must be modular in a way so that it does not rely on pre-definitions, like macros or declarations, or post-undefinitions (macros).

For example, an `include` directive like `#include <iostream>` will be automatically mapped to an `import` of that header. Fortunately, as specified by the C++20 standard, compiler vendors have to provide their Standard Library headers in an importable format. In contrast, all C++ wrappers for C Standard Libraries, for instance `<cstdio>`, `<cmath>`, or `<cstdlib>`, will not be importable. But this should not bother us as clean code developers, because most of the content of these libraries should not be used in a modern C++ program anyway.

The C++20 include translation solves a couple of issues that we still had with the old-fashioned header inclusion. First, the translation speed is increased. In addition, some ODR violations are also prevented, since identical definitions in different header files no longer cause conflicts. Header files can no longer manipulate other header files, nor can the importing translation unit change the code of imported header files.

Header Importation

The next step toward C++ modules is *header importation*, sometimes also called *header units*, which requires a few minor changes in the code on the client's side, i.e. the consumer of the module. These changes are very simple: replace each header `include` with an explicit `import` of that header. In other words, replace the `#include` directive with the new `import` keyword, as shown in Listing 6-35.

Listing 6-35. Header Importation Example

```cpp
import <iostream>; // ...instead of #include <iostream>

int main() {
  std::cout << "Header Importation" << '\n';
  return 0;
}
```

The advantages you get with header importation are basically the same as with include translation, explained in the previous section.

Module Importation

The highest level of using C++ modules is of course module importation, i.e. using modules designated for a modern C++ program. At this stage there are ideally no header files anymore, but the whole software is built of translation units and imported modules.

In Listing 6-36, you can find an example of a simple module, a small library of financial mathematical functions, which currently contains only one function.

Listing 6-36. A Simple Module That Provides Just One Function

```
module;

#include <cmath>

export module financialmath;

namespace financialmath {
  export long double calculateCompoundedInterest(const long double
  initialCapital,
    const long double rate,
    const unsigned short term) {
    return initialCapital * pow((1.0 + rate / 100.0), term);
  }
}
```

The first thing you may notice is that the usual boilerplate code that is typical for header files, such as the include guard or a #pragma once statement, is gone. Instead, we find the beginning of the so-called *global module fragment* in the first line. The content of this area is not exported and is only visible within the module. For example, preprocessor instructions can be placed here (e.g., #include directives). In our simple case, we only include <cmath> here. The following export keyword followed by the module's name introduces the *module declaration*. It declares and exposes the primary interface of a module named financialmath. Inside of the financialmath namespace, we see a function called calculateCompoundedInterest, which performs a compound interest calculation for a given initial capital at a given interest rate and a given term in years.

It is noteworthy that the function is preceded by an export keyword. Using this keyword enables a module developer to determine which parts of a module can be accessed from outside, e.g. by consumers, and which cannot. So we see another enormous advantage that we get with modules: better support of the information hiding principle, which we learned about in Chapter 3.

The use of the module is demonstrated in the unit test in Listing 6-37, which tests the exported function.

Listing 6-37. Calling the Exported Function in a Unit Test

```
import financialmath;

TEST(FinancialmathModuleTest, FinalCapitalIsCalculatedCorrectly) {
  const auto finalCapital = financialmath::calculateCompoundedInterest(
                     3500.0, 4.0, 3);
  EXPECT_DOUBLE_EQ(3937.024, finalCapital);
}
```

Module importation offers a number of additional advantages to those previously mentioned with Header translation and header importation. It is particularly noticeable that the separation between header files and source files no longer exists. Everything is located in a single module file (which also has some drawbacks, I'll get right on that). Furthermore, the ordering of the import statements of modules doesn't matter any more, because the consumer can import them in an arbitrary sequence. Cyclical imports are not possible. ODR violations are virtually a thing of the past.

Separating Interface and Implementation

As I just implied, it is not always an advantage if the module is only one single file. Especially if the module becomes very complex, it can be helpful to separate the module's interface from its implementation, because then the module interface file remains clean without any implementation details.

Therefore, even with modules, there is the possibility to separate the usually stable public interface of the module, the **Module Interface Unit**, from the probably more frequently changed module implementation, the **Module Implementation Unit**. Our small financialmath module would be divided into two units, as shown in Listings 6-38 and 6-39.

Listing 6-38. The Module Interface Unit of the financialmath Module

```
export module financialmath;

export namespace financialmath {
  long double calculateCompoundedInterest(const long double initialCapital,
    const long double rate,
    const unsigned short term);
}
```

Listing 6-39. The Module Implementation Unit of the financialmath Module

```
module;

#include <cmath>

module financialmath;

namespace financialmath {
  long double calculateCompoundedInterest(const long double initialCapital,
    const long double rate,
    const unsigned short term) {
    return initialCapital * pow((1.0 + rate / 100.0), term);
  }
}
```

Of course, this division also has some disadvantages. As with the well-known separation of header and source code files, the separation of a module into an interface and implementation unit violates the DRY principle (see Chapter 3).

Okay, that was modules in a nutshell. There is much more to tell about modules, such as module partitions, or the creation of submodules, but that would go far beyond the scope of this book. Now let's take a look at what this new concept means to clean code developers, and what impact it has on the architecture of a software.

The Impact of Modules

The most frequently mentioned advantage of C++20 modules is that with this new language feature, the compilation speed is increased. This is basically true and is also good news, but it is only a very small, and I think not the most interesting aspect.

I believe that C++20 modules will have a greater impact on the whole C++ ecosystem than any other feature added after C++98. Modules have the potential to reduce—and eventually eliminate—the preprocessor and to get rid of most or all C-style macros. They change how C++ projects are compiled, i.e., they will have an impact on build systems and CI/CD tool chains. And even if software architecture is much more than just defining components and structuring the code, modules also have an impact on how C++ projects are organized and structured.

Modules offer true encapsulation, i.e. the information hiding principle that we know from Chapter 3 is greatly supported. You can explicitly specify a module's interface that should be exported; thus, you can define what is publicly accessible and what not. We can bundle a bunch of modules into a bigger module, this enables you to build a logical structure, for instance, a hierarchical breakdown structure even on component level as depicted in Figure 6-1. All these features can significantly increase the understandability, maintainability, and extensibility of large and complex C++ development projects. And from a clean code developer's point of view, we can get rid of a lot of ugly, C-style macros.

CHAPTER 7

Functional Programming

For the past several years, a programming paradigm has experienced a renaissance that's often viewed as a kind of counterdraft to object orientation. We are talking about *functional programming.*

One of the first functional programming languages was *Lisp* (The uppercase "LISP" is an older spelling, because the name of the language is an abbreviation for "LISt Processing"). It was designed by the American computer scientist and cognitive scientist John McCarthy in 1958 at the Massachusetts Institute of Technology (MIT). McCarthy also coined the term "artificial intelligence" (AI), and he used Lisp as the programming language for AI applications. Lisp is based on the so-called *Lambda Calculus* (λ calculus), a formal model that was introduced in the 1930s by the American mathematician Alonzo Church.

THE LAMBDA CALCULUS

It is difficult to find a painless introduction into the lambda calculus. Many essays on this subject are scientifically written and require a good knowledge of mathematics and logic. I will not try to explain the lambda calculus here, because it is not the main focus of this book. But you can find countless explanations on the Internet; just use the search engine of your trust, and you will get hundreds of hits.

The lambda calculus can be regarded as the simplest and smallest programming language possible. It consists of two parts: **one single function definition scheme** and **one single transformation rule**. These two components are sufficient to create a generic model for the formal description of functional programming languages, like LISP, Haskell, Clojure, etc.

© Stephan Roth 2021
S. Roth, *Clean C++20*, https://doi.org/10.1007/978-1-4842-5949-8_7

In fact, Lisp is a family of computer programming languages. Various dialects of Lisp have emerged. For instance, everyone who has used a member of the famous Emacs text editor family, such as *GNU Emacs* or *X Emacs*, knows the dialect *Emacs Lisp* that is used as a scripting language for extension and automation.

Noteworthy functional programming languages developed using Lisp include:

- *Scheme*: A Lisp dialect with static binding that was developed in the 1970s at the MIT Artificial Intelligence Laboratory (AI Lab).

- *Miranda*: The first purely and lazy functional language that was commercially supported.

- *Haskell*: A general-purpose, purely functional programming language named after the American logician and mathematician Haskell Brooks Curry.

- *Erlang*: Developed by the Swedish telecommunication company Ericsson with a main focus on building massive scalable and high reliable real-time software systems.

- *F#* (pronounced *F sharp*): A multiparadigm programming language and a member of the Microsoft .NET Framework. The main paradigm of F# is functional programming, but it allows the developer to switch to the imperative/object-oriented world of the .NET ecosystem.

- *Clojure*: A modern dialect of the Lisp programming language created by Rich Hickey. Clojure is purely functional and runs on the Java virtual machine and the *Common Language Runtime* (CLR; the runtime environment of the Microsoft .NET Framework).

Functional programming languages are still not as widely used as their imperative relatives, such as the object-oriented ones, but they are increasing in dissemination. Examples are *JavaScript* and *Scala*, which admittedly are both multiparadigm languages (i.e., they are not purely functional). They have both become increasingly popular, especially in web development, in part due to their functional programming capabilities.

This is reason enough to dive deeper into this topic and to explore what this style of programming is all about, as well as discuss what modern C++ has to offer in this direction.

This simple formula defines the basic pattern of any function. It expresses that the value of y depends on, and solely on, the value of x. And another important point is that for the same values of x, the value of y is always the same! In other words, the function f maps any possible value of x to exactly one unique value of y. In mathematics and computer programming, this is known as *referential transparency*.

REFERENTIAL TRANSPARENCY

An essential advantage that is often mentioned in conjunction with functional programming is that pure functions are always referentially transparent.

The term *referential transparency* has its origins in analytical philosophy, which is an umbrella term for certain philosophical movements that have evolved since the beginning of the 20th Century. Analytical philosophy is based on a tradition that initially operated mainly with ideal languages (formal logics) or by analyzing the everyday language of everyday use. The term "referential transparency" is ascribed to the American philosopher and logician Willard Van Orman Quine (1908 – 2000).

If a function is referentially transparent, it means that anytime we call the function with the same input values, we will always receive the same output. In other words, we are theoretically able to substitute the function call directly with its resultant value, and this change will not have any impact. This enables us to chain together functions as if they were opaque boxes.

Referential transparency leads us directly to the concept of the pure function.

Pure vs Impure Functions

Listing 7-1 shows a simple example of a pure function in C++.

Listing 7-1. A Simple Example of a Pure Function in C++

```cpp
[[nodiscard]] double square(const double value) noexcept {
  return value * value;
};
```

As it can easily be seen, the output value of square() depends solely on the argument value that is passed to the function, so calling square() twice with the same parameter value will produce the same result each time. We have no side effects, because if any call of this function is completed, it does not leave any "dirt" behind that can influence subsequent calls of square(). Such functions, which are completely independent of an outside state without side effects, and which will produce the same output for the same inputs and are referentially transparent are called **pure functions**.

In contrast, imperative programming paradigms, such as procedural or object-oriented programming, do not provide this guarantee of side-effect freeness, as the example in Listing 7-2 shows.

Listing 7-2. An Example Demonstrating That Member Functions of Classes Can Cause Side Effects

```cpp
#include <iostream>

class Clazz {
public:
  int functionWithSideEffect(const int value) noexcept {
    return value * value + someKindOfMutualState++;
  }

private:
  int someKindOfMutualState { 0 };
};

int main() {
  Clazz instanceOfClazz { };
  std::cout << instanceOfClazz.functionWithSideEffect(3) << std::endl;
  // Output: "9"
  std::cout << instanceOfClazz.functionWithSideEffect(3) << std::endl;
  // Output: "10"
  std::cout << instanceOfClazz.functionWithSideEffect(3) << std::endl;
  // Output: "11"
  return 0;
}
```

In this case, every call of the member function with its suspicious name `Clazz::functionWithSideEffect()` will alter an internal state of the instance of class `Clazz`. As a consequence, every call of this member function returns a different result, although the given parameter for the function's argument is always the same. You can have similar effects in procedural programming with global variables that are manipulated by procedures. Functions that can produce different outputs even if they are always called with the same arguments are called **impure functions**. Another clear indicator that a function is an impure function is when it makes sense to call it without using its return value. If you can do that, this function must have any kind of side effect.

In a single-threaded execution environment, global states may cause a few problems and pain. But now imagine that you have a multithreaded execution environment, where several threads are running, calling functions in a non-deterministic order. In such an environment, global states, or object-wide states of instances, are often problematic and can cause unpredictable behavior or subtle errors.

Functional Programming in Modern C++

Believe it or not, functional programming has always been a part of C++! With this multiparadigm language, you were always able to program in a functional style, even with C++98. The reason that I can claim this is because of the existence of the known *template metaprogramming* (TMP) since the beginning of C++.

Functional Programming with C++ Templates

Many C++ developers know that *template metaprogramming* is a technique in which so-called templates are used by a compiler to generate C++ source code in a step before the compiler translates the source code to object code. What many programmers may not be aware of is the fact that template metaprogramming is functional programming, and that it is *Turing Complete*.

TURING COMPLETENESS

The term *Turing Complete,* named after the well-known English computer scientist, mathematician, logician, and cryptanalyst Alan Turing (1912 – 1954), is often used to define what makes a language a "real" programming language. A programming language is characterized as Turing Complete if you can solve any possible problem with it that can be theoretically computed by a Turing Machine. A *Turing Machine* is an abstract and theoretical machine invented by Alan Turing that serves as an idealized model for computations.

In practice, no computer system is really Turing Complete. The reason is that ideal Turing Completeness requires unlimited memory and unbounded recursions, what today's computer systems cannot offer. Hence, some systems approximate Turing Completeness by modeling unbounded memory, but they are restricted by a physical limitation in the underlying hardware.

As a proof, we will calculate the greatest common divisor (GCD) of two integers using TMP only. The GCD of two integers, which are both not zero, is the largest positive integer that divides both of the given integers. See Listing 7-3.

Listing 7-3. Calculating the Greatest Common Divisor Using Template Metaprogramming

```
01  #include <iostream>
02
03  template< unsigned int x, unsigned int y >
04  struct GreatestCommonDivisor {
05    static const unsigned int result = GreatestCommonDivisor< y, x % y
      >::result;
06  };
07
08  template< unsigned int x >
09  struct GreatestCommonDivisor< x, 0 > {
10    static const unsigned int result = x;
11  };
12
13  int main() {
```

```
14    std::cout << "The GCD of 40 and 10 is: " << GreatestCommonDivisor
      <40u, 10u>::result
15      << std::endl;
16    std::cout << "The GCD of 366 and 60 is: " << GreatestCommonDivisor
      <366u, 60u>::result <<
17      std::endl;
18    return 0;
19  }
```

This is the output that the program generates:

```
The GCD of 40 and 10 is: 10
The GCD of 366 and 60 is: 6
```

What is remarkable about this style of calculating the GCD at compile time using templates is that it is real functional programming. The two class templates used are completely free of states. There are no *mutable variables*, meaning that no variable can change its value once it has been initialized. During template instantiation, a recursive process is initiated that stops when the specialized class template on Lines 9-11 come into play. And, as mentioned, we have Turing Completeness in template metaprogramming, meaning that any conceivable computation can be done at compile time using this technique.

Well, template metaprogramming is undoubtedly a powerful tool, but also has some disadvantages. Particularly the readability and understandability of the code can suffer drastically if a great deal of template metaprogramming is used. The syntax and idioms of TMP are sometimes not easy to understand. Users can be confronted with extensive and often cryptic error messages when something goes wrong, even if this can now be greatly reduced by using C++20 concepts (see Chapter 5). And, of course, the compile time also increases with an extensive use of template metaprogramming. Therefore, TMP is certainly a proper way of designing and developing generic multi-purpose libraries (an outstanding example is undoubtedly the C++ Standard Library), but should only be used in modern and well-crafted application code if this kind of generic programming is required (e.g., to minimize code duplication).

Since C++11, it is no longer necessary to use only template metaprogramming for compile-time computations. With the help of constant expressions (constexpr; see the section about computations during compile time in Chapter 5), the GCD can easily be implemented as a usual recursive function, as shown in Listing 7-4.

Listing 7-4. A GCD Function Using Recursion That Can Be Evaluated at Compile Time

```
constexpr unsigned int greatestCommonDivisor(const unsigned int x,
                                             const unsigned int y) noexcept
{
  return y == 0 ? x : greatestCommonDivisor(y, x % y);
}
```

By the way, the mathematical algorithm behind this is called *Euclidean algorithm*, or *Euclid's algorithm*, named after the ancient Greek mathematician Euclid.

And since C++17, the numeric algorithm std::gcd() has become part of the C++ Standard Library (defined in the <numeric> header), so it is not necessary to implement it on your own. See Listing 7-5.

Listing 7-5. Using the std::gcd Function from the <numeric> Header

```
#include <iostream>
#include <numeric>

int main() {
  constexpr auto result = std::gcd(40, 10);
  std::cout << "The GCD of 40 and 10 is: " << result << std::endl;
  return 0;
}
```

Function-Like Objects (Functors)

What was also always possible in C++ from the very beginning was the definition and use of so-called *function-like objects*, also known as *functors* (another synonym is *functionals*) in short. Technically speaking, a functor is more or less just a class that defines the parenthesis operator, that is, the operator(). After the instantiation of these classes, they can pretty much be used like functions.

Depending on whether the operator() has none, one, or two parameters, the functor is called a *generator, unary function*, or *binary function*. Let's look at a generator first.

Generator

As the name "generator" reveals, this type of functor is used to produce something. See Listing 7-6.

Listing 7-6. An Example of a Generator, a Functor That Is Called With No Argument

```
class IncreasingNumberGenerator {
public:
  [[nodiscard]] int operator()() noexcept { return number++; }

private:
  int number { 0 };
};
```

The working principle is quite simple: every time IncreasingNumberGenerator::operator() is called, the actual value of the member variable number is returned to the caller, and the value of this member variable is increased by 1. The following usage example prints a sequence of the numbers 0 to 2 on standard output:

```
int main() {
  IncreasingNumberGenerator numberGenerator { };
  std::cout << numberGenerator() << std::endl;
  std::cout << numberGenerator() << std::endl;
  std::cout << numberGenerator() << std::endl;
  return 0;
}
```

Remember the quote from Sean Parent that I presented in the section on algorithms in Chapter 5: no raw loops! To fill a std::vector<T> with a certain amount of increasing values, we should not implement a handcrafted loop. Instead, we can use std::generate or std::ranges::generate (since C++20), both defined in the <algorithm> header. Both are function templates that assign each element in a certain range a value generated by a given generator object. Hence, we can write the simple and well-readable code shown in Listing 7-7 to fill a vector with an increasing number sequence using IncreasingNumberGenerator.

Listing 7-7. Filling a Vector with an Increasing Number Sequence Using
std::ranges::generate

```
#include <algorithm>
#include <vector>

using Numbers = std::vector<int>;

int main() {
  const std::size_t AMOUNT_OF_NUMBERS { 100 };
  Numbers numbers(AMOUNT_OF_NUMBERS);
  std::ranges::generate(numbers, IncreasingNumberGenerator());
  // ...now 'numbers' contains values from 0 to 99...
  return 0;
}
```

As one can easily imagine, these kinds of functors do **not** fulfill the strict
requirements for pure functions. Generators do commonly have a mutable state, that is,
when operator() is called, these functors usually have some side effect. In our case, the
mutable state is represented by the private member variable called IncreasingNumberGe
nerator::number, which is incremented after each call of the parenthesis operator.

STD::IOTA (SINCE C++11) AND STD::RANGES::IOTA_VIEW (SINCE C++20)

Since C++11, the <numeric> header has contained a function template called
std::iota(), named after the functional symbol ι (Iota) from the programming language
APL. It's not a generator functor, but it can be used to fill a container with an ascending
sequence of values in an elegant way. Since C++20, this function template is also specified as
constexpr and thus usable in compile-time computations.

Thus, the line from the previous code example where the vector is filled can also be written as
follows:

```
std::iota(begin(numbers), end(numbers), 0);
```

With the introduction of the Ranges library since C++20, there is another way to generate a sequence of elements by repeatedly incrementing an initial value: the Range factory std::ranges::iota_view (defined in the <ranges> header):

```
auto view = std::ranges::iota_view { 0, 100 };
std::vector<int> numbers(std::begin(view), std::end(view));
// ...now 'numbers' contains values from 0 to 99...
```

Another example of a function-like object of type generator is the random number generator functor class template shown in Listing 7-8. This functor encapsulates all the stuff that is necessary for the initialization and usage of a pseudorandom number generator (PRNG) based on the so-called *Mersenne Twister* algorithm (defined in the <random> header).

Listing 7-8. A Generator Functor Class Template Encapsulating a Pseudorandom Number Generator

```
#include <random>

template <typename NUMTYPE>
class RandomNumberGenerator {
public:
  RandomNumberGenerator() {
    mersenneTwisterEngine.seed(randomDevice());
  }

  [[nodiscard]] NUMTYPE operator()() {
    return distribution(mersenneTwisterEngine);
  }

private:
  std::random_device randomDevice;
  std::uniform_int_distribution<NUMTYPE> distribution;
  std::mt19937_64 mersenneTwisterEngine;
};
```

Listing 7-9 shows how the RandomNumberGenerator functor could then be used.

Listing 7-9. Filling a Vector with 100 Random Numbers

```
#include "RandomGenerator.h"
#include <algorithm>
#include <functional>
#include <iostream>
#include <vector>

using Numbers = std::vector<short>;
const std::size_t AMOUNT_OF_NUMBERS { 100 };

Numbers createVectorFilledWithRandomNumbers() {
  RandomNumberGenerator<short> randomNumberGenerator { };
  Numbers randomNumbers(AMOUNT_OF_NUMBERS);
  std::generate(begin(randomNumbers), end(randomNumbers), std::ref(randomNu
  mberGenerator));
  return randomNumbers;
}

void printNumbersOnStdOut(const Numbers& numbers) {
  for (const auto& number : numbers) {
    std::cout << number << std::endl;
  }
}

int main() {
  auto randomNumbers = createVectorFilledWithRandomNumbers();
  printNumbersOnStdOut(randomNumbers);
  return 0;
}
```

Unary Function

Next, let's look at an example of a unary function-like object, which is a functor whose parenthesis operator has one parameter. See Listing 7-10.

Listing 7-10. An Example of a Unary Functor

```
class ToSquare {
public:
  [[nodiscard]] constexpr int operator()(const int value) const noexcept {
  return value * value; }
};
```

As its name suggests, this functor squares the values passed to it in the parenthesis operator. This does not necessarily always have to be the case, because, a unary functor can also have private member variables, and thus a mutable state. Read or write access to global variables is also possible (...although this should not be the normal case nowadays).

With the ToSquare functor, we can now extend the previous example and apply it to the vector with the ascending integer sequence. See Listing 7-11.

Listing 7-11. All 100 Numbers in a Vector Are Squared

```
#include <algorithm>
#include <vector>

using Numbers = std::vector<int>;

int main() {
  const std::size_t AMOUNT_OF_NUMBERS { 100 };
  Numbers numbers(AMOUNT_OF_NUMBERS);
  std::generate(begin(numbers), end(numbers), IncreasingNumberGenerator());
  std::transform(begin(numbers), end(numbers), begin(numbers), ToSquare());
  // ...to be continued...
  return 0;
}
```

The used algorithm std::transform (defined in the <algorithm> header) applies the given function or function object to a range (defined by the first two parameters) and stores the result in another range (defined by the third parameter). In our case, these ranges are the same.

Predicate

Predicates are a special kind of functor. A unary functor is called a *unary predicate* if it has one parameter and a Boolean return value indicating a true or false result of some test, such as shown in Listing 7-12.

Listing 7-12. An Example of a Predicate

```
class IsAnOddNumber {
public:
  [[nodiscard]] constexpr bool operator()(const int value) const noexcept {
    return (value % 2) != 0;
  }
};
```

This predicate can now be applied to our number sequence using the std::erase_ if algorithm to get rid of all the odd numbers. See Listing 7-13.

Listing 7-13. All Odd Numbers From the Vector Are Deleted Using std::erase_if

```
#include <algorithm>
#include <vector>

// ...

using Numbers = std::vector<int>;

int main() {
  const std::size_t AMOUNT_OF_NUMBERS = 100;
  Numbers numbers(AMOUNT_OF_NUMBERS);
  std::generate(begin(numbers), end(numbers), IncreasingNumberGenerator());
  std::transform(begin(numbers), end(numbers), begin(numbers), ToSquare());
  std::erase_if(numbers, IsAnOddNumber());
  // ...
  return 0;
}
```

Note   Unless you are using the C++20 language standard, you will need to apply the Erase-Remove idiom to remove the odd numbers from the vector, which is explained in a sidebar in the section entitled "Building Abstractions Is Sometimes Hard" in Chapter 3.

In order to use a functor in a more flexible and generic way, it is usually implemented as a class template. Therefore, we can refactor our unary functor IsAnOddNumber into a class template so that it can be used with all integral types, such as short, int, unsigned int, uint64_t, etc. This can easily be done with the new C++20 concepts, as shown in Listing 7-14.

Listing 7-14. Ensuring That the Template Parameter Is an Integral Data Type

```
#include <concepts>

template <std::integral T>
class IsAnOddNumber {
public:
  [[nodiscard]] constexpr bool operator()(const T value) const noexcept {
    return (value % 2) != 0;
  }
};
```

The location within the body of the main() function, where our predicate is used (the call of the std::erase_if function), must now be adjusted a little bit:

```
// ...
std::erase_if(numbers, IsAnOddNumber<Numbers::value_type>());
// ...
```

If we inadvertently use the IsAnOddNumber template with a non-integral data type, such as a double, we would get a meaningful error message from the compiler.

Listing 7-15 shows the entire example, completed with an output of the contents of the vector on stdout, using std::for_each and the PrintOnStdOut functor.

Listing 7-15. The Whole Code Example with All Three Types of Functors

```cpp
#include <algorithm>
#include <concepts>
#include <iostream>
#include <vector>

class IncreasingNumberGenerator {
public:
  [[nodiscard]] int operator()() noexcept { return number++; }

private:
  int number { 0 };
};

class ToSquare {
public:
  [[nodiscard]] constexpr int operator()(const int value) const noexcept {
    return value * value;
  }
};

template <std::integral T>
class IsAnOddNumber {
public:
  [[nodiscard]] constexpr bool operator()(const T value) const noexcept {
    return (value % 2) != 0;
  }
};

class PrintOnStdOut {
public:
  void operator()(const auto& printable) const {
    std::cout << printable << '\n';
  }
};

using Numbers = std::vector<int>;
```

```
int main() {
  const std::size_t AMOUNT_OF_NUMBERS = 100;
  Numbers numbers(AMOUNT_OF_NUMBERS);
  std::generate(begin(numbers), end(numbers), IncreasingNumberGenerator());
  std::transform(begin(numbers), end(numbers), begin(numbers), ToSquare());
  std::erase_if(numbers, IsAnOddNumber<Numbers::value_type>());
  std::for_each(cbegin(numbers), cend(numbers), PrintOnStdOut());
  return 0;
}
```

The reason I show the example here again in its entirety is because we will be improving it later in this chapter.

Last but not least, let's finalize this section about functors and look at the binary functor.

Binary Functors

As mentioned, a binary functor is a function-like object that takes two parameters. If such a functor operates on its two parameters to perform some calculation (e.g., addition) and returns the result of this operation, it is called a *binary operator*. If such a functor has a Boolean return value as a result of some test, as shown in Listing 7-16, it is called a *binary predicate*.

Listing 7-16. An Example of a Binary Predicate That Compares its Two Parameters

```
class IsGreaterOrEqual {
public:
  [[nodiscard]] bool operator()(const auto& value1, const auto& value2)
  const noexcept {
    return value1 >= value2;
  }
};
```

Note   Until C++11, it was a good practice that functors, depending on their number of parameters, were derived from the templates `std::unary_function` and `std::binary_function` (both defined in the `<functional>` header). **These templates have been labeled as deprecated with C++11 and have been removed from the Standard Library since C++17.**

Binders and Function Wrappers

The next development step in terms of functional programming in C++ was made with the publication of the draft *C++ Technical Report 1* (TR 1) in 2005, which is the common name for the standard ISO/IEC TR 19768:2007 *C++ Library Extensions*. The TR 1 specifies a series of extensions to the C++ Standard Library, including, among other things, extensions for functional programming. This technical report was the library extension proposal for the later C++11 standard, and in fact, 12 of the 13 proposed libraries (with slight modifications) also made it into the new language standard published in 2011.

In terms of functional programming, the TR 1 introduced the two function templates `std::bind` and `std::function`, which are defined in the `<functional>` library header.

The function template `std::bind` is a binder wrapper for functions and their arguments. You can take a function (or a function pointer, or a functor), and "bind" actual values to one or all of the function's parameters. In other words, you can create new function-like objects from existing functions or functors. Let's start with a simple example, as shown in Listing 7-17.

Listing 7-17. Using std::bind to Wrap the multiply() Binary Function

```cpp
#include <functional>
#include <iostream>

[[nodiscard]] constexpr double multiply(const double multiplicand,
  const double multiplier) noexcept {
  return multiplicand * multiplier;
}

int main() {
  const auto result1 = multiply(10.0, 5.0);
```

```
  auto boundMultiplyFunctor = std::bind(multiply, 10.0, 5.0);
  const auto result2 = boundMultiplyFunctor();

  std::cout << "result1 = " << result1 << ", result2 = " << result2 <<
  std::endl;
  return 0;
}
```

In this example, the multiply() function is wrapped, together with two floating-point number literals (10.0 and 5.0), using std::bind. The number literals represent the actual parameters that are bound to the two function arguments multiplicand and multiplier. As a result, we get a new function-like object that is stored in the boundMultiplyFunctor variable. It can then be called like an ordinary functor using the parenthesis operator.

Maybe you are wondering, nice, but I don't get it. What's the purpose of that? What is the practical benefit of the binder function template?

Well, std::bind allows something that is known as *partial application* (or *partial function application*) in programming. Partial application is a process by which only a subset of the function parameters is bound to values or variables, whereas the other part is not yet bound. The unbound parameters are replaced with the placeholders _1, _2, _3, and so on, which are defined in the namespace std::placeholders. See Listing 7-18.

Listing 7-18. An Example of Partial Function Application

```
#include <functional>
#include <iostream>

[[nodiscard]] constexpr double multiply(const double multiplicand,
  const double multiplier) noexcept {
  return multiplicand * multiplier;
}

int main() {
  using namespace std::placeholders;

  auto multiplyWith10 = std::bind(multiply, _1, 10.0);
  std::cout << "result = " << multiplyWith10(5.0) << std::endl;
  return 0;
}
```

In this example, the second parameter of the multiply() function is bound to the floating-point number literal 10.0, but the first parameter is bound to a placeholder. The function-like object, which is the return value of std::bind(), is stored in the multiplyWith10 variable. This variable can now be used like a function, but we only need to pass one parameter: the value that is to be multiplied by 10.0.

Partial function application is an adaptation technique that allows us to use a function or a functor in various situations, when we need their functionality, but when we can supply some but not all of the arguments. In addition, with the help of the placeholders, the order of the functions parameters can be adapted to the order that the client code expects. For example, the position of the multiplicand and the multiplier in the parameter list can be interchanged by mapping them to a new function-like object in the following way:

```
auto multiplyWithExchangedParameterPosition = std::bind(multiply, _2, _1);
```

In our case with the multiply() function, this is obviously senseless (remember the commutative property of multiplication), because the new function object will produce the same results as the original multiply() function. However, in other situations, adapting the order of the parameters can improve the usability of a function. Partial function application is a tool for interface adaptation.

By the way, especially in conjunction with functions as return parameters, the automatic type deduction with its keyword auto (see the section entitled "Automatic Type Deduction" in Chapter 5) can provide valuable services, because if we inspect what the GCC compiler returns from the call to std::bind(), it is an object of the following complex type:

```
std::_Bind_helper<bool0,double (&)(double, double),const _Placeholder<int2>
&,const _Placeholder<int1> &>::type
```

Terrifying, isn't it? Writing down such a type explicitly in source code is not only less helpful, but apart from that the readability of the code also suffers considerably. Thanks to the keyword auto, it is not necessary to define these types explicitly. But in those rare cases, where you must do it, the class template std::function comes into play, which is a general-purpose polymorphic function wrapper. This template can wrap an arbitrary callable object (an ordinary function, a functor, a function pointer, etc.) and manages the memory used to store that object. For example, to wrap our multiplication function multiply() into a std::function object, the code looks as follows:

```
std::function<double(double, double)> multiplyFunc = multiply;
auto result = multiplyFunc(10.0, 5.0);
```

Now that we've discussed std::bind, std::function, and the technique of partial application, I have a possibly disappointing message for you: since C++11 and the introduction of lambda expressions, most of this template stuff from the C++ Standard Library is only seldom required.

Lambda Expressions

With the advent of C++11, the language has been extended with a new and noteworthy feature: lambda expressions! Other frequently used terms for them are *lambda functions*, *function literals*, or just *lambdas*. Sometimes they are also called *closures*, which is actually a general term from functional programming, and which, incidentally, is also not entirely correct.

CLOSURE

In imperative programming languages, we are accustomed to the fact that a variable is no longer available when the program execution leaves the scope within which the variable is defined. For instance, if a function is done and returns to its caller, all local variables of that function are removed from the call stack and deleted from memory.

On the other hand, in functional programming, we can build a *closure*, which is a function object with a persistent local variable scope. In other words, closures allow a scope with some or all of its local variables to be tied to a function, and this scope object will persist as long as that function exists.

In C++, such closures can be created with the help of lambda expressions due to the capture list in the lambda introducer. A closure is not the same as a lambda expression, just like an object (instance) in object orientation is not the same as its class.

What is special about lambda expressions is that they are usually implemented inline, that is, at the point of their application. This can sometimes improve the readability of the code, and compilers can apply their optimization strategies even more efficiently. Of course, lambda functions can also be treated as data, for example, stored in variables or passed as a function argument to a so-called high-order function (see the next section about this topic).

The basic structure of a lambda expression looks as follows:

```
[ capture list ](parameter list) -> return_type_declaration { lambda body }
```

Since this book is not a C++ language introduction, I will not explain all the basics of lambda expressions here. Even if you are seeing something like this for the first time, it should be relatively clear that the return type, the parameter list, and the lambda body are pretty much the same as with ordinary functions. What might seem unusual at first glance are two things. For example, a lambda expression has no name like an ordinary function or a function-like object. This is the reason that one speaks in this context of *anonymous functions*. The other conspicuousness is the square bracket at the beginning, which is also called the *lambda introducer*. As the name suggests, the lambda introducer marks the beginning of a lambda expression. In addition, the introducer also optionally contains something called a *capture list*.

What makes this capture list so important is that all the variables from the outside scope are listed, which should be available inside of the lambda body, and whether they should be captured by value (copying) or by reference. In other words, these are the closures of the lambda expression.

An example lambda expression is defined as follows:

```
[](const double multiplicand, const double multiplier) { return
multiplicand * multiplier; }
```

This is our good old multiplication function from the previous section as a lambda. The introducer has a blank capture list, which means that nothing from the surrounding scope is used. The return type is not specified in this case either, because the compiler can easily deduce it.

By assigning the lambda expression to a variable, a corresponding runtime object is created, the so-called closure. And this is actually true: the compiler generates a functor class of an unspecified type from a lambda expression, which is instantiated at runtime and assigned to the variable. The captures in the capture list are converted into constructor parameters and member variables of the functor object. The parameters in the lambda's parameter list are turned into parameters for the functor's parenthesis operator (operator()). See Listing 7-19.

Listing 7-19. Using the Lambda Expression to Multiply Two Doubles

```
#include <iostream>

int main() {
  auto multiply = [](const double multiplicand, const double multiplier) {
    return multiplicand * multiplier;
  };
  std::cout << multiply(10.0, 50.0) << std::endl;
  return 0;
}
```

However, the whole thing can be shorter, because a lambda expression can be called directly at the place of its definition by appending parentheses with arguments behind the lambda body. See Listing 7-20.

Listing 7-20. Defining and Calling a Lambda Expression in One Go

```
int main() {
  std::cout <<
    [](const double multiplicand, const double multiplier) {
      return multiplicand * multiplier;
    }(50.0, 10.0) << std::endl;
  return 0;
}
```

The previous example is, of course, for demonstration purposes only, since the use of a lambda in this style makes no sense. The example in Listing 7-21 uses two lambda expressions. One is used by the algorithm called std::transform to envelop the words in the string vector called quote with angle brackets and store them in another vector named result. The other lambda expression is used by std::for_each to output the content of result on standard output.

Listing 7-21. Putting Every Single Word in a List in Angle Brackets

```cpp
#include <algorithm>
#include <iostream>
#include <string>
#include <vector>

int main() {
  std::vector<std::string> quote { "That's", "one", "small", "step", "for",
  "a", "man,", "one", "giant", "leap", "for", "mankind." };
  std::vector<std::string> result;

  std::transform(begin(quote), end(quote), back_inserter(result),
    [](const std::string& word) { return "<" + word + ">"; });
  std::for_each(begin(result), end(result),
    [](const std::string& word) { std::cout << word << " "; });

  return 0;
}
```

The output of this small program is as follows:

```
<That's> <one> <small> <step> <for> <a> <man,> <one> <giant> <leap> <for>
<mankind.>
```

Generic Lambda Expressions (C++14)

With C++14, lambda expressions experienced additional improvements. Since C++14, it is okay to use auto (see the section about automatic type deduction in Chapter 5) as the return type of a function or a lambda. In other words, the compiler will deduce the type. Such lambda expressions are called *generic lambda expressions*.

Listing 7-22 shows an example.

Listing 7-22. Applying a Generic Lambda Expression on Values of Different Data Type

```cpp
#include <complex>
#include <iostream>

int main() {
  auto square = [](const auto& value) noexcept { return value * value; };

  const auto result1 = square(12.56);
  const auto result2 = square(25u);
  const auto result3 = square(-6);
  const auto result4 = square(std::complex<double>(4.0, 2.5));

  std::cout << "result1 is " << result1 << "\n";
  std::cout << "result2 is " << result2 << "\n";
  std::cout << "result3 is " << result3 << "\n";
  std::cout << "result4 is " << result4 << std::endl;

  return 0;
}
```

The parameter type as well as the result type are derived automatically depending on the type of the concrete parameter (literal) when the function is compiled (in the previous example, double, unsigned int, int, and a complex number of type std::complex<T>). Generalized lambdas are extremely useful in interaction with Standard Library algorithms, because they are universally applicable.

Lambda Templates (C++20)

The C++17 language standard that followed C++14 extended the capabilities of C++ lambdas. For instance, with C++17, it became possible to evaluate lambdas at compile-time, so-called *constexpr lambdas*. The new C++20 standard also offers further, mostly smaller improvements regarding more convenient uses of lambdas and to allow some advanced use cases.

However, one new C++20 add-on regarding lambda expressions is explicitly noteworthy: *lambda templates*!

Maybe you are a little surprised now and ask yourself, wait a minute! We have had generic lambdas since C++14. That is actually something like templates. For what purpose do we still need lambda templates now?

Let's compare two lambda expressions for a multiplication, one implemented as a generic lambda (C++14) and one as a template lambda (C++20):

```
auto multiply1 = [](const auto multiplicand, const auto multiplier) {
  return multiplicand * multiplier;
};
auto multiply2 = []<typename T>(const T multiplicand, const T multiplier) {
  return multiplicand * multiplier;
};
```

If you would call them with identical parameters for both arguments, you will not notice a difference:

```
auto result1 = multiply1(10, 20);
auto result2 = multiply2(10, 20);
```

In both cases, the value 200 can be found in the variables that receive the results. But what will happen if we call both variants with parameters of different types, e.g., an int for the multiplicand and a bool for the multiplier?

```
auto result3 = multiply1(10, true);
auto result4 = multiply2(10, true);
```

Also in this case the compiler manages to translate the generic template multiply1 without complaint. (By the way, the result in result3 is 10 because the compiler expands the true to an int [*integral promotion*] and has the value 1.) However, we get a compiler error for the instantiation of the lambda template multiply2; for instance something like this:

```
error: deduced conflicting types for parameter 'T' ('int' and 'bool')
```

With lambda templates, developers cannot be prevented from accidental wrong instantiations or usages of lambdas. Furthermore, C++20 concepts (see the section entitled "Concepts: Requirements for Template Arguments" in Chapter 5) can of course be used to perform compile-time validations of a lambda's template arguments. See Listing 7-23.

Listing 7-23.   Lambda Templates Can Also Be Equipped with Constraints Using C++20 Concepts

```cpp
#include <concepts>
#include <iostream>
#include <string>

template <typename T>
concept Number = std::integral<T> || std::floating_point<T>;

int main() {
  auto add = [] <Number T> (const T addend1, const T addend2) {
    return addend1 + addend2;
  };

  const std::string string1 { "Hello" };
  const std::string string2 { "World" };

  auto result1 = add(10, 20);              // OK
  auto result2 = add('x', 'y');            // OK
  auto result3 = add(10.0, 20.0);          // OK
  auto result4 = add(string1, string2); // Compiler-error: constraints not
                                         //                 satisfied!

  std::cout << result1 << ", " << result2 << ", " << result3 << std::endl;

  return 0;
}
```

In this example, the lambda template is allowed only for use with numeric data types (int, float, double, ...). Although there is an operator called std::string::operator+ that allows two strings to be concatenated, an instantiation of the lambda template is prohibited by the Number<T> concept.

Higher-Order Functions

A central concept in functional programming is so-called *higher-order functions*. They are the pendant to first-class functions. A higher-order function is a function that takes one or more other functions as arguments, or they can return a function as a result. In C++, any callable object—for example, an instance of the std::function wrapper, a function pointer, a closure created from a lambda expression, a handcrafted functor, and anything else that implements operator()—can be passed as an argument to a higher-order function.

We can keep this introduction relatively short, because we have already seen and used several higher-order functions. Many of the algorithms (see the section about algorithms in Chapter 5) in the C++ Standard Library are these kinds of functions. Depending on their purpose, they take a unary operator, unary predicate, or binary predicate and apply it to a container or to a sub-range of elements in a container.

Of course, despite the fact that the <algorithm> and <numeric> headers provide a comprehensive selection of powerful higher-order functions for different purposes, you can also implement higher-order functions or higher-order function templates by yourself. See Listing 7-24.

Listing 7-24. An Example of Self-Made Higher-Order Functions

```cpp
#include <functional>
#include <iostream>
#include <vector>

template<typename CONTAINERTYPE, typename UNARYFUNCTIONTYPE>
void myForEach(const CONTAINERTYPE& container, UNARYFUNCTIONTYPE
unaryFunction) {
  for (const auto& element : container) {
    unaryFunction(element);
  }
}

template<typename CONTAINERTYPE, typename UNARYOPERATIONTYPE>
void myTransform(CONTAINERTYPE& container, UNARYOPERATIONTYPE
unaryOperator) {
```

```
  for (auto& element : container) {
    element = unaryOperator(element);
  }
}

template<typename NUMBERTYPE>
class ToSquare {
public:
  NUMBERTYPE operator()(const NUMBERTYPE& number) const noexcept {
    return number * number;
  }
};

template<typename TYPE>
void printOnStdOut(const TYPE& thing) {
  std::cout << thing << ", ";
}

int main() {
  std::vector<int> numbers { 1, 2, 3, 4, 5, 6, 7, 8, 9, 10 };
  myTransform(numbers, ToSquare<int>());
  std::function<void(int)> printNumberOnStdOut = printOnStdOut<int>;
  myForEach(numbers, printNumberOnStdOut);
  return 0;
}
```

In this case, our two self-made higher-order function templates myTransform() and myForEach() are only applicable to entire containers because, unlike the Standard Library algorithms, they have no iterator interface. The crucial point, however, is that developers can provide custom higher-order functions that do not exist in the C++ Standard Library.

We will now look at three of these high-order functions in greater detail, because they play an important role in functional programming.

Map, Filter, and Reduce

Each serious functional programming language must provide at least three useful higher-order functions: *map*, *filter*, and *reduce* (called *fold*). Even if they have different names depending on the programming language, you can find this triumvirate in Haskell, Erlang, Clojure, JavaScript, Scala, and many other languages with functional programming capabilities. Hence, we can claim justifiably that these three higher-order functions form a very common functional programming design pattern.

It should therefore hardly surprise you that these higher-order functions are also contained in the C++ Standard Library. And maybe you will also not be surprised that we have already used some of these functions.

Let's look at each of these functions in the following sections.

Map

Map might be the easiest to understand of the three. With the help of this higher-order function, we can apply an operator function to each single element of a list. In C++, this function is provided by the Standard Library algorithm `std::transform` (defined in the `<algorithm>` header), which you've seen in some previous code examples.

Filter

Filter is also pretty simply. As the name suggests, this higher-order function takes a predicate (see the section about predicates earlier in this chapter) and a list, and it removes any element from the list that does not satisfy the predicate's condition. In C++, this function is provided by the Standard Library algorithm `std::remove_if` (defined in the `<algorithm>` header), which you've seen in some previous code examples.

Nevertheless, here's another nice example of the `std::remove_if` filter. If you are suffering from a disease called "aibohphobia," which is a humorous term for the irrational fear of palindromes, you could filter out palindromes from word lists, as shown in Listing 7-25.

Listing 7-25. Removing All Palindromes from a Vector of Words

```
#include <algorithm>
#include <iostream>
#include <string>
```

```cpp
#include <vector>

class IsPalindrome {
public:
  bool operator()(const std::string& word) const {
    const auto middleOfWord = begin(word) + word.size() / 2;
    return std::equal(begin(word), middleOfWord, rbegin(word));
  }
};

int main() {
  std::vector<std::string> someWords { "dad", "hello", "radar", "vector",
  "deleveled", "foo", "bar", "racecar", "ROTOR", "", "C++", "aibohphobia" };
  someWords.erase(std::remove_if(begin(someWords), end(someWords),
  IsPalindrome()),
    end(someWords));
  std::for_each(begin(someWords), end(someWords), [](const auto& word) {
    std::cout << word << ",";
  });
  return 0;
}
```

The output of this program is as follows:

```
hello,vector,foo,bar,C++,
```

Reduce (Fold)

Reduce (also called fold, collapse, or aggregate) is the most powerful of the three higher-order functions and might be a bit hard to understand at first glance. Reduce (fold) is a higher-order function to get a single resultant value by applying a binary operator to a list of values. In C++, this function is provided by the Standard Library algorithm `std::accumulate` (defined in the `<numeric>` header). Some say that `std::accumulate` is the most powerful algorithm in the Standard Library.

To start with a simple example, you can easily get the sum of all integers in a vector, as shown in Listing 7-26.

Listing 7-26. Building the Sum of All Values in a Vector Using std::accumulate

```cpp
#include <numeric>
#include <iostream>
#include <vector>

int main() {
  std::vector<int> numbers { 12, 45, -102, 33, 78, -8, 100, 2017, -110 };

  const int sum = std::accumulate(begin(numbers), end(numbers), 0);
  std::cout << "The sum is: " << sum << std::endl;
  return 0;
}
```

The version of std::accumulate we used does not expect an explicit binary operator in the parameter list. Using this version of the function, the sum of all values is calculated. Of course, you can provide your own binary operator, as in the example through a lambda expression in Listing 7-27.

Listing 7-27. Finding the Highest Number in a Vector Using std::accumulate

```cpp
int main() {
  std::vector<int> numbers { 12, 45, -102, 33, 78, -8, 100, 2017, -110 };

  const int maxValue = std::accumulate(begin(numbers), end(numbers), 0,
    [](const int value1, const int value2) {
    return value1 > value2 ? value1 : value2;
  });
  std::cout << "The highest number is: " << maxValue << std::endl;
  return 0;
}
```

LEFT AND RIGHT FOLD

Functional programming often distinguishes between two ways to fold a list of elements: a *left fold* and a *right fold*.

If we combine the first element with the result of recursively combining the rest, this is called a right fold. Instead, if we combine the result of recursively combining all elements but the last one with the last element, this operation is called a left fold.

If, for example, we take a list of values that are to be folded with a + operator to a sum, the parentheses are as follows for a left fold operation: ((A + B) + C) + D. Instead, with a right fold, the parentheses would be set like this: A + (B + (C + D)). In the case of a simple associative + operation, the result does not change whether it is formed with a left fold or a right fold. But in the case of non-associative binary functions, the order in which the elements are combined may influence the final result's value.

Also in C++, we can distinguish between a left fold and a right fold. If we use `std::accumulate` with normal iterators, we get a left fold:

`std::accumulate(begin, end, init_value, binary_operator)`

Instead, if we use `std::accumulate` with a reverse iterator, we get a right fold:

`std::accumulate(rbegin, rend, init_value, binary_operator)`

Fold Expressions in C++17

Starting with C++17, the language has gained an interesting new feature called *fold expressions*. Fold expressions are implemented as so-called *variadic templates* (available since C++11); that is, as templates that can take a variable number of arguments in a type-safe way. This arbitrary number of arguments is held in a so-called *parameter pack*.

What has been added with C++17 is the possibility to reduce the parameter pack directly with the help of a binary operator, that is, to perform a folding. The general syntax of C++17 fold expressions are as follows:

```
( ... operator parampack )                        // left fold
( parampack operator ... )                        // right fold
( initvalue operator ... operator parampack )     // left fold with an init
                                                       value
( parampack operator ... operator initvalue )     // right fold with an init
                                                       value
```

Listing 7-28 shows an example, a left fold with an init value.

Listing 7-28. An example of a Left Fold

```cpp
#include <iostream>

template<typename... PACK>
int subtractFold(int minuend, PACK... subtrahends) {
  return (minuend - ... - subtrahends);
}

int main() {
  const int result = subtractFold(1000, 55, 12, 333, 1, 12);
  std::cout << "The result is: " << result << std::endl;
  return 0;
}
```

Note that a right fold cannot be used in this case due to the lack of associativity of operatort. Fold expressions are supported for 32 operators, including logical operators like ==, &&, and ||.

Listing 7-29 shows another example, which tests that a parameter pack contains at least one even number.

Listing 7-29. Checking Whether a Parameter Pack Contains an Even Value

```cpp
#include <iostream>

template <typename... TYPE>
bool containsEvenValue(const TYPE&... argument) {
  return ((argument % 2 == 0) || ...);
}
```

```
int main() {
  const bool result1 = containsEvenValue(10, 7, 11, 9, 33, 14);
  const bool result2 = containsEvenValue(17, 7, 11, 9, 33, 29);

  std::cout << std::boolalpha;
  std::cout << "result1 is " << result1 << "\n";
  std::cout << "result2 is " << result2 << std::endl;
  return 0;
}
```

The output of this program is as follows:

```
result1 is true
result2 is false
```

Pipelining with Range Adaptors (C++20)

People who like to work with UNIX or Linux operating systems emphasize, among other things, a particularly convenient and efficient way to perform tasks on these operating systems: using shell programming. Basically, a UNIX/Linux shell is a command-line-based human-machine interface. There are a number of text-based shells available for UNIX/Linux OS, such as Bash (an acronym for *Bourne Again Shell*), the Korn Shell, and the Z Shell.

One of the reasons that you can perform complex tasks very elegantly and efficiently with the help of these shells is the possibility of *pipelining*. Some people say the concept of pipelining, introduced in 1972, has been one of the most important UNIX innovations in history, perhaps apart from regular expressions. Basically, a pipeline is a message-passing pattern and describes a chain of processing elements. In a shell, a pipeline is a set of processes, usually small programs, chained together by their standard streams, so that the output text of each process (stdout) is passed directly as input (stdin) to the next one.

As an example, suppose we have a text file named customers.txt, in which hundreds of customer names are listed line-by-line, preceded by a date, as follows (an excerpt):

```
2020-11-05,Stephan Roth
2020-11-22,John Doe
2020-10-15,Mark Powers
[...]
```

On the Bash command line, we now execute the following command sequence:

```
$ cat customers.txt | sort -r > customers2.txt
```

What will happen here? Well, first the cat command (short for "concatenate") lists the contents of the text file customers.txt on stdout. This output stream is redirected with the help of the *pipe operator* (a vertical bar: |) and is used as the input stream for the program sort. The sort command is used to sort lines in a text file. In our case, we have specified by the command-line option -r that the sort order should be reversed. Instead of descending sorting, ascending sorting is used. The output stream of the sort command is redirected again, because we don't want to see its output on the screen. Instead, it should be written to a new text file. The greater than symbol, >, tells the shell to redirect the sort's output to the customers2.txt file.

In Chapter 5 I briefly introduced the new C++20 Ranges library. However, I neglected a few of the new features there: range adaptors and chaining using the pipe operator! Just as you can chain commands together on a UNIX shell using pipes, this is also possible with C++20 Range adaptors.

You may remember the following small code example (excerpt) from Listing 5-26? It's shown in again in Listing 7-30.

Listing 7-30. The Code Snippet from Listing 5-26

```
#include <iostream>
#include <ranges>
#include <vector>

std::vector<int> integers = { 2, 5, 8, 22, 45, 67, 99 };
auto view = std::views::reverse(integers); // does not change 'integers'
```

Recall that a view is lazy evaluated, i.e., whatever transformation it applies, the view performs it at the moment someone requests an element. And as a range adaptor, it does not modify the underlying range, in our case the vector named integers.

Due to their property as adaptors, views can be easily chained. We now extend this example by adding more views and some lambda expressions; see Listing 7-31.

Listing 7-31. Chaining Range Adaptors

```
#include <algorithm> // required for std::ranges::for_each
#include <iostream>
#include <ranges>
#include <vector>

int main() {
  std::vector<int> integers = { 2, 5, 8, 22, 45, 67, 99 };
  auto isOdd = [] (const int value) { return value % 2 != 0; };
  auto square = [] (const int value) { return value * value; };
  auto printOnStdOut = [] (const int value) { std::cout << value << '\n';
};

  auto view = std::views::transform(std::views::reverse(std::views::filter(
integers, isOdd)),
    square);

  std::ranges::for_each(view, printOnStdOut);
  return 0;
}
```

The output of the program is as follows:

```
9801
4489
2025
25
```

Well, from a clean code developer's perspective, this code sample still has one unsightly flaw: the nested Range adaptors for creating the view. This is just one line of code, but it is not easy to comprehend on first sight what's happening here. Just think about that in a real software application; nested Range adaptors could become much more complex than in this relatively simple example.

This is where the new C++20 pipe operator comes into play. It is "syntactic sugar"[1] and can be used for easier function chaining. The line of code in which the view view is created can also be written as follows:

```
auto view = integers | std::views::filter(isOdd) | std::views::reverse |
   std::views::transform(square);
```

That's pretty convenient, isn't it? This looks very similar to building pipelines in a UNIX shell, as we saw it at the beginning of this section. You can simply read the expression from left to right and easily understand how the view is composed. Thanks to the power of views, the C++20 Ranges Library enables developers to write code in an even more functional programming-style.

Before we come to the end of this chapter on functional programming, I previously announced that I would revisit and improve the code example in Listing 7-15 once again. With all the new functional programming concepts we have now learned, we can refactor this example and make it much more compact and elegant; see Listing 7-32.

Listing 7-32. The Refactored Code Example

```
#include <concepts>
#include <iostream>
#include <ranges>

template <typename T>
concept Streamable = requires (std::ostream& os, const T& value) {
  { os << value };
};

int main() {
  auto toSquare = [] (const auto value) { return value * value; };
  auto isAnEvenNumber = [] <std::integral T> (const T value) {
    return (value % 2) == 0;
  };
  auto print = [] <Streamable T> (const T& printable) {
    std::cout << printable << '\n';
  };
```

---

[1]The term "syntactic sugar" describes syntax within a programming language that is designed to make parts of the code easier to read or to express.

```
for (const auto& value : std::views::iota(0, 100)
  | std::views::transform(toSquare)
  | std::views::filter(isAnEvenNumber)) {
  print(value);
}

  return 0;
}
```

Clean Code in Functional Programming

No doubt, the functional programming movement has not stopped with C++, and that's basically good. Many useful concepts have been incorporated into our somewhat aged programming language during the last decade, starting with C++11.

But code that is written in a functional style is not automatically good or clean code. The increasing popularity of functional programming languages during the last few years could make you believe that functional code is per se better to maintain, to read, to test, and is less error prone than, for instance, object-oriented code. **But that's not unconditionally true!** On the contrary, nifty elaborated functional code that is doing non-trivial things can be very difficult to understand.

Let's, for example, look at a simple fold operation that is very similar to one of the previous examples:

```
// Build the sum of all product prices
const Money sum = std::accumulate(begin(productPrices),
end(productPrices), 0.0);
```

If you read this without the explaining source code comment...is this intention revealing code? Remember what you learned in Chapter 4 about comments. Whenever you feel the urge to write a source code comment, you should first think about how to improve the code so that the comment becomes superfluous.

So, what we really want to read or write is something like this:

```
const Money totalPrice = buildSumOfAllPrices(productPrices);
```

You prefer the functional programming style over OO? Okay, but I'm sure that you will agree that KISS, DRY, and YAGNI (see Chapter 3) are also very good principles in functional programming! Do you think that you can ignore the *single responsibility principle* (see Chapter 6) in functional programming? Forget it! If a function does more than one thing, it will lead to similar problems as in object orientation. I hope do not have to mention that good and expressive naming (see Chapter 4 about good names) is also enormously important for the understandability and maintainability of code in a functional environment. Always keep in mind that developers spend much more time reading code than writing code.

Note   The principles of good software design still apply, regardless of the programming style you use!

Thus, we can conclude that most design principles used by object-oriented software designers and programmers can also be used by functional programmers.

Personally, I prefer a balanced mix of both programming styles. There are many design challenges that can be solved perfectly using object-oriented paradigms. Polymorphism is a great benefit of OO. We can take advantage of the dependency inversion principle (see the eponymous section in Chapter 6), which allows us to invert source code and runtime dependencies.

Instead, complex mathematical computations and algorithms can be better solved using a functional programming style. And if high and ambitious performance and efficiency requirements must be fulfilled, which will inevitably require a parallelization of certain tasks, functional programming can play its trump card.

Regardless of whether you prefer to write software in an object-oriented way, or in a functional style, or in an appropriate mixture of both, you should always remember the following quote:

"Always code as if the guy who ends up maintaining your code will be a violent psychopath who knows where you live."

—John F. Woods, 1991,
in a post to the comp.lang.c++ newsgroup

CHAPTER 8

Test-Driven Development

"Project Mercury ran with very short (half-day) iterations that were time boxed. The development team conducted a technical review of all changes, and, interestingly, applied the Extreme Programming practice of test-first development, planning, and writing tests before each micro-increment."

—Craig Larman and Victor R. Basili,
Iterative and Incremental Development: A Brief History. IEEE, 2003

In Chapter 2, "Build a Safety-Net," we learned that a suite of well-crafted and fast unit tests can ensure that our code works correctly. So far, so good. But what is so special about test-driven development (TDD) so that this topic justifies a dedicated chapter?

Especially in recent years, the discipline of test-driven development, a so-called test-first approach, has gained in popularity. TDD has become an important ingredient of the toolbox of software craftspeople. That's a little bit surprising, because the basic idea of test-first approaches is nothing new. *Project Mercury*, which is mentioned in the opening quote, was the first human spaceflight program of the United States and was conducted under the direction of NASA from 1958 through 1963. Although what was practiced in that project about 60 years ago as "test-first development" certainly is not exactly the kind of TDD as we know it today, we can say that the basic idea was present quite early in professional software development.

But then it seemed that this approach was forgotten for decades. In countless projects with billions of lines of code, the tests were postponed at the end of the development process. The sometimes-devastating consequences of this right-shifting of the tests in the project's schedules are known: if time is getting short in the project, one of the first things usually abandoned by the development team are the important tests.

© Stephan Roth 2021
S. Roth, *Clean C++20*, https://doi.org/10.1007/978-1-4842-5949-8_8

With the increasing popularity of agile practices in software development and the coming up of a new method called *eXtreme Programming* (XP) at the beginning of the 2000s, test-driven development was rediscovered. Kent Beck wrote his famous book *Test-Driven Development: By Example* [Beck02], and test-first approaches like TDD experienced a renaissance and became increasingly important tools in the toolbox of software craftspeople.

In this chapter, I not only explain that although the term "test" is included in test-driven development, it is not primarily about quality assurance. TDD offers many more benefits than just a simple validation of the correctness of the code. Rather I explain the differences between TDD and what is sometimes called *plain old unit testing* (POUT), followed by the discussion of the workflow of TDD in detail, supported by a detailed practical example that shows how to do it in C++.

The Drawbacks of Plain Old Unit Testing (POUT)

No doubt, as we've seen in Chapter 2, a suite of unit tests is basically a much better situation than having no tests in place. But in many projects the unit tests are written somehow parallel to the implementation of the code to be tested, sometimes even completely after finalization of the module to be developed. The UML activity diagram depicted in Figure 8-1 visualizes this process.

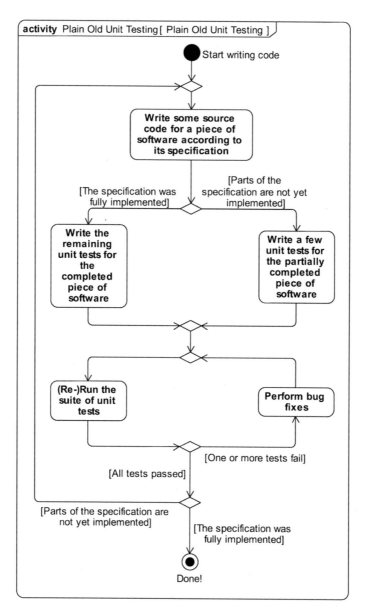

Figure 8-1. *The typical process flow in traditional unit testing*

This widespread approach is occasionally also referred to as plain old unit testing (POUT). Basically, POUT means that the software will be developed "code first", and not test first; meaning that the unit tests are written always after the code to be tested has been written. And to many developers this order appears to be the only logical sequence. They argue that to test something, obviously the thing to be tested needs to have been built previously. And in some development organizations, this approach is even mistakenly named as "test-driven development," which is flat wrong.

Like I said, plain old unit testing is better than no unit testing at all. Nonetheless, this approach has a few disadvantages:

- There is no compulsion to write the unit tests afterward. Once a feature works (...or rather seems to work), there is little motivation to retrofit the code with unit tests. It's no fun, and the temptation to move on to the next exciting task is just too great for many developers.

- The resulting code can be difficult to test. Often it is not so easy to retrofit existing code with unit tests, because the initial developers didn't set great store by its testability. This tends to favor the emergence of tightly coupled code.

- It is not easy to reach pretty-high test coverage with retrofitted unit tests. The writing of unit tests after the code has the tendency that some issues or bugs can slip through.

Test-Driven Development as a Game Changer

Test-driven development (TDD) turns traditional development completely around. For developers who have not yet dealt with TDD, this approach represents a paradigm shift.

As a so-called test-first approach and in contrast to POUT, TDD does not allow any production code to be written before the associated test has been written that justifies that code. In other words, TDD means that we write the test for a new feature or function always **before** we write the corresponding production code. This is done strictly step by step: after each implemented test, just enough production code is written that the test will pass and no more! And it is done as long as there are still unrealized requirements for the module to be developed.

At first glance, it seems to be paradoxical and a little bit absurd to write a unit test for something that does not yet exist. How can this work?

Don't worry, it works. After we have discussed the process behind TDD in detail in the next section, all doubts will hopefully be eliminated.

The Workflow of TDD

When performing test-driven development, the steps depicted in Figure 8-2 are run through repeatedly until all known requirements for the unit to develop are satisfied.

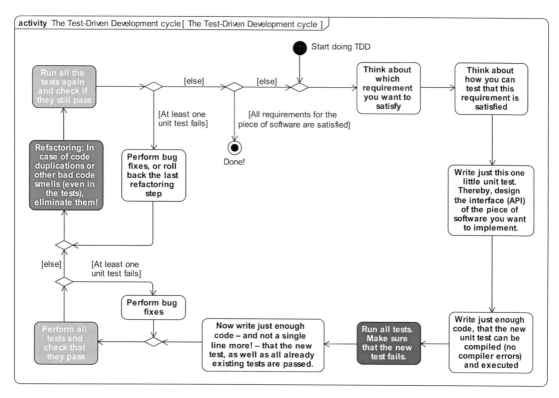

Figure 8-2. *The detailed workflow of TDD as an UML activity diagram*

First of all, it is remarkable that the first action after the initial node that is labeled with "Start Doing TDD" is that the developer should think about which requirement to satisfy. Which kinds of requirements are meant here?

Well, first and foremost there are requirements that must be fulfilled by a software system. This applies both to the requirements of the business stakeholders on the top level regarding the whole system, as well as to the requirements residing on lower abstraction levels, that is, requirements for components, classes, and functions, which were derived from the business stakeholders' requirements. With TDD and its test-first approach, requirements are nailed down firmly by unit tests. In fact, before the production code is written. In our case of a test-first approach for the development of units, that is, at the lowest level of the test pyramid (see Figure 2-1 in Chapter 2), of course the requirements at the lowest level are meant here. Naturally, such a test-first approach can also be applied at the higher levels of abstraction, such as in an approach named *acceptance test–driven development* (ATDD), which is a development methodology that encompasses acceptance testing, but claims writing acceptance tests before developers begin coding.

Next, a small test is to be written, whereby the public interface (API) is to be designed. This might be surprising, because in the first run through this cycle, we still have not written any production code. So, what interface can be designed here if we have a blank piece of paper?

Well, the simple answer is this: that "blank piece of paper" is exactly what we want to fill in now, but coming from a different perspective than usual. We take the perspective of a future external client of the piece of software to be developed. We use a small test to define how we want to use the code to be developed. In other words, this is the step that should lead to well-testable and thus also well-usable software units.

After we have written the appropriate lines in the test, we must, of course, also satisfy the compiler and provide the interface requested by the test.

Then immediately the next surprise: the newly written unit test must (initially) fail. Why?

Simple answer: we have to make sure that the test can fail at all. Even a unit test can itself be implemented incorrectly and, for example, always pass, no matter what we're doing in the production code. So, we have to ensure that the newly written test is armed.

Now we are getting to the climax of this small workflow: we write just enough production code—and not a single line more!—so that the new unit test (… and any previously existing tests) is passed! It is very important to be disciplined at this point and not write more code than required (remember the KISS principle from Chapter 3). It's up to the developer to decide what is appropriate in each situation. Sometimes a single line of code, or even just one statement, is sufficient; in other cases you need to call a library function. If the latter is the case, the time has now come to think about how to integrate and use this library, and especially how to replace it with a test double (see the section about test doubles in Chapter 2).

If we now run the unit tests and we have done everything right, the tests will pass.

We have reached a remarkable point in the process. **If the tests pass, we always have 100% unit test coverage at this step.** Always! Not only 100% in the sense of a technical test coverage metric, such as condition coverage, branch coverage, or statement coverage. No, much more important is that we have 100% unit test coverage regarding the requirements that were already implemented at this point! And yes, at this point possibly there may be still some or many non-implemented requirements for the piece of code to be developed. This is okay, because we will go through the TDD cycle again and again until all requirements are satisfied. But for a subset of requirements that are already satisfied at this point, we have 100% unit test coverage.

This fact gives us tremendous power! With this gapless safety net of unit tests, we can now carry out fearless refactorings. Code smells (e.g., duplicated code) or design issues can be fixed. We do not need to be afraid to break functionality, because regularly executed unit tests will give us immediate feedback about that. And the pleasant thing is this: if one or more tests fail during the refactoring phase, the code change that led to it was a very small one.

After the refactoring has been completed, we can implement another requirement that has not yet been fulfilled by continuing the TDD cycle. If there are no more requirements, we are ready.

Figure 8-2 depicts the TDD cycle with many details. Boiled down to its three essential main steps as depicted in Figure 8-3, the TDD cycle is often referred to as "RED – GREEN – REFACTOR."

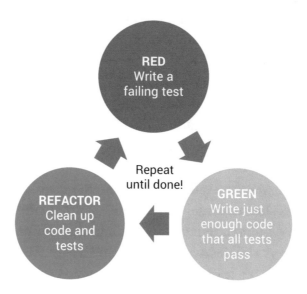

Figure 8-3. *The core workflow of TDD*

- **RED**: We write one failing unit test.

- **GREEN**: We write just enough production code—and not one line more!—so that the new test and all previously written tests will pass.

- **REFACTOR**: Code duplication and other code smells are eliminated, both from the production code as well as from the unit tests.

The terms RED and GREEN refer to typical unit test framework integrations that are available for a variety of IDEs (Integrated Development Environments), where tests that passed are displayed in green and tests that failed are shown in red.

Enough of theory, I will now explain the complete development of a piece of software using TDD and a small example.

TDD by Example: The Roman Numerals Code Kata

The basic idea for what is nowadays called a *code kata* was first described by Dave Thomas, one of the two authors of the remarkable book, *The Pragmatic Programmer* [Hunt99]. Dave was of the opinion that developers should practice on small, not job-related, code bases repeatedly so that they can master their profession like a musician. He said that developers should constantly learn and improve themselves, and for that purpose, they need practice sessions to apply the theory over and over again, using feedback to get better every time.

A code kata is a small exercise in programming, which serves exactly this purpose. The term *kata* is inherited from the martial arts. In far-eastern combatant sports, they use katas to practice their basic moves over and over again. The goal is to bring the course of motion to perfection.

This kind of practice was devolved to software development. To improve their programming skills, developers should practice their craft with the help of small exercises. Katas became an important facet of the Software Craftsmanship movement. They can address different abilities a developer should have, for example, knowing the keyboard shortcuts of the IDE, learning a new programming language, focusing on certain design principles, or practicing TDD. On the Internet, several catalogues with suitable katas for different purposes exist, for example, the collection by Dave Thomas on `http://codekata.com`.

For our first steps with TDD, we use a code kata with an algorithmic emphasis: the well-known Roman numerals code kata.

TDD KATA: CONVERT ARABIC NUMBERS TO ROMAN NUMERALS

The Romans wrote numbers using letters. For instance, they wrote "V" for the Arabic number 5.

Your task is to develop a piece of code using the test-driven development (TDD) approach that translates the Arabic numbers between 1 and 3,999 into their respective Roman representations.

Numbers in the Roman system are represented by combinations of letters from the Latin alphabet. Roman numerals, as used today, are based on seven characters:

$$1 \Rightarrow I$$
$$5 \Rightarrow V$$
$$10 \Rightarrow X$$
$$50 \Rightarrow L$$
$$100 \Rightarrow C$$
$$500 \Rightarrow D$$
$$1,000 \Rightarrow M$$

Numbers are formed by combining characters together and adding the values. For instance, the Arabic number 12 is represented by "XII" (10 + 1 + 1). And the number 2017 is "MMXVII" in its Roman equivalent.

Exceptions are 4, 9, 40, 90, 400, and 900. To avoid that four equal characters must be repeated in succession, the number 4, for instance, is not represented by "IIII", but "IV". This is known as subtractive notation, that is, the number that is represented by the preceding character I is subtracted from V (5 - 1 = 4). Another example is "CM," which is 900 (1,000 - 100).

By the way, the Romans had no equivalent for 0 (zero); furthermore, they didn't know negative numbers.

Preparations

Before we can write our first test, we need to make some preparations and set up the test environment.

As the unit test framework for this kata, I use *Google Test* (https://github.com/
google/googletest), a platform-independent C++ unit test framework released under
the *New BSD License*. Of course, any other C++ unit testing framework can be used for
this kata as well.

It is also strongly recommended to use a version control system. Apart from a few
exceptions, we will perform a commit to the version control system after each pass-
through of the TDD cycle. This has the great advantage that we can walk back and
regress possibly wrong decisions.

Furthermore, we have to think about how the source code files will be organized. My
suggestion for this kata is initially to start with just one file, the file that will take up all
future unit tests: `ArabicToRomanNumeralsConverterTestCase.cpp`. Since TDD guides us
incrementally through the formation process of a software unit, it is possible to decide
later if additional files are required.

For a fundamental function check, we write a main function that initializes
Google Test and runs all tests, and we write one simple unit test (named
`PreparationsCompleted`) that always fails intentionally, as shown in the code example in
Listing 8-1.

Listing 8-1. The Initial Content of ArabicToRomanNumeralsConverterTestCase.cpp

```cpp
#include <gtest/gtest.h>

int main(int argc, char** argv) {
  testing::InitGoogleTest(&argc, argv);
  return RUN_ALL_TESTS();
}

TEST(ArabicToRomanNumeralsConverterTestCase, PreparationsCompleted) {
  GTEST_FAIL();
}
```

After compiling and linking, we execute the resulting binary file to run the test.
The output of our small program on standard output (`stdout`) should be as shown in
Listing 8-2.

Listing 8-2. The Output of the Test Run

```
[==========] Running 1 test from 1 test case.
[----------] Global test environment set-up.
[----------] 1 test from ArabicToRomanNumeralsConverterTestCase
[ RUN      ] ArabicToRomanNumeralsConverterTestCase.PreparationsCompleted
../ ArabicToRomanNumeralsConverterTestCase.cpp:9: Failure
Failed
[  FAILED  ] ArabicToRomanNumeralsConverterTestCase.PreparationsCompleted
(0 ms)
[----------] 1 test from ArabicToRomanNumeralsConverterTestCase (2 ms total)

[----------] Global test environment tear-down
[==========] 1 test from 1 test case ran. (16 ms total)
[  PASSED  ] 0 tests.
[  FAILED  ] 1 test, listed below:
[  FAILED  ] ArabicToRomanNumeralsConverterTestCase.PreparationsCompleted

 1 FAILED TEST
```

Note   Depending on the unit test framework and its version used, the output may be different than what is presented in this example.

As expected, the test fails. The output on stdout is pretty helpful to imagine what went wrong. It specifies the name of the failed tests, the filename, the line number, and the reason that the test failed. In this case, it is a failure that was enforced by a special Google Test macro.

If we now exchange the GTEST_FAIL() macro with the GTEST_SUCCEED() macro inside the test, after a recompilation the test should pass, as shown in Listing 8-3.

Listing 8-3. The Output of the Successful Test Run

```
[==========] Running 1 test from 1 test case.
[----------] Global test environment set-up.
[----------] 1 test from ArabicToRomanNumeralsConverterTestCase
[ RUN      ] ArabicToRomanNumeralsConverterTestCase.PreparationsCompleted
[       OK ] ArabicToRomanNumeralsConverterTestCase.PreparationsCompleted (0 ms)
```

```
[----------] 1 test from ArabicToRomanNumeralsConverterTestCase (0 ms total)

[----------] Global test environment tear-down
[==========] 1 test from 1 test case ran. (4 ms total)
[  PASSED  ] 1 test.
```

That's good, because now we know that everything is prepared properly and we can start with our kata.

The First Test

The first step is to decide which first small requirement we want to implement. Then we will write a failing test for it. For our example, we've decided to start with converting a single Arabic number into a Roman numeral: We want to convert the Arabic number 1 into an "I."

Hence, we take the already existing dummy test and convert it into a real unit test, which can prove the fulfillment of this small requirement. Thereby we also have to consider how the interface to the conversion function should look (Listing 8-4).

Listing 8-4. The First Test (Irrelevant Parts of the Source Code Were Omitted)

```
TEST(ArabicToRomanNumeralsConverterTestCase, 1_isConvertedTo_I) {
  ASSERT_EQ("I", convertArabicNumberToRomanNumeral(1));
}
```

As you can see, we have decided for a simple function that takes an Arabic number as a parameter and has a string as a return value.

But the code cannot be compiled without compiler errors, because the convertArabicNumberToRomanNumeral() function does not yet exist. Uncompilable test code is considered like a failed unit test in TDD.

That means that we now have to stop writing test code to write just enough production code that it can be compiled without errors. Thus, we're going to create the conversion function now, and we'll even write that function directly into the source code file, which also contains the test. Of course, we are aware of the fact that it cannot permanently remain this way. See Listing 8-5.

Listing 8-5. The Function Stub Satisfies the Compiler

```cpp
#include <gtest/gtest.h>
#include <string>

int main(int argc, char** argv) {
  testing::InitGoogleTest(&argc, argv);
  return RUN_ALL_TESTS();
}

std::string convertArabicNumberToRomanNumeral(const unsigned int
arabicNumber) {
  return "";
}

TEST(ArabicToRomanNumeralsConverterTestCase, 1_isConvertedTo_I) {
  ASSERT_EQ("I", convertArabicNumberToRomanNumeral(1));
}
```

Now the code can be compiled again without errors. And for the moment the function returns only an empty string.

In addition, we now have our first executable test, which must fail (RED), because the test expects an "I," but the function returns an empty string (Listing 8-6).

Listing 8-6. The Output of Google Test After Executing the Deliberately Failing Unit Test (RED)

```
[==========] Running 1 test from 1 test case.
[----------] Global test environment set-up.
[----------] 1 test from ArabicToRomanNumeralsConverterTestCase
[ RUN      ] ArabicToRomanNumeralsConverterTestCase.1_isConvertedTo_I
../ArabicToRomanNumeralsConverterTestCase.cpp:14: Failure
Value of: convertArabicNumberToRomanNumeral(1)
  Actual: ""
Expected: "I"
[  FAILED  ] ArabicToRomanNumeralsConverterTestCase.1_isConvertedTo_I (0 ms)
[----------] 1 test from ArabicToRomanNumeralsConverterTestCase (0 ms total)

[----------] Global test environment tear-down
```

```
[==========] 1 test from 1 test case ran. (6 ms total)
[  PASSED  ] 0 tests.
[  FAILED  ] 1 test, listed below:
[  FAILED  ] ArabicToRomanNumeralsConverterTestCase.1_isConvertedTo_I

 1 FAILED TEST
```

Okay, that's what we expected.

Now we need to change the implementation of the convertArabicNumberToRomanNumeral() function so that the test will pass. The rule is this: do the simplest thing that could possibly work. And what could be easier than returning an "I" from the function? See Listing 8-7.

Listing 8-7. The Changed Function (Irrelevant Parts of the Source Code Were Omitted)

```cpp
std::string convertArabicNumberToRomanNumeral(const unsigned int
arabicNumber) {
  return "I";
}
```

You will probably say, "Wait a minute! That's not an algorithm to convert Arabic numbers into their Roman equivalents. That's cheating!"

Of course, the algorithm isn't ready yet. You have to change your mind. The rules of TDD state that we should write the simplest bit of code that passes the current test. It is an incremental process, and we are just at its beginning.

```
[==========] Running 1 test from 1 test case.
[----------] Global test environment set-up.
[----------] 1 test from ArabicToRomanNumeralsConverterTestCase
[ RUN      ] ArabicToRomanNumeralsConverterTestCase.1_isConvertedTo_I
[       OK ] ArabicToRomanNumeralsConverterTestCase.1_isConvertedTo_I (0 ms)
[----------] 1 test from ArabicToRomanNumeralsConverterTestCase (0 ms total)

[----------] Global test environment tear-down
[==========] 1 test from 1 test case ran. (1 ms total)
[  PASSED  ] 1 test.
```

Excellent! The test passed (GREEN) and we can go to the refactoring step. Actually, there is no need to refactor something yet, so we can just proceed with the next run-through the TDD cycle. But first we have to commit our changes to the source code repository.

The Second Test

For our second unit test, we will take a 2, which has to be converted into "II".

```
TEST(ArabicToRomanNumeralsConverterTestCase, 2_isConvertedTo_II) {
  ASSERT_EQ("II", convertArabicNumberToRomanNumeral(2));
}
```

Unsurprisingly, this test must immediately fail (RED), because our convertArabicNumberToRomanNumeral() function returns an "I." After we have verified that the test fails, we complement the implementation so that the test can pass. Once again, we do the simplest thing that could possibly work (Listing 8-8).

Listing 8-8. We Add Some Code to Pass the New Test

```
std::string convertArabicNumberToRomanNumeral(const unsigned int
arabicNumber) {
  if (arabicNumber == 2) {
    return "II";
  }
  return "I";
}
```

Both tests pass (GREEN).

Should we refactor something now? Maybe not yet, but you might get a sneaking suspicion that we will need a refactoring soon. At the moment, we continue with our third test...

The Third Test and the Tidying Afterward

Unsurprisingly, the third test will test the conversion of the number 3:

```
TEST(ArabicToRomanNumeralsConverterTestCase, 3_isConvertedTo_III) {
```

```
  ASSERT_EQ("III", convertArabicNumberToRomanNumeral(3));
}
```

Of course, this test will fail (RED). The code to pass this test, and all previous tests (GREEN), could look as follows:

```
std::string convertArabicNumberToRomanNumeral(const unsigned int
arabicNumber) {
  if (arabicNumber == 3) {
    return "III";
  }
  if (arabicNumber == 2) {
    return "II";
  }
  return "I";
}
```

The bad gut feeling about the emerging design, which you might have had on the second test, was not unsubstantiated. At least now we, as skilled clean code developers, should be completely dissatisfied with the obvious code duplication. It's pretty evident that we cannot continue this path. An endless sequence of if statements cannot be a solution, because we will end up with a horrible design. It's time for refactoring, and we can do it without fear, because 100% unit test coverage creates a comfortable feeling of safety!

If we take a look at the code inside function convertArabicNumberToRomanNumeral(), a pattern is recognizable. The Arabic number is like a counter of the I-characters of its Roman equivalent. In other words, as long as the number to be converted can be decremented by 1 before it reaches 0, an "I" is added to the Roman numeral string.

Well, this can be done in an elegant way using a while loop and string concatenation, as shown in Listing 8-9.

Listing 8-9. The Conversion Function After Refactoring

```
std::string convertArabicNumberToRomanNumeral(unsigned int arabicNumber) {
  std::string romanNumeral;
  while (arabicNumber >= 1) {
    romanNumeral += "I";
```

```
    arabicNumber--;
  }
  return romanNumeral;
}
```

That looks pretty good. We removed code duplication and found a compact solution. We also had to remove the `const` declaration from the `arabicNumber` parameter because we have to manipulate the Arabic number in the function. And the three existing unit tests are still passed.

We can proceed to the next test. Of course, you can also continue with the 5, but I decided for "10-is-X". I have the hope that the group of 10 will reveal a similar pattern as 1, 2, and 3. The Arabic number 5 will, of course, be treated later. See Listing 8-10.

Listing 8-10. The Fourth Unit Test

```
TEST(ArabicToRomanNumeralsConverterTestCase, 10_isConvertedTo_X) {
  ASSERT_EQ("X", convertArabicNumberToRomanNumeral(10));
}
```

Well, it shouldn't surprise anyone that this test fails (RED). Here is what Google Test writes on `stdout` about this new test:

```
[ RUN      ] ArabicToRomanNumeralsConverterTestCase.10_isConvertedTo_X
../ArabicToRomanNumeralsConverterTestCase.cpp:31: Failure
Value of: convertArabicNumberToRomanNumeral(10)
  Actual: "IIIIIIIIII"
Expected: "X"
[  FAILED  ] ArabicToRomanNumeralsConverterTestCase.10_isConvertedTo_X (0 ms)
```

The test fails, because 10 is not "IIIIIIIIII," but "X". However, if we see the output of Google Test, we could get an idea. Maybe the same approach that we used for the Arabic numbers 1, 2, and 3, could be used also for 10, 20, and 30?

STOP! Well, that's imaginable, but we should not yet create something for the future without unit tests that lead us to such a solution. We would not work test-driven anymore, if we implement the production code for 20 and 30 in one go with the code for 10. So, we do again the simplest thing that could possibly work. See Listing 8-11.

Listing 8-11. The Conversion Function Can Now Also Convert 10

```cpp
std::string convertArabicNumberToRomanNumeral(unsigned int arabicNumber) {
  if (arabicNumber == 10) {
    return "X";
  } else {
    std::string romanNumeral;
    while (arabicNumber >= 1) {
      romanNumeral += "I";
      arabicNumber--;
    }
    return romanNumeral;
  }
}
```

Okay, the test and all previous tests are passed (GREEN). We can stepwise add a test for the Arabic number 20, and then for 30. After we run through the TDD cycle for both cases, our conversion function looks like Listing 8-12.

Listing 8-12. The Result During the Sixth TDD Cycle Before Refactoring

```cpp
std::string convertArabicNumberToRomanNumeral(unsigned int arabicNumber) {
  if (arabicNumber == 10) {
    return "X";
  } else if (arabicNumber == 20) {
    return "XX";
  } else if (arabicNumber == 30) {
    return "XXX";
  } else {
    std::string romanNumeral;
    while (arabicNumber >= 1) {
      romanNumeral += "I";
      arabicNumber--;
    }
    return romanNumeral;
  }
}
```

At least now a refactoring is urgently required. The emerged code has some bad smells, like some redundancies and a high cyclomatic complexity. However, our suspicion has also been confirmed that the processing of the numbers 10, 20, and 30 follows a similar pattern to processing the numbers 1, 2, and 3. Let's try it; see Listing 8-13.

Listing 8-13. After the Refactoring All if-else Decisions Are Gone

```
std::string convertArabicNumberToRomanNumeral(unsigned int arabicNumber) {
  std::string romanNumeral;
  while (arabicNumber >= 10) {
    romanNumeral += "X";
    arabicNumber -= 10;
  }
  while (arabicNumber >= 1) {
    romanNumeral += "I";
    arabicNumber--;
  }
  return romanNumeral;
}
```

Excellent, all tests passed immediately! It seems that we are on the right track.

We must, however, have the goal in mind of the refactoring step in the TDD cycle. Further up in this section, you can read the following: Code duplication and other code smells are eliminated, both from the production code **as well as from the unit tests**.

We should take a critical look at our test code. Currently it looks like Listing 8-14.

Listing 8-14. The Emerged Unit Tests Have a Lot of Code Duplications

```
TEST(ArabicToRomanNumeralsConverterTestCase, 1_isConvertedTo_I) {
  ASSERT_EQ("I", convertArabicNumberToRomanNumeral(1));
}

TEST(ArabicToRomanNumeralsConverterTestCase, 2_isConvertedTo_II) {
  ASSERT_EQ("II", convertArabicNumberToRomanNumeral(2));
}

TEST(ArabicToRomanNumeralsConverterTestCase, 3_isConvertedTo_III) {
  ASSERT_EQ("III", convertArabicNumberToRomanNumeral(3));
```

```
}

TEST(ArabicToRomanNumeralsConverterTestCase, 10_isConvertedTo_X) {
  ASSERT_EQ("X", convertArabicNumberToRomanNumeral(10));
}

TEST(ArabicToRomanNumeralsConverterTestCase, 20_isConvertedTo_XX) {
  ASSERT_EQ("XX", convertArabicNumberToRomanNumeral(20));
}

TEST(ArabicToRomanNumeralsConverterTestCase, 30_isConvertedTo_XXX) {
  ASSERT_EQ("XXX", convertArabicNumberToRomanNumeral(30));
}
```

Remember what I wrote about test code quality in Chapter 2: the quality of the test code must be as high as the quality of the production code. In other words, our tests need to be refactored, because they contain a lot of duplication and should be designed more elegantly. Furthermore, we want to increase their readability and maintainability. But what can we do?

Take a look at the six tests. The verification in the tests is always the same and could be read more generally as: "Check if Arabic number <x> is converted to the Roman numeral <string>."

A solution could be to provide a dedicated assertion (also known as *custom assertion* or *custom matcher*) for that purpose, which can be read in the same way:

```
checkIf(x).isConvertedToRomanNumeral("string");
```

More Sophisticated Tests with a Custom Assertion

To implement our custom assertion, we first of all write a unit test that fails, but different from the unit tests we've written before:

```
TEST(ArabicToRomanNumeralsConverterTestCase, 33_isConvertedTo_XXXIII) {
  checkIf(33).isConvertedToRomanNumeral("XXXII");
}
```

The probability is very high that the conversion of 33 already works. Therefore, we force the test to fail (RED) by specifying an intentionally wrong result as the expected value ("XXXII"). But this new test also fails due to another reason: the compiler cannot compile the unit test without errors. A function named checkIf() does not exist yet, equally there is no isConvertedToRomanNumeral().

So, we must first satisfy the compiler by writing the custom assertion. This will consist of two parts (Listing 8-15):

- A free checkIf(<parameter>) function, returning one instance of a custom assertion class.

- The custom assertion class that contains the real assertion method, verifying one or various properties of the tested object.

Listing 8-15. A Custom Assertion for Roman Numerals

```
class RomanNumeralAssert {
public:
  RomanNumeralAssert() = delete;
  explicit RomanNumeralAssert(const unsigned int arabicNumber) :
      arabicNumberToConvert(arabicNumber) { }
  void isConvertedToRomanNumeral(std::string_view expectedRomanNumeral)
const {
    ASSERT_EQ(expectedRomanNumeral,
    convertArabicNumberToRomanNumeral(arabicNumberToConvert));
  }

private:
  const unsigned int arabicNumberToConvert;
};

RomanNumeralAssert checkIf(const unsigned int arabicNumber) {
  RomanNumeralAssert assert { arabicNumber };
  return assert;
}
```

> **Note**   Instead of a free function `checkIf()`, a static and public class method can also be used in the assertion class. This can be necessary when you're facing ODR violations, for example, clashes of identical function names. Of course, then the namespace name must be prepended when using the class method:
>
> ```
> RomanNumeralAssert::checkIf(33).isConvertedToRomanNumeral
> ("XXXIII");
> ```

Now the code can be compiled without errors, but the new test will fail as expected during execution. See Listing 8-16.

Listing 8-16. An Excerpt from the Output of Google Test on stdout

```
[ RUN      ] ArabicToRomanNumeralsConverterTestCase.33_isConvertedTo_XXXIII
../ArabicToRomanNumeralsConverterTestCase.cpp:30: Failure
Value of: convertArabicNumberToRomanNumeral(arabicNumberToConvert)
  Actual: "XXXIII"
Expected: expectedRomanNumeral
Which is: "XXXII"
[  FAILED  ] ArabicToRomanNumeralsConverterTestCase.33_isConvertedTo_XXXIII
(0 ms)
```

So, we need to modify the test and correct the Roman numeral that we expect as the result. See Listing 8-17.

Listing 8-17. Our Custom Asserter Allows a More Compact Spelling of the Test Code

```
TEST(ArabicToRomanNumeralsConverterTestCase, 33_isConvertedTo_XXXIII) {
  checkIf(33).isConvertedToRomanNumeral("XXXIII");
}
```

Now we can sum up all previous tests into a single one, as shown in Listing 8-18.

Listing 8-18. All Checks Can Be Elegantly Pooled Into One Test Function

```
TEST(ArabicToRomanNumeralsConverterTestCase,
conversionOfArabicNumbersToRomanNumerals_Works) {
```

```
checkIf(1).isConvertedToRomanNumeral("I");
checkIf(2).isConvertedToRomanNumeral("II");
checkIf(3).isConvertedToRomanNumeral("III");
checkIf(10).isConvertedToRomanNumeral("X");
checkIf(20).isConvertedToRomanNumeral("XX");
checkIf(30).isConvertedToRomanNumeral("XXX");
checkIf(33).isConvertedToRomanNumeral("XXXIII");
}
```

Take a look at our test code now: redundancy-free, clean, and easily readable. The directness of our self-made assertion is quite elegant. And it is blindingly easy to add more tests now, because we have just to write a single line of code for every new test.

You might complain that this refactoring also has a small disadvantage. The name of the test method is now less specific than the name of all test methods prior to the refactoring (see the section on unit test names in Chapter 2). Can we tolerate these small drawbacks? I think yes. We've made a compromise here: This little disadvantage is compensated by the benefits in terms of maintainability and extensibility of our tests.

Now we can continue the TDD cycle and implement the production code successively for the following three tests:

```
checkIf(100).isConvertedToRomanNumeral("C");
checkIf(200).isConvertedToRomanNumeral("CC");
checkIf(300).isConvertedToRomanNumeral("CCC");
```

After three iterations, the code will look like Listing 8-19 prior to the refactoring step.

Listing 8-19. Our Conversion Function in the Ninth TDD Cycle Before Refactoring

```cpp
std::string convertArabicNumberToRomanNumeral(unsigned int arabicNumber) {
  std::string romanNumeral;
  if (arabicNumber == 100) {
    romanNumeral = "C";
  } else if (arabicNumber == 200) {
    romanNumeral = "CC";
  } else if (arabicNumber == 300) {
    romanNumeral = "CCC";
  } else {
```

```cpp
    while (arabicNumber >= 10) {
      romanNumeral += "X";
      arabicNumber -= 10;
    }
    while (arabicNumber >= 1) {
      romanNumeral += "I";
      arabicNumber--;
    }
  }
  return romanNumeral;
}
```

And again, the same pattern emerges as before with 1, 2, 3; and 10, 20, and 30. We can also use a similar loop for the hundreds, as shown in Listing 8-20.

Listing 8-20. The Emerging Pattern, as Well as Which Parts of the Code Are Variable and Which Are Identical, Is Clearly Recognizable

```cpp
std::string convertArabicNumberToRomanNumeral(unsigned int arabicNumber) {
  std::string romanNumeral;
  while (arabicNumber >= 100) {
    romanNumeral += "C";
    arabicNumber -= 100;
  }
  while (arabicNumber >= 10) {
    romanNumeral += "X";
    arabicNumber -= 10;
  }
  while (arabicNumber >= 1) {
    romanNumeral += "I";
    arabicNumber--;
  }
  return romanNumeral;
}
```

It's Time to Clean Up Again

At this point we should take a critical look at our code once again. If we continue like this, the code will contain many code duplications, because the three `while` statements look very similar. We can, however, take advantage of these similarities by abstracting the code parts that are equal in all three `while` loops.

It's refactoring time! The only code parts that are different in all three `while` loops are the Arabic number and its corresponding Roman numeral. The idea is to separate these variable parts from the stable rest of the loop.

In a first step, we introduce a `struct` that maps Arabic numbers to their Roman equivalents. In addition, we need an array (we will use `std::array` from the C++ Standard Library here) of that struct. Initially, we will only add one element to the array that allocates letter "C" to the number 100. See Listing 8-21.

Listing 8-21. Introducing an Array that Holds Mappings Between Arabic Numbers and Their Roman Equivalents

```
struct ArabicToRomanMapping {
  unsigned int arabicNumber;
  std::string romanNumeral;
};

const std::array arabicToRomanMappings {
  ArabicToRomanMapping { 100, "C" }
};
```

After these preparations, we modify the first `while` loop in the conversion function to verify if the basic idea will work. See Listing 8-22.

Listing 8-22. Replacing the Literals with Entries from the New Array

```
std::string convertArabicNumberToRomanNumeral(unsigned int arabicNumber) {
  std::string romanNumeral;
  while (arabicNumber >= arabicToRomanMappings[0].arabicNumber) {
    romanNumeral += arabicToRomanMappings[0].romanNumeral;
    arabicNumber -= arabicToRomanMappings[0].arabicNumber;
  }
```

```
  while (arabicNumber >= 10) {
    romanNumeral += "X";
    arabicNumber -= 10;
  }
  while (arabicNumber >= 1) {
    romanNumeral += "I";
    arabicNumber--;
  }
  return romanNumeral;
}
```

All tests pass. So, we can continue to fill the array with the mappings "10-is-X" and "1-is-I". See Listing 8-23.

Listing 8-23. Again a Pattern Emerges: The Obvious Code Redundancy Can Be Eliminated by a Loop

```
const std::array arabicToRomanMappings {
  ArabicToRomanMapping { 100, "C" },
  ArabicToRomanMapping {  10, "X" },
  ArabicToRomanMapping {   1, "I" }
};

std::string convertArabicNumberToRomanNumeral(unsigned int arabicNumber) {
  std::string romanNumeral;
  while (arabicNumber >= arabicToRomanMappings[0].arabicNumber) {
    romanNumeral += arabicToRomanMappings[0].romanNumeral;
    arabicNumber -= arabicToRomanMappings[0].arabicNumber;
  }
  while (arabicNumber >= arabicToRomanMappings[1].arabicNumber) {
    romanNumeral += arabicToRomanMappings[1].romanNumeral;
    arabicNumber -= arabicToRomanMappings[1].arabicNumber;
  }
  while (arabicNumber >= arabicToRomanMappings[2].arabicNumber) {
    romanNumeral += arabicToRomanMappings[2].romanNumeral;
    arabicNumber -= arabicToRomanMappings[2].arabicNumber;
  }
  return romanNumeral;
}
```

And again, all tests are passed. Excellent! But there is still a lot of duplicated code, so we have to continue our refactoring. The good news is that we can now see that the only difference in all three while loops is just the array index. This means that we can get along with just one while loop if we iterate through the array. See Listing 8-24.

Listing 8-24. Through the Range Based for Loop, the DRY Principle Is No Longer Violated

```
std::string convertArabicNumberToRomanNumeral(unsigned int arabicNumber) {
  std::string romanNumeral;
  for (const auto& mapping : arabicToRomanMappings) {
    while (arabicNumber >= mapping.arabicNumber) {
      romanNumeral += mapping.romanNumeral;
      arabicNumber -= mapping.arabicNumber;
    }
  }
  return romanNumeral;
}
```

All tests pass. Wow, that's great! Just take a look at this compact and well-readable piece of code. More mappings of Arabic numbers to their Roman equivalents can now be supported by adding them to the array. We will try this for 1,000, which must be converted into an M. Here is our next test:

```
checkIf(1000).isConvertedToRomanNumeral("M");
```

The test failed as expected. By adding another element for "1000-is-M" to the array, the new test, and of course all previously tests, should pass.

```
const std::array arabicToRomanMappings {
  ArabicToRomanMapping { 1000, "M" },
  ArabicToRomanMapping {  100, "C" },
  ArabicToRomanMapping {   10, "X" },
  ArabicToRomanMapping {    1, "I" }
};
```

A successful test run after this small change confirms our assumption: it works! That was quite easy. We can add more tests now, for example, for 2,000 and 3,000. And even 3,333 should work immediately:

```
checkIf(2000).isConvertedToRomanNumeral("MM");
checkIf(3000).isConvertedToRomanNumeral("MMM");
checkIf(3333).isConvertedToRomanNumeral("MMMCCCXXXIII");
```

Good. Our code works even with these cases. However, there are some Roman numerals that have not yet been implemented. For example, the 5 that has to be converted to "V".

```
checkIf(5).isConvertedToRomanNumeral("V");
```

As expected, this test fails. The interesting question is the following: what should we do now so that the test gets passed? Maybe you think about a special treatment of this case. But is this really a special case, or can we treat this conversion in the same way as the previous and already implemented conversions?

Probably the simplest thing that could possibly work is to just add a new element at the correct index to our array? Well, maybe it's worth it to try it out...

```cpp
const std::array arabicToRomanMappings {
  ArabicToRomanMapping { 1000, "M" },
  ArabicToRomanMapping {  100, "C" },
  ArabicToRomanMapping {   10, "X" },
  ArabicToRomanMapping {    5, "V" },
  ArabicToRomanMapping {    1, "I" }
};
```

Our assumption was true: All tests are passed! Even Arabic numbers like 6 and 37 should be converted correctly to their Roman equivalent. We verify that by adding assertions for these cases:

```
  checkIf(6).isConvertedToRomanNumeral("VI");
//...
  checkIf(37).isConvertedToRomanNumeral("XXXVII");
```

Approaching the Finish Line

And it comes as no surprise that we can use basically the same approach for "50-is-L" and "500-is-D".

Next, we need to deal with the implementation of the so-called subtraction notation; for example, the Arabic number 4 has to be converted to the Roman numeral "IV". How could we implement these special cases elegantly?

Tip   If you ask yourself how to find all the important test cases for this code kata, I just want to remind you about the topics of equivalence partitioning and boundary value analysis discussed in Chapter 2.

Well, after a short consideration it becomes obvious that these cases are nothing really special! Ultimately, it is of course not forbidden to add a mapping rule to our array where the string contains two characters instead of one. For instance, we can just add a new "4-is-IV" entry to the arabicToRomanMappings array. Maybe you will say, "Isn't that a hack?" No, I don't think so. It is pragmatic and easy, without making things unnecessarily complicated.

Therefore, we first add a new test that will fail:

```
checkIf(4).isConvertedToRomanNumeral("IV");
```

For the new test to be passed, we add the corresponding mapping rule for 4 (see the penultimate entry in the array):

```
const std::array arabicToRomanMappings {
  ArabicToRomanMapping { 1000, "M"  },
  ArabicToRomanMapping {  500, "D"  },
  ArabicToRomanMapping {  100, "C"  },
  ArabicToRomanMapping {   50, "L"  },
  ArabicToRomanMapping {   10, "X"  },
  ArabicToRomanMapping {    5, "V"  },
  ArabicToRomanMapping {    4, "IV" },
  ArabicToRomanMapping {    1, "I"  }
};
```

After we've executed all tests and verified that they passed, we can be certain that our solution also works for 4! Hence, we can repeat that pattern for "9-is-IX," "40-is-XL," "90-is-XC," and so on. The schema is always the same, so I do not show the resulting source code here (the final result with the complete code is shown in Listing 8-25), but I think it's not hard to comprehend.

Done!

The interesting question is this: When do we know that we are done? When the piece of software that we have to implement is finished and all requirements are satisfied? When we can discontinue running through the TDD cycle? Do we really have to test all the numbers from 1 up to 3999 each by a unit test to know that we're done?

The simple answer: **If all requirements on our piece of code have been successfully implemented, and we do not find a new unit test that would lead to new production code, we are done!**

And that is exactly the case with our TDD kata. We could still add many more assertions to the test method; the test would pass each time without the necessity to change the production code. This is the way TDD "speaks" to us: "Hey, my friend, you're done!"

The result is shown in Listing 8-25.

Listing 8-25. This Version Has Been Checked In at GitHub with the Commit Message "Done"

```
#include <gtest/gtest.h>
#include <string>
#include <array>

int main(int argc, char** argv) {
  testing::InitGoogleTest(&argc, argv);
  return RUN_ALL_TESTS();
}

struct ArabicToRomanMapping {
  unsigned int arabicNumber;
  std::string romanNumeral;
};

const std::string arabicToRomanMappings {
  ArabicToRomanMapping { 1000, "M"  },
  ArabicToRomanMapping {  900, "CM" },
  ArabicToRomanMapping {  500, "D"  },
  ArabicToRomanMapping {  400, "CD" },
  ArabicToRomanMapping {  100, "C"  },
```

```
  ArabicToRomanMapping {   90, "XC" },
  ArabicToRomanMapping {   50, "L"  },
  ArabicToRomanMapping {   40, "XL" },
  ArabicToRomanMapping {   10, "X"  },
  ArabicToRomanMapping {    9, "IX" },
  ArabicToRomanMapping {    5, "V"  },
  ArabicToRomanMapping {    4, "IV" },
  ArabicToRomanMapping {    1, "I"  }
};

std::string convertArabicNumberToRomanNumeral(unsigned int arabicNumber) {
  std::string romanNumeral;
  for (const auto& mapping : arabicToRomanMappings) {
    while (arabicNumber >= mapping.arabicNumber) {
      romanNumeral += mapping.romanNumeral;
      arabicNumber -= mapping.arabicNumber;
    }
  }
  return romanNumeral;
}

// Test code starts here...

class RomanNumeralAssert {
public:
  RomanNumeralAssert() = delete;
  explicit RomanNumeralAssert(const unsigned int arabicNumber) :
      arabicNumberToConvert(arabicNumber) { }
  void isConvertedToRomanNumeral(std::string_view expectedRomanNumeral)
  const {
    ASSERT_EQ(expectedRomanNumeral, convertArabicNumberToRomanNumeral
    (arabicNumberToConvert));
  }

private:
  const unsigned int arabicNumberToConvert;
};
```

```
RomanNumeralAssert checkIf(const unsigned int arabicNumber) {
  return RomanNumeralAssert { arabicNumber };
}

TEST(ArabicToRomanNumeralsConverterTestCase,
conversionOfArabicNumbersToRomanNumerals_Works) {
  checkIf(1).isConvertedToRomanNumeral("I");
  checkIf(2).isConvertedToRomanNumeral("II");
  checkIf(3).isConvertedToRomanNumeral("III");
  checkIf(4).isConvertedToRomanNumeral("IV");
  checkIf(5).isConvertedToRomanNumeral("V");
  checkIf(6).isConvertedToRomanNumeral("VI");
  checkIf(9).isConvertedToRomanNumeral("IX");
  checkIf(10).isConvertedToRomanNumeral("X");
  checkIf(20).isConvertedToRomanNumeral("XX");
  checkIf(30).isConvertedToRomanNumeral("XXX");
  checkIf(33).isConvertedToRomanNumeral("XXXIII");
  checkIf(37).isConvertedToRomanNumeral("XXXVII");
  checkIf(50).isConvertedToRomanNumeral("L");
  checkIf(99).isConvertedToRomanNumeral("XCIX");
  checkIf(100).isConvertedToRomanNumeral("C");
  checkIf(200).isConvertedToRomanNumeral("CC");
  checkIf(300).isConvertedToRomanNumeral("CCC");
  checkIf(499).isConvertedToRomanNumeral("CDXCIX");
  checkIf(500).isConvertedToRomanNumeral("D");
  checkIf(1000).isConvertedToRomanNumeral("M");
  checkIf(2000).isConvertedToRomanNumeral("MM");
  checkIf(2017).isConvertedToRomanNumeral("MMXVII");
  checkIf(3000).isConvertedToRomanNumeral("MMM");
  checkIf(3333).isConvertedToRomanNumeral("MMMCCCXXXIII");
  checkIf(3999).isConvertedToRomanNumeral("MMMCMXCIX");
}
```

Note   The source code of the completed Roman numerals kata, including its version history, can be found on GitHub at: `https://github.com/Apress/clean-cpp20`.

Wait! There is still one really important step to be taken: we must separate the production code from the test code. We used the `ArabicToRomanNumeralsConverterTestCase.cpp` file all the time like our workbench, but now the time has come to remove the finished piece of work from the vise. In other words, the production code has now to be moved into a different, still-to-be created new file; but of course, the unit tests should still be able to test the code.

During this last refactoring step, some design decisions can be made. For example, does it remain with a free-standing conversion function, or should the conversion method and the array be wrapped into a new class? I would clearly favor the latter (embedding the code in a class) because it is toward an object-oriented design, and it is easier to hide implementation details with the help of encapsulation.

No matter how the production code will be provided and be integrated in its usage environment (this depends on the purpose), our gapless unit test coverage makes it unlikely that something will go wrong.

The Advantages of TDD

Test-driven development is a tool and technique for incremental design and development of a software component. That's why the acronym TDD is also often referred to as "test-driven design." It's one way, of course not the only way, to think through your requirements or design before you write the production code.

The significant advantages of TDD are the following:

- **TDD, if done right, forces you to take small steps when writing software.** The approach ensures that you always have to write just a few lines of production code to reach the comfortable state again where everything works. This also means that you are at most a few lines of code away from a situation where everything still worked. This is the main difference with the traditional approach of producing and changing a lot of production code beforehand, which goes hand in hand with the drawback that the software sometimes cannot be compiled and executed without errors for hours or days.

- **TDD establishes a very fast feedback loop.** Developers must always know if they are still working on a correct system. Therefore, it is important for them that they have a fast feedback loop to know in a split second that everything works correctly. Complex system and integration tests, especially if they are still carried out manually, are not capable of this and are much too slow (remember the test pyramid in Chapter 2).

- **Creating a unit test first helps a developer really consider what needs to be done.** In other words, TDD ensures that code is not simply hacked down from the brain into the keyboard. That's good, because code that was written that way is often error prone, difficult to read, and sometimes even superfluous. Many developers are usually going faster than their true capacity to deliver good work. TDD is a way to slow the developers down in a positive sense. Don't worry, managers, it is good that your developers slow down, because this will soon be rewarded with a noticeable increase in quality and speed in the development process when the high test-coverage reveals its positive effect.

- **With TDD, a gapless specification arises in the form of executable code.** Specifications written in natural language with a text processing program of an Office suite, for example, are not executable—they are "dead artifacts."

- **The developer deals much more consciously and responsibly with dependencies.** If another software component or even an external system (for example, a database) is required, this dependency can be defined due to an abstraction (interface) and replaced by a test double (mock object) for the test. The resulting software modules (e.g., classes) are smaller, loosely coupled, and contain only the code necessary to pass the tests.

- **The emerging production code with TDD will have 100% unit test coverage by default.** If TDD was performed correctly, there should not be a single line of production code that was not motivated by a previously written unit test.

Test-driven development can be a driver and enabler for a good and sustainable software design. As with many other tools and methods, the practice of TDD cannot guarantee a good design. It is not a silver bullet for design issues. The design decisions are still taken by the developer and not by the tool. At the least, TDD is a helpful approach to avoid what might be perceived as bad design. Many developers who use TDD in their daily work can confirm that it is extremely hard to produce or tolerate bad and messy code with this approach.

And there is no doubt about when a developer has finished implementing all required functionalities: if all unit tests are green and they cannot find any more new test cases that would lead to new code, it means that all requirements on the unit are satisfied and the job is done! And an enjoyable side effect is that it's done in high quality.

In addition, the TDD workflow also drives the design of the unit to be developed, especially its interface. With TDD and test first, the API's design and implementation are guided by its test cases. Anyone who has ever tried to retrofit legacy code with unit tests knows how difficult that could be. These systems are typically built "code first." Many inconvenient dependencies and a bad API design complicate testing in such systems. And if a software unit is hard to test, it is also hard to (re-)use. In other words, TDD gives early feedback on a software unit's usability, that is, how simple that piece of software can be integrated and used in its planned execution environment.

When We Should Not Use TDD

The final question is this: should we develop every piece of code using a test-first approach?

My clear answer is **probably not!**

No doubt, test-driven development is a great practice to guide the design and implementation of a piece of software. Theoretically, it would even be possible to develop almost all parts of a software system this way. And as a kind of positive side effect, the emerging code is 100% tested by default.

But some parts of a project are so simple, small, or less complex, that they don't justify this approach. If you can write your code quickly off the cuff, because complexity and risks are low, then of course you can do that. Examples of such situations are pure data classes without functionality (which could be, by the way, a smell, but for other reasons; see the section about anemic classes in Chapter 6), or simple glue code that couples together two modules.

Furthermore, prototyping can be a very difficult task with TDD. When you enter new territory, or you should develop software in a very innovative environment without domain experience, you're sometimes not sure what road you're going to take to a solution. Writing unit tests first in projects with very volatile and fuzzy requirements can be an extremely challenging task. Sometimes it's better to write down a rudimentary solution easily and quickly then, and to ensure its quality in a later step with the help of retrofitted unit tests.

Another big challenge, for which TDD won't help, is getting a good architecture. TDD does not replace the necessary reflecting on the coarse-grained structures (subsystems, components, etc.) of your software system. When you are faced with fundamental decisions about frameworks, libraries, technologies, or architecture patterns, TDD might not be the appropriate approach to make them.

UI code also seems to resists this practice. It seems difficult to impossible to develop the (graphical) user interface of an application in a test-driven way. Among other things, this may be due to the fact that it takes a certain amount of imagination to get an idea of what the UI should look like: How should the user be guided visually through the flow of an use case? How many screens or dialogs are we talking about? What are the preconditions? What does visual feedback to the user look like in the event of an error? All of these questions may not be easily answered, even by domain experts and other stakeholders.

In such cases, a method called *behavior driven development* (BDD) might be helpful, an extension of TDD. BDD promotes writing specification stories with acceptance criteria together with the people from business and QA. These stories can be—virtually or real—executed step by step, stimulating the software to be developed to change its state. With BDD, the user's interaction with the software can be systematically explored and requirements for the UI can be derived.

For anything else, I strongly recommend TDD. This approach can save a lot of time, headaches, and false starts when you must develop a software unit, like a function or class, in C++.

> *"For anything that is more complex than just a few lines of code, software craftsmen can test-drive code as fast as other developers can write code without tests, if not faster."*
>
> —Sandro Mancuso

Tip   If you want to dive deeper into test-driven development with C++, I recommend the excellent book *Modern C++ Programming with Test-Driven Development* [Langr13] by Jeff Langr. Jeff's book offers much deeper insights into TDD and gives you hands-on lessons about the challenges and rewards of doing TDD in C++.

TDD Is Not a Replacement for Code Reviews

"Given enough eyeballs, all bugs are shallow."

—Eric S. Raymond, Linus's law,
The Cathedral and the Bazaar, 1999

Let's conclude this chapter with a topic that plays a major role not only in the environment of C++ development projects: code reviews.

The so-called multi-eye principle applied in code reviews may seem somewhat old-fashioned and time-consuming in today's world, but it is a proven means of knowledge sharing and quality assurance in software development. Who hasn't had this experience—that sometimes it's enough just to have a colleague take a quick look at a tricky problem you've been brooding over for hours and she can immediately give you the decisive tip to solve it?

A code review is much more than just reviewing and improving a piece of code by another developer. In a team, code reviews also help developers get to know their code base better. They can share ideas about how to implement a piece of software better, and they also learn new technologies and practices that enhance their skills. A code review simplifies conversations about the code base, making it easier and faster for new team members to understand the system being developed.

The following questions and points can be clarified and discussed in a code review:

- Are there any obvious bugs in the reviewed code?

- Does the reviewed code meet the requirements for readable, understandable and well-maintainable code? Were clean code principles followed? Are there any bad and unwanted dependencies?

371

- Have all requirements for the reviewed piece of code been considered and implemented?

- Are the tests sufficient for the reviewed piece of code?

- Does new code conform to existing style and formatting guidelines?

- Is the implementation of the reviewed piece of code appropriate and efficient, or are there shorter, more elegant, and better ways to achieve the same result (e.g., a library function that the developers didn't know about)?

- Is there anything I can learn, take, or draw a lesson from the developers of the piece of code being reviewed, e.g., a particularly elegant and good solution, or a library feature that was previously unknown to me?

Code reviews can be performed in a variety of ways. An informal code review can be that you simply ask your colleagues to take a quick look at the code you just wrote and to see if they notice anything ("over-the-shoulder review"). In some development organizations, reviews are formalized and there is even a defined process for them. In some other organizations, code reviews are organized as a regular and social team event, e.g., once a week the development team meets for one or two hours over coffee and cake to review and discuss some code. With pair programming, a continuous code review takes place, so to speak, because the multiple-eyes principle is already in effect while the code is written.

In addition to physical (peer) code review techniques, where a few team members get together for an hour or two, there are also centralized software tools with code review capabilities, often integrated with the version control system and the developers IDEs. These have advantages as well as disadvantages. Advantages are that such tools automatically ensure traceability, and they often provide reporting as well. In addition, they also seem to save time, since a time-consuming meeting for reviewing a piece of code is not required.

The downside of these tools is that you have to find one that fits well into your development process. Moreover, it should be ensured that such tools in no way replace the indispensable face-to-face communication of the team: software development is also a social activity, and direct communication is a crucial factor for success.

Some people say that with test-driven development, you can largely do without code reviews. They argue that with the help of TDD, developers are enforced to produce code of such high quality that a review then no longer brings any further improvements.

But beware: This is a fallacy! If each developer writes test cases, code, and APIs for himself alone, the view of another developer is missing, i.e., someone who can check the aforementioned points from a different perspective. Every developer would stew in her own juice. Thus, no knowledge sharing can take place, nor can people learn from each other. In the medium to long term, code quality will suffer.

One way to combine code reviews and TDD and perform both in parallel is the aforementioned *pair programming*. The pairing partners can discuss test cases, algorithms, structure, naming, and API design and thus improve together. Bugs can be spotted much earlier, because four eyes see more than two. Early and frequent feedback can raise the code quality significantly, and you can't get an earlier feedback than from your pairing partner. And by changing pairings, knowledge is continuously distributed throughout the team.

CHAPTER 9

Design Patterns and Idioms

Good craftspeople can draw on a wealth of experience and knowledge. Once they've found a good solution for a certain problem, they take this solution into their repertoire to apply it in the future to a similar problem. Ideally, they transform their solution into something that is known as a *canonical form* and document it, both for themselves and for others.

CANONICAL FORM

The term *canonical form* in this context describes a representation of something that is reduced to its simplest and most significant form without losing generality. Related to design patterns, the canonical form of a pattern describes its most basic elements: name, context, problem, forces, solution, examples, drawbacks, etc.

This is also true for software developers. Experienced developers can draw on a wealth of sample solutions for constantly recurring design problems in software. They share their knowledge with others and make it reusable for similar problems. The principle behind this is **don't reinvent the wheel!**

In 1995, a much-noticed and famous book was published. Some people even say that it was one of the most important books that has ever been written in software history. The book's title is *Design Patterns: Elements of Reusable Object-Oriented Software* [Gamma95]. Its four authors, Erich Gamma, Richard Helm, Ralph Johnson, and John Vlissides, also known as the *Gang of Four* (GoF), introduced the concept of design patterns into software development and presented a catalogue of 23 object-oriented design patterns.

© Stephan Roth 2021
S. Roth, *Clean C++20*, https://doi.org/10.1007/978-1-4842-5949-8_9

Some people believe that Gamma et al. had invented all the design patterns that are described in their book. But that's not true. Design patterns are not invented by someone, they are usually discovered. The authors have examined software systems that were well made regarding certain qualities, especially flexibility, maintainability, and extendibility. They found the cause of these positive characteristics in the code base and described them in a canonical form.

After the book of the Gang of Four was published, it was thought that many other authors would join the bandwagon and there would be a flood of pattern books in the following years. But this did not happen. Indeed, in the following years there were a few other important books on the subject pattern, such as *Pattern-Oriented Software Architecture* (also known under the acronym "POSA") [Busch96] or *Patterns of Enterprise Application Architecture* [Fowler02], both about architectural patterns, but the expected huge mass stayed out. But from time to time a few new patterns appear, especially in the light of new trends in software development. In recent years, for example, special patterns have become known for the environment of highly distributed, highly available and hyperscaling software systems, which are often based on so-called *microservice architectures*. One example is the Circuit Breaker [Nygard18], a fault-tolerance pattern that can handle the problem that remote requests to other systems or processes can either fail or take too long.

Design Principles vs Design Patterns

In the previous chapters, we discussed a lot of design principles. But how are these principles related to design patterns? What is more important?

Well, let's assume just hypothetically that perhaps one day object-orientation will become totally unpopular, and functional programming (see Chapter 7) will be the dominating programming paradigm. Do principles like KISS, DRY, YAGNI, single responsibility principle, open-closed principle, information hiding, etc., become invalid and thus worthless? The clear answer is **no!**

A principle is a fundamental "truth" or "law" that serves as the foundation for decisions. Therefore, a principle is in most cases independent of a certain programming paradigm or technology. The KISS principle (see Chapter 3), for instance, is a very universal principle. No matter if you are programming in an object-oriented or a functional style, or using different languages like C++, C#, Java, or Erlang: trying to do something as simple as possible is always a worthwhile attitude!

In contrast, a design pattern is a solution for a concrete design problem in a certain context. Especially those ones that are described in the famous *Design Pattern* book of the Gang of Four are closely related to object-orientation. Therefore, principles are more long-lasting and more important. You can find a design pattern for a certain programming problem by yourself, if you have internalized all the valuable principles.

"Decisions and patterns give people solutions; principles help them design their own."

—Eoin Woods in a keynote on
the Joint Working IEEE/IFIP Conference on
Software Architecture 2009 (WICSA2009)

Some Patterns and When to Use Them

As mentioned, besides the 23 design patterns described in the Gang of Four book, there are of course more patterns. Even nowadays, new patterns appear from time to time. Particularly in the context of highly distributed and concurrent systems, specific patterns of resilience, consistency ensurance, and fault tolerance have emerged in recent years. Some patterns are often being found in many code bases, while others are more or less rare or exotic.

The following sections discuss some of the in my opinion most important design patterns.

By the way, we used a few design patterns in the previous chapters, some even relatively intense, but I did not mentioned it. Just a slight hint: In the book of the Gang of Four [Gamma95], you can find a design pattern that is called... *Iterator*!

Before we continue with the discussion of individual design patterns, a warning must be pointed out here.

Warning   Don't overuse design patterns! No doubt, design patterns are cool and sometimes even fascinating. But an overplayed use of them, especially if there are no good reasons to justify it, can have catastrophic consequences. Your software design will suffer from useless overengineering. Always remember KISS and YAGNI (see Chapter 3).

Let's take a look at a few patterns.

Dependency Injection (DI)

"Dependency Injection is a key element of agile architecture."

—Ward Cunningham, paraphrased from the
"Agile and Traditional Development" panel discussion at Pacific
NW Software Quality Conference (PNSQC) 2004

The fact that I start the section about specific design patterns with one that is not mentioned in the famous book of the Gang of Four has weighty reasons, of course. I am convinced that *dependency injection* is by far the most important pattern that can help software developers significantly improve their software design. This pattern can be regarded quite rightly as a game changer.

Before we dive deeper into dependency injection, I want to reckon with another pattern that is detrimental to good software design: the singleton!

The Singleton Anti-Pattern

I'm pretty sure that you already know the design pattern named *singleton*. It is, on first sight, a simple and widespread pattern, not only in the C++ domain (we will see soon that its supposed simplicity can be deceptive). Some code bases are even littered with singletons. This pattern is, for instance, often used for so-called *loggers* (objects for logging purposes), for database connections, for central user management, or to represent things from the physical world (e.g., hardware such as USB or printer interfaces). In addition, factories and so-called utility classes, which are a colorful hodgepodge of helper functions, are often implemented as singletons. The latter are a code smell, because they are a sign of weak cohesion (see Chapter 3).

The authors of *Design Patterns* have been regularly asked by journalists when they will revise their book and publish a new edition. And their regular answer was that they do not see any reason for this, because the contents of the book are still largely valid. In an interview with the online journal *InformIT*, however, they allowed themselves to give a more detailed answer. Here is a small excerpt from the entire interview, which reveals an interesting opinion from Gamma about singletons (Larry O'Brien was the interviewer, and Erich Gamma gives the answer):

> *[...]*
>
> **Larry:** *How would you refactor "Design Patterns"?*

Erich: We did this exercise in 2005. Here are some notes from our session. We have found that the object-oriented design principles and most of the patterns haven't changed since then. (...)

When discussing which patterns to drop, we found that we still love them all. (Not really—I'm in favor of dropping Singleton. Its use is almost always a design smell.)

—Design Patterns 15 Years Later: An Interview
with Erich Gamma, Richard Helm, and
Ralph Johnson, 2009 [InformIT09]

So, why did Erich Gamma say that the Singleton pattern is almost always a design smell? What's wrong with it?

To answer this, let's first look at what goals are achieved by means of singletons. What requirements can be fulfilled with this pattern? Here is the mission statement of the Singleton pattern from the GoF book:

"Ensure a class only has one instance and provide a global point of access to it."

—Erich Gamma, et al., *Design Patterns* [Gamma95]

This statement contains two conspicuous aspects. On the one hand, the mission of this pattern is to control and manage the whole lifecycle of its one-and-only instance. In accordance with the principle of *separation of concerns*, the management of the lifecycle of an object should be independent and separated from its application—or domain-specific business logic. In a singleton, these two concerns are mixed together.

On the other hand, a global access to its one-and-only instance is provided, so that every other object in the application can use it. This talk about a "global point of access" in the context of object-orientation appears fishy and should raise red flags.

Let's first look at a general implementation style of a singleton in C++, the so-called *Meyers' Singleton*, named after Scott Meyers, the author of the *Effective C++* book [Meyers05]. See Listing 9-1.

Listing 9-1. An Implementation of Meyers' Singleton in Modern C++

```cpp
#pragma once

class Singleton final {
public:
  static Singleton& getInstance() {
    static Singleton theInstance { };
    return theInstance;
  }

  int doSomething() {
    return 42;
  }

  // ...more member functions doing more or less useful things here...

private:
  Singleton() = default;
  Singleton(const Singleton&) = delete;
  Singleton(Singleton&&) noexcept = delete;
  Singleton& operator=(const Singleton&) = delete;
  Singleton& operator=(Singleton&&) noexcept = delete;
  // ...
};
```

One of the main advantages of this implementation style of a singleton is that since C++11, the construction process of the one-and-only instance using a static variable inside getInstance() is thread-safe by default. Be careful, because that does not automatically mean that all the other member functions of the singleton are thread-safe too! The latter must be ensured by the developer.

In source code, the use of such a global singleton instance typically looks like Listing 9-2.

Listing 9-2. An Excerpt from the Implementation of an Arbitrary Class That Uses the Singleton

```cpp
001  #include "AnySingletonUser.h"
002  #include "Singleton.h"
```

```
003  #include <string>
004
...  // ...
024
025  void AnySingletonUser::aMemberFunction() {
...    // ...
040    std::string result = Singleton::getInstance().doThis();
...    // ...
050  }
051
...  // ...
089
090  void AnySingletonUser::anotherMemberFunction() {
...    //...
098    int result = Singleton::getInstance().doThat();
...    //...
104    double value = Singleton::getInstance().doSomethingMore();
...    //...
110  }
111  // ...
```

I think it should now be clear what one of the main problems with singletons is. Due to their global visibility and accessibility, they are simply used anywhere inside the implementation of other classes. That means that in the software design, all the dependencies to this singleton are hidden inside the code. You cannot see these dependencies by examining the interfaces of your classes, that is, their attributes and methods.

And the AnySingletonUser class exemplified in Listing 9-2 is only representative of perhaps hundreds of classes within a large code base, many of which also use the Singleton at different places. In other words, **a singleton in OO is like a global variable in procedural programming.** You can use this global object everywhere, and you cannot see that usage in the interface of the using class, but only in its implementation.

This has a significant negative impact on the dependency situation in a project, as depicted in Figure 9-1.

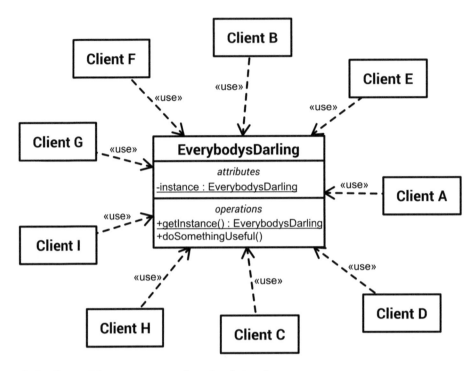

Figure 9-1. *Loved by everyone: the singleton!*

Note   Perhaps you are wondering why, when looking at Figure 9-1, there is a private member variable `instance` inside the `Singleton` class `EverybodysDarling`, which cannot be found in this form in Meyers's recommended implementation. Well, UML is programming language agnostic, that is, as a multipurpose modeling language it does not know about C++, Java, or other OO languages. In fact, in Meyers's Singleton there is a variable that holds the one-and-only instance, but there is not a graphical notation for a variable with static storage duration in UML, because this feature is proprietary in C++. Therefore, I chose to represent this variable as a private static member. This makes the representation compatible with the no longer recommended Singleton implementation described in the GoF book [Gamma95].

I think it's easy to imagine that all these dependencies will have major drawbacks regarding reusability, maintainablility, and testability. All those client classes of the singleton are tightly coupled to it (remember the good property of loose coupling discussed in Chapter 3).

As a consequence, we completely forfeit the possibility to take advantage of polymorphism to supply an alternative implementation. Just think about unit testing. How can it succeed at all to implement a real unit test, if something is used inside the implementation of the class to be tested that cannot be replaced easily by a test double? See the section about test doubles in Chapter 2.

And remember all the rules for good unit tests discussed in Chapter 2, especially unit-test independence. A global object like a singleton sometimes holds a mutable state. How can the independence of tests be ensured, if many or nearly all of the classes in a code base are dependent on one single object that has a lifecycle that ends with the termination of the program, and that possibly holds a state that is shared between them?

Another disadvantage of singletons is that if they have to be changed due to new or changing requirements, this change could trigger a cascade of changes in all the dependent classes. All the dependencies visible in Figure 9-1 pointing to the singleton are potential propagation paths for changes.

Finally, it is also very difficult to ensure in a distributed system—which, by the way, is the normal case in software architecture nowadays—that exactly one instance of a class exists. Just imagine the Microservices pattern, where a complex software system is composed of many small, independent, and distributed processes. In such an environment, singletons are not only difficult to protect against multiple instantiations, but they are also problematic because of the tight coupling they foster.

So, maybe you will ask now: "Okay, I've got it, singletons are basically bad, but what are the alternatives?" The perhaps surprisingly simple answer, which of course requires some further explanation, is this: **Just create one and inject it everywhere its needed!**

Dependency Injection to the Rescue

In the aforementioned interview with Erich Gamma et al., the authors also made a statement about those design patterns, which they would like to include in a new revision of their book. They nominated only a few patterns that would possibly make it into their legendary work and one of them is dependency injection.

Basically, dependency injection (DI) is a technique in which the independent service objects needed by a dependent client object are supplied from the outside. The client object does not have to take care of its required service objects itself, or actively request the service objects, for example, from a factory (see the Factory pattern later in this chapter), or from a service locator.

The intent behind DI could be formulated as follows:

"Decouple components from their required services in such a way that the components do not have to know the names of these services, nor how they have to be acquired."

Let's look at a specific example, the Logger already mentioned, for example, a service class, which offers the possibility to write log entries. Such loggers have often been implemented as singletons. Hence, every client of the logger is dependent on that global singleton object, as depicted in Figure 9-2.

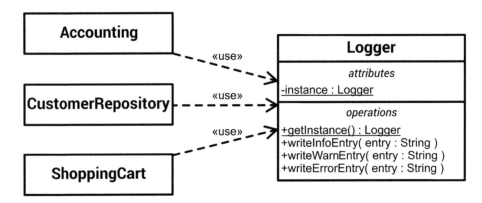

Figure 9-2. *Three domain-specific classes of a web shop are dependent on the logger singleton*

Listing 9-3 shows how the logger singleton class might look in source code (only the relevant parts are shown).

Listing 9-3. The Logger Implemented as a Singleton

```cpp
#include <string_view>

class Logger final {
public:
  static Logger& getInstance() {
    static Logger theLogger { };
    return theLogger;
  }
```

```cpp
  void writeInfoEntry(std::string_view entry) {
    // ...
  }

  void writeWarnEntry(std::string_view entry) {
    // ...
  }

  void writeErrorEntry(std::string_view entry) {
    // ...
  }
};
```

STD::STRING_VIEW [SINCE C++17]

Since C++17, there is a new class available in the C++ language standard: std:: string_
view (defined in the <string_view> header). Objects of this class are very performant
proxies (Proxy is, by the way, also a design pattern) of a string, which are cheap to construct
(there is no memory allocation for raw string data) and thus also cheap to copy.

Another nice feature is that std::string_view can also serve as an adaptor for C-style
strings (char*), character arrays, and even for proprietary string implementations from
different frameworks such as CString (MFC) or QString (Qt):

```cpp
CString aString("I'm a string object of the MFC type CString");
std::string_view viewOnCString { (LPCTSTR)aString };
```

Therefore, it is the ideal class to represent strings whose data is already owned by someone
else and if read-only access is required, for example, for the duration of a function's
execution. For instance, instead of the widespread constant references to std::string,
now std::string_view should be used as a replacement for read-only string function
parameters in a modern C++ program.

We now just pick out for demonstration purposes one of those many classes that use
the logger singleton in its implementation to write log entries, the CustomerRepository
class, shown in Listing 9-4.

Listing 9-4. An Excerpt from the CustomerRepository Class

```cpp
#include "Customer.h"
#include "Identifier.h"
#include "Logger.h"

class CustomerRepository {
public:
  //...
  Customer findCustomerById(const Identifier& customerId) {
    Logger::getInstance().writeInfoEntry("Starting to search for a customer
    specified by a
      given unique identifier...");
    // ...
  }
  // ...
};
```

In order to get rid of the singleton and replace the Logger object with a test double during unit tests, we must first apply the *dependency inversion principle* (DIP; see Chapter 6). This means that we have to introduce an abstraction (an interface) and make both the CustomerRepository and the concrete Logger dependent on that interface, as depicted in Figure 9-3.

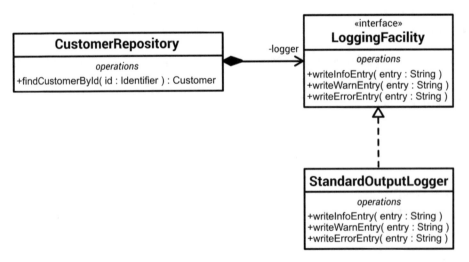

Figure 9-3. *Decoupling through the applied dependency inversion principle*

Listing 9-5 shows how the newly introduced LoggingFacility interface looks in source code.

Listing 9-5. The LoggingFacility Interface

```
#include <memory>
#include <string_view>

class LoggingFacility {
public:
  virtual ~LoggingFacility() = default;
  virtual void writeInfoEntry(std::string_view entry) = 0;
  virtual void writeWarnEntry(std::string_view entry) = 0;
  virtual void writeErrorEntry(std::string_view entry) = 0;
};

using Logger = std::shared_ptr<LoggingFacility>;
```

The StandardOutputLogger is one example of a specific Logger class that implements the LoggingFacility interface and writes the log on standard output, as its name suggests. See Listing 9-6.

Listing 9-6. One Possible Implementation of a LoggingFacility: the StandardOutputLogger

```
#include "LoggingFacility.h"
#include <iostream>

class StandardOutputLogger : public LoggingFacility {
public:
  void writeInfoEntry(std::string_view entry) override {
    std::cout << "[INFO] " << entry << std::endl;
  }

  void writeWarnEntry(std::string_view entry) override {
    std::cout << "[WARNING] " << entry << std::endl;
  }
```

```
  void writeErrorEntry(std::string_view entry) override {
    std::cout << "[ERROR] " << entry << std::endl;
  }
};
```

Next, we need to modify the CustomerRepository class. First, we create a new member variable of the smart pointer type alias Logger. This pointer instance is passed into the class via an initialization constructor. In other words, we allow an instance of a class that implements the LoggingFacility interface **to be injected into** the CustomerRepository object during construction. We also delete the default constructor, because we do not want to allow a CustomerRepository to be created without a logger. Furthermore, we remove the direct dependency in the implementation to the singleton and instead use the smart pointer Logger to write log entries. See Listing 9-7.

Listing 9-7. The Modified Customer Repository Class

```
#include "Customer.h"
#include "Identifier.h"
#include "LoggingFacility.h"

class CustomerRepository {
public:
  CustomerRepository() = delete;
  explicit CustomerRepository(const Logger& loggingService) : logger {
  loggingService } { }
  //...

  Customer findCustomerById(const Identifier& customerId) {
    logger->writeInfoEntry("Starting to search for a customer specified by
    a given unique identifier...");
  // ...

  }
  // ...

private:
  // ...
  Logger logger;
};
```

As a consequence of this refactoring, the CustomerRepository class is no longer dependent on a specific logger. Instead, the CustomerRepository simply has a dependency on an abstraction (interface) that is now explicitly visible in the class and its interface, because it is represented by a member variable and a constructor parameter. That means that the CustomerRepository class now accepts service objects for logging purposes that are passed in from outside, as shown in Listing 9-8.

Listing 9-8. The Logger Object Is Injected Into the Instance of CustomerRepository

```
Logger logger = std::make_shared<StandardOutputLogger>();
CustomerRepository customerRepository { logger };
```

This design change has significantly positive effects. A loose coupling is promoted, and the client object CustomerRepository can now be configured with various service objects that provide logging functionality, as can be seen in the UML class diagram in Figure 9-4.

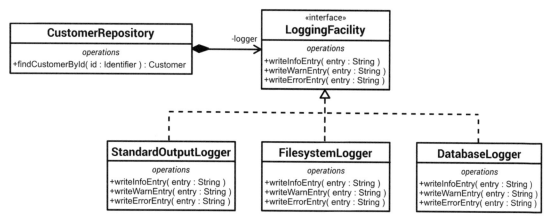

Figure 9-4. *The CustomerRepository class can be supplied with specific logging implementations via its constructor*

Moreover, the testability of the CustomerRepository class has been significantly improved. There are no hidden dependencies to singletons anymore. Now we can easily replace a real logging service by a mock object (see Chapter 2 about unit tests and test doubles). We can equip the mock object with spy methods, for example, to check inside the unit test and determine which data would leave the CustomerRepository object via the LoggingFacility interface. See Listing 9-9.

Listing 9-9. A Test Double (Mock Object) to Unit Test Classes That Have a Dependency on LoggingFacility

```cpp
namespace test {

#include "../src/LoggingFacility.h"
#include <string>
#include <string_view>

class LoggingFacilityMock : public LoggingFacility {
public:
  void writeInfoEntry(std::string_view entry) override {
    recentlyWrittenLogEntry = entry;
  }

  void writeWarnEntry(std::string_view entry) override {
    recentlyWrittenLogEntry = entry;
  }

  void writeErrorEntry(std::string_view entry) override {
    recentlyWrittenLogEntry = entry;
  }

  std::string_view getRecentlyWrittenLogEntry() const {
    return recentlyWrittenLogEntry;
  }

private:
  std::string recentlyWrittenLogEntry;
};

using MockLogger = std::shared_ptr<LoggingFacilityMock>;

}
```

In the unit test in Listing 9-10, you can see the mock object in action.

Listing 9-10. An Example Unit Test Using the Mock Object

```cpp
#include "../src/CustomerRepository.h"
#include "LoggingFacilityMock.h"
#include <gtest/gtest.h>

namespace test {

TEST(CustomerTestCase, WrittenLogEntryIsAsExpected) {
  MockLogger logger = std::make_shared<LoggingFacilityMock>();
  CustomerRepository customerRepositoryToTest { logger };
  Identifier customerId { 1234 };

  customerRepositoryToTest.findCustomerById(customerId);

  ASSERT_EQ("Starting to search for a customer specified by a given unique
  identifier...",
    logger->getRecentlyWrittenLogEntry());}

}
```

In the previous example, I presented dependency injection as a pattern to remove annoying singletons, but of course this is only one of many applications. Basically, a good object-oriented software design should ensure that the involved modules or components are as loosely coupled as possible, and dependency injection is the key to this goal. By consistently applying this pattern, a software design will emerge that has a very flexible plug-in architecture. As a kind of positive side effect, this technique results in highly testable objects as well.

The responsibility for object creation and linking is removed from the objects themselves and is centralized in an infrastructure component, the so-called *assembler* or *injector*. This component (see Figure 9-5) usually operates at program startup and processes something like a "construction plan" (e.g., a configuration file) for the whole software system; that is, it instantiates the objects and services in the correct order and injects the services into the objects that needs them.

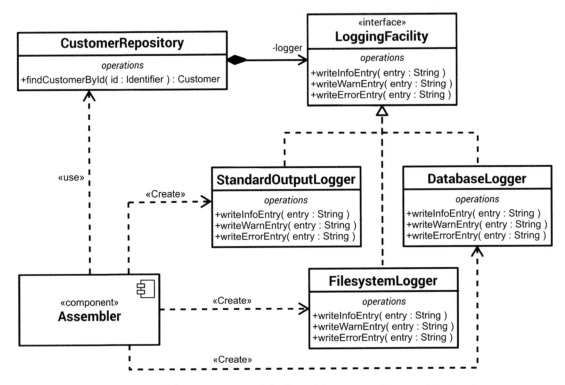

Figure 9-5. *The assembler is responsible for object creation and injection*

Pay attention to the pleasant dependency situation. The direction of the creation dependencies (dashed arrows with stereotype «Create») leads away from the Assembler to the other modules (classes). In other words, no class in this design "knows" that such an infrastructure element like an Assembler exists. (That's not completely correct, because at least one other element in the software system knows about the existence of this component, because the assemble process must be triggered by someone, usually at program start.)

Somewhere within the Assembler component, something like the code in Listing 9-11 could possibly be found.

Listing 9-11. Parts of the Implementation of the Assembler Could Look Like This

```
// ...
Logger loggingServiceToInject = std::make_shared<StandardOutputLogger>();
auto customerRepository = std::make_shared<CustomerRepository>
(loggingServiceToInject);
// ...
```

This DI technique is called *constructor injection*, because the service object to be injected is passed as an argument to an initialization constructor of the client object. The advantage of constructor injection is that the client object gets completely initialized during its construction and is immediately usable then.

But what do we do if service objects are to be injected into client objects while the program is running, for instance, if a client object is only occasionally created during program execution, or the specific logger should be exchanged at runtime? Then the client object must provide a setter for the service object, as in the example in Listing 9-12.

Listing 9-12. The Customer Class Provides a Setter to Inject a Logger

```cpp
#include "Address.h"
#include "LoggingFacility.h"

class Customer {
public:
  Customer() = default;

  void setLoggingService(const Logger& loggingService) {
    logger = loggingService;
  }

  //...

private:
  Address address;
  Logger logger;
};
```

This DI technique is called *setter injection*. And, of course, it is also possible to combine constructor injection and setter injection.

Dependency injection is a design pattern that makes a software design loosely coupled and eminently configurable. It allows the creation of different product configurations for different customers or intended purposes of a software product. It greatly increases the testability of a software system, since it enables developers to inject mock objects very easily. Therefore, this pattern should not be ignored when designing any serious software system. If you want to dive deeper into this pattern, I recommend you read the trend-setting blog article "Inversion of Control Containers and the Dependency Injection pattern" written by Martin Fowler [Fowler04].

In practice, dependency injection frameworks are available as commercial and open source solutions.

Adapter

I'm sure the Adapter (Wrapper) is one of the most commonly used design patterns. The reason for this is that the adaptation of incompatible interfaces is certainly a case that's often necessary in software development, such as when a module developed by another team has to be integrated, or when using third-party libraries.

Here is the mission statement of the Adapter pattern:

> *"Convert the interface of a class into another interface clients expect. Adapter lets classes work together that couldn't otherwise because of incompatible interfaces."*
>
> —Erich Gamma et al., *Design Patterns* [Gamma95]

Let's further develop the example from the previous section about dependency injection. Let's assume that we want to use *BoostLog v2* (see `www.boost.org`) for logging purposes, but we want to keep a usage of this third-party library exchangeable with other logging approaches and technologies.

The solution is simple: we just have to provide another implementation of the `LoggingFacility` interface, which adapts the interface of BoostLog to the interface that we want, as depicted in Figure 9-6.

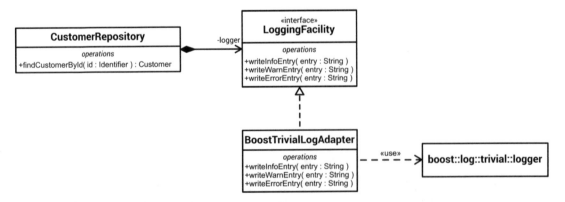

Figure 9-6. *An adapter for a boost logging solution*

In source code, the additional implementation of the LoggingFacility interface BoostTrivialLogAdapter is shown in Listing 9-13.

Listing 9-13. The Adapter for BoostLog Is Just Another Implementation of LoggingFacility

```cpp
#include "LoggingFacility.h"
#include <boost/log/trivial.hpp>

class BoostTrivialLogAdapter : public LoggingFacility {
public:
  void writeInfoEntry(std::string_view entry) override {
    BOOST_LOG_TRIVIAL(info) << entry;
  }

  void writeWarnEntry(std::string_view entry) override {
    BOOST_LOG_TRIVIAL(warn) << entry;
  }

  void writeErrorEntry(std::string_view entry) override {
    BOOST_LOG_TRIVIAL(error) << entry;
  }
};
```

The advantages are obvious: through the Adapter pattern, there is now exactly one class in the entire software system that has a dependency to the third-party logging solution. This also means that the code is not contaminated with proprietary logging statements, like BOOST_LOG_TRIVIAL(). And because this Adapter class is just another implementation of the LoggingFacility interface, we can also use dependency injection (see the previous section) to inject instances—or just exactly the same instance—of this class into all client objects that want to use it.

Adapters can facilitate a broad range of adaptation and conversion possibilities for incompatible interfaces. This ranges from simple adaptations, such as operations names and data type conversions, right up to supporting an entirely different set of operations. In our case, a call of a member function with a string parameter is converted into a call of the insertion operator for streams.

Interface adaptations are of course easier if the interfaces to be adapted are similar. If the interfaces are very different, an adapter can also become a very complex piece of code.

Strategy

If you remember the open-closed principle (OCP) described in Chapter 6 as a guideline for an extensible object-oriented design, the Strategy design pattern can be considered as the "celebrity gig" of this important principle. Here is the mission statement of this pattern:

> *"Define a family of algorithms, encapsulate each one, and make them interchangeable. Strategy lets the algorithm vary independently from clients that use it."*
>
> —Erich Gamma et al., *Design Patterns* [Gamma95]

Doing tings in different ways is a common requirement in software design. Just think of sorting algorithms for lists. There are various sorting algorithms that have different characteristics regarding the time complexity (number of operations required) and the space complexity (additional required storage space in addition to the input list). Examples are Bubble-Sort, Quick-Sort, Merge-Sort, Insert-Sort, and Heap-Sort.

For instance, Bubble-Sort is the least complex one and it is very efficient regarding memory consumption, but also one of the slowest sorting algorithms. In contrast, Quick-Sort is a fast and efficient sorting algorithm that is easy to implement through its recursive structure and does not require additional memory, but it is very inefficient with presorted and inverted lists. With the help of the Strategy pattern, a simple exchange of the sorting algorithm can be implemented, for example, depending on the properties of the list to be sorted.

Let's consider another example. Assume that we want to have a textual representation of an instance of a Customer class in an arbitrary business IT system. A stakeholder requirement states that the textual representation should be formatted in various output formats: as plain text, as XML (Extensible Markup Language), and as JSON (JavaScript Object Notation).

First of all, let's introduce an abstraction for our various formatting strategies, the abstract class Formatter. See Listing 9-14.

Listing 9-14. The Abstract Formatter Class Contains Everything That All Specific Formatter Classes Have in Common

```cpp
#include <memory>
#include <string>
#include <string_view>

class Formatter {
public:
  virtual ~Formatter() = default;

  Formatter& withCustomerId(std::string_view customerId) {
    this->customerId = customerId;
    return *this;
  }

  Formatter& withForename(std::string_view forename) {
    this->forename = forename;
    return *this;
  }

  Formatter& withSurname(std::string_view surname) {
    this->surname = surname;
    return *this;
  }

  Formatter& withStreet(std::string_view street) {
    this->street = street;
    return *this;
  }

  Formatter& withZipCode(std::string_view zipCode) {
    this->zipCode = zipCode;
    return *this;
  }

  Formatter& withCity(std::string_view city) {
    this->city = city;
    return *this;
  }
```

```cpp
  virtual std::string format() const = 0;
protected:
  std::string customerId { "000000" };
  std::string forename { "n/a" };
  std::string surname { "n/a" };
  std::string street { "n/a" };
  std::string zipCode { "n/a" };
  std::string city { "n/a" };
};

using FormatterPtr = std::unique_ptr<Formatter>;
```

The three specific formatters that provide the formatting styles that are requested by the stakeholders are shown in Listing 9-15.

Listing 9-15. The Three Specific Formatters Override the Pure Virtual format() Member Function of Formatter

```cpp
#include "Formatter.h"
#include <sstream>

class PlainTextFormatter : public Formatter {
public:
  std::string format() const override {
    std::stringstream formattedString { };
    formattedString << "[" << customerId << "]: "
      << forename << " " << surname << ", "
      << street << ", " << zipCode << " "
      << city << ".";
    return formattedString.str();
  }
};
class XmlFormatter : public Formatter {
public:
  std::string format() const override {
    std::stringstream formattedString { };
    formattedString <<
      "<customer id=\"" << customerId << "\">\n" <<
```

```
    "  <forename>" << forename << "</forename>\n" <<
    "  <surname>" << surname << "</surname>\n" <<
    "  <street>" << street << "</street>\n" <<
    "  <zipcode>" << zipCode << "</zipcode>\n" <<
    "  <city>"  << city << "</city>\n" <<
    "</customer>\n";
    return formattedString.str();
  }
};

class JsonFormatter : public Formatter {
public:
  std::string format() const override {
    std::stringstream formattedString { };
    formattedString <<
      "{\n" <<
      "  \"CustomerId : \"" << customerId << END_OF_PROPERTY <<
      "  \"Forename: \"" << forename << END_OF_PROPERTY <<
      "  \"Surname: \"" << surname << END_OF_PROPERTY <<
      "  \"Street: \"" << street << END_OF_PROPERTY <<
      "  \"ZIP code: \"" << zipCode << END_OF_PROPERTY <<
      "  \"City: \"" << city << "\"\n" <<
      "}\n";
    return formattedString.str();
  }

private:
  static constexpr const char* const END_OF_PROPERTY { "\",\n" };
};
```

As can be seen clearly here, the OCP is particularly well supported. As soon as a new output format is required, another specialization of the abstract class Formatter has to be implemented. Modifications to the already existing formatters are not required. See Listing 9-16.

Listing 9-16. How the Passed-In Formatter Object Is Used Inside the Member
Function getAsFormattedString()

```cpp
#include "Address.h"
#include "CustomerId.h"
#include "Formatter.h"

class Customer {
public:
  // ...
  std::string getAsFormattedString(Formatter& formatter) const {
    return formatter.
    withCustomerId(customerId.toString()).
    withForename(forename).
    withSurname(surname).
    withStreet(address.getStreet()).
    withZipCode(address.getZipCodeAsString()).
    withCity(address.getCity()).
    format();
  }
  // ...

private:
  CustomerId customerId;
  std::string forename;
  std::string surname;
  Address address;
};
```

The Customer::getAsFormattedString() member function has a parameter that
expects a non-const reference to a formatter object. This parameter can be used to
control the format of the string that can be retrieved through this member function,
or in other words, the member function Customer::getAsFormattedString() can be
supplied with a formatting strategy.

Perhaps you've noticed the special design of the public interface of the Formatter
with its numerous chained with...() member functions. Here also another design
pattern has been used, which is called *Fluent Interface*. In object-oriented programming,

a fluent interface is a style to design APIs in a way that the readability of the code is close to that of ordinary written prose. In Chapter 8, we saw such an interface. That chapter introduced a custom assertion (see the section entitled "More Sophisticated Tests with a Custom Assertion") to write more elegant and better readable tests. In this case here, the trick is that every `with...()` member function is self-referential, that is, the new context for calling a member function on the formatter is equivalent to the previous context, unless when the final `format()` function is called.

A graphical visualization of the class structure of our code example (a UML class diagram) is shown in Figure 9-7.

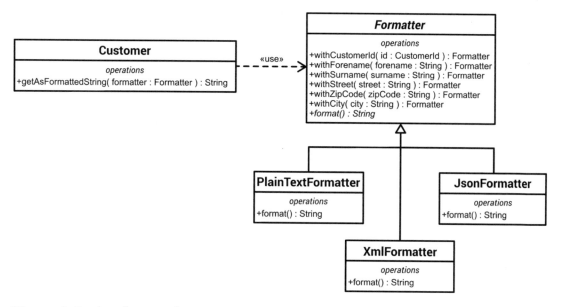

Figure 9-7. *An abstract formatting strategy and its three concrete formatting strategies*

As you can see, the Strategy pattern in this example ensures that the caller of the `Customer::getAsFormattedString()` member function can configure the output format as it wants. You want to support another output format? No problem: thanks to the excellent support of the open-closed principle, another concrete formatting strategy can be easily added. The other formatting strategies, as well as the `Customer` class, remain completely unaffected by this extension.

CLASS HIERARCHY VS TYPE ERASURE IDIOM

As we know from the section about object-orientation in Chapter 6, polymorphism in general means providing a single interface to entities of different types. Many object-oriented design patterns, including most of those in the *Design Patterns* book, rely on class hierarchies with dynamic (runtime) polymorphism realized by virtual member function overrides.

You may also remember the section on type erasure techniques in Chapter 6. There, I presented an alternative way to realize dynamic polymorphism that did not rely on a class hierarchy: the Type Erasure idiom. At this point I would like just to remind you that Strategy, as well as other design patterns, could also be implemented with the help of this idiom.

Command

Software systems usually have to perform a variety of actions due to the reception of instructions. Users of text processing software, for example, issue a variety of commands by interacting with the software's user interface. They want to open a document, save a document, print a document, copy a piece of text, paste a copied piece of text, etc. This general pattern is also observable in other domains. For example, in the financial world, there could be orders from a customer to his securities dealer to buy shares, sell shares, etc. And in a more technical domain like manufacturing, commands are used to control industrial facilities and machines.

When implementing software systems that are controlled by commands, it is important to ensure that the request for an action is separated from the object that actually performs the action. The guiding principle behind this is loose coupling (see Chapter 3) and separation of concerns.

A good analogy is a restaurant. In a restaurant, the waiter accepts the customer's order, but she is not responsible for cooking the food. That is a task for the restaurant's kitchen. Actually, it is even transparent for the customer how the food is prepared. Maybe someone at the restaurant prepares the food, but the food might also be delivered from somewhere else.

In object-oriented software development, there is a behavioral pattern named *Command* (*Action*) that fosters this kind of decoupling. Its mission statement is as follows:

"Encapsulate a request as an object, thereby letting you parameterize clients with different requests, queue or log requests, and support undoable operations."

—Erich Gamma et al., *Design Patterns* [Gamma95]

A good example of the Command pattern is a client/server architecture, where a client—the so-called *invoker*—sends commands that should be executed on a server, which is referred to as the *receiver*.

Let's start with the abstract Command, which is a simple and small interface shown in Listing 9-17.

Listing 9-17. The Command interface

```
#include <memory>

class Command {
public:
  virtual ~Command() = default;
  virtual void execute() = 0;
};

using CommandPtr = std::shared_ptr<Command>;
```

We've also introduced a type alias (CommandPtr) for a smart pointer to commands.

This abstract Command interface can now be implemented by various concrete commands. Let's first take a look at a very simple command, the output of the string "Hello World!". See Listing 9-18.

Listing 9-18. A First and Very Simple Implementation of a Concrete Command

```
#include <iostream>

class HelloWorldOutputCommand : public Command {
public:
  void execute() override {
    std::cout << "Hello World!" << "\n";
  }
};
```

Next, we need the element that accepts and executes the commands. This element is called `Receiver` in the general description of this design pattern. In our case, it is a class named `Server` that plays this role. See Listing 9-19.

Listing 9-19. The Receiver Command

```
#include "Command.h"

class Server {
public:
  void acceptCommand(const CommandPtr& command) {
    command->execute();
  }
};
```

Currently, this class contains only one simple public member function that can accept and execute commands.

Finally, we need the so-called invoker, which is the `Client` class in our client/server architecture. See Listing 9-20.

Listing 9-20. The Client Sends Commands to the Server

```
class Client {
public:
  void run() {
    Server theServer { };
    CommandPtr helloWorldOutputCommand = std::make_shared<HelloWorldOutput
    Command>();
    theServer.acceptCommand(helloWorldOutputCommand);
  }
};
```

Inside the `main()` function, we find the simple code shown in Listing 9-21.

Listing 9-21. The main() Function

```
#include "Client.h"

int main() {
  Client client { };
```

```
  client.run();
  return 0;
}
```

If this program is now being compiled and executed, the "Hello World!" output will appear on stdout. Well, at first sight, this may seem not very exciting, but what we have achieved through the Command pattern is that the origination and sending off of the command is decoupled from its execution. We can now handle command objects as well as other objects.

Since this design pattern supports the open-closed principle (OCP; see Chapter 6) very well, it is also very easy to add new commands with negligible minor modifications of existing code. For instance, if we want to force the Server to wait for a certain amount of time, we can just add the new command shown in Listing 9-22.

Listing 9-22. Another Concrete Command That Instructs the Server to Wait

```
#include "Command.h"
#include <chrono>
#include <thread>

class WaitCommand : public Command {
public:
  explicit WaitCommand(const unsigned int durationInMilliseconds) noexcept :
    durationInMilliseconds{durationInMilliseconds} { };

  void execute() override {
    std::chrono::milliseconds timespan(durationInMilliseconds);
    std::this_thread::sleep_for(timespan);
  }

private:
  unsigned int durationInMilliseconds { 1000 };
};
```

Now we can use the new WaitCommand, as shown in Listing 9-23.

Listing 9-23. The New WaitCommand in Use

```cpp
class Client {
public:
  void run() {
    Server theServer { };
    const unsigned int SERVER_DELAY_TIMESPAN { 3000 };

    CommandPtr waitCommand = std::make_shared<WaitCommand>(SERVER_DELAY_
    TIMESPAN);
    theServer.acceptCommand(waitCommand);

    CommandPtr helloWorldOutputCommand = std::make_shared<HelloWorldOutputC
    ommand>();
    theServer.acceptCommand(helloWorldOutputCommand);
  }
};
```

Figure 9-8 shows an overview of the structure that has been originated so far in the form of an UML class diagram.

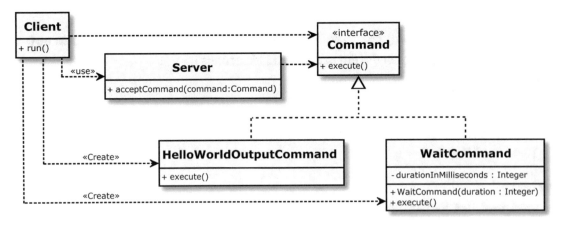

Figure 9-8. *The server knows the Command interface, but not any concrete command*

As can be seen in this example, we can parameterize commands with values. Since the signature of the pure virtual execute() member function is specified as parameterless by the Command interface, the parameterization is done with the help of an initialization constructor. Furthermore, we didn't have to change anything in the Server class, because it was able to treat and execute the new command immediately.

The Command pattern provides manifold possibilities of applications. For example, commands can be queued. This also supports an asynchronous execution of the commands: The invoker sends the command and can then do other things immediately, but the command is executed by the receiver at a later time.

However, something is missing! In the quoted mission statement of the Command pattern, you can read something about "...support undoable operations." Well, the following section is dedicated to that topic.

Command Processor

In our small example of a client/server architecture from the previous section, I cheated a bit. In reality, a server would not execute the commands in the manner I demonstrated. The command objects that are arriving at the server would be distributed to the internal parts of the server that are responsible for the execution of the command. This can, for example, be done with the help of another pattern that is called *Chain of Responsibility* (this pattern is not described in this book).

Let's consider another, more complex example. Assume that we have a drawing program. Users of this program can draw many different shapes, for instance, circles and rectangles. For this purpose, corresponding menus are available in the program's user interface via that these drawing operations can be invoked. I'm pretty sure that you've guessed it: the well-skilled software developers of this program implemented the Command pattern to perform these drawing operations. A stakeholder requirement, however, states that a user of the program can also undo drawing operations.

To fulfill this requirement, we need, first of all, undoable commands. See Listing 9-24.

Listing 9-24. The UndoableCommand Interface Is Created by Combining Command and Revertable

```
#include <memory>

class Command {
public:
  virtual ~Command() = default;
  virtual void execute() = 0;
};
```

```cpp
class Revertable {
public:
  virtual ~Revertable() = default;
  virtual void undo() = 0;
};

class UndoableCommand : public Command, public Revertable { };

using CommandPtr = std::shared_ptr<UndoableCommand>;
```

According to the interface segregation principle (ISP; see Chapter 6), we've added another interface called Revertable that supports the Undo functionality. This new interface can be combined with the existing Command interface using inheritance to an UndoableCommand.

As an example of many, different undoable drawing commands, I just show the concrete command for the circle in Listing 9-25.

Listing 9-25. An Undoable Command for Drawing Circles

```cpp
#include "Command.h"
#include "DrawingProcessor.h"
#include "Point.h"

class DrawCircleCommand : public UndoableCommand {
public:
  DrawCircleCommand() = delete;
  DrawCircleCommand(DrawingProcessor& receiver, const Point& centerPoint,
    const double radius) noexcept :
    receiver { receiver }, centerPoint { centerPoint }, radius { radius } {
}

  void execute() override {
    receiver.drawCircle(centerPoint, radius);
  }

  void undo() override {
    receiver.eraseCircle(centerPoint, radius);
  }
```

```
private:
  DrawingProcessor& receiver;
  const Point centerPoint;
  const double radius;
};
```

It is easy to imagine that the commands for drawing a rectangle and other shapes look very similar. The executing receiver of the command is a class named DrawingProcessor, which is the element that performs the drawing operations. A reference to this object is passed along with other arguments during the construction of the command (see initialization constructor). At this place I show only a small excerpt of the presumably complex class DrawingProcessor, because it does not play an important role for the understanding of the pattern. See Listing 9-26.

Listing 9-26. The DrawingProcessor Is the Element that Will Perform the Drawing Operations

```
class DrawingProcessor {
public:
  void drawCircle(const Point& centerPoint, const double radius) {
    // Instructions to draw a circle on the screen...
  };

  void eraseCircle(const Point& centerPoint, const double radius) {
    // Instructions to erase a circle from the screen...
  };

  // ...
};
```

Now we come to the centerpiece of this pattern, the CommandProcessor; see Listing 9-27.

Listing 9-27. The CommandProcessor Class Manages a Stack of Undoable Command Objects

```
#include <stack>

class CommandProcessor {
public:
```

```
void execute(const CommandPtr& command) {
  command->execute();
  commandHistory.push(command);
}

void undoLastCommand() {
  if (commandHistory.empty()) {
    return;
  }
  commandHistory.top()->undo();
  commandHistory.pop();
}

private:
  std::stack<std::shared_ptr<Revertable>> commandHistory;
};
```

The CommandProcessor class (which is by the way not thread-safe when using the above implementation) contains a std::stack<T> (defined in the <stack> header), which is an abstract data type that operates as a LIFO (Last-In First-Out). After an execution of a command has been triggered by the CommandProcessor::execute() member function, the command object is stored on the commandHistory stack. When calling the CommandProcessor::undoLastCommand() member function, the last command stored on the stack is undone and then removed from the top of the stack.

The undo operation can now be modeled as a command object. In this case, the command receiver is, of course, the CommandProcessor itself. See Listing 9-28.

Listing 9-28. The UndoCommand Prompts the CommandProcessor to Perform an Undo

```
#include "Command.h"
#include "CommandProcessor.h"

class UndoCommand : public UndoableCommand {
public:
  explicit UndoCommand(CommandProcessor& receiver) noexcept :
    receiver { receiver } { }
```

```cpp
  void execute() override {
    receiver.undoLastCommand();
  }

  void undo() override {
    // Intentionally left blank, because an undo should not be undone.
  }

private:
  CommandProcessor& receiver;
};
```

Lost the overview? It's once again time for a "big picture" in the form of a UML class diagram, as shown in Figure 9-9.

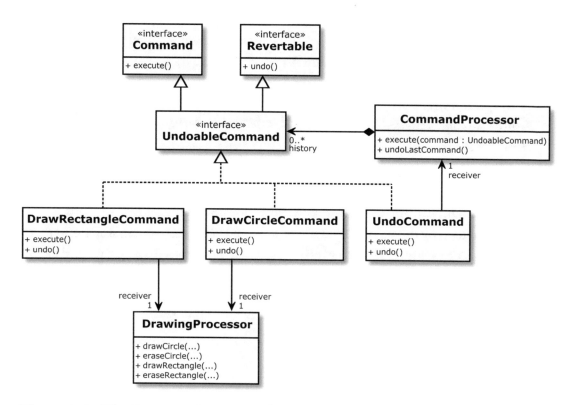

Figure 9-9. *The CommandProcessor (on the right) executes the commands it receives and manages a command history*

When using the Command pattern in practice, you're often confronted with the need to be able to compose a more complex command from several simple commands or to record and replay commands (scripting). In order to be able to implement such requirements in an elegant manner, the following design pattern is suitable.

Composite

A data structure widely used in computer science is that of a tree. Trees can be found everywhere. For instance, the hierarchical organization of a filesystem on a data media (e.g., a hard disk) conforms to that of a tree. The project browser of an integrated development environment (IDE) usually has a tree structure. In compiler design, the abstract syntax tree (AST), is, as the name suggests, a tree representation of the abstract syntactic structure of the source code that is usually the result of the syntax analysis phase of a compiler.

The object-oriented blueprint for a tree-like data structure is called the *Composite* pattern. This pattern has the following intent:

> *"Compose objects into tree structures to represent part-whole hierarchies. Composite lets clients treat individual objects and compositions of objects uniformly."*
>
> —Erich Gamma et al., *Design Patterns* [Gamma95]

Our previous example from the "Command" and "Command Processor" sections should be extended by the possibility that we can build composite commands, and that commands can be recorded and replayed. So we add a new class to the previous design, a CompositeCommand. See Listing 9-29.

Listing 9-29. A New Concrete UndoableCommand That Manages a List of Commands

```
#include "Command.h"
#include <ranges>
#include <vector>

class CompositeCommand : public UndoableCommand {
public:
```

```cpp
  void addCommand(CommandPtr& command) {
    commands.push_back(command);
  }

  void execute() override {
    for (const auto& command : commands) {
      command->execute();
    }
  }

  void undo() override {
    const auto& commandsInReverseOrder = std::ranges::reverse_
    view(commands);
    for (const auto& command : commandsInReverseOrder) {
      command->undo();
    }
  }

private:
  std::vector<CommandPtr> commands;
};
```

The composite command has a member function called addCommand(), which allows you to add commands to an instance of CompositeCommand. Since the CompositeCommand class also implements the UndoableCommand interface, its instances can be treated like ordinary commands. In other words, it is also possible to assemble composite commands with other composite commands hierarchically. Through the recursive structure of the Composite pattern, you can generate command trees.

The UML class diagram in Figure 9-10 depicts the extended design.

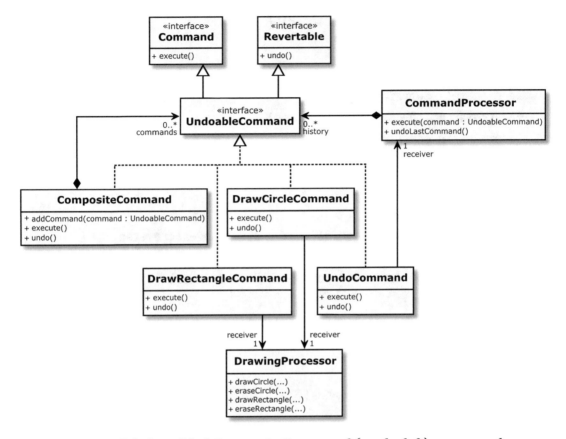

Figure 9-10. *With the added CompositeCommand (on the left), commands can now be scripted*

The newly added CompositeCommand class can now be used, for example, as a macro recorder in order to record and replay command sequences. See Listing 9-30.

Listing 9-30. The New CompositeCommand in Action as a Macro Recorder

```cpp
int main() {
  CommandProcessor commandProcessor { };
  DrawingProcessor drawingProcessor { };

  auto macroRecorder = std::make_shared<CompositeCommand>();

  Point circleCenterPoint { 20, 20 };
  CommandPtr drawCircleCommand = std::make_shared<DrawCircleCommand>
  (drawingProcessor, circleCenterPoint, 10);
  commandProcessor.execute(drawCircleCommand);
```

```
macroRecorder->addCommand(drawCircleCommand);

Point rectangleCenterPoint { 30, 10 };
CommandPtr drawRectangleCommand = std::make_shared<DrawRectangleCommand>
(drawingProcessor, rectangleCenterPoint, 5, 8);
commandProcessor.execute(drawRectangleCommand);
macroRecorder->addCommand(drawRectangleCommand);

commandProcessor.execute(macroRecorder);
commandProcessor. undoLastCommand();

  return 0;
}
```

With the help of the Composite pattern, it is now very easy to assemble complex command sequences from simple commands (the latter are referred to as "leafs" in the canonical form). Since CompositeCommand also implements the UndoableCommand interface, they can be used exactly like the simple commands. This greatly simplifies the usage through client code.

On closer inspection, there is a small disadvantage. You may have noticed that an access to the member function CompositeCommand::addCommand() is possible only if you use an instance (macroRecorder) of the concrete type CompositeCommand (see the source code). This member function is not available via the UndoableCommand interface. In other words, the promised equal treatment (remember the pattern's intent) of composites and leafs is not given here!

If you look at the general Composite pattern in [Gamma95], you'll see that the administrative functions for managing child elements are declared in the abstraction. In our case, however, this would mean that we would have to declare an addCommand() in the UndoableCommand interface (which would be a violation of the ISP, by the way). The fatal consequence would be that the leaf elements would have to override addCommand(), and must provide a meaningful implementation for this member function. This is not possible! What should happen, what doesn't violate the principle of least astonishment (see Chapter 3), if we add a command to an instance of DrawCircleCommand?

If we do that, it would be a violation of the Liskov Substitution Principle (LSP; see Chapter 6). Therefore, it is better to make a tradeoff in this case and do without the equal treatment of composites and leafs.

Observer

A well-known architecture pattern for the structuring of software systems is *Model-View-Controller* (MVC). With the help of this architecture pattern, which is described in detail in the book *Pattern-Oriented Software Architecture* [Busch96], the presentation part (User Interface) of an application is usually structured. The principle behind it is separation of concerns (SoC). Among other things, the data to be displayed, which is held in the model, is separated from the manifold visual representations (so-called views) of these data.

In MVC, the coupling between the views and the model should be as loose as possible. This loose coupling is usually realized with the *Observer* pattern. The Observer is a behavioral pattern that is described in [Gamma95] and it has the following intent:

> *"Define a one-to-many dependency between objects so that when one object changes state, all its dependents are notified and updated automatically."*
>
> —Erich Gamma et al., *Design Patterns* [Gamma95]

As usual, the pattern can best be explained using an example. Let's consider a spreadsheet application, which is a natural constituent of many office software suites. In such an application, the data can be displayed in a worksheet, in a pie chart graphic, and in many other presentation forms; the so-called views. Different views on the data can be created and closed again.

First we need an abstract element for the views that is called `Observer`. See Listing 9-31.

Listing 9-31. The Observer Abstract

```cpp
#include <memory>

class Observer {
public:
  virtual ~Observer() = default;
  virtual int getId() const noexcept = 0;
  virtual void update() = 0;
};

bool operator==(const Observer& lhs, const Observer& rhs) {
```

```
  return lhs.getId() == rhs.getId();
}

using ObserverPtr = std::shared_ptr<Observer>;
```

The Observers observe a so-called Subject. For this purpose, they can be registered at the Subject, and they can also be deregistered. See Listing 9-32.

Listing 9-32. Observers Can Be Added to and Removed From a Subject

```
#include "Observer.h"
#include <algorithm>
#include <vector>

;
class Subject {
public:
  void addObserver(const ObserverPtr& observerToAdd) {
    if (isNotYetObservingThisSubject(observerToAdd)) {
      observers.push_back(observerToAdd);
    }
  }

  void removeObserver(ObserverPtr& observerToRemove) {
    std::erase(observers, observerToRemove);
  }
protected:
  void notifyAllObservers() const {
    for (const auto& observer : observers) {
      observer->update();
    }
  }
private:
  std::vector<ObserverPtr> observers;
};
```

In addition to the Subject class, a functor named IsEqualTo is also defined (see Chapter 7 about functors), which is used for comparisons when adding and removing observers. The functor compares the IDs of the Observer. It would also be conceivable that it compares the memory addresses of the Observer instances. Then it would even be possible for several observers of the same type to register at the Subject.

The core is the notifyAllObservers() member function. It is protected since it is intended to be called by the concrete subjects that are inherited from this one. This function iterates over all registered observers and calls their update() member function.

Let's look at a concrete subject, the SpreadsheetModel. See Listing 9-33.

Listing 9-33. The SpreadsheetModel Is a Concrete Subject

```
#include "Subject.h"
#include <iostream>
#include <string_view>

class SpreadsheetModel : public Subject {
public:
  void changeCellValue(std::string_view column, const int row, const double
  value) {
    std::cout << "Cell [" << column << ", " << row << "] = " << value <<
    std::endl;
    // Change value of a spreadsheet cell, and then...
    notifyAllObservers();
  }
};
```

This, of course, is only an absolute minimum of a SpreadsheetModel. It just serves to explain the functional principle of the pattern. The only thing you can do here is call a member function that calls the inherited notifyAllObservers() function.

The three concrete observers in our example that implement the update() member function of the Observer interface are the three views TableView, BarChartView, and PieChartView. See Listing 9-34.

Listing 9-34. Three Concrete Views Implement the Abstract Observer Interface

```cpp
#include "Observer.h"
#include "SpreadsheetModel.h"

class TableView : public Observer {
public:
  explicit TableView(SpreadsheetModel& theModel) :
    model { theModel } { }
  int getId() const noexcept override {
    return 1;
  }

  void update() override {
    std::cout << "Update of TableView." << std::endl;
  }
private:
  SpreadsheetModel& model;
};

class BarChartView : public Observer {
public:
  explicit BarChartView(SpreadsheetModel& theModel) :
    model { theModel } { }
  int getId() const noexcept override {
    return 2;
  }

  void update() override {
    std::cout << "Update of BarChartView." << std::endl;
  }
private:
  SpreadsheetModel& model;
};

class PieChartView : public Observer {
public:
```

```
explicit PieChartView(SpreadsheetModel& theModel) :
  model { theModel } { }
int getId() const noexcept override {
  return 3;
}

void update() override {
  std::cout << "Update of PieChartView." << std::endl;
}

private:
  SpreadsheetModel& model;
};
```

I think it is time again to show an overview in the form of a class diagram. Figure 9-11 depicts the structure (classes and dependencies) that have arisen.

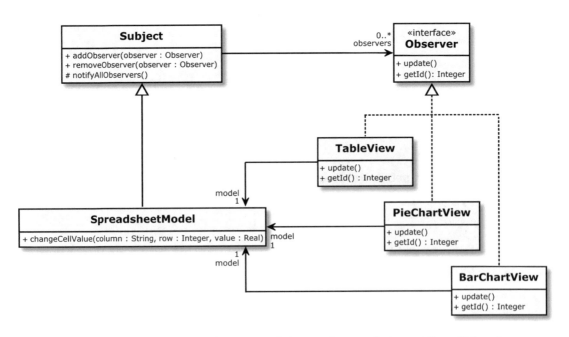

Figure 9-11. *When the SpreadsheetModel gets changed, it notifies all its observers*

In the main() function, we now use the SpreadsheetModel and the three views, as shown in Listing 9-35.

Listing 9-35. Our SpreadsheetModel and the Three Views Assembled Together and in Action

```
#include "SpreadsheetModel.h"
#include "Views.h"

int main() {
  SpreadsheetModel spreadsheetModel { };

  ObserverPtr observer1 = std::make_shared<TableView>(spreadsheetModel);
  spreadsheetModel.addObserver(observer1);

  ObserverPtr observer2 = std::make_shared<BarChartView>(spreadsheetModel);
  spreadsheetModel.addObserver(observer2);

  spreadsheetModel.changeCellValue("A", 1, 42);

  spreadsheetModel.removeObserver(observer1);

  spreadsheetModel.changeCellValue("B", 2, 23.1);

  ObserverPtr observer3 = std::make_shared<PieChartView>(spreadsheetModel);
  spreadsheetModel.addObserver(observer3);

  spreadsheetModel.changeCellValue("C", 3, 3.1415926);

  return 0;
}
```

After compiling and running the program, we see the following on the standard output:

```
Cell [A, 1] = 42
Update of TableView.
Update of BarChartView.
Cell [B, 2] = 23.1
Update of BarChartView.
Cell [C, 3] = 3.14153
Update of BarChartView.
Update of PieChartView.
```

In addition to the positive feature of loose coupling (the concrete subject knows nothing about the Observers), this pattern also supports the open-closed principle very well. New concrete observers (in our case, new views) can be added very easily since nothing needs to be adjusted or changed in the existing classes.

Factories

According to the *separation of concerns* (SoC) principle, object creation or procurement should be separated from the domain-specific tasks that an object has. The dependency injection pattern follows this principle in a straightforward way, because the whole object creation and dependency resolution process is centralized in an infrastructure element, and the objects themselves do not have to worry about it.

But what should we do if an object must be dynamically created at some point at runtime? Well, this task can then be taken over by an object factory.

The *Factory* design pattern is basically relatively simple and appears in code bases in many different forms and varieties. In addition to the SoC principle, information hiding (see Chapter 3) is also greatly supported, because the creation process of an instance should be concealed from its users.

As stated, factories can be found in countless forms and variants. We discuss only a simple variant.

Simple Factory

The simplest implementation of a Factory probably looks like Listing 9-36 (we take up the Logging example from the DI section).

Listing 9-36. Probably the Simplest Imaginable Object Factory

```cpp
#include "LoggingFacility.h"
#include "StandardOutputLogger.h"

class LoggerFactory {
public:
  static Logger create() {
    return std::make_shared<StandardOutputLogger>();
  }
};
```

Usage of this very simple factory looks like Listing 9-37.

Listing 9-37. Using the LoggerFactory to Create a Logger Instance

```cpp
#include "LoggerFactory.h"

int main() {
  Logger logger = LoggerFactory::create();
  // ...log something...
  return 0;
}
```

Maybe you'll ask now, whether it is at all worth it to spend an extra class for such a puny task. Well, maybe not. It's more sensible, if the factory were able to create various loggers, and decides which type it will be. This can be done, for example, by reading and evaluating a configuration file, or a certain key is read out from the Windows Registry database. It is also imaginable that the type of the generated object is made dependent on the time of the day. The possibilities are endless. It is important that this should be completely transparent to the client class. Listing 9-38 shows a slightly more sophisticated LoggerFactory that reads a configuration file (e.g., from hard disk) and decides which specific Logger is created based on the current configuration.

Listing 9-38. A More Sophisticated Factory That Reads and Evaluates a Configuration File

```cpp
#include "LoggingFacility.h"
#include "StandardOutputLogger.h"
#include "FilesystemLogger.h"

#include <fstream>
#include <string>
#include <string_view>

class LoggerFactory {
private:
  enum class OutputTarget : int {
    STDOUT,
    FILE
  };
```

```cpp
public:
  explicit LoggerFactory(std::string_view configurationFileName) :
    configurationFileName { configurationFileName } { }

  Logger create() const {
    const std::string configurationFileContent = readConfigurationFile();
    OutputTarget outputTarget = evaluateConfiguration(configurationFileContent);
    return createLogger(outputTarget);
  }

private:
  std::string readConfigurationFile() const {
    std::ifstream filestream(configurationFileName);
    return std::string(std::istreambuf_iterator<char>(filestream),
      std::istreambuf_iterator<char>());   }

  OutputTarget evaluateConfiguration(std::string_view
  configurationFileContent) const {
    // Evaluate the content of the configuration file...
    return OutputTarget::STDOUT;
  }

  Logger createLogger(OutputTarget outputTarget) const {
    switch (outputTarget) {
    case OutputTarget::FILE:
      return std::make_shared<FilesystemLogger>();
    case OutputTarget::STDOUT:
    default:
      return std::make_shared<StandardOutputLogger>();
    }
  }

  const std::string configurationFileName;
};
```

The UML class diagram in Figure 9-12 depicts the structure that we basically know from the section about dependency injection (Figure 9-5), but now with our simple LoggerFactory instead of an assembler.

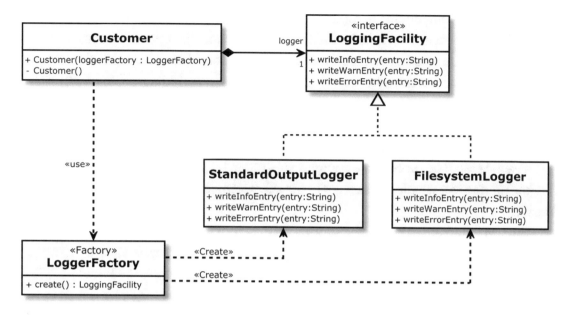

Figure 9-12. *The Customer uses a LoggerFactory to obtain concrete loggers*

Comparing this diagram with Figure 9-5 shows a significant difference: while the
`CustomerRepository` class has no dependency on the assembler, the customer "knows"
the factory class when using the Factory pattern. Presumably, this dependency is not
a serious problem, but it makes clear once again that loose coupling is brought to the
maximum extent with dependency injection.

Facade

The *Facade* pattern is a structural pattern that is often used on an architectural level and
has the following intent:

> *"Provide a unified interface to a set of interfaces in a subsystem. Facade
> defines a higher-level interface that makes the subsystem easier to use."*
>
> —Erich Gamma et al., *Design Patterns* [Gamma95]

Structuring a large software system according to the separation of concerns and
single responsibility principles (see Chapter 6), and information hiding (see Chapter 3)
usually has the result that some kind of bigger components or modules are originated.

Generally, these components or modules can sometimes be referred to as "subsystems." Even in a layered architecture, individual layers can be considered subsystems.

In order to promote encapsulation, the internal structure of a component or subsystem should be hidden from its clients (see information hiding in Chapter 3). The communication between subsystems, and thus the amount of dependencies between them, should be minimized. It would be fatal, if clients of a subsystem must know details about the internal structure and the interaction of its parts.

A Facade regulates access to a complex subsystem by providing a well-defined and simple interface for clients. Any access to the subsystem must solely be done over the Facade.

The UML diagram in Figure 9-13 shows a subsystem named Billing for preparing invoices. Its internal structure consists of several interconnected parts. Clients of the subsystem cannot access these parts directly. They have to use the Facade BillingService, which is represented by a UML port (stereotype «facade») on the border of the subsystem.

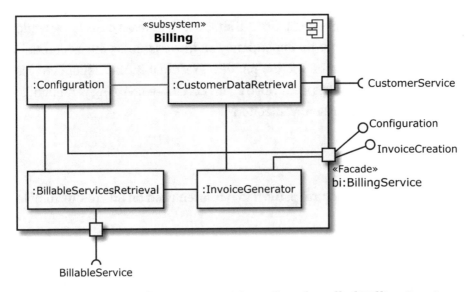

Figure 9-13. *The Billing subsystem provides a facade called BillingService as an access point for clients*

In C++, and also in other languages, a Facade is nothing special. It is often just a simple class that is receiving calls at its public interface and forwarding them to the internal structure of the subsystem. Sometimes it is only a simple forwarding of a call to one of the internal structural elements of the subsystem, but occasionally a Facade also carries out data conversions, in which case it's also an adapter (see the section about adapters).

In our example, the Facade class BillingService implements two interfaces, represented by the UML ball-notation. According to the interface segregation principle (ISP; see Chapter 6), the configuration of the Billing subsystem (the Configuration interface) is separated from the generation of bills (the InvoiceCreation interface). Thus, the Facade must override operations that are declared in both interfaces.

The Money Class

If high accuracy is of any importance, you should avoid floating-point values. Floating-point variables of type float, double, or long double fail in simple additions, as this small example demonstrates. See Listing 9-39.

Listing 9-39. When Adding Ten Floating-Point Numbers This way, the Result Is Possibly Not Accurate Enough

```
#include <assert.h>
#include <iostream>

int main() {

  double sum = 0.0;
  double addend = 0.3;

  for (int i = 0; i < 10; i++) {
    sum = sum + addend;
  };

  assert(sum == 3.0);
  return 0;
}
```

If you compile and run this small program, this is what you'll see as its console output:

```
Assertion failed: sum == 3.0, file ..\main.cpp, line 13
```

I think that the cause for this deviation is generally known. Floating-point numbers are stored in a binary format internally. Due to this, it is impossible to store a value of 0.3 (and others) precisely in a variable of type float, double, or long double, because it has no exact representation of finite length in binary. In decimal, we have a similar problem. We can't represent the value 1/3 (one-third) using only decimal notation. 0.33333333 isn't completely accurate.

There are several solutions for this problem. For currencies it can be a suitable approach to store the money value in an integer with the required precision, for example, $12.45 will be stored as 1245. If requirements are not very high, an integer can be a feasible solution. Note that the C++ standard does not specify the size of integral types in bytes; thus you must be careful with very big amounts since an integer overflow can occur. If in doubt, a 64-bit integer should be used, as it can hold very large amounts of money.

DETERMINING THE RANGE OF AN ARITHMETIC TYPE

The actual implementation-specific ranges for arithmetic types (either integral or floating-point) can be found as class templates in the <limits> header. For example, this is how you would find the maximum range for int:

```
#include <limits>
constexpr auto INT_LOWER_BOUND = std::numeric_limits<int>::min();
constexpr auto INT_UPPER_BOUND = std::numeric_limits<int>::max();
```

Another popular approach is to provide a special class for this purpose, the so-called *Money class*:

"Provide a class to represent exact amounts of money. A Money class handles different currencies and exchanges between them."

—Martin Fowler, Patterns of Enterprise Application Architecture
[Fowler02]

The Money Class pattern is basically a class encapsulating a financial amount and its currency, but dealing with money is just one example of this category of classes. There are many other properties, or dimensions, that must be accurately represented, for example, precise measurements in physics (time, voltage, current, distance, mass, frequency, amount of substances, and so on).

1991: PATRIOT MISSILE MISTIMING

MIM-104 Patriot is a surface-to-air missile (SAM) system that was designed and manufactured by the *Raytheon Company* of the United States. Its typical application was to counter high-altitude tactical ballistic missiles, cruise missiles, and advanced aircraft. During the first Persian Gulf War (1990 – 1991), also called operation "Desert Storm," Patriot was used to shoot down incoming Iraqi SCUD or Al Hussein short-range ballistic missiles.

On February 25, 1991, a battery in Dhahran, a city located in the Eastern Province of Saudi Arabia, failed to intercept a SCUD. The missile struck an Army barracks and caused 28 deaths and 98 injuries.

An investigation report [GAOIMTEC92] revealed that the cause of this failure was an inaccurate calculation of the time since power-up of the system due to computer arithmetic errors. So that Patriot's missiles can detect and hit the target after launch, they must be spatially approximated to the target, the "range gate." To predict where the target will appear next (the deflection angle), some calculations with the system's time and the target's flying speed had to be performed. The elapsed time since system's start was measured in tenths of a second and expressed as an integer. The target's speed was measured in miles per second and expressed as a decimal value. To calculate the "range gate," the value of the system's timer has to be multiplied by 1/10 to get the time in seconds. This calculation was done using registers that were only 24 bits long.

The problem was that the value of 1/10 in decimal cannot be accurately represented in a 24-bit register. The value was chopped at 24 bits after the radix point. The consequence was that the conversion of time from an integer to a real number results in a small loss of precision causing a less accurate time calculation. This accuracy error would probably not have been a problem if the system would only been in operation for a few hours, according to its concept of operation as a mobile system. But in this case, the system has been running for more than

100 hours. The number representing the system's up-time was quite large. This meant that the small conversion error of 1/10 into its decimal 24-bit representation resulted in a large deviation error of nearly half of a second! An Iraqi SCUD missile travels approximately 800 meters in that time span—far enough to be outside the "range gate" of an approaching Patriot missile.

Although the accurate dealing with amounts of money is a very common case in many business IT systems, you will struggle in vain to find a Money class in most mainstream C++ base class libraries. But don't reinvent the wheel! There are multitudes of different C++ Money class implementations out there, just search and you will get thousands of hits. As is often the case, one implementation doesn't satisfy all requirements. The key is to understand your problem domain. While choosing (or designing) a Money class, you may consider several constraints and requirements. Here are a few questions that you may have to clarify first:

- What is the full range of values to be handled (minimum, maximum)?

- Which rounding rules apply? There are national laws or practices for roundings in some countries.

- Are there legal requirements for accuracy?

- Which standards must be considered (e.g., ISO 4217 *International Standard for Currency Codes*)?

- How will the values be displayed to the user?

- How often will conversion take place?

From my perspective, it is absolutely essential to have 100% unit test coverage (see Chapter 2 about unit tests) for a Money class to check whether the class is working as expected under all circumstances. Of course, the Money class has a small drawback compared to the pure number representation with an integer: you lose a smidgen of performance. This might be an issue in some systems. But I'm convinced that in most cases the advantages will predominate (always keep in mind that premature optimization is bad).

Special Case Object (Null Object)

In the section "Don't Pass or Return 0 (NULL, nullptr)" in Chapter 4, you learned that returning a `nullptr` from a function or method is bad and should be avoided. There we also discussed various strategies to avoid regular (raw) pointers in a modern C++ program. In the section "An Exception Is an Exception, Literally!" in Chapter 5, you learned that exceptions should only be used for truly exceptional cases and not for the purpose of controlling the normal program flow.

The open and interesting question is now this: How do we treat special cases that are not real exceptions (e.g., a failed memory allocation), without using a non-semantic `nullptr` or other weird values?

Let's pick up our code example again, which we have seen several times before: the query of a `Customer` by name. See Listing 9-40.

Listing 9-40. A Lookup Method for Customers by Name

```
Customer CustomerService::findCustomerByName(const std::string& name) {
  // Code that searches the customer by name...
  // ...but what shall we do, if a customer with the given name does not
  exist?!
}
```

Well, one possibility would be to return lists instead of a single instance. If the returned list is empty, the queried business object does not exist. See Listing 9-41.

Listing 9-41. An Alternative to nullptr: Returning an Empty List if the Lookup for a Customer Fails

```
#include "Customer.h"
#include <vector>

using CustomerList = std::vector<Customer>;

CustomerList CustomerService::findCustomerByName(const std::string& name) {
  // Code that searches the customer by name...
  // ...and if a customer with the given name does not exist:
  return CustomerList();
}
```

The returned list can now be queried in the program sequence whether it is empty. But what semantics does an empty list have? Was an error responsible for the emptiness of the list? Well, the member function `std::vector<T>::empty()` cannot answer this question. Being empty is a state of a list, but this state has no domain-specific semantics.

Folks, no doubt, this solution is much better than returning a `nullptr`, but maybe not good enough in some cases. What would be much more comfortable is a return value that can be queried about its origination cause, and about what can be done with it. The answer is the *Special Case* pattern!

> *"A subclass that provides special behavior for particular cases."*
>
> —Martin Fowler, Patterns of
> Enterprise Application Architecture [Fowler02]

The idea behind the Special Case pattern is that we take advantage of polymorphism, and that we provide classes representing the special cases, instead of returning `nullptr` or some other odd value. These special case classes have the same interface as the "normal" class that is expected by the callers. The class diagram in Figure 9-14 depicts such a specialization.

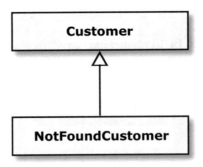

Figure 9-14. *The class(es) representing a special case are derived from the Customer class*

In C++ source code, an implementation of the `Customer` class and the `NotFoundCustomer` class representing the special case looks something like Listing 9-42 (only the relevant parts are shown).

Listing 9-42. An Excerpt from the Customer.h File with the Customer and NotFoundCustomer Classes

```
#ifndef CUSTOMER_H_
#define CUSTOMER_H_

#include "Address.h"
#include "CustomerId.h"
#include <memory>
#include <string>

class Customer {
public:
  // ...more member functions here...
  virtual ~Customer() = default;

  virtual bool isPersistable() const noexcept {
    return (customerId.isValid() && ! forename.empty() && ! surname.empty()
    &&
      billingAddress->isValid() && shippingAddress->isValid());
  }

private:
  CustomerId customerId;
  std::string forename;
  std::string surname;
  std::shared_ptr<Address> billingAddress;
  std::shared_ptr<Address> shippingAddress;
};

class NotFoundCustomer final : public Customer {
public:
  bool isPersistable() const noexcept override {
    return false;
  }
};
using CustomerPtr = std::unique_ptr<Customer>;

#endif /* CUSTOMER_H_ */
```

433

The objects that represent the special case can now be used largely as if they were valid (normal) instances of class Customer. Permanent null-checks, even when the object is passed around between different parts of the program, are superfluous, since there is always a valid object. Many things can be done with the NotFoundCustomer object, as if it were an instance of Customer, for example, presenting it in a user interface. The object can even reveal whether it is persistable. For the "real" Customer, this is done by analyzing its data fields. In the case of the NotFoundCustomer, however, this check always has a negative result.

Compared to the meaningless null-checks, a statement like the following one makes significantly more sense:

```
if (customer.isPersistable()) {
    // ...write the customer to a database here...
}
```

STD::OPTIONAL<T> [C++17]

Since C++17, there is another interesting alternative that could be used for a possibly missing result or value: std::optional<T> (defined in the <optional> header). Instances of this class template represent an "optional contained value," that is, a value that may or may not be present.

The Customer class can be used as an optional value using std::optional<T> by introducing a type alias as follows:

```
#include "Customer.h"
#include <optional>
using OptionalCustomer = std::optional<Customer>;
```

Our search function CustomerService::findCustomerByName() can now be implemented as follows:

```
class CustomerRepository {
public:
    OptionalCustomer findCustomerByName(const std::string& name) {
        if ( /* the search was successful */ ) {
            return Customer();
        } else {
```

```
      return {};
    }
  }
};
```

At the call site of the function, you now have two ways to handle the return value, as illustrated in the following example:

```
int main() {
  CustomerRepository repository { };
  auto optionalCustomer = repository.findCustomerByName("John Doe");

  // Option 1: Catch an exception, if 'optionalCustomer' is empty
  try {
    auto customer = optionalCustomer.value();
  } catch (std::bad_optional_access& ex) {
    std::cerr << ex.what() << std::endl;
  }

  // Option 2: Provide a substitute for a possibly missing object
  auto customer = optionalCustomer.value_or(NotFoundCustomer());

  return 0;
}
```

In the second option, for instance, it is possible to either provide a standard (default) customer, or—as in this case—an instance of a special case object, if optionalCustomer is empty. I recommend choosing the first option when the absence of an object is unexpected and is a clue that a serious error must have been occurred. For the other cases, where a missing object is nothing unusual, I recommend option 2.

What Is an Idiom?

A programming idiom is a special kind of pattern to solve a problem in a specific programming language or technology. That is, unlike the more general design patterns, idioms are limited in their applicability. Often, their applicability is limited to exactly one specific programming language or a certain technology, for example, a framework.

Idioms are typically used during detailed design and implementation, if programming problems must be solved at a low level of abstraction. A well-known idiom in the C and C++ domain is the so-called *Include Guard*, sometimes also called *Macro Guard* or *Header Guard*, which is used to avoid double inclusion of the same header file:

```
#ifndef FILENAME_H_
#define FILENAME_H_

// ...content of header file...

#endif
```

One disadvantage of this idiom is that a consistent naming scheme for filenames, and thus also for Include Guard macro names, must be ensured. Hence, most modern C and C++ compilers support a non-standard #pragma once directive. This directive, inserted at the top of a header file, will ensure that the header file is included only once.

By the way, we have already gotten to know a few idioms. In Chapter 4, we discussed the Resource Acquisition Is Initialization (RAII) idiom, and in Chapter 6, I presented the Type Erasure idiom that I also used earlier in this chapter to implement the State pattern.

Some Useful C++ Idioms

It is not a joke, but you can actually find an exhaustive collection of nearly 100(!) C++ idioms on the Internet (WikiBooks: *More C++ Idioms*; URL: https://en.wikibooks. org/wiki/More_C++_Idioms). The problem is that not all of these idioms are conducive to a modern and clean C++ program. They are sometimes very complex and barely comprehensible (e.g., *Algebraic Hierarchy*), even for fairly skilled C++ developers. Furthermore, some idioms have become largely obsolete by the publishing of C++11 and subsequent standards. Therefore, I present here a small selection, which I consider interesting and still useful.

The Power of Immutability

Sometimes it's very helpful to have classes for objects that cannot change their states once they have been created, a.k.a. immutable classes (what is really meant by this are in fact immutable objects, because properly speaking a class can only be altered by a developer). For instance, immutable objects can be used as key values in a hashed data structure, since the key value should never change after creation. Another known example of an immutable object is the String class in several other languages like C# or Java.

The benefits of immutable classes and objects are the following:

- Immutable objects are thread-safe by default, so you will not have any synchronization issues if several threads or processes access those objects in a non-deterministic way. Thus, immutability makes it easier to create a parallelizable software design as there are no conflicts among objects.

- Immutability makes it easier to write, use, and reason about the code, because a class invariant, that is, a set of constraints that must always be true, is established once at object creation and is ensured to be unchanged during the object's lifetime.

To create an immutable class in C++, the following measures must be taken:

- The member variables of the class must all be made immutable, that is, they must all be made const (see the section about const correctness in Chapter 4). This means that they can only be initialized once in a constructor, using the constructor's member initializer list.

- Manipulating methods do not change the object on which they are called, but return a new instance of the class with an altered state. The original object is not changed. To emphasize this, there should be no setter, because a member function whose name starts with set...() is misleading. There is nothing to set on an immutable object.

- The class should be marked as final. This is not a hard rule, but if a new class can be inherited from an allegedly immutable class, it might be possible to circumvent its immutability (remember the history constraint described in Chapter 4).

Listing 9-43 shows an example of an immutable class in C++.

Listing 9-43. Employee Is Designed as an Immutable Class

```cpp
#include "Identifier.h"
#include "Money.h"
#include <string>
#include <string_view>

class Employee final {
public:
  Employee(std::string_view forename,
    std::string_view surname,
    const Identifier& staffNumber,
    const Money& salary) noexcept :
    forename { forename },
    surname { surname },
    staffNumber { staffNumber },
    salary { salary } { }

  Identifier getStaffNumber() const noexcept {
    return staffNumber;
  }

  Money getSalary() const noexcept {
    return salary;
  }

  Employee changeSalary(const Money& newSalary) const noexcept {
    return Employee(forename, surname, staffNumber, newSalary);
  }

private:
  const std::string forename;
  const std::string surname;
  const Identifier   staffNumber;
  const Money        salary;
};
```

Substitution Failure Is Not an Error (SFINAE)

In fact, *substitution failure is not an error* (SFINAE) is not a real idiom but a feature of the C++ compiler. It has already been a part of the C++98 standard, but with C++11 several new features have been added. However, it is still referred to as an idiom, also because it is used in a very idiomatic style, especially in template libraries, such as the C++ Standard Library, or Boost.

The defining text passage in the standard can be found in Section 14.8.2 about template argument deduction. There we can read in §8 the following statement:

> *"If a substitution results in an invalid type or expression, type deduction fails. An invalid type or expression is one that would be ill-formed if written using the substituted arguments. Only invalid types and expressions in the immediate context of the function type and its template parameter types can result in a deduction failure."*
>
> —Standard for Programming Language C++ [ISO11]

Error messages in case of a faulty instantiation of C++ templates, for example, with wrong template arguments, can be very verbose and cryptic. SFINAE is a programming technique that ensures that a failed substitution of template arguments does not create an annoying compilation error. Simply put, it means that if the substitution of a template argument fails, the compiler continues with the search for a suitable template instead of aborting with an error.

Listing 9-44 shows a very simple example with two overloaded function templates.

Listing 9-44. SFINAE by Example of Two Overloaded Function Templates

```cpp
#include <iostream>

template <typename T>
void print(typename T::type) {
  std::cout << "Calling print(typename T::type)" << std::endl;
}

template <typename T>
void print(T) {
  std::cout << "Calling print(T)" << std::endl;
}
```

```
struct AStruct {
  using type = int;
};

int main() {
  print<AStruct>(42);
  print<int>(42);
  print(42);

  return 0;
}
```

The output of this small example on `stdout` will be:

```
Calling print(typename T::type)
Calling print(T)
Calling print(T)
```

As can be seen, the compiler uses the first version of `print()` for the first function call, and the second version for the two subsequent calls. This code also works in C++98.

Well, but SFINAE prior C++11 had several drawbacks. The previous very simple example is a bit deceptive regarding the real effort to use this technique in real projects. The application of SFINAE this way in template libraries has led to very verbose and tricky code that is difficult to understand. Furthermore, it is badly standardized and sometimes compiler specific.

With the advent of C++11, the so-called Type Traits library was introduced, which we got to know in Chapter 7. The meta function `std::enable_if()` (defined in the `<type_traits>` header), which is available since C++11, played a central role in SFINAE. With this function we got a conditionally "remove functions capability" from overload resolution based on type traits. C++14 added a helper template for `std::enable_if` that has a shorter syntax: `std::enable_if_t`. With the help of this template, and the miscellaneous template-based type checks from the `<type_traits>` header, we can, for example, pick an overloaded version of a function depending on the argument's type at compile-time. See Listing 9-45.

Listing 9-45. SFINAE By Using the Function Template std::enable_if<>

```
#include <iostream>
#include <type_traits>

template <typename T>
void print(T var, std::enable_if_t<std::is_enum_v<T>, T>* = nullptr) {
  std::cout << "Calling overloaded print() for enumerations." << std::endl;
}

template <typename T>
void print(T var, std::enable_if_t<std::is_integral_v<T>, T> = 0) {
  std::cout << "Calling overloaded print() for integral types." <<
  std::endl;
}

template <typename T>
void print(T var, std::enable_if_t<std::is_floating_point_v<T>, T> = 0.0) {
  std::cout << "Calling overloaded print() for floating point types." <<
  std::endl;
}

template <typename T>
void print(const T& var, std::enable_if_t<std::is_class_v<T>, T>* =
nullptr) {
  std::cout << "Calling overloaded print() for classes." << std::endl;
}
```

The overloaded function templates can be used by simply calling them with arguments of different types, as shown in Listing 9-46.

Listing 9-46. Thanks to SFINAE, There Is a Matching print() Function for Arguments of Different Types

```
enum Enumeration1 {
  Literal1,
  Literal2
};
```

```
enum class Enumeration2 : int {
  Literal1,
  Literal2
};

class Clazz { };

int main() {
  Enumeration1 enumVar1 { };
  print(enumVar1);

  Enumeration2 enumVar2 { };
  print(enumVar2);

  print(42);

  Clazz instance { };
  print(instance);

  print(42.0f);

  print(42.0);

  return 0;
}
```

After compiling and executing, we see the following result on the standard output:

```
Calling overloaded print() for enumerations.
Calling overloaded print() for enumerations.
Calling overloaded print() for integral types.
Calling overloaded print() for classes.
Calling overloaded print() for floating point types.
Calling overloaded print() for floating point types.
```

The Copy-and-Swap Idiom

In the section "Prevention Is Better Than Aftercare" in Chapter 5, we learned the four levels of exception-safety guarantee: no exception-safety, basic exception-safety, strong exception-safety, and the no-throw guarantee. What member functions of a class should always guarantee is the basic exception-safety, because this exception-safety level is usually easy to implement.

In the section "The Rule of Zero" in Chapter 5, we learned that we should design classes in a way that the compiler-generated special member functions (copy constructor, copy assignment operator, etc.) automatically do the right things. Or in other words, when we are forced to provide a non-trivial destructor, we are dealing with an exceptional case that requires special treatment during destruction of the object. As a consequence, it follows that the special member functions generated by the compiler are not sufficient to deal with this situation, and we have to implement them by ourselves.

However, it is inevitable that the Rule of Zero will occasionally not be fulfilled, that is, a developer has to implement the special member functions by herself. In this case, it may be a challenging task to create an exception-safe implementation of an overloaded assignment operator. In such a case, the *Copy-and-Swap* idiom is an elegant way to solve this problem.

Hence, the intent of this idiom is as follows:

"Implement the copy assignment operator with strong exception safety."

The simplest way to explain the problem and its solution is with a small example. Consider the class shown in Listing 9-47.

Listing 9-47. A Class That Manages a Resource That Is Allocated on the Heap

```cpp
#include <cstddef>

class Clazz final {
public:
  explicit Clazz(const std::size_t size) : resourceToManage { new
  char[size] }, size { size } { }
  ~Clazz() {
    delete [] resourceToManage;
  }
```

```
private:
  char* resourceToManage;
  std::size_t size;
};
```

This class is, of course, only for demonstration purposes and should not be part of a real program.

Let's assume that we want to do the following with the class `Clazz`:

```
int main() {
  Clazz instance1 { 1000 };
  Clazz instance2 { instance1 };
  return 0;
}
```

We know from Chapter 5 that the compiler-generated version of a copy constructor does the wrong thing here: it only creates a flat copy of the character pointer resourceToManage!

Hence, we have to provide our own copy constructor, like so:

```
#include <algorithm>

class Clazz final {
public:
  // ...
  Clazz(const Clazz& other) : Clazz { other.size } {
    std::copy(other.resourceToManage, other.resourceToManage + other.size,
    resourceToManage);
  }
  // ...
};
```

So far, so good. Now the copy construction will work fine. But now we'll also need a copy assignment operator. If you are not familiar with the copy-and-swap idiom, an implementation of an assignment operator might look like this:

```
#include <algorithm>

class Clazz final {
```

444

```
public:
  // ...
  Clazz& operator=(const Clazz& other) {
    if (&other == this) {
      return *this;
    }
    delete [] resourceToManage;
    resourceToManage = new char[other.size];
    std::copy(other.resourceToManage, other.resourceToManage + other.size,
      resourceToManage);
    size = other.size;
    return *this;
  }
  // ...
};
```

Basically, this assignment operator will work, but it has several drawbacks. For instance, the constructor and destructor code is duplicated in it, which is a violation of the DRY principle (see Chapter 3). Furthermore, there is a self-assignment check at the beginning. But the biggest disadvantage is that we cannot guarantee exception-safety. For example, if the new statement causes an exception, the object can be left behind in a weird state that violates elementary class invariants.

Now the copy-and-swap idiom comes into play, also known as "Create-Temporary-and-Swap"!

For a better understanding, I present the whole class Clazz in Listing 9-48.

Listing 9-48. A Much Better Implementation of an Assignment Operator Using the Copy-and-Swap Idiom

```
#include <algorithm>
#include <cstddef>

class Clazz final {
public:
  explicit Clazz(const std::size_t size) : resourceToManage { new
  char[size] },
    size { size } { }
```

```
  ~Clazz() {
    delete [] resourceToManage;
  }

  Clazz(const Clazz& other) : Clazz { other.size } {
    std::copy(other.resourceToManage, other.resourceToManage + other.size,
      resourceToManage);
  }

  Clazz& operator=(Clazz other) {
    swap(other);
    return *this;
  }
private:
  void swap(Clazz& other) noexcept {
    using std::swap;
    swap(resourceToManage, other.resourceToManage);
    swap(size, other.size);
  }

  char* resourceToManage{ nullptr };
  std::size_t size{ 0 };
};
```

What is the trick here? Let's look at the completely different assignment operator. This no longer has a const reference (const Clazz& other) as a parameter, but an ordinary value parameter (Clazz other). This means that when this assignment operator is called, the copy constructor of Clazz is called. The copy constructor, in turn, calls the default constructor that allocates memory for the resource. And that is exactly what we want: we need a temporary copy of other!

Now we come to the heart of the idiom: the call of the private member function Clazz::swap(). Within this function, the contents of the temporary instance other, that is, its member variables, are exchanged ("swapped") with the contents of the same member variables of our own class context (this). This is done by using the non-throwing std::swap() function (defined in the <utility> header). After the swap operations, the temporary object called other now owns the resources that were previously owned by the this object, and vice versa.

Additionally, the `Clazz::swap()` member function now makes it very easy to implement a move constructor:

```
class Clazz {
public:
  // ...
  Clazz(Clazz&& other) noexcept {
    swap(other);
  }
  // ...
};
```

Of course, the major goal in good class design should be that it is not necessary to implement explicit copy constructors and assignment operators (recall the Rule of Zero). But when you are forced to do it, you should remember the copy-and-swap idiom.

Pointer to Implementation (PIMPL)

The last section of this chapter is dedicated to an idiom with the funny acronym, PIMPL. PIMPL stands for *Pointer to Implementation*; and the idiom is also known as *Handle Body*, the *Compilation Firewall,* or *Cheshire Cat technique* (The Cheshire Cat is a fictional character, a grinning cat, from Lewis Carroll's novel *Alice's Adventures in Wonderland.*) It has, by the way, some similarities with the *Bridge* pattern described in [Gamma95].

The intent of the PIMPL could be formulated as follows:

"Remove compilation dependencies on internal class implementation details by relocating them into a hidden implementation class and thus improve compile times."

Let's look at an excerpt from the `Customer` class, a class that we've seen in many examples before. See Listing 9-49.

Listing 9-49. An Excerpt from the Contents of the Customer.h Header File

```
#ifndef CUSTOMER_H_
#define CUSTOMER_H_

#include "Address.h"
#include "Identifier.h"
```

```cpp
#include <string>

class Customer {
public:
  Customer();
  virtual ~Customer() = default;
  std::string getFullName() const;
  void setShippingAddress(const Address& address);
  // ...

private:
  Identifier customerId;
  std::string forename;
  std::string surname;
  Address shippingAddress;
};

#endif /* CUSTOMER_H_ */
```

Let's assume that this is a central business entity in our commercial software system and that it is used (#include "Customer.h") by many other classes. When this header file changes, any files that use that file will need to be recompiled, even if only one private member variable is added, renamed, etc.

In order to reduce these recompilations to the absolute minimum, the PIMPL idiom comes in to play.

First we rebuild the class interface of the Customer class, as shown in Listing 9-50.

Listing 9-50. The Altered Customer.h Header File

```cpp
#ifndef CUSTOMER_H_
#define CUSTOMER_H_

#include <memory>
#include <string>

class Address;

class Customer {
public:
  Customer();
```

```
  virtual ~Customer();
  std::string getFullName() const;
  void setShippingAddress(const Address& address);
  // ...

private:
  class Impl;
  std::unique_ptr<Impl> impl;
};

#endif /* CUSTOMER_H_ */
```

It is conspicuous that all previous private member variables, as well as their associated include-directives, have now disappeared. Instead, a forward declaration for a class named Impl, as well as a std::unique_ptr<T> to this forward-declared class, is present.

Let's look at the corresponding implementation file, shown in Listing 9-51.

Listing 9-51. The Contents of the Customer.cpp File

```
#include "Customer.h"

#include "Address.h"
#include "Identifier.h"

class Customer::Impl final {
public:
  std::string getFullName() const;
  void setShippingAddress(const Address& address);

private:
  Identifier customerId;
  std::string forename;
  std::string surname;
  Address shippingAddress;
};

std::string Customer::Impl::getFullName() const {
  return forename + " " + surname;
}
```

```
void Customer::Impl::setShippingAddress(const Address& address) {
  shippingAddress = address;
}

// Implementation of class Customer starts here...

Customer::Customer() : impl { std::make_unique<Customer::Impl>() } { }

Customer::~Customer() = default;

std::string Customer::getFullName() const {
  return impl->getFullName();
}

void Customer::setShippingAddress(const Address& address) {
  impl->setShippingAddress(address);
}
```

In the upper part of the implementation file (up to the source code comment), we can see the Customer::Impl class. Everything has been relocated in this class, which formerly was done directly by the Customer class. Here we also find all member variables.

In the lower section (beginning with the comment), we now find the implementation of the Customer class. The constructor creates an instance of Customer::Impl and holds it in the smart pointer impl. As to the rest, any call of the API of the Customer class is delegated to the internal implementation object.

If something has to be changed in the internal implementation in Customer::Impl, the compiler must only compile Customer.h/Customer.cpp, and then the linker can start its work immediately. Such changes do not have an effect on the outside, and a time-consuming compilation of the almost entire project is avoided.

APPENDIX A

Small UML Guide

"Learn the rules so you know how to break them properly."

—Rule no. 5 of the Dalai Lama's "18 Rules for Living"

The OMG Unified Modeling Language (OMG UML)[1] is a standardized graphical language used to create models of software and other systems. Its main purpose is to enable developers, software architects, and other stakeholders to design, specify, visualize, construct, and document artifacts of a software system. The language supports both the modeling of structures (the building blocks of a software and their relationships), as well as their behavior (how those building blocks interact and collaborate at runtime). Well-crafted UML models support the discussion between different stakeholders, serve as an aid to clarify requirements and other issues related to the system of interest, and can capture design decisions.

The vocabulary range of the UML is very extensive. The language offers 15 different diagram types for different purposes. However, as with any other language, it is not usually necessary to use all the vocabulary you know in daily communication. The "art of omission" is also essential here. In practice, there is always a limitation on the language elements you need, and a limitation on a few diagram types.

This appendix provides a brief overview of that subset of UML notations that are used in this book. Each UML element is illustrated (syntax) and briefly explained (semantic). The short definition for an element is based on the current UML specification [OMG15], which can be downloaded for free from OMG's website. An in-depth introduction to the Unified Modeling Language should be made with the help of appropriate literature, or by taking a course at a training provider.

---

[1]OMG, Unified Modeling Language, and UML are registered trademarks of the Object Management Group, Inc.

Structural Modeling

This section introduces the UML notations used to model structures, i.e. the building blocks of a software system, their interfaces, and their relationships (dependencies). Among the most important structural diagrams in UML are the component diagram and the class diagram.

Component

The UML element **component** represents a modular part of a system that is usually on a high abstraction level, for example at the level of software architecture. A component serves as a kind of "capsule" or "envelope" for a set of smaller components or classes that together fulfill certain functionality.

COMPONENT

A *component* represents a modular part of a system that encapsulates its contents and whose manifestation is replaceable within its environment.

The notation (syntax) of a component is a rectangular symbol with the component's name, as depicted in Figure A-1. Above the component's name (Billing), the keyword «component» appears within French quotation marks, which are also called guillemets. The icon in the upper-right corner is optional.

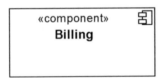

Figure A-1. An example of the notation of a billing component

Due to the fact that a component encapsulates its content, its services are defined in terms of so-called provided and required interfaces. Only these interfaces are available to the environment for the use of a component. That means that a component is a substitutable unit that can be replaced at design time or at runtime by another component that has compatible interfaces and offers equivalent functionality.

Class and Object

Among various other applications, class diagrams are typically used to depict structures of an object-oriented software design. Class diagrams are at a lower level of abstraction than the previously discussed component diagrams. The central element in class diagrams is the **class**.

CLASS

A *class* describes a set of objects that share the same specifications of features, constraints, and semantics.

The notation (symbol) for a class is a simple rectangle with the name of the class, as depicted in Figure A-2.

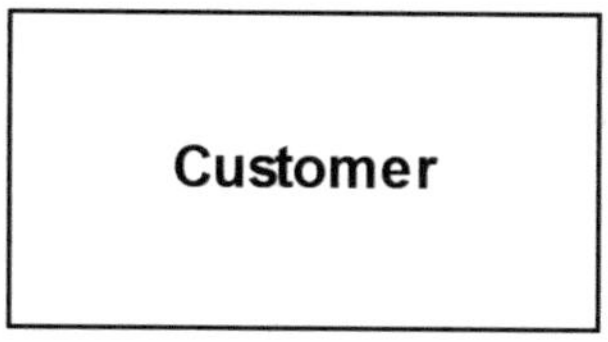

Figure A-2. *A class named Customer*

An instance of a class is commonly referred to as an **object**. Therefore, classes can be considered as blueprints for similar objects. If such objects are presented in a UML diagram, they are called **instance specifications**.[2] The notation of an instance specification is very similar to that of a class, with the difference that its name is underlined. Figure A-3 depicts three instance specifications ("peter", "mary", and "sheila") that were created by instantiating the same class.

---

[2]A linguistic subtlety: The background for this very special term "instance specification" is that the graphical representation of an instance (object) on a UML diagram is not the real object at all, it is just a specification of it in a model. The real object can be found in the memory of the running software system.

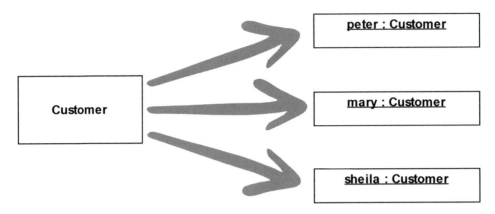

Figure A-3. *Three instance specifications created from the Customer class*

Usually, classes have both structural and behavioral features. These are called **attributes** and **operations**.[3] Attributes are usually shown in the second compartment of the class and operations in the third, as depicted in Figure A-4.

Customer
attributes
-identifier : GUID -name : String -billingAddress : Address -shippingAddress : Address -isRegular : Boolean
operations
«Create» +Customer(idProvider : UniqueIdentifierFactory, name : String, isRegular : Boolean) +setShippingAddress(address : Address) +setBillingAddress(address : Address) +getShippingAddress() : Address {query} +getBillingAddress() : Address {query} +isRegular() : Boolean {query} +getIdentifierAsString() : String {query} +getIdentifier() : GUID {query}

Figure A-4. *The Customer class with attributes and operations*

---

[3]In C++, the attributes of a class are sometimes called "members," and the operations are sometimes called "methods" or "member functions," whereby the last term is properly speaking not quite correct, because they are normally not true pure functions.

The type of an attribute is noted separated by a colon after the attribute's name. The same applies to the type of the return value of an operation. Operations can have parameters that are specified within parentheses. If an operation has more than one parameter, the parameters are noted as a comma-separated list. Static attributes or operations are underlined.

Classes have a mechanism to regulate the access to their attributes and operations. In UML they are called visibilities. The **visibility kind** is placed in front of the attribute's or operation's name and may be one of the characters described in Table A-1.

Table A-1. *Visibilities*

Character	Visibility Kind
+	**public:** This attribute or operation is visible to all elements that can access the class.
#	**protected:** This attribute or operation is not only visible inside the class itself, but also visible to elements that are derived from the class that owns it (see the section entitled "Generalization").
~	**package:** This attribute or operation is visible to elements that are in the same package as its owning class. This kind of visibility cannot be realized in a language like C++ and is therefore not used in this book.
-	**private:** This attribute or operation is only visible inside the class, nowhere else.

A C++ class definition corresponding to the UML class shown in Figure A-4 may look like Listing A-1.

Listing A-1. The Customer Class Implemented in C++

```cpp
#include <string>
#include <string_view>
#include "Address.h"
#include "UniqueIdentifierFactory.h"

class Customer {
public:
  Customer() = delete;
  Customer(const UniqueIdentifierFactory& idProvider,
    std::string_view name, const bool isRegular);
  virtual ~Customer() = default;
```

```
  void setShippingAddress(const Address& address);
  void setBillingAddress(const Address& address);
  Address getShippingAddress() const;
  Address getBillingAddress() const;
  bool isRegular() const;
  GUID getIdentifier() const;
  std::string getIdentifierAsString() const;

private:
  void requestUniqueIdentifier(const UniqueIdentifierFactory&
    identifierFactory);

  GUID identifier;
  std::string name;
  Address billingAddress;
  Address shippingAddress;
  bool isRegular;
};
```

Note   Due to the fact that a UML model is an abstraction in most cases
(exception: when their purpose is to generate source code), diagrams often do not
depict all existing properties of a described element, i.e., diagrams usually have a
lower level of detail.

If a class is abstract, that is, it cannot be instantiated due to an incomplete
specification, its name is typically shown in italicized letters, as depicted in Figure A-5.
Abstract classes serve as base classes in inheritance hierarchies (see the section entitled
"Generalization").

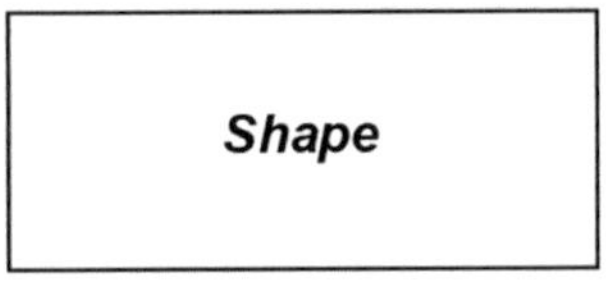

Figure A-5. An abstract class called Shape

Interface

An **interface** defines a kind of a contract. A component or class that realizes the interface must fulfill that contract. Another component or class that uses the interface expects that it is supplied with an element that fulfills the contract.

INTERFACE

An *interface* is a declaration of a set of coherent public obligations.

Interfaces are always abstract, that is, they cannot be instantiated by default. The UML symbol for an interface is very similar to a class, with the keyword «interface» above its name, as depicted in Figure A-6.

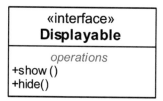

Figure A-6. *The Displayable interface with two declared operations*

To express, for example, that a class realizes (synonym: implements) an interface, a special relationship exists in UML. The **realization relationship** is a dashed arrow with a closed but not filled arrowhead. This relationship points, as depicted in Figure A-7, from the class (the realizing element) to the interface (the specification).

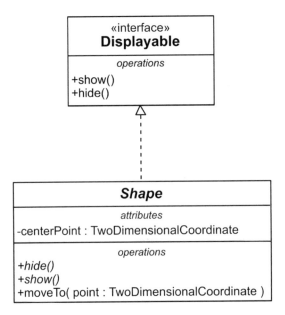

Figure A-7. *The Shape class realizes the Displayable interface*

It is, of course, allowed that a class implements multiple interfaces.

Unlike some other object-oriented languages, such as Java and C#, there is no `interface` keyword in C++. Interfaces are therefore usually emulated with the help of abstract classes that solely consist of pure virtual member functions, as shown in Listing A-2.

Listing A-2.   The Displayable Interface in C++

```cpp
class Displayable {
public:
  virtual ~Displayable() = default;
  virtual void show() = 0;
  virtual void hide() = 0;
};
```

To show that a class or component provides or requires interfaces, you can use the so-called **ball-and-socket notation**. A provided interface is depicted using a ball (a "lollipop"), whereas a required interface is depicted with a socket (a symbol that looks like a claw). Strictly speaking, this is an alternative notation, as Figure A-8 clarifies. (The association relationship that appears in this figure between Account and Owner is explained in detail in the following section.)

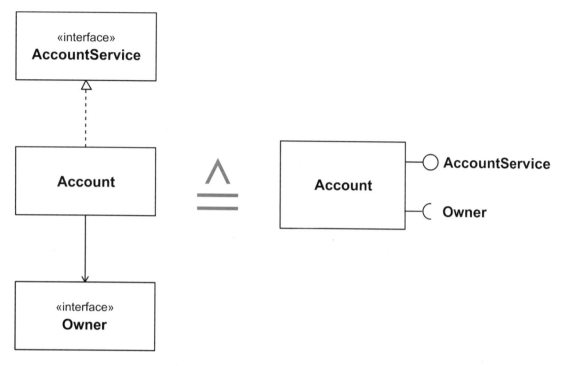

Figure A-8. *The so-called "ball-and-socket-notation" for provided (AccountService) and required (Owner) interfaces*

Association

Classes usually have static relationships to other classes. The UML **association** specifies such a relationship.

ASSOCIATION

An *association* relationship allows one instance of a classifier (e.g., a class or a component) to access another.

In its simplest form, the UML syntax for an association is a solid line between two classes, as depicted in Figure A-9.

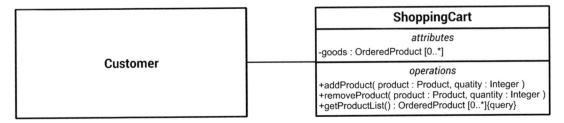

Figure A-9. *A simple association relationship between two classes*

This simple association is often not sufficient to properly specify the relationship between both classes. For instance, the navigation direction across such a simple association, that is, who is able to access whom, is undefined by default. However, navigability in this case is often interpreted as bidirectional by convention, that is, Customer (whose internals have been completely hidden here) has an attribute to access ShoppingCart and vice versa. Therefore, more information can be provided to an association. Figure A-10 illustrates a few of the possibilities.

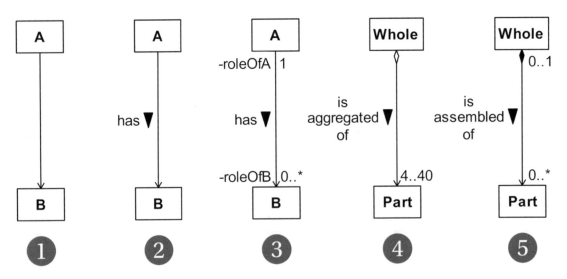

Figure A-10. *Some examples of associations between classes*

1. This example shows an association with one end **navigable** (depicted by an arrowhead) and the other having unspecified navigability. The semantic is: class A is able to navigate to class B. In the other direction it is unspecified, that is, class B might be able to navigate to class A.

Note   It is strongly recommended to define the interpretation of the navigability of such an unspecified association end in your project. **My recommendation is to consider them as non-navigable.** This interpretation is also used in this book.

2. This navigable association has a **name** ("has"). The solid triangle indicates the direction of reading. Apart from that, the semantics of this association is fully identical to Example 1.

3. In this example, both association ends have **labels** (names) and **multiplicities**. The labels are typically used to specify the roles of the classes in an association.

   A multiplicity specifies the allowed quantity of instances of the classes that are involved in an association. It is an inclusive interval of non-negative integers beginning with a lower bound and ending with an (possibly infinite) upper bound. In this case, any A has zero to any number of Bs, whereas any B has exactly one A. Table A-2 shows some examples of valid multiplicities.

4. This is a special association called **aggregation**. It represents a whole-part-relationship; that is, the one class (the part) is hierarchically subordinated to the other class (the whole). The hollow diamond is just a marker in this kind of association and identifies the whole. Otherwise, everything that applies to associations applies to an aggregation.

5. This is a **composite aggregation**, which is a strong form of aggregation. It expresses that the whole is the owner of the parts, and thus also responsible for the parts. If an instance of the whole is deleted, all of its part instances are normally deleted with it.

Note   Note that a part can (where allowed) be removed from a composite before the whole is deleted, and thus not be deleted as part of the whole. This can be made possible by a multiplicity of 0..1 at the association end that is connected to the whole, that is, the end with the filled diamond. The only allowed multiplicities at this end are 1 or 0..1; all other multiplicities are prohibited.

Table A-2. *Multiplicity Examples*

Multiplicity	Meaning
1	Exactly one. If no multiplicity is shown on an association end, this is the default.
1..10	An inclusive interval between 1 and 10.
0..*	An inclusive interval between 0 and any number (zero-to-many). The star character (*) is used to represent the unlimited (or infinite) upper bound.
*	Abbreviated form of 0..*.
1..*	An inclusive interval between 1 and any number (one-to-many).

In programming languages, associations and the mechanism of navigation from one class to another can be implemented in various ways. In C++, associations are usually implemented by members having the other class as its type, for example, as a reference or a pointer, as shown in Listing A-3.

Listing A-3. Sample Implementation of a Navigable Association Between Classes A and B

```
class B; // Forward declaration

class A {
private:
  B* b;
  // ...
};

class B {
  // No pointer or any other reference to class A here!
};
```

Generalization

A central concept in object-oriented software development is the so-called inheritance. In UML there is a different and better fitting term for this concept: **generalization**. What is meant by this is the generalization of, for instance, classes or components.

GENERALIZATION

A *generalization* is a taxonomic relationship between a general class and a more specific class.

The generalization relationship is used in UML diagrams to represent the concept of inheritance: the specific class (subclass) inherits attributes and operations of the more general class (base class). The UML syntax of the generalization relationship is a solid arrow with a closed but not filled arrowhead, as depicted in Figure A-11.

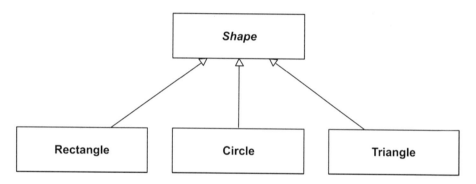

Figure A-11. *An abstract base class called Shape and three concrete classes that are specializations of it*

In the direction of the arrow, this relationship is read as the following: "<Subclass> is a kind of <Baseclass>," for example, "Rectangle is a kind of Shape."

Dependency

In addition to the already mentioned associations, classes (and components) can have further relationships with other classes (and components). For instance, if a class is used as a type for a parameter of a member function, this is not an association, but it is a kind of dependency to that used class.

DEPENDENCY

A *dependency* is a relationship that signifies that a single or a set of elements requires other elements for their specification or implementation.

As depicted in Figure A-12, a dependency is shown as a dashed arrow between two elements, for example, between two classes or components. It implies that the element at the arrowhead is required by the element at the tail of the arrow, for example, for implementation purposes. In other words, the dependent element is incomplete without the independent element.

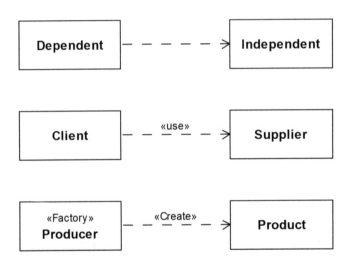

Figure A-12. *Miscellaneous dependencies*

In addition to its simple form (see the first example in Figure A-12), two special types of dependency can be distinguished:

- The **usage dependency** («use») is a relationship in which one element requires another element (or set of elements) for its full implementation or operation.

- The **creation dependency** («Create») is a special kind of usage dependency indicating that the element at the tail of the arrow creates instances of the type at the arrowhead.

Template and Template Binding

In C++, templates are well known as the foundation of generic programming. In contrast, the possibility of depicting class templates in UML class diagrams is largely unknown, as is the possibility to show how template parameters are substituted with concrete types or values.

The example in Figure A-13 shows a **class template** named std::vector with two formal **template parameters** named T and Allocator. Template parameters of a Class template are shown in a dashed rectangle that overlaps the class' rectangle in the upper-right corner. In our example, there is even a default value (std::allocator) with which the Allocator template parameter is substituted.

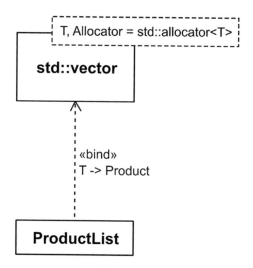

Figure A-13. *The class template std::vector and a bound class ProductList*

There is also a bound class (named ProductList) that substitutes the template parameter T with the type Product (which is another class that is not shown here). The **TemplateBinding** is depicted with a dashed arrow («bind») showing the substitution of template parameters (T -> Product).

Behavioral Modeling

In addition to modeling static structures, UML also offers various possibilities to model the behavior of software, i.e. dynamic aspects and processes during the operation of the software. The three diagram types most commonly used for this purpose are activity diagrams, sequence diagrams, and state diagrams.

Since the total vocabulary range of UML is also relatively large, we will confine ourselves in this small introduction only to the elements that are necessary for understanding the behavioral diagrams presented in this book.

Activity Diagram

An activity diagram is suitable for describing complex processes (e.g., procedures, operations, etc.). The paths through the process described by an activity diagram can be divided and reunited, decisions can be made, and parallel regions may also exist, i.e. you can also describe concurrently running processes.

In general, an activity diagram consists of **nodes** and **edges**. The edges determine the processing order. The nodes are the elements that are brought into a certain order by the edges.

Figure A-14 depicts a simple example of an activity diagram. It shows that there are two alternative flows for regular customers and new customers, because regular customers already have a customer account, whereas new customers first have to provide their data and then their credit card is charged. The diagram also shows that for regular customers, debiting the customer account and crediting the bonus points can run in parallel.

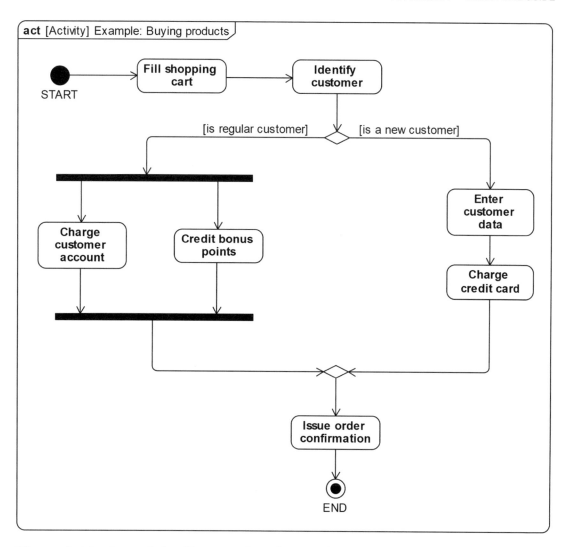

Figure A-14. *An activity diagram that depicts the process of purchasing products*

Action

A very central element in activity diagrams is an executable node that is called **action**.

ACTION

An *action* is the fundamental unit of executable functionality.

Actions are used to describe that something is happening in the modeled system, i.e. some kind of function or processing. The syntax (notation) of an action is a rectangle with rounded corners, as depicted in Figure A-15. The name of the action is usually the description of what is executed. Good and well-understandable action names consist of a noun and a verb.

```
┌──────────────┐
│   Identify   │
│   customer   │
└──────────────┘
```

Figure A-15. *The notation of a simple action*

There are many special kinds of actions in UML. For our purposes, the simple standard action (also called an opaque action), which describes by an expressive name what happens within the modeled system, is sufficient.

Control Flow Edge

In Figure A-16, the solid line with an open arrowhead connecting the action called "Fill shopping cart" to "Identify customer" is a control flow edge. This means that when the "Fill shopping cart" behavior is completed, control is passed to the action named "Identify customer".

Figure A-16. *A control flow edge connects two actions*

A control flow edge can also have a so-called **guard**. Guards can be used, for example, to decide how a process in an activity will continue. A guard is depicted by a condition, which is a (Boolean) expression that can be evaluated to true or false, surrounded with square brackets, e.g., [is regular customer].

Other Activity Nodes

Table A-3 provides an overview with brief descriptions of the other nodes that can be seen in the activity diagram in Figure A-14.

Table A-3. *Other Frequently Used Activity Nodes*

Notation	Name of the Element and its Semantic
	Initial node Represents the point at which flow starts when the activity is invoked. An activity may contain more than one initial node; in this case invoking the activity will start multiple flows simultaneously.
	Activity final node This kind of node stops all flows in an activity. An activity may contain more than one activity final node; in this case the first one reached stops all flows and terminates the whole activity.
	Decision node This kind of node has one incoming edge and selects one outgoing edge from two or more possible outgoing flows. So-called guards (see the section called "Control Flow Edge") are typically used to select the outgoing edge.
	Merge node This kind of node brings together multiple incoming alternate flows and has one single outgoing flow.
	Fork node This kind of node has one incoming edge and multiple outgoing edges and is used to split an incoming flow into multiple concurrent (parallel) flows.
	Join node This kind of node has multiple incoming edges and one outgoing edge and is used to synchronize incoming concurrent (parallel) flows.

Sequence Diagram

Unlike the previously discussed activity diagrams, a sequence diagram depicts the interaction of, or communication between, elements of the modeled system in a specific, limited situation. They thus represent a different view of the behavior of the modeled system.

The sequence diagram in Figure A-17 depicts the sequence of interactions, that is, the ordered exchange of messages between all software modules involved in creating a new posting in an account.

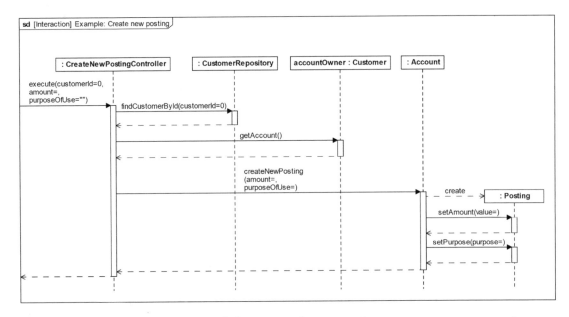

Figure A-17. *The interaction of elements when creating a new account posting*

Lifeline

The central element in sequence diagrams is the so-called **lifeline**.

LIFELINE

A *lifeline* represents an individual participant in an interaction.

The syntax (notation) of a lifeline, as depicted in Figure A-18, is a symbol that consists of a rectangle forming its "head" followed by a vertical dashed line that represents the lifetime of the participant. The head of the lifeline contains the information about the participant in the format elementName : elementType, whereby the elementName is optional.

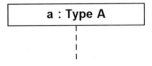

Figure A-18. *A lifeline representing the element a of type Type A*

Message

A **message** is a communication between participants of an interaction in which a sender makes a request for either an operation call or signal reception by a receiver. Figure A-19 depicts different sorts of messages.

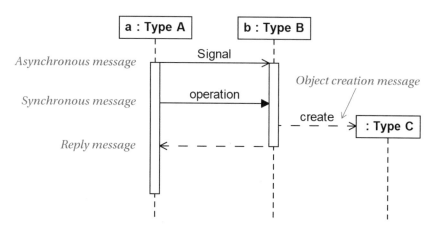

Figure A-19. *Different sorts of messages*

The difference between a synchronous and asynchronous message is that with an asynchronous message, the sender can do other things immediately after the message has been sent ("fire and forget"). On the other hand, the sender of a synchronous message is blocked until the message recipient has finished processing the message and returns to the caller with a so-called Reply message.

An object creation message (depicted by a dashed line with an open arrow head pointing to the head of a lifeline) designates the creation of another lifeline object.

State Diagram

In addition to processes (depicted with the help of activity diagrams) and interactions (depicted with the help of sequence diagrams), a third aspect of behavior is the state and the change of states, i.e. event-driven behaviors of parts of a system. These states and transitions between states are usually modeled with the help of state machines and depicted in state diagrams. UML state machine is an object-based variant of Harel statechart [Harel87], adapted and extended by UML. Thus, it offers more possibilities than the traditional Finite State Machine (FSM).

Figure A-20 depicts an example of a state diagram with the most common notation elements. The diagram frame represents the context of the state machine.

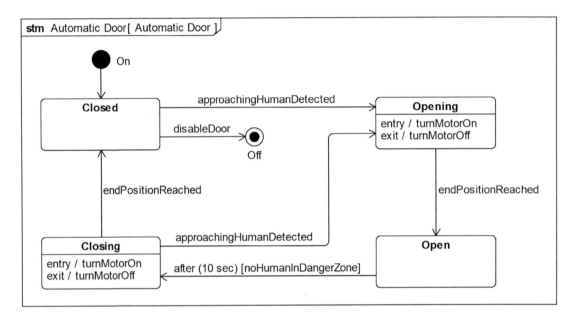

Figure A-20. *An example of a state diagram*

State

The central element in state diagrams is the **state**.

STATE
A *state* models a situation during which some (usually implicit) invariant condition holds.

A state is depicted as a rectangle with rounded corners. A distinction is made between simple and composite states, as depicted in Figure A-21. The latter are states that have a region with sub-states, i.e. hierarchically nested states.

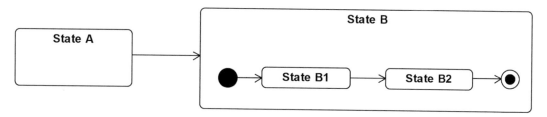

Figure A-21. *A simple state (State A) and a composite state (State B), with nested sub-states (State B1 and State B2)*

Transitions

Transitions are basically distinguished between external and internal transitions.

External Transitions

An external transition usually leads to a change of state. Switching from one state to another is called **state transition**. However, it is also possible that the start and end state of an external transition are the same. The syntax (notation) of an external transition is a solid line with an open arrowhead, as depicted in Figure A-22.

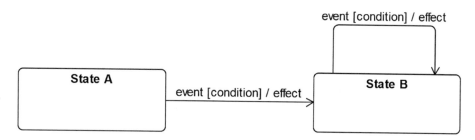

Figure A-22. *External transitions*

Internal Transitions

Sometimes an event causes some internal behavior to execute but does not lead to a state change. This is called an **internal transition**. Internal transitions are noted within a state's compartment, as depicted in Figure A-23.

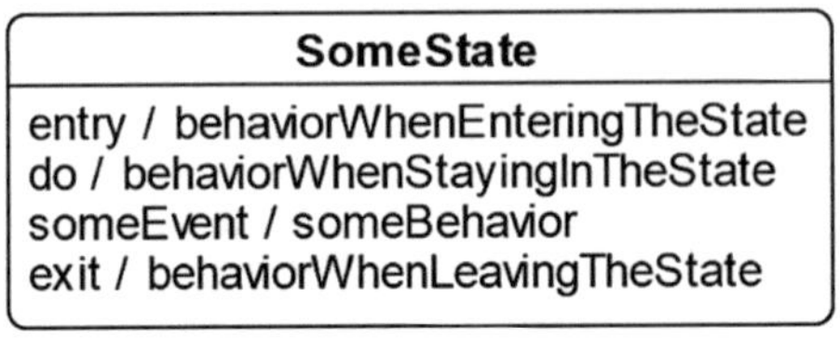

```
┌─────────────────────────────────────────┐
│              SomeState                    │
├─────────────────────────────────────────┤
│ entry / behaviorWhenEnteringTheState      │
│ do / behaviorWhenStayingInTheState        │
│ someEvent / someBehavior                  │
│ exit / behaviorWhenLeavingTheState        │
└─────────────────────────────────────────┘
```

Figure A-23. *A state with internal transitions*

Besides self-defined events, the following predefined events can optionally be used for internal transitions in order to execute some specified behavior:

- entry: A behavior that is performed upon entry to a state.

- do: An ongoing behavior that is performed as long as the modeled element is in the state.

- exit: A behavior that is performed upon exit from a state.

Trigger

A transition may own a set of so-called triggers. A **trigger** specifies an event whose occurrence, when dispatched, may trigger traversal of the transition. Triggers can be noted on a transition according to the following template:

```
[event1, event2, ...][condition][/behavior]
```

All elements, i.e. the explicit events, the so-called guard (that's the part that contains the condition), as well as the executed behavior if a transition is triggered, are optional. Even if no explicit trigger is annotated at a transition, there is one. This implicit event is called a **completion event** and it signifies that all behaviors associated with the source state (e.g., the possibly existing behaviors that are associated with the entry- and do- events) have completed execution.

Stereotypes

Among other ways, the vocabulary of UML can be extended with the help of so-called stereotypes. This lightweight mechanism allows the introduction of platform- or domain-specific extensions of standard UML elements. For instance, by the application of the stereotype «Factory» on the standard UML element Class, designers can express that those specific classes are object factories.

The name of an applied stereotype is shown within a pair of guillemets (French quotation marks) above or before the name of the model element. Some stereotypes also introduce a new graphical symbol, an icon. Table A-4 contains a list of the stereotypes used in this book.

Table A-4. *Stereotypes Used in This Book*

Stereotype	Meaning
«Factory»	A class that creates objects without exposing the instantiation logic to the client.
«Facade»	A class that provides a unified interface to a set of interfaces in a complex component or subsystem.
«Include»	A stereotype applied to a directed relationship (dependency) to indicate that one source code file requires the contents of another source code file.
«ModuleImport»	A stereotype applied to a directed relationship (dependency) to indicate that a C++ source code file imports a C++ module, which is a set of source code files that were precompiled independently of the units that are importing the module.
«Subsystem»	A UML standard stereotype. It is used to mark a component that represents a large-scale module within a system, which may have characteristics of a self-contained system.
«SUT»	The System Under Test (SUT). Classes or components with this stereotype are the entities to be tested, for example, with the help of unit tests.
«System»	This stereotype, which can be applied to both the UML component and the class, marks the element that represents the so-called "system of interest," i.e., the entire software system.
«TestContext»	A software entity, for example, a class that acts as a grouping mechanism for a set of test cases (see stereotype «TestCase»).
«TestCase»	An operation that interacts with the «SUT» to verify its correctness. Test cases are grouped in a «TestContext».

Bibliography

[Abrahams98] David Abrahams. "Exception-Safety in Generic Components." Appeared in "Selected Papers from the International Seminar on Generic Programming' (pp 69–79), Proceedings of the ACM. Springer, 1998.

[Beck01] Kent Beck, Mike Beedle, Arie van Bennekum, et al. "Manifesto for Agile Software Development." 2001. `http://agilemanifesto.org`, retrieved 3-21-2021.

[Beck02] Kent Beck. *Test-Driven Development: By Example.* Addison-Wesley Professional, 2002.

[Beizer90] Boris Beizer. *Software Testing Techniques (2nd Edition).* Itp – Media, 1990.

[Busch96] Frank Buschmann, Regine Meunier, Hans Rohnert, and Peter Sommerlad. *Pattern-Oriented Software Architecture Volume 1: A System of Patterns.* Wiley, 1996.

[Cohn09] Mike Cohn. *Succeeding with Agile: Software Development Using Scrum (1st Edition).* Addison-Wesley, 2009.

[Cppcore21] Bjarne Stroustrup, Herb Sutter. *C++ Core Guidelines.* `https://isocpp.github.io/CppCoreGuidelines/CppCoreGuidelines.html`, retrieved 3-21-2021.

[Evans04] Eric J. Evans. *Domain-Driven Design: Tackling Complexity in the Heart of Software (1st Edition).* Addison-Wesley, 2004.

[Feathers07] Michael C. Feathers. *Working Effectively with Legacy Code.* Addison-Wesley, 2007.

[Fernandes12] R. Martinho Fernandes. "Rule of Zero." `https://github.com/rmartinho/flamingdangerzone/blob/master/_posts/cxx11/2012-08-15-rule-of-zero.md`, retrieved 3-22-2021.

[Fowler02] Martin Fowler. *Patterns of Enterprise Application Architecture.* Addison-Wesley, 2002.

[Fowler03] Martin Fowler. "Anemic Domain Model." November 2003. `https://martinfowler.com/bliki/AnemicDomainModel.html`, retrieved 5-1-2017.

[Fowler04] Martin Fowler. "Inversion of Control Containers and the Dependency Injection Pattern." January 2004. `https://martinfowler.com/articles/injection.html`, retrieved 7-19-2017.

BIBLIOGRAPHY

[Gamma95] Erich Gamma, Richard Helm, Ralph Johnson, and John Vlissides. *Design Patterns: Elements of Reusable, Object-Oriented Software.* Addison-Wesley, 1995.

[GAOIMTEC92] United States General Accounting Office. GAO/IMTEC-92-26: "Patriot Missile Defense: Software Problem Led to System Failure at Dhahran, Saudi Arabia," 1992. `https://www.gao.gov/products/imtec-92-26`, retrieved 3-22-2021.

[Hunt99] Andrew Hunt, David Thomas. *The Pragmatic Programmer: From Journeyman to Master.* Addison-Wesley, 1999.

[InformIT09] Larry O'Brien. "Design Patterns 15 Years Later: An Interview with Erich Gamma, Richard Helm, and Ralph Johnson." InformIT/Pearson Education, 2009. `https://www.informit.com/articles/article.aspx?p=1404056`, retrieved 3-22-2021

[ISO11] International Standardization Organization (ISO), JTC1/SC22/WG21 (The C++ Standards Committee). ISO/IEC 14882:2011, Standard for Programming Language C++.

[ISO14] International Standardization Organization (ISO), JTC1/SC22/WG21 (The C++ Standards Committee). ISO/IEC 14882:2014, Standard for Programming Language C++.

[ISO17] International Standardization Organization (ISO), JTC1/SC22/WG21 (The C++ Standards Committee). ISO/IEC 14882:2017, Standard for Programming Language C++.

[ISO20] International Standardization Organization (ISO), JTC1/SC22/WG21 (The C++ Standards Committee). ISO/IEC 14882:2020, Standard for Programming Language C++.

[Jain15] Naveen Jain. Naveen Jain Blog: "Why You Should Always Bet on Dreams, Not Experts." `http://www.naveenjain.com/why-you-should-always-bet-on-dreams-not-experts/`, retrieved 3-22-2021.

[Jeffries98] Ron Jeffries. "You're NOT Gonna Need It!" `http://ronjeffries.com/xprog/articles/practices/pracnotneed/`, retrieved 3-21-2021.

[JPL99] NASA Jet Propulsion Laboratory (JPL). "Mars Climate Orbiter Team Finds Likely Cause of Loss." September 1999. `https://solarsystem.nasa.gov/news/156/mars-climate-orbiter-team-finds-likely-cause-of-loss/`, retrieved 3-22-2021.

[Knuth74] Donald E. Knuth. "Structured Programming with Go To Statements." *ACM Journal Computing Surveys*, 6 (4), December 1974. `https://dl.acm.org/doi/10.1145/356635.356640`, retrieved 3-22-2021.

[Koenig01] Andrew Koenig and Barbara E. Moo. "C++ Made Easier: The Rule of Three." June 2001. `http://www.drdobbs.com/c-made-easier-the-rule-of-three/184401400`, retrieved 3-22-2021.

[Langr13] Jeff Langr. *Modern C++ Programming with Test-Driven Development: Code Better, Sleep Better.* Pragmatic Bookshelf, 2013.

[Liskov94] Barbara H. Liskov and Jeanette M. Wing. "A Behavioral Notion of Subtyping." *ACM Transactions on Programming Languages and Systems* (TOPLAS), 16 (6): 1811–1841. November 1994. `http://dl.acm.org/citation.cfm?doid=197320.197383`, retrieved 12-30-2014.

[Martin03] Robert C. Martin. *Agile Software Development: Principles, Patterns, and Practices.* Prentice Hall, 2003.

[Meyers05] Scott Meyers. *Effective C++: 55 Specific Ways to Improve Your Programs and Designs (Third Edition).* Addison-Wesley, 2005.

[Nygard18] Michael T. Nygard. *Release It!: Design and Deploy Production-Ready Software (2nd Edition).* O'Reilly UK Ltd., 2018.

[OMG17] Object Management Group. OMG Unified Modeling Language (OMG UML), Version 2.5.1. OMG Document Number: formal/17-12-05. `http://www.omg.org/spec/UML/2.5.1`, retrieved 3-22-2021.

[Parnas07] ACM Special Interest Group on Software Engineering: ACM Fellow Profile of David Lorge Parnas. `http://www.sigsoft.org/SEN/parnas.html`, retrieved 9-24-2016.

[Ram03] Stefan Ram. Dr. Alan Kay on the Meaning of "Object-Oriented Programming." `http://www.purl.org/stefan_ram/pub/doc_kay_oop_en`, retrieved 3-22-2021.

[Rivera19] Rene Rivera. "C++ Tooling Statistics: Are Modules Fast?" February 2019. `https://www.bfgroup.xyz/cpp_tooling_stats/modules/modules_perf_D1441R1.html`, retrieved 3-21-2021.

[Sommerlad13] Peter Sommerlad. "Meeting C++ 2013: Simpler C++ with C++11/14." November 2013. `http://wiki.hsr.ch/PeterSommerlad/files/MeetingCPP2013_SimpleC++.pdf`, retrieved 1-2-2014.

[Stroustrup16] Bjarne Stroustrup. "C++11 – The New ISO C++ Standard." September 2016. `https://www.stroustrup.com/C++11FAQ.html`, retrieved 3-21-2021.

[Sutter04] Herb Sutter. "The Free Lunch Is Over: A Fundamental Turn Toward Concurrency in Software." `http://www.gotw.ca/publications/concurrency-ddj.htm`, retrieved 3-21-2021.

[Thought08] ThoughtWorks, Inc. (multiple authors). *The ThoughtWorks Anthology: Essays on Software Technology and Innovation.* Pragmatic Bookshelf, 2008.

[Wipo1886] World Intellectual Property Organization (WIPO): Berne Convention for the Protection of Literary and Artistic Works. `https://www.wipo.int/treaties/en/ip/berne/index.html`, retrieved 3-22-2021.

Index

A

Abstract Syntax Tree (AST), 282, 412
Activity diagram
    action, 467, 468
    activity final node, 469
    control flow edge, 468
    decision node, 469
    fork node, 469
    guards, 468, 469
    initial node, 469
    merge node, 469
    nodes/edges, 466
Anemic Domain Model, 276, 277
Anti-pattern, *see also* Code smell
    abuse of exceptions, 204
    anemic classes, 275
    circular dependencies, 258
    god class, 231, 279
    Not invented here
        syndrome, 182
    reinventing the wheel, 182
    singleton, 25, 378
        disadvantage, 383
        global variable, 381
        hidden dependencies, 381
        Meyers' Singleton, 379, 380
        utility classes, 378
Apache OpenOffice, 66, 83

B

Behavior driven development (BDD), 370
Big Ball of Mud, 2
Boundary Value Analysis, extreme values,
    33, 35
Built Module Interface (BMI), 283
Broken window theory, 4

C

C++ programming language, 65
    Apache OpenOffice, 66
    appropriate level, 72
    ADL, 160
    arithmetic types, 428
    array default delete, 171
    auto keyword, 159
    automatic type deduction, 159, 160
    brownfield/greenfield projects, 8
    C++11, 6, 7
    C++14, 7
    C++17, 7
    C++20, 7
    comments
        block comments, 80–84
        definition, 77
        disable code, 79, 80
        documentation generator, 86–89

K

L

W, X, Y, Z

Printed in the United States
by Baker & Taylor Publisher Services